# Religions and Dialogue

# Religions in Dialogue

Series of the Academy of World Religions,
University of Hamburg

No. 7

Waxmann 2014
Münster • New York

Wolfram Weisse, Katajun Amirpur,
Anna Körs & Dörthe Vieregge (Eds.)

# Religions and Dialogue

International Approaches

Waxmann 2014
Münster • New York

SPONSORED BY THE

 Federal Ministry
of Education
and Research

**Bibliographic information published by die Deutsche Nationalbibliothek**
Die Deutsche Nationalbibliothek lists this publication in
the Deutsche Nationalbibliografie; detailed bibliographic
data are available in the internet at http://dnb.d-nb.de.

**Religions in Dialogue, No. 7**

Series of the Academy of World Religions

ISSN 1867-1292
Print-ISBN 978-3-8309-3036-5
E-Book-ISBN 978-3-8309-8036-0

© Waxmann Verlag GmbH, 2014
Postfach 8603, 48046 Münster, Germany

© Waxmann Publishing Co.
P. O. Box 1318, New York, NY 10028, U. S. A.

www.waxmann.com
info@waxmann.com

Cover Design: Plessmann Design, Ascheberg
Cover Picture: Window designed by students at the Helmut-Schmidt-Gymnasium in
Hamburg-Wilhelmsburg, © Andreas Gloy
Setting: Sven Solterbeck, Münster
Print: CPI buchbücher.de; Birkach

Printed on age-resistant paper, acid-free as per ISO 9706

Printed in Germany

# Contents

## Dialogue in Christianity

## Dialogue in Islam

## Dialogue in Hinduism

## Dialogue in Buddhism

*Katajun Amirpur, Anna Körs, Dörthe Vieregge & Wolfram Weisse*

# Introduction

## The Challenge of Pluralisation and the Relevance of Encounter

Responding to plurality is a demanding task. Nonetheless it is one of the challenges that European countries are facing today, and perhaps the greatest among them. Over the past decades, the social and religious make-up of Central Europe has changed, and this has led to resentment and fears of mass immigration, social disintegration and the emergence of parallel societies.

A study conducted by Bielefeld University in 2008 identified strong resentments against a number of groups. 41 per cent of respondents in several European countries believe: "The Jews are trying to take advantage of the fact that they were victimised during the Nazi era."[1] Throughout Europe, 31 per cent agree that: "There is a natural hierarchy between black and white peoples."[2] That puts them squarely in the racist and anti-Semitic camp.

Muslims suffer especially. According to the findings of this study, only 16.6 per cent of the German respondents agree with the statement: "Muslim culture fits well with Germany".[3] In Great Britain and the Netherlands, 39 per cent of respondents agree. Half the Germans consider Islam a threat, while 19 per cent of both East and West Germans think the same of Judaism. This was found by the Bertelsmann Foundation's *Religionsmonitor* survey published in May 2013.[4]

These are surprisingly unequivocal and high figures. Still, they are no reason to panic or give up. Encounters between people from diverse backgrounds will naturally be fraught with problems. Integrating large immigrant minorities with the social mainstream has always been difficult. The Polish population of the Ruhr area and the Catholic Irish immigrants in the United States are two often-cited historical examples, and some even considered the integration of German immigrants in America an impossible task.

Thomas Jefferson and James Madison both expressed considerable reservation about German-speaking immigrants. They considered Germans, Austri-

---

1   Zick, A. & Küpper, B.: Gruppenbezogene Menschenfeindlichkeit in Europa. http://www.uni-bielefeld.de/ikg/projekte/GMF/Gruppenbezogene_Menschenfeindlichkeit_in_Europa_Zusammenfassung.pdf (p. 8), last accessed 26.11.2013.
2   Ibid.: Meinungen zum Islam und Muslimen in Deutschland und Europa. Ausgewählte Ergebnisse der Umfrage Gruppenbezogene Menschenfeindlichkeit in Europa: http://www.uni-bielefeld.de/ikg/zick/Islam_GFE_zick.pdf (p. 4), last accessed 26.11.2013.
3   Ibid. (p. 2).
4   Bertelsmann Stiftung (Ed.): Religionsmonitor 2013. Verstehen was verbindet. Religion und Zusammenhalt in Deutschland. Die wichtigsten Ergebnisse im Überblick. http://www.bertelsmann-stiftung.de/cps/rde/xbcr/SID-BAEC7F5C-7223950E/bst/RelMo_Befunde_Deutschland_final_130428.pdf (pp. 3), last accessed 26.11.2013.

ans, and other newcomers from 'backward' absolutist countries a threat to the American culture of liberty. Martin Scorsese's epic movie *Gangs of New York* portrays the problems of integrating immigrant communities that culminated in street battles between English-speaking Protestant 'natives' and the Irish Catholics who came to America later. These conflicts are hardly remembered today. The Catholic Irish are now as thoroughly integrated as the 42.8 million German-Americans, serving as examples that immigrants, even if they are initially conceived of as strangers and the Other, ultimately gain acceptance, join and influence mainstream society. By way of a more recent German example, it seems impossible to be more integrated than Lukas Podolski, the star player of the football club 1. FC Köln. '*Prinz Poldi*' joined the 2012 carnival procession on the float of the honour guard. This realisation of every Cologne boy's dream – to be carnival prince – was easily compatible with him speaking Polish on the pitch with his colleague Miroslav Klose, shortly before both proceeded to score goals for the German national team against Poland.

Encountering strangers and facing differences can lead to fears and resentment in any human society, including the fear of being 'swamped' by foreigners. However, we also find empirical proof that prejudice is lowest where there is direct contact; where the stranger is not so strange after all. Conversely, surveys have found that fear of Islam is most pronounced in countries where few Muslims live. For example, 50 per cent of Italians agree that there are "too many Muslims" living in Italy. In fact, the number of practising Muslims in the country is estimated at two per cent at most. In Poland (47 per cent agreement) and Hungary (60.7 per cent), Muslims make up less than one per cent of the population.[5]

The differences between urban and rural areas also demonstrate that resentment and fear flourish in the absence of contact. The 2009 referendum banning minarets in Switzerland was decided by 'yes' votes from rural areas that very likely never saw an actual Muslim. In the rural district of Frutigen (Canton Berne), two thirds voted in favour of the ban while in the city of Berne itself, two thirds of voters were opposed.

The votes on the minaret ban as much as survey data on attitudes towards Islam in Europe support what is known as the contact hypothesis that posits a causal relationship between contacts with members of minority groups and hostile attitudes towards those groups. Empirical studies have demonstrated that personal contact can have a stronger influence on attitudes towards people of different race, nationality, religion or culture than either political or economic deprivation. Encountering members of a minority group can counter the emergence of negative stereotypes and behaviour while simultaneously reducing

---

5    Zick, A. & Küpper, B.: Meinungen zum Islam und Muslimen in Deutschland und Europa. Ausgewählte Ergebnisse der Umfrage Gruppenbezogene Menschenfeindlichkeit in Europa: http://www.uni-bielefeld.de/ikg/zick/Islam_GFE_zick.pdf (p. 3), last accessed 26.11.2013.

hostile attitudes. Dialogue – active contact – is of particular importance in this process. This was demonstrated clearly in the Swiss case:

Of the four Swiss communities that already host minarets (Zurich, Winterthur, Geneva and Wangen bei Olten), the ban found a majority in only one (Wangen bei Olten). In Zurich, where the country's first mosque had been built as early as 1963, a similar ban was rejected at the cantonal level in 2006. There was also a pronounced difference in voting patterns on both sides of the so-called *Röstigraben*. This notional line, originally a humorous reference to perceived cultural difference, divides the two largest linguistic regions of Switzerland. It also traces a noticeable divide in voting patterns between the German-speaking majority and French-speaking Swiss. In the referendum, 11.5 per cent more votes for the ban were recorded in German-speaking parts of Switzerland while the largest Muslim communities are found in country's francophone west.

Frequent exhortations by politicians and commentators to take fears seriously can blind us to the fact that these fears are often deliberately stoked. Taking concerns about mass immigration, of the Other and the stranger, seriously must not mean kowtowing to right-wing populism by banning its visible manifestations, be they minarets or burkas, from the public sphere. Fears should be reduced by offering perspectives that solve problems. Those can be language learning opportunities in early childhood, shelters for women, investment in education, measures to prevent ghettoisation, and above all, dialogue. Indeed, there appears to be an increasing need for more dialogue in order to make the stranger less strange, the unknown known, the other no longer entirely other.

This is equally true in academic research: There is a definite need, yet research on questions of interreligious dialogue remains in its infancy throughout the various disciplines engaged in it. The international project *Religion and Dialogue in Modern Societies* (ReDi) at the Academy of World Religions of Hamburg University that started in 2011 seeks to contribute to remedying this deficit. Most articles in this book were created in the course of the project's preliminary study phase that included two conferences held in 2011 where all their authors met. Like the ReDi-Project, this book, too, looks at dialogue from different perspectives. It includes both theoretical and empirical approaches as well as a variety of theological viewpoints on a theology of plurality and dialogue from the perspective of different religions.

## The Contributions of this Volume

Religion, Society and Dialogue: Theoretical Approaches

First, *José Casanova* takes a critical look at the current state of European debates on secularisation, religion, and multicultural citizenship. He points to the need for a critical reflection of the European secularisation process and its specific relationship with modernisation to arrive at viable conceptions of multicultural citizenship and a modern nation state.

*Hans Joas* puts forward a plea for a process of dialogue in steps as a realistic mode of interreligious communication in a plural society. In this process, other religions must not merely be understood as value systems, but as efforts to interpret human experience. Only readiness to enter into a genuine encounter with the Other without relinquishing the Own can result in productive dialogue.

*Morteza Ghasempour's* contribution emphasises the necessity of a culture of mutual recognition. He understands dialogue as a mode of being that abjures any absolute truth claims in order to "make the Other possible". Such a mode of dialogically encountering the world would result in a radical "revaluation of values" and necessarily require opposition to social structures that stand against a culture of recognition.

Religious Diversity and the Need for Dialogue: Empirical Approaches

While the need for dialogue in religiously plural societies is obvious and expectations of it are high, the empirical study of dialogue is still in its infancy, facing a subject that is as broad as it is immediately relevant for modern society. The following four articles address key aspects of interreligious dialogue from global, European and national perspectives.

*Peter Beyer* emphasises that (world) religions as well as religious diversity are not self-evident, but the contingent outcome of historical developments. In this situation, interreligious dialogue occurs as a way of positively structuring religious differences within a unity that realises religion as a singular orientation. However, drawing on his current research from Canada it becomes clear that the actual religious identities, including vast and ambiguous 'in-between' identities as well as non-religious standpoints, are much more varied than the defined religions as categories can grasp. This raises the two central questions of who is actually (not) represented by the dialogue partners as well as what operates as the unit of this diversity.

*Nils Friedrichs* and *Alexander Yendell* study the attitudes towards religious communities and their adherents based on a survey from 2010 in five European countries: Denmark, France, Germany, Portugal and the Netherlands. They find that especially Islam as a religion, but also Muslims are viewed negatively in all five countries, but most strongly in Germany. Analysing theory-derived explanations they "confirm the importance of the contact hypothesis in all countries surveyed". Reservations against Islam and Muslims therefore do not result from actual encounters but, quite the reverse, from a lack of contact. This provides further impetus to investigate dialogical practices, which the next two articles do with a focus on Germany.

In view of the high normatively conditioned expectations of interreligious dialogue as an instrument for integration, *Gritt Klinkhammer* studies Christian-Muslim-dialogue in Germany, its conditions, and its impact in the Dialogos project. Besides finding that interreligious dialogue does not function easily once established, but is a demanding endeavour, she demonstrates that such initiatives are more than an integrative tool for governance. Instead, her emphasis is on their effect on individual religiosity by facilitating new spiritual experiences and thereby leading to "a dynamisation of religious practice".

Proceeding from established typologies of the various forms of interreligious dialogue, *Alexander-Kenneth Nagel* and *Mehmet Kalender* pose the question what motivates parties to participate in them. Their article offers a systematic review of motivations for interreligious activities based on interviews with promoters and organisers, addressing both exogenous motivations such as political expectations and endogenous ones, such as the wish to symbolically strengthen the presence of religion in secular society. Through this, they reveal the many faces of interreligious dialogue and at the same time show the need for further theoretical work on the nexus between exogenous and endogenous motivating factors.

Theology in the Plural: Interreligious and Dialogical Approaches

In his essay "Intercultural Theology as Interreligious Theology", *Perry Schmidt-Leukel* formulates the vision of an interreligious theology. This grew and emerged with increasing clarity through the twentieth century, and it grew out of intercultural theology. Yet what exactly does interreligious theology mean? Schmidt-Leukel writes: "Interreligious theology proceeds from the positive assumption that theologically relevant truth is not only found in one's own tradition, but also in those of other religions."

*Wolfram Weisse* draws attention to the contemporary roots of dialogical theology. He presents two core concepts of an interreligious, encounter-orientated dialogue which were developed in 1970s and 1980s by the Christian theologian Hans Jochen Margull and the Muslim theologian Abdoldjavad Falaturi. Although developed separately, their ideas show remarkable similarities, taking into account the daily experiences of people with their different religions and world views. They continue to be a valuable resource for the development of a dialogically orientated theology.

Dialogue in Jewish Thinking

*Ephraim Meir* explains in his contribution the conviction that all religions are windows to an Ultimate Reality. This fact gives us, as Meir puts it, the rationale for the realisation of an interreligious religiosity. Given that contacts with different cultures and religions have become the norm, an interreligious religiosity and a pluralisation of theologies are simply a necessity. He argues that this aim cannot be reached by integrating different theological traditions, but by taking them seriously while at the same time transcend them. His key term for this process is 'transdifference'.

## Dialogue in Christianity

Yet, for all it being necessary, dialogue is not easy to achieve. *Reinhold Bernhardt* explores the difficulties in his article "Jesus Christ as a Stumbling Block in Interreligious Dialogue?" where he also makes the point that different Christian traditions may result in different degrees of openness towards dialogue. He argues that a Christology which derives from a Johannine universalism will likely pave the way for interreligious dialogue more effectively than a Christology proceeding from the Pauline centrality of the cross. It is his aim to discuss a type of Christological approach and understanding of the truth of the Christian faith that is open to interreligious dialogue.

*Manuela Kalsky* goes in a different direction: Her article focuses on interreligious dialogue that is reflected in new identities; that can lead to new identities, as in the case of little Blume Yamina, the daughter of a Jewish mother and a Muslim father. Her bi-cultural and bi-religious upbringing makes her a *Jewslim*. Kalsky considers her an example of the situation young people are facing in a globalised world: The cultural and religious identities of future generations are becoming much more hybrid.

Yet another dimension of 'Dialogue in Christianity' is addressed by *Julia Ipgrave*. Her article views interreligious engagement in England from a specifically Church of England perspective. Her paper first characterises the English church establishment in relation to other faiths, then describes a shift in the nature of interfaith involvement over the last ten years and the place of the established Church in these, and further outlines some of the issues for the Church of England's interfaith involvement that were raised by the people she interviewed.

## Dialogue in Islam

Three essays investigate the question of 'Dialogue in Islam'. *Katajun Amirpur* sees a fundamental prerequisite of dialogue in the recognition of the 'religious other'. She therefore seeks evidence for this recognition in Islamic exegesis. As examples, she mentions the Mawlana Jalal-ud-Din, better known in the West as Rumi, the contemporary Iranian theologian Mohammad Mojtahed Shabestari, and Abdulkarim Soroush, referred to as the Iranian John Hick.

*Mahmoud Ayoub* seamlessly dovetails with this approach in that he, too, assumes that religious pluralism is already anchored in the Qur'an itself. Using numerous Qur'anic examples, he supports the view – shared by all Muslims that support religious pluralism – "that the Qur'anic worldview, with its emphasis on the diversity of human, racial and cultural identities and man's innate capacity to know and have faith in God, recognises the diverse religions of humankind as divinely preordained ways to this ultimate goal".

This opinion is shared by *Mahmut Aydın*. He discusses the Qur'anic teaching of the religious other. In his article he first deals with the issue of living together with the other within the context of the Qur'an's dialogue with Jews and Christians and then extends his findings to all non-Muslims. He, too, starts with the Qur'anic teaching. Muslims, in his opinion, must regulate their relationship in the light of the Qur'anic teaching since it is the centre of the Muslim faith. Aydın further believes that a better understanding of each other and living together can be achieved if Muslims – and Jews and Christians too – only listened to what their Holy Scripture tells them.

## Dialogue in Hinduism

*Anantanand Rambachan* explains how dialogical approaches in Hinduism can be strengthened. He considers dialogue an important element in the Hindu tradition, but sees it being weakened by a focus on individual spiritual experience without enough impulses from the sacred scriptures. To him, an intense and critical reflection of the Vedas is necessary to be better equipped for an interreligious dialogue e.g. with Christian partners. He therefore advocates a "more creative relationship between revelation, reason and experience."

## Dialogue in Buddhism

Last but not least, we are able to include articles on Buddhism. This is important since Buddhism is not only one of the oldest and largest religions worldwide, but also plays a growing role in Western societies.

*Carola Roloff*, one of our staff members at the Academy of World Religions and a Tibetan Buddhist nun, covers the theme of interreligious dialogue from a Buddhist perspective in general and focuses on the role of gender in its context. Stressing the importance of both inter- and intra-religious dialogue, she points to Buddhist scriptures and traditions which encourage and even demand it. She also presents different forms of dialogue and explains why the full ordination of nuns in Buddhism could become "a driving force for interreligious dialogue".

*André van der Braak* looks to the fundamental question of our understanding of texts in general and advocates a critical hermeneutics for the interpretation of texts in order to foster dialogue from the perspective of Zen-Buddhism. He stresses the relevance of a comparative approach to which Western scholars bring an active awareness of their religious traditions in order to be able to reflect more productively on the significance of Buddhist texts. With respect for the 'otherness' of Buddhist traditions, he reminds us to take the role of language more seriously and warns us not to "jump to interpretations too quickly", so as to avoid romantic or orientalist misinterpretations.

*Anna Alomes* presents a Buddhist vision of multi-faith dialogue. She frames her analysis by referring to the importance of such a dialogue in our time of profound change. Two examples illustrate how important the Buddhist teaching of empathy and the practice of meditation could be. One example looks at to the Truth and Reconciliation Commission in South Africa, the other at recent neurological research showing the effects of meditation on the brain. In the second part of her paper, the great relevance of an interfaith dialogue for Buddhists is demonstrated with reference to the planned "Charter for Universal Responsibility". This charter – which is advocated by the Dalai Lama – views the strengthening of respect and trust as the cornerstone for developing dialogue and global responsibility.

*Parichart Suwanbubbha* combines general reflections on forms and levels of dialogue in Buddhist thinking with concrete examples and experiences of conflict resolution through dialogue in Thailand. She stresses that the Buddha himself advocated and practiced dialogue with other religions and world views. The core elements of dialogue are seen in the Buddhist concept of 'compassionate' or 'deep' listening. She recommends verifying Buddhist concepts of interreligious dialogue by using them in concrete processes of dialogue. In order to show how this can be put into practice, she provides the example of a conflict resolution initiative in Southern Thailand.

## The international research project "Religion and Dialogue in Modern Societies" (ReDi) at the Academy of World Religions

As we were working and writing on dialogue it became more and more obvious for us that the growing religious pluralisation of modern societies has placed the question of religions and dialogue at the centre of public attention, with great expectations for the peaceful coexistence of people from different faiths and cultures tied to it.

That is why we are grateful that the Federal Ministry for Education and Research has decided to fund the project *Religion and Dialogue in Modern Societies* (ReDi) at the Academy of World Religions of Hamburg University starting in 2013 and scheduled for completion over five years in 2018. It is designed as practice-oriented research addressing the fundamental questions of interreligious dialogue both regarding its possibilities and limitations. Its interdisciplinary approach including theology (and the humanities in general) along with social sciences and education has been chosen to study complex phenomena of interreligious dialogical activity with regard to their impact on social processes of integration and peace-making and thus gain practically applicable insight for their realisation.

At the level of dialogical theology, our project identifies and explores the potential and limitations to dialogue in different religious traditions in order to base an open, dialogical theology on extant approaches of openness to pluralism. This work is undertaken by a team of experts from different religious traditions including Hamburg-based researchers and cooperation partners from both within Germany and abroad. The dialogical theology thus developed is to integrate empirical findings on the theological conceptions of laypeople, especially young people, rooted in the everyday experience of religious pluralism and living dialogical practice. A further aspect is the question what impulses interreligious dialogue may gain by integrating gendered perspectives.

At the level of research into dialogical practice, the project deploys empirical surveys to gauge the possibilities and limitations of living dialogue between people from different religious and cultural backgrounds and to study the forms, functions and potentials of dialogical practices. In this effort, two fields are in primary focus. On the one hand, we are studying the practices, opinions and reflections of lived religions in urban areas on different levels (different age groups and genders, lay people and clergy) in order to work out a differentiated structure of thinking and practice on dialogue and interaction across the range of lived religions. Furthermore, we analyse the ties and interactions of religious communities and organisations – both amongst each other and with secular actors (e.g. public authorities, politicians, NGOs, associations and other members of civil society). On the other hand, the broad field of religious education, both scholastic and extramural, is studied with a view to the possibilities and limitations it has for fostering interreligious understanding.

While the main focus lies on dialogue between religions (or religious actors), our project also encompasses dialogue within a given religious tradition as well as between religious and secular actors within the term 'interreligious dialogue'. Its initial understanding remains deliberately heuristic, and no final definition is attempted at the outset. Rather, it is the task of our research work to explore interreligious dialogue in its fundamental preconditions, applications and functions through interdisciplinary and complementary approaches and thus to contribute to a better understanding of the concept.

As interreligious dialogue always occurs within a specific context whose religious, political and socioeconomic conditions, societal discourses and other local factors shape it, this contextual dependence must also be taken into account. We are carrying out our research as an internationally comparative study whose horizon extends beyond Hamburg to other European metropolitan regions. In Germany, the Rhine-Ruhr region in Germany will be studied. Internationally surveys will also be carried out in Scandinavia, focusing on the cities of Oslo and Stockholm, and in London.

In Germany, public discourse on religious pluralism mostly focuses on Islam, usually viewed as a single entity and referred to as *"der Islam"*, using a definite article. This predominance is defended by pointing to over four million Muslims living in Germany and their justified calls for greater recognition and participation in public affairs. For example, the Federal Ministry of Education and Research has been supporting the introduction of Islamic Studies or Islamic Theology as a subject taught at public universities based on recommendations of the German Science Council.

The current – and even more so future – situation in Germany will have to take account not only of Christian and Muslim theologies, though, but also of a growing number of other faiths, an increasing intrareligious differentiation into separate traditions or confessions, and individualised forms of religiosity and spirituality that defy traditional religious affiliation. Developing an analytical perspective on religious pluralism and the relations between people from different religious traditions or belief systems thus is a vital task for academia and society at large. That is what our project aims to do.

Its two central perspectives exemplify the unique position the Academy of World Religions of Hamburg University has in German academia. The approach is deliberately dialogue-oriented, focusing not only on a coexistence of different religions, but on the interaction between them, especially with a view to extant dialogue orientation and future potential. Also, it integrates religions beyond Christianity and Islam, namely Judaism, Buddhism, Hinduism and Alevism while also taking into account the perspective of the religiously unaffiliated and people or groups whose positions on religious questions are socially relevant, but underresearched. Thus, the Academy's research profile matches the central characteristics of the religious landscape in Germany and other European countries: pluralism, internal differentiation, individualisation and secularisation. In this context it must be pointed out, though, that the latter aspect tends to be overestimated in its importance and that we can expect growing religiosity, or at least interest in religion, in Western Europe as well as the rest of the world. This makes us even more grateful to be able to study religion and dialogue in modern societies in such detail.

## Acknowledgements

We would like to express our gratitude to the Federal Ministry of Education and Research for funding our work in general and also providing support for this publication. Further, we wish to thank the authors whose work is collected in this volume not only for allowing us to publish their contributions, but also for the knowledge and commitment they brought to the table at our conferences. They have contributed greatly to the development of the project and will continue to do so during its main phase. We are indebted to the Senate of the Free and Hanseatic City of Hamburg, especially to Dr. Dorothee Stapelfeldt, senator of the Authority for Science and Research. We also express our gratitude to the President of Hamburg University, Prof. Dieter Lenzen, and the Dean of the Faculty of Education of our University, Prof. Eva Arnold, for their support of our Academy of World Religions and our research on religions and dialogue. We are also indebted to the *Udo Keller Foundation Forum Humanum* for their longstanding and generous support and to the *Volker and Veronika Putz Foundation*. Moreover, we would like to thank Volker Bach for his excellent work translating articles for this book into English and proofreading others, and Heike Stamer for her critical re-reading and her professional editing of the texts. Thanks are also due to Stela Muminovic for formatting the contributions with the help of Habib Khenkhar. Finally, we also wish to express our thanks to Beate Plugge of our publisher Waxmann Verlag for the great help and support we have received from her, as always.

# Religion, Society and Dialogue:
# Theoretical Approaches

*José Casanova*

# Secularisation, Religion and Multicultural Citizenship[1]

Each of these terms, 'secularisation', 'religion' and 'multicultural citizenship', would require a separate and more systematic elaboration than the one I can offer in a single lecture. My aim in this chapter is simply to explore some interrelations between contemporary debates about secularisation, religion, and multicultural citizenship by adopting a global comparative perspective which may help to illuminate critically the European debates.

## 1.   Secularisation

Rather than viewing secularisation as a general universal process of human and societal development culminating in secular modernity, one should begin with the recognition that the very term secularisation derives from a unique Western Christian theological category, that of the *saeculum*, which has no equivalent term not only in other world religions, but even in Eastern Christianity. Originally, the Latin world *saeculum*, as in *per saecula saeculorum* only meant an indefinite period of time, but eventually it became one of the terms of a dyad, religious/secular, which served to structure the entire spatial and temporal reality of medieval Christendom into a binary system of classification separating two worlds, the religious-spiritual-sacred world of salvation and the secular-temporal-profane world. Thus, the distinction between the 'religious' or regular clergy, who withdrew from the world into the monasteries to lead a life of Christian perfection, and the 'secular' clergy who lived in the world along with the laity.

In this respect, to secularise means to "make worldly", to convert religious persons or things into secular ones, as when a religious person abandons the monastic rule to live in the world, or when monastic property is secularised. This is the original Christian theological meaning of the term secularisation that may serve, however, as the basic metaphor of the historical process of Western secularisation. This historical process needs to be understood as a particular reaction to the structuring dualism of Medieval Christendom, as an attempt to bridge, eliminate or transcend the dualism between the religious and the secular world. Even in the West, however, this process of secularisation follows two different dynamics.

One is the dynamic of internal Christian secularisation which aims to spiritualise the temporal and to bring the religious life of perfection out of the monasteries into the secular world. It tends to transcend the dualism by blurring

---

1   Public lecture within the symposium *Islamic Theology in Dialogue*, University of Hamburg, January 14–15, 2010.

the boundaries between the religious and the secular, by making the religious secular and the secular religious through mutual reciprocal infusion. This path was initiated by the various medieval movements of Christian reform of the *saeculum,* was radicalised by the Protestant Reformation and has attained its paradigmatic expression in the Anglo-Saxon Calvinist cultural area, particularly in the United States.

The other different, indeed almost opposite dynamic of secularisation takes the form of laicisation. It aims to emancipate all secular spheres from clerical-ecclesiastical control and in this respect it is marked by a laic-clerical antagonism. Unlike in the Protestant path, however, here the boundaries between the religious and the secular are rigidly maintained, but those boundaries are pushed into the margins, aiming to contain, privatise and marginalise everything religious, while excluding it from any visible presence in the secular public sphere, now defined as the realm of *laïcité,* freed from religion. This is the paradigmatic French-Latin-Catholic path of secularisation, but it will find diverse manifestations throughout continental Europe.

With many variations these are the two main dynamics of secularisation which culminate in our secular age. In different ways both paths lead to an overcoming of the medieval Christian dualism through a positive affirmation and revaluation of the *saeculum,* that is, of the secular age and the secular world, imbuing the immanent secular world with a quasi-transcendent meaning as the place for human flourishing. In this broad sense of the term 'secular', we are all secular and all modern societies are secular and are likely to remain so for the foreseeable future, one could almost say *per saecula saeculorum.*

There is a second, narrower meaning of the term secular, that of self-sufficient and exclusive secularity, when people are simply 'irreligious', that is, devoid of religion and closed to any form of transcendence beyond the purely secular immanent frame. Here, secular is not anymore one of the units of a dyadic pair, but is constituted as a self-enclosed reality. To a certain extent, this constitutes one possible end-result of the process of secularisation, of the attempt to overcome the dualism between religious and secular, by freeing oneself of the religious component.

In his recent work, *A Secular Age,* Charles Taylor has reconstructed the process through which the phenomenological experience of what he calls "the immanent frame" becomes constituted as an interlocking constellation of the modern differentiated cosmic, social and moral orders. All three orders, the cosmic, the social, and the moral are understood as purely immanent secular orders, devoid of transcendence, and thus functioning *etsi Deus non daretur,* "as if God would not exist". It is this phenomenological experience that, according to Taylor, constitutes our age paradigmatically as a secular one, irrespective of the extent to which people living in this age may still hold religious or theistic beliefs.

The question is whether the phenomenological experience of living within such an immanent frame is such that people within it will also tend to function *etsi Deus non daretur.* Taylor's phenomenological account of the secular "conditions" of belief is meant to explain the change from a Christian society around 1500CE in which belief in God was unchallenged and unproblematic, indeed 'naïve' and taken for granted, to a post-Christian society today in which belief in God not only is no longer axiomatic but is becoming increasingly problematic, so that even those who adopt an 'engaged' standpoint as believers tend to experience reflexively their own belief as an option among many others, one moreover requiring an explicit justification. Secularity, being without religion, by contrast tends to become increasingly the default option, which can be naively experienced as natural and, thus, no longer in need of justification.

This naturalisation of 'unbelief' or 'non-religion' as the normal human condition in modern societies corresponds to the assumptions of the dominant theories of secularisation, which have postulated a progressive decline of religious beliefs and practices with increasing modernisation, so that the more modern a society the more secular, i.e. the less 'religious' it is supposed to become. That the decline of religious beliefs and practices is a relatively recent meaning of the term secularisation is indicated by the fact that it does not yet appear in the dictionary of most modern European languages.

The fact that there are some modern non-European societies, such as the United States or South Korea, that are fully secular in the sense that they function within the same immanent frame and yet their populations are also at the same time conspicuously religious, or the fact that the modernisation of so many non-Western societies is accompanied by processes of religious revival, should put into question the premise that the decline of religious beliefs and practices is a quasi-natural consequence of processes of modernisation. If modernisation per se does not necessarily produce the progressive decline of religious beliefs and practices, then we need a better explanation for the radical and widespread secularity one finds among the population of Western European societies.

Secularisation, in this second meaning of the term secular, that of being "devoid of religion", does not happen automatically as a result of processes of modernisation, but it needs to be mediated phenomenologically by some other particular historical experience.

Self-sufficient secularity, that is, the absence of religion, has a better chance of becoming the normal taken-for-granted position if it is experienced not as an unreflexively naïve condition, as just a fact, but actually as the meaningful result of a quasi-natural process of development. As Taylor has pointed out, modern unbelief is not simply a condition of absence of belief, nor merely indifference. It is a historical condition that requires the perfect tense, "a condition of 'having overcome' the irrationality of belief".[2] Intrinsic to this phenomenological experience is a modern "stadial consciousness", inherited from the Enlightenment, which understands this anthropocentric change in the conditions of belief as a process of maturation and growth, as a "coming of age" and as progressive

---

2    Taylor, C. (2007) *A Secular Age* Cambridge, MA: Harvard University Press, 269.

emancipation. For Taylor, this stadial phenomenological experience serves in turn to ground the phenomenological experience of exclusive humanism as the positive self-sufficient and self-limiting affirmation of human flourishing and as the critical rejection of transcendence beyond human flourishing as self-denial and self-defeating.

In this respect, the historical self-understanding of secularism has the function of confirming the superiority of our present modern secular outlook over other supposedly earlier and therefore more primitive religious forms of understanding. To be secular means to be modern, and therefore by implication to be religious means to be somehow not yet fully modern. This is the ratchet effect of a modern historical stadial consciousness, which turns the very idea of going back to a surpassed condition into an unthinkable intellectual regression.

The function of secularism as a philosophy of history, and thus as ideology, is to turn the particular Western Christian historical process of secularisation into a universal teleological process of human development from belief to unbelief, from primitive irrational or metaphysical religion to modern rational post-metaphysical secular consciousness. Even when the particular role of internal Christian developments in the general process of secularisation is acknowledged, it is in order to stress the universal significance of the uniqueness of Christianity as, in Marcel Gauchet's expressive formulation, "the religion to exit from religion".[3]

I would like to propose that this secularist stadial consciousness is a crucial factor in the widespread secularisation that has accompanied the modernisation of Western European societies. Europeans tend to experience their own secularisation, that is, the widespread decline of religious beliefs and practices in their midst as a natural consequence of their modernisation. To be secular is not experienced as an existential choice which modern individuals or modern societies make, but rather as a natural outcome of becoming modern. In this respect, the theory of secularisation mediated through this historical stadial consciousness tends to function as a self-fulfilling prophecy. It is, in my view, the presence or absence of this secularist historical stadial consciousness that explains when and where processes of modernisation are accompanied by radical secularisation. In places where such secularist historical stadial consciousness is absent or less dominant, as in the United States or in most non-Western post-colonial societies, processes of modernisation are unlikely to be accompanied by processes of religious decline. On the contrary, they may be accompanied by processes of religious revival.

In our global age it has become increasingly evident that European secular developments are not a universal norm for the rest of the world and that, as the rest of the world modernises, its people are not becoming more secular like us, but are becoming more religious, or actually they are becoming simultaneous-

---

3    Gauchet, M. (1999) *The Disenchantment of the World* Princeton: Princeton University
     Press.

ly both more secular and more religious, which of course only muddles and confuses our binary categories. Indeed, one must admit that the whole world is becoming simultaneously both more 'religious' and more 'secular' since the Western Christian binary classification system of religious versus secular reality has been adopted globally. Indeed, the categories of 'religious' and 'secular' have recently become globalised for the first time in all non-Western cultures.

## 2.    Religion

Whereas the social sciences, and particularly my own discipline, i.e. the sociology of religion, still function with a relatively unreflexive general category of religion, within the newer discipline of "religious studies" (which in German would be called *Religionswissenschaft*) the very category of 'religion' has undergone numerous challenges as well as all kinds of critical deconstructions. There has been much debate in the last two decades concerning the competing genealogies of the 'modern' category of religion and its complex relation to various phenomena like the pluralisation of Christian confessions and denominations in early modernity, the Western colonial expansion and the encounter with the religious 'other', the Enlightenment critique of religion and the triumph of 'secular reason', the hegemony of the secular state and the disciplinary institutionalisation of the scientific study of religion, as well as the Western 'invention of the world religions' and the classificatory taxonomies of religion which have now become globalised.

But, paradoxically, scholars of religion are questioning the validity of the category of 'religion' at the very same moment when the discursive reality of religion is more widespread than ever and has become, for the first time, global. I am not claiming that people today everywhere are either more or less religious than they may have been in the past. Here I am bracketing out altogether the question which has dominated most theories of secularisation, namely whether religious beliefs and practices are declining or growing as a general modern trend throughout the world. I am only claiming that 'religion' as a discursive reality, indeed as an abstract category and as a system of classification of reality, used by modern individuals as well as by modern societies across the world, by religious as well as by secular authorities, has become an undisputable global social fact.

It is obvious that, when people around the world use the same category of religion, they actually mean very different things. The actual concrete meaning of whatever people denominate as 'religion' can only be elucidated in the context of their particular discursive practices. But the very fact that the same category of religion is being used globally across cultures and civilisations testifies to the global expansion of the modern secular/religious system of classification of reality which first emerged in the modern Christian West.

Moreover, while the religious/secular system of classification of reality may have become globalised, what remains hotly disputed and debated almost everywhere in the world today is how, where, and by whom the proper boundaries between the religious and the secular ought to be drawn. There are in this respect multiple competing secularisms, as there are multiple and diverse forms of religious fundamentalist resistance to those secularisms. For example, American, French, Turkish, Indian and Chinese secularism – to name only some paradigmatic and distinctive modes of drawing the boundaries between the religious and the secular – represent not only very different patterns of separation of the secular state and religion, but very different models of state regulation and management of religion and of religious pluralism in society.

Similarly, despite 'family resemblances' observed among the diverse religious fundamentalisms, one should resist the temptation to view them all as diverse manifestations of a single process of religious fundamentalist reaction against a single general global process of progressive secularisation. Each of the so-called religious fundamentalist movements – American Protestant, Jewish, Muslim, Hindu, etc., each of which is moreover internally plural and diverse – are particular responses to particular ways of drawing the boundaries between the religious and the secular. Moreover, those responses are not only reactive, but also proactive attempts to seize the opportunity offered by processes of globalisation to redraw the boundaries. Above all, always and everywhere the religious and the secular are mutually constituted through socio-political struggles and cultural politics. Not surprisingly, one also finds diverse resistances to attempts to impose the European, or any other particular pattern of secularisation as a universal, teleological model everywhere.

It is no longer the United States alone which appears to be an exception to the European rule of secularisation, but the rest of the world appears to be equally exceptional to the point in which we are now talking of the European exception. But we should be cautious with the new discourse of European exceptionalism, because when it comes to 'religion' and its antonym 'the secular', there is no global rule. We must humbly recognise that many of our received categories, derived from our Christian-secular European developments, fail us when we try to understand developments in the rest of the world, in that they, rather than facilitating understanding, actually lead to fundamental misunderstanding. Neither the category of religious fundamentalism, as if we were witnessing a single global anti-modern reaction to secular modernity, nor the term proposed by Peter Berger "the de-secularisation of the world" (*Entsäkularisierung der Welt*), as if we were witnessing simply a reversal of a previous process of secularisation, nor even the expression "return of religion" or "religious revival", as if we were simply witnessing the return of the old traditional religions, none of these categories are very helpful in trying to understand contemporary religious developments around the world. We first need a 'de-secularisation' of our consciousness and of our secularist and modernist categories before we can develop better concepts to understand the novelty and the modernity of these developments.

The very category of secularisation becomes deeply problematic once it is conceptualised in a Euro-centric way as a universal process of progressive human societal development from 'belief' to 'unbelief' and from traditional 'religion' to modern 'secularity' and once it is transferred to other world religions and other civilisational areas with very different dynamics of structuration of the relations and tensions between religion and world, or between cosmological transcendence and worldly immanence. Moreover, in the same way as Western secular modernity is fundamentally and inevitably post-Christian, the emerging multiple modernities in the different post-axial civilisational areas are likely to be post-Hindu, or post-Confucian, or post-Muslim, i.e. they will also be particular and contingent refashionings and transformations of existing civilisational patterns and social imaginaries mixed with modern secular ones.

We need to recognise the particular historical character of European developments, not only in relation to non-Western cultures, but even more importantly in relation to other Western non-European developments, such as those in the United States.

The drastic decline in church attendance across Europe since the 1950s constitutes the strongest evidence for the defenders of the traditional theory of secularisation. When compared with the very different evidence of continuing vitality in congregational, associational religion in the United States across all denominations – Protestant and Catholic, Jewish and Muslim, and now Hindu and Buddhist – it is obvious that this is the fundamental difference between American and European religiosity. Secularisation in Europe takes primarily the form of 'unchurching' (*Entkirchlichung*), which should be understood as a form of liberation from the type of territorialised confessional religiosity which was the legacy of the Westphalian system. European Christianity, for all kinds of reasons, never made the full historical transition from territorial national churches based on the territorial parish (*Pfarrgemeinde*) to competing denominations of civil society based on voluntary religious associations, a modern form of religious community.

The analytical distinction between "church" and "denomination" is the key to any comparative analysis of religious developments and patterns of secularisation in Europe and the United States. Following Max Weber's definition, sociologically, a "church" is an ecclesiastical institution which claims the monopoly of the means of salvation over a territory. The territorialisation of religion and the corresponding confessionalisation of state, nation and peoples are the fundamental facts and formative principles of the Westphalian system of sovereign territorial states which emerged in early modern Europe out of the so-called wars of religion. The principle *cuius regio eius religio* is the general formative principle of such a system, a principle moreover which was already well established before the wars of religion and even before the Protestant Reformation, as shown by the expulsion of Jews and Muslims from Spain by the Catholic monarchs in order to establish a territorial Catholic state ruling over a homogeneously religious Catholic society. What the Peace of Westphalia represented was the generalisation of this dual model of confessionalisation of states, nations and peoples and territorialisation of ecclesiastical religion among the emerging European territorial states. Every early modern European state (with the exception of the Polish-Lithuanian Commonwealth), was defined confessionally as Catholic, Anglican, Lutheran, Calvinist, or Orthodox. In this respect, religious homogenisation and in many instances ethno-religious cleansing are found at the very origin of the modern European state.

This is the fundamental factor of early modern European history which will determine the various patterns of European secularisation. Comparatively speaking, European secularisation can be best understood as a process of successive de-confessionalisations of states, nations and peoples, which has been phenomenologically experienced as a process of liberation from confessional identities. This is what determines the historically unique character of European secularisation, which is now increasingly being recognised as a form of 'European exceptionalism' rather than as a general model of modernisation that is likely to be replicated elsewhere. In fact, the European pattern of secularisation can hardly be replicated in other contexts in which there was no previous historical pattern of confessionalisation of states, nations and peoples requiring their secularisation, that is, their de-confessionalisation.

## 3.    Multicultural Citizenship

It should be obvious that this interrelation between confessionalisation, de-confessionalisation and European secularisation is also intrinsically related with issues of multicultural citizenship. In fact, without taking into account this longue durée European pattern of confessionalisation and de-confessionalisation, it is not possible to understand the difficulties which every continental European state has – irrespective of whether they have maintained formal establishment or are constitutionally secular – and the difficulties which every European society has – the most secular as well as the most religious ones – in accommodating religious diversity, and particularly in incorporating immigrant religions.[4] This is one of the fundamental differences between Europe and the United States, which never underwent a process of confessionalisation and developed a radically different model of religious denominationalism.

Paraphrasing Karl Marx in "On the Jewish Question" one could say that if America can be characterised simultaneously as the model of "perfect disestablishment" and the "land of religiosity par excellence", European societies offer by contrast the inverse combination of different forms of "imperfect disestab-

---

4    Casanova, J. (2007) Immigration and the New Religious Pluralism: A EU/US Comparison. In: T. Banchoff (Ed.) *Democracy and the New Religious Pluralism* New York: Oxford University Press, 59–84.

lishment" and "lands of secularity par excellence".[5] The United States never had to undergo a formal process of separation of church and state, since it never had either a confessional state or an established state church, from which the state had to separate itself. Unlike most Europeans, Americans also did not need to undergo a process of de-confessionalisation from any national ecclesiastical institution, since even the established colonial churches – Congregational, Presbyterian and Anglican – remained minoritarian institutions and the majority of the population remained unchurched. The American state was born as a modern secular state, without having to undergo any process of de-confessionalisation. The dual constitutional formula of no establishment of religion at the state level and free exercise of religion in society guaranteed the development of denominationalism as a system of free and open religious pluralism in society.

American denominationalism is a system of mutual recognition of de-territorialised voluntary religious institutions and associations within civil society without any state regulation or interference other than through the courts when there are legal conflicts within or among religious organisations. The American state not only has no office of regulation or registration of religious associations, but does not even have the right to register or survey the religious denomination of its individual citizens.

It should be obvious that the different American model of religious denominationalism within a pluralistic civil society and the European model of confessional national churches with limited pluralism have important consequences for the constitution of civil society on both sides of the Atlantic, but also for the development of inclusionary, more egalitarian and solidaristic welfare states in Europe and the weak development of a welfare state in the USA. As the polemical debates around the attempts of the Obama administration to reform the American health system clearly indicate, the very discursive legitimation of what is a taken for granted principle in most European nation states, namely the principle a of public national health system which guarantees a minimum egalitarian access of health care for all its citizens, is immediately suspect as an etatist, socialist un-American project and susceptible to the most irrational debates. One can certainly find close elective affinities between the anti-etatist model of state-civil society relations and the model of free exercise of religion protected from any kind of state regulation or control.

American religious pluralism and the multicultural model of society are historically related to the continuous waves of immigration from all over the world. Indeed, there is compelling historical evidence that immigrants to America throughout history, throughout the 19th century as well as in the late 20th century, become increasingly more religious, not less, as they settle in the new country. In fact, most immigrant groups – Protestants and Catholics, Jews and Muslims, Hindus and Buddhists – today as in the past claim to be more con-

---

5   Berger, P. et al. (2008) *Religious America, Secular Europe? A Theme and Variations* Hampshire: Ashgate.

sciously and reflexively religious in the United States than they were in their old countries before immigration. In this respect, American religiosity is not a traditional survival from traditional societies which is bound to disappear with increasing modernisation, but is actually an immigrant response to the conditions of denominational religious pluralism in American society.

The conditions in Europe in this respect are significantly different. European societies, after many centuries of religious homogeneity, are becoming again, in some cases for the first time, religiously pluralistic. This novel phenomenon is related, on the one hand, to processes of increasing religious individuation linked to ongoing de-confessionalisation and, on the other, and more importantly to increasing immigration. The new religious pluralism presents a challenge not only to the traditional model of the homogeneous nation-state, but even more so to the equally homogeneous conceptions of modern secular societies and to secularist conceptions of liberal democracy and the public sphere.

It is important to recognise that the Westphalian principle, *cuius regio eius religio,* and the principle of a homogeneous national society that it entails, were not significantly altered either by the critical transition from royal to national or popular sovereignty after the French Revolution, or by the expansion and consolidation of democracy in Western European societies after World War II. Neither the limited secularisation of the European state nor the more drastic secularisation of European societies altered the dynamics of religious and cultural homogeneity. Secularisation, to be sure, brought the de-confessionalisation of individuals and peoples, as well as increasing individualisation, liberalisation, and moral pluralism. But it did not create the conditions for new forms of religious or cultural pluralism.

In the past, 'the Jewish question' served as the catalyst of all the unresolved tensions in conceptions of civic as well as ethnic nationalism in Europe. Today 'the Muslim question' serves as a similar catalyst in all the debates concerning competing conceptions of liberal secular democracy and multicultural citizenship. The difficulty which most European societies have with the integration of Muslim immigrants could be viewed not so much, or at least not only, as a sign that 'Islam' might be 'the problem', but rather as an indication of the still unresolved problems which the model of the European nation-state has – whether it is formally secular or not – in regulating deep religious pluralism. One should question the problematic notion that the European secular state is de facto a religiously neutral state and therefore already contains within itself the proper solution to the management of religious pluralism in society. In order to be more neutral the state will need to become not only post-Christian, but also post-secularist.

The same could be said about 'secularist' conceptions of the liberal public sphere.

In this context I would like to introduce a distinction between secularism as statecraft principle and secularism as ideology. By secularism as statecraft principle, I understand simply some principle of separation between religious and political authority, either for the sake of the neutrality of the state vis-à-vis each and all religions, or for the sake of protecting the freedom of conscience of each individual, or for the sake of facilitating the equal access of all citizens, religious as well as non-religious, to democratic participation. Such a statecraft doctrine neither presupposes nor needs to entail any substantive 'theory', positive or negative, of 'religion'. Indeed the moment the state holds a particular view of 'religion' one enters the realm of ideology.

Secularism becomes an ideology the moment it entails a theory of what 'religion' is or does. It is this assumption that 'religion', in the abstract, is a thing that has an essence or that produces certain particular and predictable effects, which is the defining characteristic of modern secularism. It is the essentialising of 'the religious', based on problematic assumptions of what 'religion' is or does, which is in my view the fundamental problem of secularism as ideology. One can distinguish two basic types of secularist ideologies. The first type is secularist theories of religion grounded in some progressive stadial philosophies of history which relegates religion to a superseded stage. The second type is secularist political theories which presuppose that religion is either an irrational force or a non-rational form of discourse which should be banished from the democratic public sphere. They can be called respectively 'philosophico-historical' and 'political' secularisms.

At the phenomenological level of everyday life philosophico-historical secularist prejudices are manifested in the assumption that to be secular means to leave religion behind, to emancipate oneself from religion, thus overcoming the non-rational forms of being, thinking and feeling associated with religion. It also means growing up, becoming mature, becoming autonomous, thinking and acting on one's own. It is precisely this assumption that secular people think and act on their own and are rational autonomous free agents, while religious people somehow are unfree, heteronomous, non-rational agents, which constitutes the foundational premise of secularist ideology.

On its part, political secularism falls easily into secularist ideology the moment 'the political' arrogates for itself an absolute, sovereign, quasi-sacred, quasi-transcendent character or when 'the secular' arrogates for itself the mantle of rationality and universality, while claiming that 'religion' is essentially non-rational, particularistic, and intolerant (or illiberal) and as such dangerous and a threat to democratic politics once it enters the public sphere. It is the essentialising of 'the religious', but also of 'the secular' or 'the political', based on problematic assumptions of what 'religion' is or does, which is in my view the fundamental problem of secularism as ideology.

Overcoming, or at least being reflexively aware of such secular prejudices would seem to be a necessary condition for any viable conception of multicultural citizenship. We need to be more reflexively aware of the complex historical process of Western Christian secularisation and its relation to allegedly general processes of modernisation, as well as to the processes of modern state formation and modern nationalism. We must avoid the false dichotomies built into our binary categories, either religious or secular, either traditional or modern. Above all, we must be more critically reflexive of the stadial consciousness built into our "secular self-interpretation of modernity." Becoming post-secular does not mean necessarily becoming religious again, but questioning our stadial consciousness as well as our Euro-centric conceptions of secular modernity.

*Hans Joas*

## Values and Religion

The Transmission of Values and Interreligious Dialogue Today[1]

Whenever there is talk of the necessity of a clear value-orientation, of the urgency of a reflection on one's own values, or of the difficulties of transmitting values to the next generation, the question concerning religion is not far off. This is not surprising because religions do indeed give values a graphic form. Believers gain motivation and orientation from their faith and position themselves within traditions which they also try to pass on to their children and pupils. On closer examination, however, difficulties also reveal themselves. The Christian churches, for instance, despite all the achievements in the area of transmitting values, are like other religious communities by no means unanimously enthusiastic when, in view of social ills or conflicts, they are given a kind of commission to reconstitute social cohesion. They then feel themselves to be degraded to mere tools or functional social systems, and resist faith's being put into service for exogenous ends. Their objection is that faith does not arise through a rational conviction that it is useful for the individual, or for others, or for society. Conversely, some warn against regarding religions at all as a possible source of social cohesion. Their argument is that religions are necessarily particular formations borne by particular communities. Quite independently of their orientation, they are therefore said to have a divisive potential which the state and society have to tame and to overarch with religiously neutralised institutions.

The following considerations represent a modest attempt to sketch a realistic path for religiously founded transmission of values and interreligious dialogue in a time when the various religions are coming into ever closer contact with one another through migration and globalisation, but at the same time, especially in Europe, the Christian tradition has been pushed onto the defensive, and even partially marginalised through various forms of secularisation.

The starting-point must be the insight that religions are indeed more than value systems.[2] Those who believe certainly regard their faith not primarily as a logically consistent system of statements about the good, or even as a merely emotionally coloured morality. Faith is based on intensive experiences; it enables participation in rituals which themselves are in turn sources of experience;

---

1   This article is the revised version of an essay that appeared in: L. Mohn et al. (Eds.) (2006) *Werte. Was die Gesellschaft zusammenhält* Gütersloh: Verlag Bertelsmann-Stiftung, 19–32. An English version of the original article appeared in the Korean periodical *Indigo* 2 (2010), 72–80.

2   For details on the understanding of religions, faith and values: Joas, H. (2008) *Do We Need Religion? On the Experience of Self-Transcendence* Boulder, CO/London: Paradigm Publishers; Id. (2000) *The Genesis of Values* Chicago: University of Chicago Press.

it offers exemplary models that invite us to imitate them; and it contains stories and myths that provide a thread when interpreting our own lives and history, helping us to answer questions concerning the meaning of life. What is decisive is that all these experiences, symbolisations and narratives are far too rich to be reduced to formulae. Instead of reducing religions to value-systems or systems of doctrinal propositions, it would therefore be more plausible to ask converse-ly for the experiential foundations, symbolic and narrative structures in all non-religious value-systems. To be sure, orientations arise for the faithful from faith, but they are not derived from it in an abstract, logical way, but through the concrete interpretation of invariably risky situations of decision and action.

This insight into the character of religions, and in part even of stable and widespread secular interpretations of the world as well, must be taken as starting-point because it makes an effect comprehensible that many feel to be paradoxical and which recurs in attempts to provide an overview of the world's religions or competing value-systems. When religions are presented as mere systems of values or statements of faith held to be true, whether it be in school-teaching, or in a social-scientific form, the effect is initially mostly confusion, then indifference. Even when the intention of this preoccupation consists in facilitating for participants a free, individual decision in the market for systems of meaning, in such a presentation, the individual religions must appear as formations that are difficult to understand, stretch the limits of com-prehensibility and in part are even odd and peculiar. And this holds not only for the religions of exotic cultures but, in such a presentation, even for those that in the past have left a deep impression on their own culture; even these religions can provoke perplexity about the irrationality of our forebears. Non-believers thus usually find a confirmation of their prepossession about how healthy it is to keep a safe distance from the peculiarities of religious life. If mere distance does not suffice for them, they can only attempt to assume an objectifying per-spective on religions in their diversity, to conceive of them as the consequence of economic, political or social conditions, or to attribute them to psychologi-cal, and perhaps even biological, phenomena of human existence.

In such confrontations with the diversity of religions (and secular world-interpretations) there are for believers in principle two options. They too, like the self-assured secular thinker, can on the one hand, attribute truth, and even evidence, to their own faith only; for them, too, then all other religions are a cabinet of curiosities, a 'gobbledygook', as missionaries sometimes called the religions of their mission districts. On the other hand, some missionaries, by contrast, developed an understanding of, sometimes even gaining admiring access to the religions they found in foreign parts. They regarded the religions they struck upon as impressive interpretations of authentic experiences that people had gone through in other times and cultures in their lives, including in their dealings with the divine. According to this view, many or all religions contain an element of divine revelation.

A precondition for such a productive relationship to religions is to regard them not as value-systems, and also not as quasi-scientific doctrines, but as attempted interpretations of human experiences. Secular and religious ways of dealing with experiences are then distinguished by the fact that the former hold that which is encountered in human experience as a purely inner-worldly phenomenon, whereas the latter declare that a genuine encounter with the divine is possible, and therefore presuppose that in experiences of self-transcendence there is also an opportunity to encounter transcendence per se. The obverse side of productive curiosity about religious interpretations of the world is thus a certain humility toward one's own interpretive background. It, too, then becomes recognizable as an expression of constitutive experiences, and the thought becomes plausible that also one's own interpretation of experiences of self-transcendence is to be regarded as never quite successful, never quite exhausting the richness of experience. This must hold true all the more when a real encounter with divine transcendence is seen in these experiences. The divine can only ever reveal itself comprehensibly in the words and symbols of human beings, but never can present itself to us as it is in itself. In such a perspective, the word of God, as it has been laid down in the holy scriptures, is not the immediate self-expression of God, but the passing-on of God's communicative intention within the referential frame of the recipients, that is, of people who are always situated distinctively in history and culture, and thus within the limits of their knowledge and imaginative powers.

Accordingly, the preoccupation with religions generates not merely confusion and indifference if it takes place with an open mind toward the other and humility regarding one's own worldview. Now, it is easy to demand open-mindedness and to declare that one is prepared to be so. A general open-mindedness, however, does not achieve any more than a search for common features, the formation of a smallest common denominator. It does not open up anything really new and therefore does not lead to any change in one's own standpoint. In this sense, open-mindedness is only a minimum condition that has to be fulfilled if an exacting process is to get underway, for the serious engrossment with religions is a strenuous process challenging one's own certainties. As in the case of understanding other people or cultures in general, a comparison with the acquisition of foreign languages helps here. When we learn a foreign language, our sensibility for the contingencies of one's own language is enhanced. We see that semantic structures and syntactic rules are not necessary per se, and are not demanded by the inherent structure of the world. The acquisition of every further language is tedious. Through the attempt to acquire several languages simultaneously, we become confused and do not make headway with any of them. A comparative lecture about the grammars of the world's languages may provide us with some information, but certainly does not teach us the use of a single language. This can be regarded as an analogy to the attempt to gain an overview of the religions. It seems as if the acquisition of further foreign languages becomes easier if we have already learned some; but there is no completely generalised ability to learn languages which would obviate the acquisition of each concrete language.

George Santayana has put this into the famous formula: "The attempt to speak without speaking a concrete language is just as much doomed to failure as the attempt, without a calling, to be religious in a certain religion."[3] In a context marked by Christianity, the 'realistic' path which is to be sketched here must therefore begin with the ecumenical dialogue as soon as the transmission of one's own tradition of faith is to be transcended. The opportunities and difficulties of the intra-Christian ecumenical dialogue are necessary training for a more comprehensive understanding among the religions. The ecumenical dialogue can indeed lead to the overcoming of only apparent existing differences, whether these exist in theological doctrines or in mere stereotypes of mentality as they have come down from history or arise recurrently from the needs of denominations or confessions to mark oneself off and sharpen one's own profile. This dialogue can also lead to the sobering insight that the differences are not even described in a common language, and even the offers of common ground from one side are perceived by the other as mere strategies for co-option and absorption. In Germany, the ecumenical dialogue is simplified by the fact that it takes into consideration only a small segment of the Christian spectrum. The orthodox and oriental forms of Christianity play only a minor role in it, and the Protestant spectrum comprises practically none of the fundamentalist currents that are so significant in the United States, nor the Pentecostal movement whose rapid spread in parts of Latin American and Africa is nothing less than spectacular.

Apart from the ecumenical dialogue, in the second half of the 20th century, the Judaeo-Christian dialogue has become more intense. Racist anti-Semitism, and especially the murder of millions of Jews by the Nazis, have confronted the Christian churches with the inescapable task of rethinking the traditions of Christian anti-Judaism and posing the question concerning one's own guilt and responsibility for the Holocaust. The talk of the Judaeo-Christian tradition so easily spoken of by Christians today is itself only a product of the 20th century. This is often forgotten. It is itself an expression of the praiseworthy attempt to overcome a self-presentation of Christianity against the foil of a distortedly presented Judaism. Even this apparently unproblematic composite, even when it is free of all undertones that Judaism is only a preliminary step toward true faith, can be felt from the Jewish side as a smothering co-option. The deceased Pope John-Paul II sought a way out of this dilemma by taking up a formulation referring to the Jews as the "elder brothers in faith" from a 19th century Polish poem. Following the Jewish religious thinkers Franz Rosenzweig and Martin Buber, Wolfgang Huber speaks of "two ways of faith" which only come

---

3   Santayana, G. (1936) Reason in Religion. In: Id. *Works* Vol. IV. New York: Scribner's, 3–206, 4.

together in an eschatological perspective.[4] Without a dialogue with Judaism Christianity cannot be.

Neither the ecumenical nor the Judaeo-Christian dialogue have so far attained their goal, but it cannot be overlooked that at the beginning of the 21st century a high-priority task is posed which could be called the dialogue among the Abrahamic religions, that is, a dialogue among Judaism, Christianity and Islam. The political charging-up of Islam in the present day can lead to Islamophobia, which does injustice to this great religion, and even transfers stereotypes of Christian anti-Judaism to Islam. Of course, anti-Jewish and anti-Christian images cultivated by Muslims are just as dangerous. Rémi Brague is certainly right to demand that a dialogue among these religions, whose history is marked by a diversity of intensive interactions, cross-influences and hostility, must not gloss over the deep differences for the sake of intellectual ease, but presupposes the endeavour "to understand the other just as he understands himself, to comprehend the meaning of words in the way he uses them, to accept the initial situation of disunity in order to attempt to achieve a better understanding starting from this situation".[5] It then quickly becomes apparent that it is not sufficient to conceive of the relation to a holy book or to Abraham or to monotheism as an assured common basis, since even the status of the book and genealogy and the conception of God differ greatly from one another. A central place in this dialogue on the theological plane seems to me to be the Christian doctrine of the Divine Trinity. What appears from a Muslim perspective as a relapse into polytheism must be an occasion for the Christians to reflect upon the depth of their own conception of God. Islam has always considered itself a purification and critique of a Christianity that is seen as a falsification even of the true message of Jesus. For that reason Islam needs the dialogue with Christianity as Christianity needs the dialogue with Judaism. And Christianity needs the dialogue with Islam for an examination and potential correction of its self-perception.

Although the political priority of the 'Abrahamic dialogue' today seems indisputable, the next great task is already announced: the dialogue of the Abrahamic religions with the forms of religiosity in southern and eastern Asia. Like the other attempts at reaching an understanding discussed here, this dialogue, too, has already begun, in this case, at the latest in the 19th century. Very frequently, however, it is not really a dialogue with representatives, for instance, of Buddhism itself, but with European or American experts or converts or contemporaries who merely flirt with dropping out of the Jewish-Christian-Muslim tradition and thus out of the monotheistic reference-system. This will change, and that not only because of the growing economic and political significance of Asia, because of migration and politicisation also of Hinduism (in India) and

---

4   Huber, W. (2008) The Judeo-Christian Tradition. In: H. Joas & K. Wiegandt (Eds.) *The Cultural Values of Europe* Liverpool: Liverpool University Press, 43–58.
5   Brague, R. (2007) Schluß mit den "drei Monotheismen"!. In: *Communio*, 2, 98–113.

in part even of Buddhism (in Sri Lanka), but also because of the considerable attractiveness, especially of Buddhism, in the West. In his speculations on an imminent "age of conciliation"[6] Max Scheler already anticipated this necessity. Not only the murmuring praise of Asian mysticism as an alternative to mono-theistic faith, but also the general claim that the mystical traditions of the Jews or Christians or Moslems already contained what was to be learnt from Asia, are of no assistance here. Once again it is only the willingness to enter into a genuine confrontation with the other without renouncing one's own standpoint that can be productive.

My plea is thus for the thesis that today, only such a form of the transmission of faith is in keeping with the times which poses these tasks of dialogue for itself, and which also, conversely, does not bracket off its own tradition of faith, but regards it as a necessary precondition for a productive confrontation with the other. Two objections against this thesis are close at hand. Some will object that religions mutually exclude each other. The perspective sketched here of a multi-stage, difficult dialogue would then be simply illusory; much more likely would be the conflict among the religions which, when religions become polit-ical, must become a clash of civilisations. Others will object that, at least in the radically secularised parts of Europe, a link with one's own tradition precisely cannot be assumed. The multi-stage interreligious dialogue would then have to fail even at the first stage and, despite all the disadvantages, only a neutral overview of the diversity of worldviews and religions would remain.

Both objections should be briefly responded to. The first objection proceeds from a fundamentally false premise, namely, that religions or cultures could act at all. In contrast to this premise, the preceding considerations presuppose that it is always only people who act, that is, individuals and their associations, or-ganisations and institutions.[7] These people believe and disseminate their faith; they go through experiences and interpret them; they have many different needs and interests, aims and values. Therefore, religions or cultures as such cannot clash, but only human beings who define their faith or their political objectives, among other things, in certain ways. People, however, can join together in joint actions, even when their culturally shaped motives differ. They can also bring together impulses from different traditions in new, creative ways; they can dis-cover new shared interests and values; and they can orient themselves toward precisely such values which cannot be conceived as the exclusive property of their own community. The dissemination of Christianity in late antiquity seems to have been significantly furthered by a willingness of the Christians to assist not only other Christians, but all people.[8] This does not yet say anything about

---

6   Scheler, M. (1927) Der Mensch im Weltalter des Ausgleichs. In: M. S. Frings (Ed.) (1976) *Späte Schriften Gesammelte Werke* Vol. IX. Berne/Munich: Francke, 145–170.

7   This seems to me to be a common feature of the research programs of Max Weber and the American pragmatists.

8   Runciman, W. G. argues thus in (2004) The Diffusion of Christianity in the Third Centu-ry AD as a Case-Study in the Theory of Cultural Selection. In: *Archives européennes de*

the concrete dangers of religiously motivated political, or politically motivated religious conflicts. It is only a matter of repudiating the thought of inevitable clashes among differing religious traditions.

The second objection takes a real situation seriously, namely the extensive de-christianisation, for instance, of eastern Germany, but also of many cities in the old West Germany. Nevertheless, this objection does not describe the situation precisely enough. Intact religious milieus, namely, still coexist with largely secularised milieus; innumerable buildings, symbols, rituals, norms and values are witnesses of a religious past which in this way is once again raised to awareness and then quickly made recognizable at least as a force leaving its imprint upon a culture. To this is added the fact that the religious vitality of immigrants partly, as Muslims, represents a challenge to a secularised self-conception, and partly, as Christians, also contributes to a revitalisation of Christian communities. From low numbers of church-goers or church members, it also does not follow necessarily that all people lacking such activity or membership regard themselves as being non-religious. What is called for, therefore, is a self-conception of religions that, in its articulation, reaches both those schooled in a certain faith and those whose knowledge is sparse or who have turned away from faith on the basis of a good level of knowledge. At least for the latter two groups, what has been asserted as a precondition for a productive interreligious dialogue holds true. Without a relation of faith and all binding values and interpretations of the world to constitutive experiences, no genuine and honest discussion between the faithful and non-believers can get underway. Through this relation, however, the interpretation of the world by non-believers can become more transparent to them, just as the meaning of the truths of faith can be made freshly aware to the faithful.

So far these considerations have left one aspect largely to one side, namely, that of a properly political ethics and the affinities between religions and specifically political values, such as those of democracy. The emphasis on the religious in the narrow sense derives from caution about attributing at all to religions a kind of inherent political ethics. Today we are inclined to attribute to Christianity a self-evident tendency toward democracy and human rights. Historically, however, that is untenable. It would be more appropriate to trace the historical path on which Christian foundations for democracy and human rights were developed. From this self-critical, careful and non-triumphalist perspective on the history of Christianity, a bridge could then be built in search of religious foundations for democracy and human rights in other religious traditions. In this way, the religious traditions could enter into an interreligious dialogue also about political ethics without having their dialogue reduced to it. It has

*sociologie*, 45, 3–21. An overview of competing explanations is provided by Markschies, C. (2004) Warum hat das Christentum in der Antike überlebt? Ein Beitrag zum Gespräch zwischen Kirchengeschichte und Systematischer Theologie. In: *Forum Theologische Literaturzeitung*, 13, Leipzig: Evangelische Verlagsanstalt.

also become apparent that it is the ethos of democracy and human rights that has inspired this idea of interreligious dialogue. It is a matter of a universalism that does not impose upon people any breach with the particular binding powers of those traditions out of which they understand themselves. The demand for such a rupture, for a transition to rational universalisms, for foundational arguments without any self-reflective anchoring in experience and binding power is downright counter-productive in this context. We remain obliged to adopt this stance in our preoccupation with other religions, even when there is no concrete partner to the dialogue or the partner denies us a dialogue. Politically, we may and must fight religiously motivated opposition against democracy and human rights; but our transmission of values must be oriented not toward struggle but toward productive dialogue.

This dialogue connects religious and secular forms of moral and legal universalism. They stand united against racist and other forms of anti-universalism, against a post-modern indifference with regard to universal validity claims and against the exaggeration of a single one of the competing universalisms to be the only one. In dialogue the coexisting universalisms may discover their hidden particularities.

*Morteza Ghasempour*

# Philosophy of Dialogical Encounter with the World[1]

The inflationary use of the word 'dialogue' is increasingly diluting its meaning today. Thus, a philosophical treatment of the matter must seek to contextualise the term and its content in such a way as to render it distinct from its commonplace, diffuse understandings.

Dialogue is neither a partial form of behaviour that can be reduced to verbal articulations as a specific form of linguistic exchange, nor is it a facility with rhetorical technique that can be deployed to legitimise a given position. It can also not be classed as a functional approach to palliating and resolving extant conflicts, subordinated to a compromise of opposing interests. Finally, it cannot be classed as an epistemologically foreshortened mode of thought aiming to discursively establish the 'truth'.

This common view of dialogue, which is based on the Platonic dialogues as a model, overlooks the fact that the deployment of any given method to establish truth presupposes the truth of the method itself. Such truth, however, cannot be posited pre-dialogically, but must be established dialogically. A theory of dialogue that is conscious of its own pre-judgements must therefore question the unquestioned premises of Platonic practice.

It was this Platonic view of dialogue as the locus of discursive truth-seeking that gave dialogue its epistemological meaning and has led to it being classed as a category of hermeneutics. This goes hand in hand with a rationalistic reduction to an intellectual tool defined by its intended objective of truth. Thus instrumentalising and reducing the concept of dialogue subordinates its value to its superordinate purpose without considering the need to defend the creation of such a hierarchy. This dogmatic assumption, evidently the sediment of still contemporary consensualist communication theories, is the epiphenomenon of a fundamentally ideologically truth-centred conception of dialogue that discards the truth of dialogue over the dialogue on truth.

Though all of these understandings of dialogue encompass and accentuate possible aspects of the whole, these aspects should be shown to be the secondary and derivative consequences of an understanding of dialogue that precedes these particular occurrences and applications and makes them possible.

We can counter such sectorally reductionist conceptions, foreshortening dialogue into a functionalist, pragmatist, instrumentalist or scientistically cognitive form, with an emphasis on the fact that dialogue is not primarily a category of knowledge, but a mode of being. It is never merely a form of linguistic articu-

---

1   This article is a translation of: Ghasempour, M. (2010) Philosophie der dialogischen Welt-begegnung. In: W. Weisse & H.-M. Gutmann (Eds.) *Religiöse Differenz als Chance? Positionen, Kontroversen, Perspektiven* Münster: Waxmann, 81–87.

lation that could be realised partially or segmentally, but refers to a concept of meaning and as such is a mode of being that encompasses all human existence.

Since dialogue is a relational concept that draws its meaning from relating to the Other, understood as a mode of being it represents a particular attitude and specific manner to exist in a social and natural environment and to act with regard to it.

Its relational nature means that the specificity of a dialogical mode of being is best identified by seeking to determine the location of the Other in the horizon of its dialogical world view.

The specificity of a dialogical encounter with the world is this: Unlike other, non-dialogical modes or relating, it replaces a hierarchical and asymmetric relationship to the Other with a symmetrical and reciprocal one. Its constitutive elements of symmetry, reciprocity and congeniality make the dialogical experience of the world an eminent form of relationship that is principally and factually different from all forms of hegemonially relating to the world. Within the horizon of dialogically encountering the Other, all reductive representations of the Other are identified as violent strategies of annective de-alienation and thus negated. The decentralisation of the Own in favour of maintaining an attitude of equality and equivalence of the other means nothing less than the acceptance (*Anerkennung*) of the Other. A dialogical culture is of necessity one of mutual acceptance. This form of acceptance cannot be equated with tolerance, which is a mere transitory preamble to true acceptance. Its deficient character stems from its dimension of sufferance which implies the undesirability of the Other by connoting him as something to be suffered. That is why Goethe only recognised tolerance as "a transient attitude" (*eine vorübergehende Gesinnung*) that must transform into acceptance.[2]

This acceptance as the mark of dialogical encounter with the world can thus be understood as a more profound and complete form of tolerance. Such a culture of acceptance radically transforms our relationship with the world by de-hierarchising and pacifying the way we relate to the Other through the introduction of equivalence and equality.

A dialogical recognition of the Other, however, necessitates the insight into his relative legitimacy and validity. From a critical stance towards truth and hermeneutics, this requires us to recognise our own validity's relativity and thereby relinquish our claim to its absoluteness. A culture of dialogue and recognition thus depends on a mutual relativisation of absolute claims in the interest of allowing for the Other. A dialogical awareness of the dependence and finiteness of our own space thus opens up the communicative space in which the Other begins to appear. Recognition and the limitation of our claims of self provides

---

2   "Toleranz sollte eigentlich nur eine vorübergehende Gesinnung sein: sie muß zur Anerkennung führen. Dulden heißt beleidigen". Goethe, J. W. von (1998) Maximen und Reflexionen 151. In: Id. *Werke, Hamburger Ausgabe in 14 Bänden*, Bd. 12, München: Beck, 385.

a sheltered space of acceptance in difference to the Other. His otherness is not merely tolerated, but desired and protected.

Just as a non-dialogical relationship with the world corresponds to a dogmatic and absolutist mental attitude, a dialogical culture of acceptance presupposes a moderate scepticism and relativism in awareness of our own limitations. Any totalisation of the Own automatically leads to the marginalisation of the Other, and setting the self absolute relativises exclusively the Other and thus becomes an act of violence. Only a mutual relativising of the self based on our understanding of the limitedness of our being lends its meaning to what we refer to as respect for others in moral terms[3] and allows for a dialogical encounter.

Insight into the conditionality of all universals, not the desire to expansively universalise the regional, is the social wisdom of dialogical being. It preserves otherness as a precondition of meaningful communication from being levelled by identity-focused rationality.

The mutual act of sensible self-limitation which stems from this wisdom simultaneously provides that which is gained: a universal and dependable space that allows for non-violent communication and prevents acceptance from deteriorating into indifference.

Thus what remains as universally binding and shared in a dialogical experience of the world is not determined through its authorisation by a given understanding of the world, but comes into being through the renunciation by all parties of absolutist claims for their perspectives. This provides a satisfactory and non-ideological answer to the question of drawing the limits of acceptance. This form of doing so is not founded on privileging one perspective to the detriment of all others, but is founded on the rights of all to equal consideration.[4]

It must be stressed that a dialogical form of being with its constitutive dimensions of reciprocity and equivalence is not limited to the creation of ideal spaces of interaction. It intends symmetry in the objective, material terms of human existence. Dialogical acceptance and respect for humanity would remain empty shells if they did not include the call for abolishing real suffering and creating justice in the concrete realities of human existence.

Thus, negating hierarchical orders of social, political and economic inequity and seeking to replace them with just conditions are necessarily part of a dialogical culture if it wants to avoid ideological perversion into theoretical naivety or complicity with the inhuman. A dialogical attitude thus understood to encompass, shape and pacify the ideal and real terms of human existence is both political from the outset and emphatic in its call for justice.

---

3   This demonstrates that the dialogical mode of being contains an ethic of humanity and solidarity. Ethics is thus not an element added on to a dialogical culture, but originally inherent in it and a consequence of a dialogical encounter with the world.

4   This problem is contextualised in terms of epistemology and truth theory by the author in Ghasempour, M. (2006) Grundthesen der interkulturellen Philosophie. In: H. Antor (Ed.) *Inter- und Transkulturelle Studien. Theoretische Grundlagen und interdisziplinäre Praxis* Heidelberg: Universitätsverlag, 95–108, 97 ff.

As this culture of humanity that addresses itself at the suffering of others, desiring to end it, a dialogical perspective not only has an ethical, but a political aspect.

It follows from this understanding of dialogue that, far beyond merely providing a technique to establish truth or arrive at a functional compromise, dialogue describes a human and nonviolent culture of coexistence and can thus claim the ontological status and axiological dignity of a purpose per se. As such an eminent entity, dialogue is not a means to truth, but itself has the dignity of truth.

The question to what extent a dialogical form of being, idealistic as it appears, can ever be realised in the face of real global suffering must be answered by, on the one hand, pointing out that such a form of being can be understood as a regulative idea approximating which would become a universal obligation, on the other by stating that no acceptable alternative to a dialogical culture exists, and that the consequences of a non-dialogical attitude are neither desirable nor more easily borne.

It would be contrary to the requirements of an understanding of dialogue that is aware of the world to limit the conception here outlined to human inter-subjectivity, thus ignoring its relation to non-human life forms and the environment.

As a cosmophile mode of being which peacefully moulds the relation of humans to the world as such, intersubjective dialogue must be organically integrated into an acceptance of the dignity of nature as an elementary precondition for biological and social life in any form.

Characteristics of dialogical culture – such as criticism of hierarchies in recognition of the Other – extend to nature as empathically as to the specifically human sphere of interpersonal socialisation.

One precondition for an understanding of dialogue that embraces nature is to reject traditional world views whose philosophical and theological incarnations anthropocentrically demote and devalue the natural environment. Dialogue in this form is the ability to adopt a mode of thought that has liberated itself from this world view and its modern ideological descendants, technicism and economism, and the political systems they adopt. The development of a dialogical culture has its objective equivalent in the development of a socio-economic order whose structural formative power does not oppose the ideal subjective impetus of a dialogical mode of being. The degree to which such a social order is realised determines the degree to which the dialogical idea can be. The structural change of social orders that are the concrete sediment of monological mis-order and the subjective transformation of undialogical attitudes are dependent on each other. Therefore, the call for dialogue within monologically ordered, structurally anti-dialogical circumstances of life at best betrays the naivety of a retreat into the private. The primacy of a communality in which cooperative intersubjectivity replaces the isolating law of confrontative subjectivity is an indispensable precondition for a society that has overcome both consensualism and dissensualism as ideologically charged wrong turns in inter-personal communication.

The determination of these basic preconditions for dialogue demonstrates that a dialogical culture requires a fundamental re-valuing of extant values in order to be realised.

In the context of further reflections on the pathology of dialogical culture, I intend to both name the institutionally solidified power relationships of social macro-communication as well as those modern aspects of life that interfere with any interpersonal and intrapersonal relationships all the way to the individual level and hinder a dialogical formation of these relations. We only need to look at the ineluctable phenomena of modern existence, mobility and rapidity, in all their anti-dialogical nature to exemplify the obstacles and adversity a dialogical mode of being faces among the realities of life.

It is above all these modern facts of life that have led to the devastating act of substituting communication as a category of meaning to existence with com-munication as a technical category of competence and have triggered harmful infantilisation by reducing the process of maturing to the earliest possible stage. When we consider that, unlike widespread functional phenomena of contact which lack depth and thoughtfulness or oppose them as obstacles, dialogue must be grouped among the eminent forms of communication that requires re-flection and thus numbers patience and slowness among the virtues necessary for its success, we see that a wisdom-guided, dialogical realisation of human existence is impossible amid our hasty, restless and reflective culture.[5]

This conflict between the necessity of a dialogical culture on the one hand and the structural impossibility of its development on the other encapsulates the tragedy of subjective efforts for dialogue. The idea of dialogue cannot be real-ised subjectively without making it realisable in the public sphere of material reality and objective feasibility, i.e. by the call for the abolition of anti-dialogi-cal macro-structures.

Alongside the philosophical and sociological preconditions of dialogue which we have emphasised here, attention needs to be drawn to its psychologi-

---

5   Hölderlin already knew of the disappearing of the socio-cultural preconditions whose absence seals the impossibility of meaningful speech: "We must often be silent; we lack sacred names" (*Schweigen müssen wir oft; es fehlen heilige Namen*), Hölderlin, F. (1969) Heimkunft. In: F. Beißner & J. Schmidt (Eds.) *Werke und Briefe*, Bd. 1, Frankfurt a. M.: Inasel Verlag, 122. Nietzsche's terminological use of the word "market" (*Markt*) to de-signate the modern nihilistic wasteland that is human existence which he counters with the concept of solitude corresponds to the empty forms of contact in which noise (*der Lärm*) as a ubiquitous cultural phenomenon decimates dialogue: "Where solitude ends, the market begins" (*Wo die Einsamkeit aufhört, da beginnt der Markt*), Nietzsche, F. (1980) *Kritische Studienausgabe in 15 Bänden* (G. Colli & M. Montinari (Eds.)), Bd. 4, München: de Gruyter, 65. Heideggers fundamentally ontological analysis of '*Gerede*' as a constitutive moment of decrepit (*verfallenen*) existence hints at the desertification of communicative speech in an age dominated by a nihilistic obliviousness being: Heidegger, M. (2001) *Sein und Zeit*, 18. Auflage, Tübingen: Max Niemeyer Verlag, 167 ff.

cal ones. The societal fixation of the individual on personal gain converges with a psychological fear of the Other as endangering the Own. The psychopathy of competition corresponds to the psychopathy of loneliness among individuals living panically against each other. Societal alienation shows its psychological deep structure in the xenophobia of a fear-filled ego pitted against the you.

Dialogue as a social and therefore communicative attitude philosophically opposes a dogmatic attitude as it morally does an egotistical and psychologically a narcissistic one. This corresponds to the ability to de-centre the self and relinquish an obsessive desire for stability. Thus, it requires a decompositive virtuosity at transcending the self that may seem like excessively demanding asceticism to an individual not accustomed to scepticism and openness.

The ascetic act of forgoing the self can be made easier to bear to narcissistic personalities by education towards an understanding of the mysterious dialectic that shows this act to be an eminent form of social and existential fulfilment by emphasising the potential creation of new communicative spaces in which the self can enjoy the privilege of dialogical experience and development.

The self- and property-addicted individual's relief from fear of the Other as the central psychological precondition of dialogue cannot be achieved purely by educational means targeting the individual psyche. The reification of psychological palliative therapy as fundamental modes of reducing suffering while silencing any mention of the necessity of real change is itself a symptom of a deceptive willingness to individual change. Providing psychological solutions for problems located outside the psychological realm exemplifies the ideological strategy of doing anything in order not to do what is necessary.

Strengthening the psyche of encapsulated individuals resistant to openness into an interior instance of dialogically relating to the world thus refers us to the need to reform the entirety of interrelations between the spheres of our being.

Thus, within the context of this description of the most important preconditions for dialogue we can say that it requires no less than the individual and institutional effort to render all aspects of human existence dialogical.

The question whether dialogue itself can be derived as a desirable collective value may be answered by resorting to the dialogical idea itself.

As dialogue constitutionally depends on the idea of mutual acceptance which, in turn, allows for the privileging of no position, it guarantees the possibility of all positions while being immune to capture by any of them. Its prescriptive character is not rooted in the partial interests of any one view of the world, but springs from its fundamentally desire to allow all perspectives to be recognised. As such, dialogue is the principle of allowing all positions and, in the interest of achieving non-violent consensus, the 'a priori' normative.

# Religious Diversity and the Need for Dialogue:
## Empirical Approaches

*Peter Beyer*

# Global Migration, Religious Diversity and Dialogue

## Religion, Religions and Interreligious Dialogue in Contemporary Global Context

The contemporary concept and practice of interreligious dialogue occur in a very specific historical, cultural, and social context which conditions their meaning and import. Above all, interreligious dialogue takes as a condition for its possibility the assumption of plurality, including a normative component that puts a positive value on this 'religious diversity', shading the perceived and institutionalised fact of religious plurality into religious *pluralism*, the principled promotion of the plurality.[1] Dialogue, in turn, denotes a particular sort of relation of the components of the religious plurality. These relations assume that the 'partners' in dialogue are formally of equal worth, that having the dialogue is important, and that the outcome of dialogue is what is sometimes called 'mutual understanding'. That is to say, dialogue maintains – and even clarifies – the differences of the dialoguing partners while also thereby structuring a commonality that at the very least consists in the identification and recognition of difference and equality; but also extends ideally to generating a sense of shared, identifiably religious, enterprise. Interreligious dialogue is a way of structuring, clarifying, institutionalizing, indeed of 'doing' religious difference or plurality *within* a commonality or unity that realises religion as a single and singular orientation and endeavour. It is a religious enterprise which includes its own observation; it is thereby also a theological undertaking.[2] These preliminary observations, however, raise some obvious questions: why is it important to dialogue? Who or what composes the religious plurality? And what is this common religion or common religious enterprise?

The first question can be addressed briefly. The importance of interreligious dialogue is contained in its very structure: its participants and observers presume the differences, but these cannot just exist side by side, or at least such isolated juxtaposition is understood as problematic, generative of *mis*understanding, *dis*harmony, conflict and social *dis*order unless there is added a positive activity that 'integrates' the differences. Interreligious dialogue wishes

---

[1] Beckford, J. A. (2003) *Social Theory and Religion* Cambridge: Cambridge University Press.

[2] I note, in this regard, that a large portion of the literature of and on interreligious dialogue is at the same time theological or theologically oriented literature. One might almost say that interreligious dialogue is often the practical theological orientation to what otherwise is treated in the literature on religious diversity and pluralism. Another large portion of the literature is, of course, descriptive of the phenomenon. For an appreciation of the balance, see the various contributions to the *Journal of Interreligious Dialogue* (http://irdialogue. org/journal/).

to contribute to the construction of a positively valued form of cohabitation of differences, under the assumption that this positive structuring will not happen by itself; rather the opposite.[3]

The second question addresses the core of my concerns in this chapter. There exists a more or less globally spread, both popular and scholarly assumption that religion, however understood more precisely, manifests itself today and historically predominantly if not exclusively as a relatively clearly demarcated set of religions. An ongoing debate among scholars – especially in religious studies – questions the reality and legitimacy of seeing religion this way[4], but there can be little doubt that the existence of these religions and the pluralist understanding of them informs the socially effective and lived realities of the majority of the global society's regions and people. The imagining and construction of these '(world) religions' is indeed a historically and socially contingent outcome; it features a good deal of 'colonialist invention' and 'Christian understanding'; it does not and never has included all that 'religion' is or was in today's or historical societies; but like the global system of sovereign nation-states, which shares analogous features, the religions form a clear structural and semantic feature of our present world, even if by no means necessarily a permanent and unquestionable one.[5]

These religions are the major part of the differences that inform interreligious dialogue, which is almost always a dialogue of representatives of these religions or of equally constructed and contingent subdivisions within them, for instance in Protestant-Catholic-Orthodox Christian dialogue. This fact, however, does not imply either a generally accepted set of such religions – there is no real equivalent of the recognition of religions, let alone whatever might count as the equivalent of their 'sovereignty', such as there exists for states – nor a consistency in what religions are included in the set from place to place and time to time. Not even what I like to call the R5 (parallel to the G8), Christianity, Judaism, Islam, Buddhism, and Hinduism, are consistent and recognised presences in all parts of the world, although the three ostensibly 'missionizing' religions

---

3   The situation is, I suggest, similar to the way interculturalism is understood in certain European countries, and Quebec: the recognition and expression of diverse 'cultures' is valued but considered problematic if it does not involve significant interaction of cultures and their 'integration' into a (usually 'national') common project. Bouchard, G. & Taylor, C. (2008) *Building the Future: A Time for Reconciliation* Quebec City: Government of Quebec; Foblets, M.-C. & Kulakowski, C. (2010) *Les assises de l'interculturalité* Bruxelles: Ministère de l'Emploi et de l'Égalité des Chances.

4   As examples: D. Peterson & D. Walhof (Eds.) (2002) *The Invention of Religion: Rethinking Belief in Politics and History* New Brunswick, NJ: Rutgers University Press; Smith, B. K. (2000) Who Does, Can, and Should Speak for Hinduism?. In: *Journal of the American Academy of Religion*, 68(4), 741–749; Smith, J. Z. (1988) 'Religion' and 'Religious Studies': No Difference at All. In: *Soundings*, 71, 231–244; Smith, W. C. (1991) *The Meaning and End of Religion* Minneapolis, MN: Fortress Press.

5   I have offered a more complete analysis in Beyer, P. (2006) *Religions in Global Society* London: Routledge.

of Christianity, Islam, and Buddhism probably come closest. In each region of the world, there appears to exist somewhat different groupings of operatively present and formally/officially legitimate (recognised) religions. Thus, for instance, in Germany the religion of Alevism may have a real and recognised presence – including in interreligious dialogue – that it has virtually nowhere else, while Scientology is quite definitely excluded. In Canada, by contrast, few people will even have heard of Alevism, but no inclusive dialogue could possibly exclude Sikhism; and Scientology, under the correct circumstances, might be given a (grudgingly) legitimate seat at the interreligious table. In the People's Republic of China, only Protestantism, Roman Catholicism (regarded as two religions), Islam, Buddhism, and Daoism are officially recognised and all other religions, by contrast, have a (more) difficult time establishing their presence, let alone taking part in dialogue. And so on for virtually every other country and region in the world. All this is to underline the degree to which religious diversity, both practical and normative, is neither something self-evident nor an ideologically driven imposition or illusion. It is rather the socially real and contingent outcome of historical developments which now ineluctably inform our world; and so we have to find ways of 'dealing with' them.

The third question points to an analogous situation with the idea and reality of religion itself. Although most of the self-identified and other-recognised religions – but especially the core R5 – trace their origins to at the very least 1,500 years ago, the global understanding and institutional manifestations of religion as a *distinct domain* of action and experience with relation to 'transcendence' have a much shorter history. Some of the features of such a differentiation of religion date back much longer, but it is really only in the modern era that it reaches sufficient clarity that other social domains can successfully be *secular*, which is to say precisely not religious.[6] The commonality which interreligious dialogue strives to identify or achieve thereby tends to be located in this differentiated religious domain; dialogue works as much towards the identification of religion as towards the solidification of the religious identities of the partners in dialogue, and this as much by virtue of the social context in which it takes place as by any overt intention. Moreover, this aspect of the identification of religion and the religions also serves to make interreligious dialogue a theological enterprise, a self-observation of and a reflection on religion (faith).

---

6   Jaspers' still relevant notion of the 'Axial Age' includes the idea that most of the so-called world religions trace their key formative stages to somewhere around 2,500 years ago, and in immediately subsequent centuries. Jaspers, K. (1953) *The Origins and Goal of History* New Haven: Yale University Press. On the distinction between the 'religious' developments of this Axial Age and the modern distinction of a religious domain differentiated from secular domains: Casanova, J. (2012) Religion, the Axial Age, and Secular Modernity in Bellah's Theory of Religious Evolution. In: R. N. Bellah & H. Joas (Eds.) *The Axial Age and Its Consequences* Cambridge, MA: Belknap Press and Harvard University Press, 191–221.

A further central contextual aspect has to do with contemporary globalisation, both in the spatial and the temporal meanings of this word. Contemporary society is becoming ever more strongly a global society; the communicative ties between the disparate parts of the world have been increasing in density and intensity for a long time, and that increase has significantly accelerated during the last two centuries, including very much the last few decades. A historically very high rate of global migration has been an important feature of these globalizing developments and these have had the effect of bringing more people of more religions and more variants of religions to parts of the world where they have not had much of an historical presence before and where they enter into contact with those religious identities that have hitherto been dominant or at least significantly present there for some time. The results are particularly evident in the majority of the rich and powerful core Western countries in Europe, North America, and Australasia; but, be it noted, not just there. This globalisation of religions in fact has created the conditions for not just 'spread' but also significant reconstruction of religions as they settle in new contexts. With globalisation has come the multiplication of religions, the increased development of authentic and even authoritative versions of those religions, and thereby the significant weakening of religious authority as centred in particular, putatively core regions for any religion, or even for religious authority as such.[7]

For interreligious dialogue, this means that the potential local partners have become more diverse in most countries, including especially the Western core countries, leading to more and different practical and theological challenges. Moreover – and this brings me to the more specific focus of my discussion in this chapter – the greater density of different religions in various countries and the diminution of religious authorities as the arbiters of religious authenticity leads to the much higher probability that dialogue will be much more than 'formal', arranged and carried out by (usually elite) representatives of the various religions and subdivisions of religions. It will also involve 'informal' interaction among adherents to the different religions and, just as importantly, the 'personal reflection' of religious individuals as they live and practice more and more in a multi-religious context that challenges them to construct, reconstruct, reflect upon, and more clearly identify themselves in a pluralistic context. In addition, greater religious diversity in the form of a greater number of self-identified and other-recognised religions points to the difficulty of establishing clear limits to this diversity, let alone maintaining some kind of dominance of one or more recognised religions, and this concerns the diversity of legitimate religions, the internal diversity within those religions, and the diversity that escapes either of these classifications.

---

7    Beyer, P. (1998) The City and Beyond as Dialogue: Negotiating Religious Authenticity in
     Global Society. In: *Social Compass*, 45, 61–73.

## Religious Identities in Canada: Some Current Research

What I mean here can be illustrated on hand of some trends taken from the Canadian national census. Canada, like other British settler countries, is a country that has few formal mechanisms for recognizing religions, whether in law or through administrative routines such as formal registration. But it does have a long-standing tradition, dating back to the middle of the nineteenth century, of counting adherents to religions and religious groups through regular censuses. Three significant trends over the past forty years – the first years in Canada of truly global immigration since its founding in the seventeenth century – are noteworthy: the number of different and recorded/reported religions has been steadily increasing, the number of subcategories within the still demographically dominant religion, Christianity, has been increasing, and so have the number and variety of 'para' and 'no' religious identities, namely 'religious' identities that fall outside the boundaries of 'the religions'. Interpreting somewhat, not only are there more religions present in the population, not only are the numbers of adherents to those religions increasing steadily (if unevenly), but those religions come in an increasing number of variants with claims to authenticity, and an increasing number of people identify themselves religiously outside their boundaries, or outside the boundaries of religion altogether. It is arguable that these trends are interconnected; that the increase of religious plural*ity* – the fact of being plural – is related to increased religious plural*ism* – the legitimacy and valuing of that plurality – and that this combination encourages the somewhat uncontrolled expansion of self-conceived and other-recognised (i.e. legitimated) religious identities, and this includes an expansion of what counts as religion (for example, under the heading of 'spirituality').

This multiplication not only in the number of religious identities that could relate to one another, but also in the variety of ways in which religious boundaries are drawn is of course not entirely the result of more intense and varied global migration; but it is probably the case that the greater presence of religiously 'others' in our various countries – in our various 'backyards', as it were – is making a significant contribution to a restructuring of how these boundaries are to be understood, how we draw them, and how we inhabit them in our personal and institutional lives.

Departing from these abstract reflections, I now move to illustrate these circumstances more concretely through an examination of the outcome of two research projects that I and a team of investigators have been conducting over the past number of years in Canada. The main purpose of this research was to discover how certain key segments of the Canadian population are understanding and living their religious identities in an increasingly pluralistic religious context and one that officially and in popular discourse explicitly espouses pluralism. The projects focused mainly on the so-called second generation of immigration to Canada, namely the segment of the population that was born and/or grew up in Canada but were of immigrant families in which the parents had arrived in Canada only during the last 40 years or so.[8] The rationale for this choice is that this population can be seen to best represent the new diversity: they are by and large not representative of the older Christian-dominated context, but rather more directly of the more recent increase in religious diversity of all stripes, including perhaps in the diversity that breaks beyond the bounds of the recognised religions and their many subdivisions. Above all, unlike their parents who come from a different context outside the country, and the longer established population that in many cases has not had to live in the new diversity as directly, this generation is both indigenous and relatively 'newly arrived'.

Briefly, the two main projects were conducted in 2004–2006 and in 2008–2010 mostly in five major urban centres of Canada, including Vancouver, Edmonton, Toronto, Ottawa, and Montreal. The urban contexts are important because that is where, typically, most of the recent immigration has settled and therefore where the greatest extent and density of the religious diversity is to be found. The data which I interpret here consists of 300 in-depth interviews with second and 1.5 generation (grew up in Canada, but were born elsewhere) young adults between 18 and 32 years old, both men and women, and from a wide range of religious backgrounds, including varieties of Christian (Protestant, Catholic, and Orthodox), Muslim (Shi'a and Sunni), Sikh, Hindu, Buddhist, and those claiming no religion at all. In other words, the 300 participants, while clearly not representative, include a broad segment of the religious diversity that is my focus.[9]

Although interreligious dialogue as such was not the focus of these projects, the way that the participants identified themselves religiously in an incontrovertibly and unavoidably interreligious context was. Almost all of them lived in cities with a high level of recent immigrants and a high level of religious diversity (both as measured by the Canadian census discussed above). Even if there exists a comparative residential concentration of the various immigrant groups, in no city does this attain a level that might be called ghettoisation.[10] Moreover, the vast majority of the participants were recruited on the campuses of postsecondary institutions, a strategy that was adopted because a very high percentage of the target populations in the 18–30 year age group in Canada either have postsecondary education or are in the process of acquiring it.[11] Being

---

8    Beyer P. & Ramji, R. (Eds.) (2013) *Growing Up Canadian: Muslims, Hindus, Buddhists* Kingston & Montreal: McGill-Queen's University Press.

9    It is for this reason that, in the analysis that follows, I do not include any numbers and percentages since such seemingly 'hard' data would just be misleading.

10   Beyer, P. & Martin, W. K. (2010) *The Future of Religious Diversity in Canada* Ottawa: Citizenship and Immigration Canada; Walks, R. A. & Bourne, L. S. (2006) Ghettos in Canadian Cities? Racial Segregation, Ethnic Enclaves and Poverty Concentration in Canadian Urban Areas. In: *The Canadian Geographer*, 50(3), 273–297.

11   Abada, T. & Lin, S. (2011) *The Educational Attainments and Labour Outcomes of Children of Immigrants in Canada* Toronto: Higher Education Quality Council of Ontario; Beyer, P. (2005) Religious Identity and Educational Attainment among Recent Immigrants to Canada: Gender, Age, and 2nd Generation. In: *Journal of International Migration and Integra-*

on average highly educated, however, does not mean that the participants were drawn disproportionately from the socio-economic elites of the post-1970s immigrant population; economic status of the first generation immigrant families in which they grew up does not correlate well with educational attainment of either that first or the second generation.[12]

Looking at the results of these research projects, it is perhaps not surprising that the great majority of the participants located their religious identities in terms of the standardly recognised world religions, in Canada mainly in terms of Christianity, Islam, Hinduism, Buddhism, Sikhism, and Judaism. The recruitment, after all, was done with reference to these religions: there was no requirement that participants identify with these religions, but we did ask that they have these religions in their family heritages. In this context, most identified clearly with one and only one religion, and among these a great many located their religious identity totally within that religion, seeking to believe and practice what they considered all the important features of that religion, and nothing else. One might say that they were exclusive and practicing Muslims, Christians, Hindus, and so on; but that does not necessarily mean that they constructed this belonging uniformly under these overarching categories. Moreover, beside these there were a high number of those with seemingly exclusive nominal identities in terms of these religions, who were not necessarily so clearly and consistently within them or outside of them. On closer examination, religious identities often crossed the lines that these clear categorisations suggest, and this in a number of ways. First, the most common were those who actually only partially identified with one of the religions. They would be somewhat within a religion, but also somewhat outside any religion, whether in the sense of being "spiritual but not religious", being highly selective with respect to what features of a religion one incorporated into one's identity (religion *à la carte*), or identifying oneself as primarily non-religious with an admixture of a small number of features of one or more religions. There were also a few people who identified with more than one religion, say Islam *and* Hinduism or Christianity *and* Buddhism; but these were a very small number. More common were those who engaged in religious *bricolage*[13], combining elements from a number of religions or from various 'spiritual' traditions (e.g. yoga, esoteri-

*tion*, 6(2), 171–199; Bonikowska, A. & Hou, F. (2011) *Reversal of Fortunes or Continued Success? Cohort Differences in Education and Earnings of Childhood Immigrants* Ottawa: Statistics Canada, Analytical Studies Branch Research Paper Series; Corak, M. (2008) Immigration in the Long Run: The Education and Earnings Mobility of Second-Generation Canadians. In: *IRPP Choices,* 14(13).

12 Beyer, P. (2011) Religion, Culture and the Economic Success of Immigrant Young Adults in Canada: International Society for the Sociology of Religion Conference, Aix en Provence, France; Beyer & Martin (2010); Model, S. & Lin, L. (2002) The Cost of Not Being Christian: Hindus, Sikhs and Muslims in Britain and Canada. In: *International Migration Review,* 36(4), 1061–1092.

13 Luckmann, T. (1967) *The Invisible Religion: The Problem of Religion in Modern Societies* New York: Macmillan.

cism, theosophy, alchemy) but perhaps not identifying themselves with any of them. Then, of course, there were those who considered themselves to be explicitly non-religious, but this all the way from express atheists who declared themselves to be against religion, to those who identified with no religion in particular but admitted that some small elements of religions made their way into their identities, into the way that they lived their lives.

The importance of this variation in identification lies in the fluid and varied relations between the recognised and defined religions as categories and institutions on the one hand, and the actual religious identities of individuals on the other. One way to represent these relations as they emerged in the data is in terms of a continuum that passes from identities (and therefore belief and practice) that are expressly and entirely outside the category of religion as such through various hybrid identities all the way to exclusive and complete identification with one of the religions, and mostly a specific subvariant of one of these. This continuum can be represented as follows:

> not religious → hybridizing → identifying → co-existing → exclusive

On the left are those who see themselves as outside of the category of religion: atheists of various stripes, 'apatheists' (people how are apathetic about the whole religious question and thus religion is not part of their identities), and those with no religion in particular. From there, moving to the right, are those people who begin to have something of a religious identity, first those who put together their own combination (bricoleurs, spiritual but not religious, etc.), then those who do this but with the idea that they are adherents of a particular religion. Farther on down the continuum are those who are in practice, belief, and identification, entirely within a particular religion, but who are so consciously in a multi-religious context. These are people who are clearly religious in an institutional and 'regular practitioner' sense[14], but who recognise and accept that they are but one legitimate possibility within a pluralistic context which includes other religions, less defined 'spiritualities', and 'secularists'/ 'atheists'. To the left of this category of the co-existing (see diagram) are included those that seek to express their religious identity in part by interacting with other religious identities; these are among those whom we might call, 'informal dialogue' partners. To the right of this category, one begins to shade into the extreme right of the continuum, the exclusive and exclusivist identifiers who strongly identify with one religion but do not recognise the validity or value of any other religious identity and therefore will generally not engage in or be interested in interaction or dialogue. From the brief outline of the character of the participants in our research projects, it will be evident that the vast majority of them find themselves somewhere on the inside of this continuum, on that part marked by the central

---

14  Hervieu-Léger, D. (1999) *Le pèlerin et le converti: La religion en mouvement* Paris: Flammarion.

three descriptors and away from either of the extremes; but the main point is that there were at least some participants virtually anywhere on this continuum, including somewhat to the left or the right of each of the named descriptors.

Locating the participants on this continuum instead of simply in terms of the distinct religious identities of the named religions points to a further very important feature of their religious identity constructions, and that is the relatively weak direct role that institutional religious *authority* or even religious tradition appears to play. The integrity, or perhaps better, *authenticity* of their identities for the vast majority of them depended on their own efforts to appropriate, understand, and consciously decide to believe and to practice in the ways that they had come to do. What religious authorities – for example, their church, religious leaders, their parents or family authorities, or just received tradition – had to say was important only in so far as they had appropriated these orientations and practices individually. That included in many cases core sacred sources like the Bible, the Qur'an, Adi Granth, Buddhist sutras, Hindu epics, etc. There was relatively little "I do or think this because this is what I have been told" or "this is what we do because we are _____". Indicative of this absence was, by contrast, the relatively frequent incidence of people who engaged in practices or (sometimes) pretended to believe only to please others like their parents or family, not because such beliefs or practices were actually part of their own religious identities. An important implication of this pattern is that it raises the question of how representative anyone can be in especially formal interreligious dialogue given that for so many of those supposedly represented, the authority to do so is conditional upon their (individual) consent. As it turns out, if the results of our research are at all indicative, the answer to this question is that it depends a great deal on which religion one is talking about.

As already noted, the significant majority of the participants identified explicitly with one and only one the religions, but large numbers of these did so selectively or ambiguously. The selective identifiers were selective precisely in that they rejected various elements of what *they* understood to belong to their religion according to religious authorities or received religious tradition. These are, for example, Hindus who recognise that performing regular puja is part of Hinduism as it has been handed down to them, but they consciously reject this practice; or Christians who know that being a Christian means believing in the divinity of Christ or praying, but they do not; and so on. In other words, there exists for these people an, even if imprecisely, understood 'orthodoxy' to which they do not hold themselves. The ambiguous identifiers were not only selective, they were also not sure whether they really were Christians, Buddhist, or Sikhs, for example, even though they did not identify with any other religion or as non-religious people. Contrasted with these individuals were a large number of others who were neither selective nor ambiguous: they were definitely and clearly Buddhist, Christian, Muslim, or another religion. Moreover, they adhered to everything that they felt belonged with that identity, everything that their recognised religious authorities dictated or their received religious tradition enjoined. Where they failed to do so, they felt this was an insufficiency on their part which they usually hoped to overcome at some point. Such adherence to 'orthodoxy' did not, of course, negate the above-discussed logically prior need to appropriate this orthodoxy for themselves, although they typically insisted that they were not themselves deciding what this orthodoxy was; from their perspective, they had simply learned to understand what it was.

What is significant with respect to these different ways of identifying with a religion is that the distribution of their incidence across the sample of participants is not even. In particular, the last group, the "orthodox and exclusive adherents" were disproportionately to be found only in two categories, Muslims and Evangelical/Conservative Protestant Christians. There were, of course, selective and ambiguous identifiers among these as well – they were spread across the above continuum, in other words – but the reverse was the case with virtually every other single-religion identity, including Roman Catholics, Orthodox Christians, Hindus, Sikhs, and Buddhists. Those who identified uniquely with one of these religions in significant majority did so ambiguously or selectively, and far less often in 'orthodox' fashion. Moreover – and this is perhaps not that surprising but it is potentially of great importance – it was also only among the Evangelical Protestants and the (mostly Sunni) Muslims that one also found a consistent sense of what the respective 'orthodoxies' comprised: most of them shared a consistent idea or description of what it was to be a Christian or a Muslim. For the former this included the belief that the Bible was the literal Word of God, that one had to make a personal decision for Jesus (usually by being 'born again'), that one had to spread one's faith, pray and go to church regularly and often, and adhere to a socially conservative set of moral attitudes. For the latter it centred on the Five Pillars of Islam, the centrality of the literal truth of the Qur'an (and usually Hadith), conservative moral attitudes, and the observance of halal dietary regulations. By contrast, among those who identified with one of other standard religions, the minority that were also 'orthodox' did not share such a common understanding of their particular orthodoxy, whether that be Roman Catholic or Orthodox Christian, Hindu, Buddhist, or Sikh. They told a far less consistent story.

## Some Possible Implications

The research I have reported here is, of course, only one relatively small project carried out in one relatively sparsely populated corner of the world at a particular time near the beginning of the 21st century. The purpose of presenting some of its results was to gain some illustrative purchase on some of the issues that pose a challenge for the idea and practicality of interreligious dialogue in contemporary circumstances. In that light, to the extent that its results may prove to be indicative of the situation with respect to religion in at least larger portions of global society, there are a number of implications to be drawn that may be significant. The first and most obvious is that identifying and including the partners in such dialogue is anything but straightforward. The institutionalised reality of the religions in global society does not appear to be in doubt, and the list of these religions, while varied depending on where one is in the world, is relatively clear.

What is not nearly as clear is the 'what' and the 'who' of these religions. The religions, while they arguably all have historical/mythical heartlands, that is, places with which they are more closely associated than others, do not (any longer, to the extent that they ever did) have clear and effective centres of authority and authenticity that dominate the religious lives of their adherents, nominal or otherwise, around the world.[15] 'Diaspora' locations and adherents in these places generate their own, for most purposes equally authentic versions of these religions. Dialogue will of necessity, therefore, always be local, but even there the critical issue will be one of representation. If the bulk of the people who enact and live a given religion do not do so with dominant reference to strong authoritative religious institutions, then it is an open question whether any dialogue partner will represent anyone much beyond themselves or a smaller group. The previously dominant institutions, like the various Christian churches in different countries, are no exception, as even their most regular participants often may not consider their leaders as representative of them[16], not to speak of those who are only selective or nominal adherents. Moreover, even with those religions or variants of religions, such as the Evangelical Protestants or Sunni Muslims in our Canadian research sample, where we can observe a strong convergence of religious content, the issue of who would actually represent them is just as open: they, after all, converge by virtue of personal decision, not simply in obedience to authorities or tradition. In that light, therefore, dialogue may have to be among religious people, not among religions as such. The labels of being Christian, Sikh, Muslim, or another religion, will be labels of convenience and self-identification, and not necessarily much more than that.

A further implication concerns the religion that is not subsumed in one of the religions, in terms of the continuum presented above, those toward the left end of the scale: those who do not identify with a particular religion, those who identify with multiple religions, those who consider themselves "spiritual but not religious", and the atheists who sometimes participate in interreligious dialogue. By all accounts, this is not an inconsiderable number, certainly not in most Western countries and in the countries of Eastern Asia.[17] The inclusion

---

15  Beyer, P. (1998) The City and Beyond as Dialogue: Negotiating Religious Authenticity in Global Society. In: *Social Compass*, 45, 61–73.

16  For the Canadian context: Grenville, A. (2000) ‚For by Him All Things Were Created … Visible and Invisible‘: Sketching the Contours of Public and Private Religion in North America. In: D. Lyon & M. Van Die (Eds.) *Rethinking Church, State, and Modernity: Canada betwee Europe and America* Toronto: University of Toronto Press, 211–227.

17  Clark, W. & Schellenberg, G. (2006) Who's Religious?. In: *Canadian Social Trends*, 81, 2–9; R. Inglehart et al. (Eds.) (2004) *Human Values and Beliefs: A Cross-Cultural*

of these identities in interreligious dialogue presents a challenge not so much in terms of who will represent the religions, as with respect to the structuring of religion as a distinct and institutionalised sphere of human – and, of course, perhaps not just human – endeavour. Put slightly differently, if the importance of interreligious dialogue, as I noted at the outset, lies in finding ways towards the cohabitation and mutual understanding of differences, then the contemporary upswing in the number of people identifying as 'spiritually', multiply, vaguely, ambiguously, or not religious points to shifts in the structuring of the very domain that is at issue. If it is difficult enough figuring out which religions will be represented in these efforts toward mutual understanding and who will represent these religions, the question of what operates as the unity – the religious – of this diversity is perhaps just as challenging.

All these questions have implications as well for the theology of interreligious dialogue, that is, the reflection on what it is and what purpose it serves religiously. If the religions end up being little more than labels of self-identification and convenience for those engaged in dialogue, and if the religious identities included are not to be limited to the (locally) usual list – especially the R5+ and the clearly structured 'orthodoxies' among them – then theological reflection will have to address the core issue of what religion is as a constant and important question that always accompanies dialogue. If, just to take an example, religion is conceived as some sort of transcendent/immanent relation, then the vexed issue of what exactly counts as transcendent, how and why we recognise it as such, and the nature of the relation between the two terms will be a logically prior question to how different expressions of that relation express themselves and can come to cohabit and come to mutual understanding.

## In Conclusion: Some Implications for Research

Conducting and reflecting on interreligious dialogue is the task of those who engage in it. Researching the issue with the tools of the social and human sciences is connected, but not the same task. Given the arguments made above, the questions that such research might address will (continue to) include the following: In contemporary interreligious dialogue, which religions are more consistently represented than others, and how does this selection come about? Is it the case, and if so under what circumstances, that such dialogue tends to be limited to the institutional representatives of the major subdivisions of Christianity, Judaism, and Islam, with the inconsistent addition of representatives from the other members of the R5+? What tends to be the outcome of such dialogue?

*Sourcebook Based on the 1999–2002 Values Surveys* Mexico City: Siglo XXI Editores; H. McLeod & W. Ustorf (Eds.) (2003) *The Decline of Christendom in Western Europe, 1750–2000* Cambridge: Cambridge University Press; Pew Research Center (2012) *"Nones" on the Rise: One-in-Five Adults Have No Religious Affiliation* n.p.: Pew Forum on Religion & Public Life (www.pewforum.org, last accessed 10.12.2013).

When does it take place? More specifically, what indications are there that such dialogue has any effect outside its necessarily narrow confines? If 'atheists' are occasionally included, what about the vast and ambiguous 'in-between' identities discussed above? Do they have any place? Depending on the answer, what are the implications of that inclusion or exclusion for the nature of the dialogue that takes place? The contemporary possibility of a major restructuring of the 'religious domain' potentially questions easy assumptions about the nature and indeed the importance of interreligious dialogue. It may be that the aims of the conception and the activity are actually – or can only hope to be – of a limited nature, for instance, of establishing better relations between the representatives of certain religious institutions. Or the possibilities might be larger. In either case, research can assist in finding out what has been or is the case, what outcomes these efforts have had and what relation there is between the form that dialogue takes and the particular local circumstances in which it takes place. And these local circumstances are not just geographically determined, but also temporally. What this dialogue is and can be today may in fact – and this is perhaps the most important conclusion to which my deliberations here might come – be quite different than it was only a couple of decades ago, and the reasons for this shift might be just as important to understand as any other question.

*Nils Friedrichs & Alexander Yendell*

# Attitudes towards Members of Different Religious Communities in Five European Countries

## Introduction

While sociological research into prejudice traditionally focused primarily on ethnic stereotyping, it is now becoming increasingly interested in religious communities and their members as societies become more religiously plural. In many public debates on the matter, it appears that nothing less is at stake than the fundamental configuration of societies subject to mass immigration.

Against this background, we must ask how different religious communities and their members are perceived. Are they widely accepted or rejected? Do people differentiate between a community and its members? We will try to provide answers to these questions by analysing the data of an extensive survey entitled "The Legitimacy of Religious Pluralism: Perception and Acceptance of Religious Diversity among the European Population". The study was carried out in 2010 in Germany, Denmark, France, the Netherlands, and Portugal. In the following, we will first briefly address key concepts and hypotheses that were used in designing the study. Secondly, we will provide descriptive analyses regarding the perception of different religious communities and their members. In our third and final section, we will study the micro-social factors influencing the acceptance or rejection of Muslims.

## Theoretical Considerations

To study perceptions of individuals or groups precisely, we need to distinguish conceptually between the cognitive dimension of an object's properties and the evaluative dimension of its perceived worth.[1] We looked at general attitudes towards Christians, Muslims, Buddhists, Hindus, Jews and atheists in the evaluative dimension. With regard to Christianity and Islam, we also studied the qualities cognitively attributed to them and their positive and/or negative connotations. These, too, express a valuation of the respective groups. Since we cannot assume that both dimensions exist independently of each other, we also studied how they might relate to each other.

Researchers studying prejudice, xenophobia and right-wing extremism have proposed numerous theories to explain the rejection of members of religious communities perceived as foreign. We will limit ourselves here to evaluating the most prominent theories. Perhaps the most widely known attempt to explain

---

1 Stolz, J. (2000) *Soziologie der Fremdenfeindlichkeit. Theoretische und empirische Analysen* Frankfurt a. M.: Campus, 77.

the phenomenon is Adorno's concept of the authoritarian personality.[2] It explains xenophobic attitudes arising from an authoritarian personality structure, one that includes strong adherence to social convention, deference to power, and submissiveness. Like other previous studies, we included items to identify religious dogmatism and authoritarian tendencies to identify the authoritarian personality with regard to religiosity.[3]

A prominent socio-psychological approach that locates the emergence of negative attitudes within a process of group comparison is Social Identity Theory (SIT), which was developed principally by Tajfel and Turner.[4] This approach assumes that the strong relational and comparative identification that individuals have with their own group means that they must view it positively. This leads to a tendency to prefer it to other groups, which are in turn seen in a negative light.[5]

A further prominent approach is the contact hypothesis,[6] which assumes that prejudice towards social groups stems from generalisations and undifferentiated simplifications created by insufficient or wrong information. According to this model, personal contact leads to improved understanding and reduced prejudice.[7]

A sociological hypothesis that has been developed in great detail is that social deprivation produces prejudice. It posits that members of a majority group who are disadvantaged in the competition for scarce socio-economic resources are particularly prone to devaluing and rejecting immigrants. In particular, a perception of disadvantage relative to others (subjective relative deprivation) fosters such negative attitudes.[8]

## Findings

Our analysis is based on data generated by a broad survey conducted by TNS Emnid in five European countries between July and August 2010. Based on

2   Adorno, T. W. et al. (1950) *The Authoritarian Personality* New York: Harper and Brothers.
3   One prominent example of this connection is found in the Allport & Ross (1967) scales on intrinsic and extrinsic religiosity that refer back to Adorno's work. Allport, G. & Ross, J. M. (1967) Personal Religious Orientation and Prejudice. In: *Journal of Personality and Social Psychology*, 4, 432–443.
4   Tajfel, H. & Turner, J. C. (1986) The Social Identity Theory of Intergroup Behavior. In: S. Worchel & W. G. Austin (Eds.) *Psychology of Intergroup Relations* Chicago: Burnham Inc Pub., 7–24.
5   Ibid., 13–16.
6   Allport, G. W. (1971) *Die Natur des Vorurteils* Köln: Kiepenheuer & Witsch.
7   Rippl does state that the reduction of prejudice depends on the type and quality of the contact. Rippl, S. (1995) Vorurteile und persönliche Beziehungen zwischen Ost- und Westdeutschen. In: *Zeitschrift für Soziologie*, 4, 273–283, 277–278.
8   Rippl, S. & Baier, D. (2005) Das Deprivationskonzept in der Rechtsextremismusforschung. Eine vergleichende Analyse. In: Kölner Zeitschrift für Soziologie und Sozialpsychologie, 4, 644–666, 647–648.

a sample derived from the ADM selection system, 1041 personal interviews (CAPI) were conducted in the states of the pre-1990 West Germany and 1002 in the states of the former East Germany. In Denmark, 1014 telephone interviews (CATI) were conducted; 1001 in France and 1000 each in the Netherlands and Portugal.[9] The data were then weighted based on standard sample distortion.[10]

## The Evaluative Dimension: Attitudes towards Christians, Muslims, Jews, Buddhists, Hindus and Atheists

What, then, are the attitudes towards members of the different religious communities in the five countries studied? The question was posed as follows: "What is your personal attitude towards members of the following religious groups?" Respondents had the option of locating their attitudes towards Christians, Muslims, Jews, Buddhists, Hindus and atheists on an even-point four-part Likert scale (very positive, rather positive, rather negative, very negative).

In the Netherlands (62.0%), France (56.1%) and Denmark (54.6%), over half of the respondents have a rather or very positive attitude towards Muslims (cf. Table 1). The reverse is true in both parts of Germany, where over half of the respondents report rather or very negative attitudes towards Muslims (West Germany: 57.8%; East Germany: 62.2%). In Portugal, a significant proportion of the respondents (14.2%) appear unsure how to react to the question. Nonetheless, more Portuguese people are welcoming towards Muslims (46.6%) than opposed to them (33.5%).

*Table 1: Attitudes towards Muslims in Countries Surveyed (per cent)*

|  | G-West | G-East | DK | F | NL | P |
|---|---|---|---|---|---|---|
| Very positive | 5.8 | 2.7 | 15.7 | 4.6 | 8.9 | 7.4 |
| Somewhat positive | 28.4 | 23.2 | 38.9 | 51.5 | 53.1 | 39.2 |
| Somewhat negative | 40.7 | 40.2 | 23.8 | 28.8 | 28.1 | 22.6 |
| Very negative | 17.1 | 22.0 | 11.9 | 8.0 | 7.8 | 10.9 |
| Don't know | 4.8 | 8.8 | 6.8 | 5.7 | 1.6 | 14.2 |
| No response | 3.3 | 3.2 | 3.0 | 1.4 | 0.5 | 5.7 |
| **Total** | **100.0** | **100.0** | **100.0** | **100.0** | **100.0** | **100.0** |

What about attitudes towards members of the other religious communities as well as towards atheists? The means and standard deviations are reported in Table 2. First of all, we can see that attitudes towards all non-Islamic religious communities as well as towards atheists are generally positive. Christians are viewed most positively. The average evaluations of the other communities

---

9   We developed a unitary questionnaire for use in all countries, though the German questionnaire was expanded by several additional questions on key aspects.

10   Age, gender and educational attainment were considered in the weighting process.

across the countries surveyed fall between the highest-scoring Christians and the lowest-scoring Muslims.[11]

*Table 2: Attitudes towards Christians, Muslims, Hindus, Buddhists, Jews and Atheists (averages)*

| n =<br>697–1009 | D-West | | D-East | | DK | | F | | NL | | P | | Total | |
|---|---|---|---|---|---|---|---|---|---|---|---|---|---|---|
| | M | SD | M | SD | M | SD | M | SD | M | SD | M | SD | M | SD |
| Attitude to Christians | 1.7 | 0.6 | 2.0 | 0.7 | 1.6 | 0.7 | 2.1 | 0.6 | 1.9 | 0.6 | 1.9 | 0.8 | 1.9 | 0.7 |
| Attitude to Muslims | 2.8 | 0.8 | 2.9 | 0.8 | 2.4 | 0.9 | 2.4 | 0.7 | 2.4 | 0.8 | 2.5 | 0.8 | 2.6 | 0.8 |
| Attitude to Hindus | 2.3 | 0.7 | 2.5 | 0.8 | 1.9 | 0.7 | 2.1 | 0.6 | 2.0 | 0.6 | 2.2 | 0.7 | 2.2 | 0.7 |
| Attitude to Buddhists | 2.1 | 0.7 | 2.4 | 0.8 | 1.8 | 0.7 | 2.1 | 0.6 | 1.9 | 0.6 | 2.1 | 0.8 | 2.0 | 0.7 |
| Attitude to Jews | 2.3 | 0.7 | 2.4 | 0.8 | 1.9 | 0.7 | 2.2 | 0.6 | 1.9 | 0.6 | 2.2 | 0.8 | 2.1 | 0.7 |
| Attitude to atheists | 2.3 | 0.8 | 1.9 | 0.8 | 1.9 | 0.8 | 2.0 | 0.7 | 2.0 | 0.7 | 2.2 | 0.8 | 2.0 | 0.8 |

Note: Average differences between countries are significant at a level of $p < 0.01$. M = mean value, SD = standard deviation

With the exception of France and the Netherlands, there is a relatively large number of people who find it hard to define their attitude towards Hinduism and Buddhism. We can therefore say that, in total, the most positive attitudes are towards Christians. They are followed by atheists, who are viewed especially positively in East Germany with its long atheist tradition (73.9) and in France (79.4).

## The Cognitive Dimension: Images of Islam and Christianity

What image do people in the countries surveyed have of Islam and Christianity? To survey the characteristics which respondents ascribe to each religion, we presented them with a list of 'images'. They were asked to select those they considered most characteristic of Islam and/or Christianity. For the sake of brevity, we will only deal in detail with the findings for the items 'fanaticism', 'tolerance' and 'discrimination against women' (cf. Picture 1).

One essential finding is that Islam is viewed equally negatively in all five countries. For instance, approximately 70 per cent associate 'fanaticism' with Islam and some 80 per cent of the population of all nations think of 'discrimination against women' when they hear the word 'Islam'. When the respond-

---

11 Taking unanswered items into account, we found no major differences between the different countries with regard to positive attitudes towards atheists (69%), Buddhists (68%), Jews (67,6%) und Hindus (60,2%).

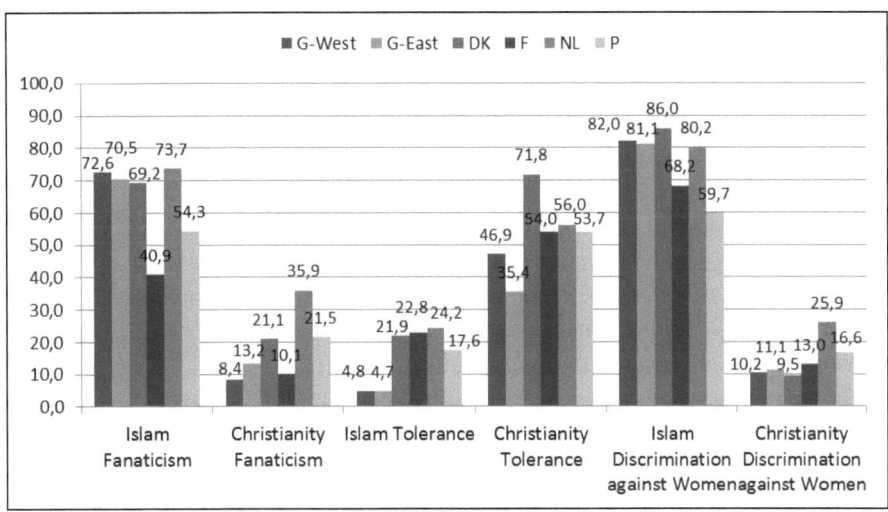

*Picture 1: Associations with Islam/Christianity of: Fanaticism/Tolerance/Discrimination against Women (agreement in per cent)*

ents are offered positive attributes to choose from, a clear difference between Germany and the other countries emerges. Fewer than 5 per cent of Germans ascribe 'tolerance' to Islam, while in Denmark, France and the Netherlands, it is more than 20 per cent. The results also reveal that Islam and Christianity are polar opposites in the minds of many people.[12] 'Fanaticism' is often associated with Islam and hardly ever with Christianity. The association of fundamentalism with Islam seems to be influencing public perception, especially since the attacks of 11 September 2001.[13] In contrast, fundamentalist Christian movements are hardly visible in Europe. Regarding the association of tolerance with Christianity and Islam, the picture is almost the reverse, although 'tolerance' is associated with Christianity to the same degree as 'fanaticism' is with Islam in no country except Denmark. Rather, people do not seem to regard 'tolerance' as a primary characteristic of religions in general; nonetheless, it is associated significantly more often with Christianity than with Islam in all countries studied. Notably, though, more than four times as many Danish, French, Dutch and Portuguese respondents ascribed 'tolerance' to Islam than German respondents. Results for 'discrimination against women' are similar to those for 'fanaticism': With the exception of France and Portugal, respondents throughout all countries

---

12  A 2006 survey conducted by the Institut für Demoskopie Allensbach arrived at similar results. Here, too, German respondents associated features such as fanaticism, violence, discrimination of women and backwardness with Islam. Allensbacher Archiv (2006) *IfD-Umfrage 7089* April/Mai 2006.

13  In their 2005 GMF survey Leibold, Kühnel & Heitmeyer (2006) found 60 per cent of German respondents agreeing that terrorists would find strong support in the Muslim community. A further 64 per cent were convinced that Muslims admired terrorists. Leibold, J. et al. (2006) Abschottung von Muslimen durch generalisierte Islamkritik? In: *Aus Politik und Zeitgeschichte*, 1–2, 3–10, 5.

surveyed agree that Islam discriminates against women (agreement: between 80.2% and 86.0%). With the exception of the Netherlands, where 'fanaticism', was also ascribed relatively broadly to Christianity, 'discrimination against women' is hardly seen in Christians (between 10.2% and 16.6%). Such decisive positions on this point may be due in part to the public debate on equality of the sexes especially in Islam. The findings indicate a level of individual identification with Christianity on the part of respondents[14] that seems to go hand in hand, at least to a degree, with their distancing themselves from Islam.[15]

How much of a homogeneous picture of Islam emerges when we include all ascriptions recorded? To study this, we summarised the frequencies of positively and negatively connoted qualities in separate indices. A variation from 0–4 possible mentions of both positive and negative qualities is used. The index is calculated solely on the distinction between positively and negatively connoted items. The fact that the different qualities may describe very different things is not considered. When we relate positive and negative qualities attributed to Islam to each other based on the indices, we find a relatively homogeneous and very negative overall picture in West Germany (cf. Table 3).

We find 32.3 per cent of respondents associating four negative, but no positive, attributes with Islam. More strikingly, 83.1 per cent of West German respondents do not associate a single positively connoted quality with Islam. If the criteria for a negative overall image of Islam are defined as ascribing between two and four negative qualities, but no more than one positive one, then almost three quarters of people in West Germany (73.5%) have an entirely negative image (bold framing). The picture in the former East Germany is practically identical at 74.0 per cent. This confirms once more that the image of Islam throughout Germany is negative. Overall negative perceptions of Islam were also found in Denmark (56.6%) and the Netherlands (50.6%). The results in France and Portugal are more positive.[16]

---

14   Detlef Pollack found around two thirds of West Germans and around a quarter of East Germans identifying with Christianity. Pollack, D. (2009) *Rückkehr des Religiösen. Studien zum religiösen Wandel in Deutschland und Europa II* Tübingen: Mohr Siebeck, 126. Gert Pickel also finds a strong Christian influence in Europe as a whole and at least the Western states of Germany, though he cautions that this must be viewed separately from individual religious affiliation. Pickel, G. (2009) Secularisation as a European Fate? – Results from the Church and Religion in an Enlarged Europe Project 2006. In: G. Pickel & O. Müller (Eds.) *Church and Religion in Contemporary Europe. Results from Empirical and Comparative Research* Wiesbaden: Verlag für Sozialwissenschaften, 89–122, 99. Olaf Müller (2011) emphasises that most people certainly regard European culture as influenced by religion (i.e. Christianity). Müller, O. (2011) *Kirchlichkeit und Religiosität in den postkommunistischen Gesellschaften Ostmittel- und Osteuropas. Entwicklungen – Muster – Bestimmungsgründe* Unveröffentlichte Dissertation, 172.

15   The pattern of agreement with the remaining image prompts for Islam is comparable. They were: Violence, peacefulness, backwardness, bigotry, solidarity and respect for human rights.

16   France: 41.2%, Portugal: 37.9%.

*Table 3: Cross-reference: Positive and Negative Attributions to Islam, West Germany*

| | | **Negative Attributions to Islam** | | | | | |
|---|---|---|---|---|---|---|---|
| | | **0** | **1** | **2** | **3** | **4** | **Total** |
| | 0 | 5.2% | 11.4% | 13.2% | 21.0% | 32.3% | 83,1% |
| **Positive** | 1 | 1.1% | 1.8% | 1.4% | 3.0% | 2.6% | 9,9% |
| **Attributions** | 2 | 0.6% | 0.7% | 0.9% | 1.0% | 1.1% | 4,1% |
| **to Islam** | 3 | 0.7% | 0.1% | 0.2% | 0.2% | 0.4% | 1,5% |
| | 4 | 0.7% | 0.1% | 0.1% | 0.0% | 0.5% | 1,3% |
| **Total** | | **8.2%** | **14.1%** | **15.8%** | **25.1%** | **36.8%** | **100.0%** |

A factor in the prevailing view of Islam by German respondents is their particularly strong sense of distance from it. In all countries surveyed, the view of Islam as a religion is much more negative than the view of its adherents. Testing whether respondents with a positive attitude towards Muslims have different views on Islam to those with a critical attitude bears this out (cf. Picture 2). Interestingly, while there is a highly significant correlation between positive attitudes towards Muslims and a less negative image of Islam, even respondents with highly positive attitudes towards Muslims had more negative than positive associations with the prompt "Islam".

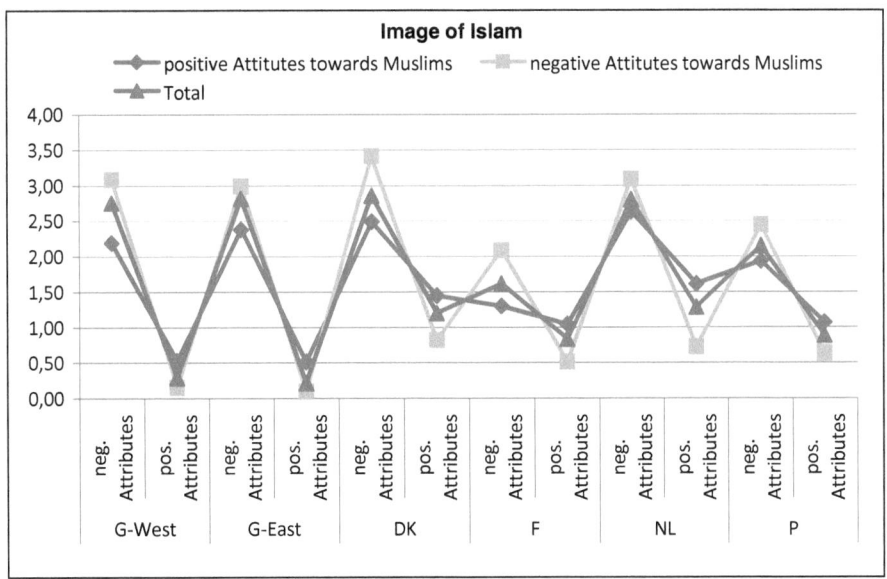

*Picture 2: Negative Traits Associated with Islam, Differentiated by Attitudes towards Muslims*

Only in France did respondents with a positive attitude towards Muslims associate as many positive as negative traits with Islam. Overall, people clearly have a different view of the religious community than they have of its adherents. This needs to be taken into account in the context of public discourse.

What are the factors influencing such negative attitudes towards Muslims? Based on the micro-social approaches mentioned in the theoretical considerations above, we calculated linear regression models separately for each country surveyed (for Germany, separately for the East and West)[17]. To survey xenophobia, we asked to what degree respondents agreed that too many foreigners were living in their country. We surveyed for national pride and related concepts through agreement with the statement "I am proud of my nationality" and self-localisation on a left-right political spectrum. Engaging with Muslims was operationalised through surveying both self-reported frequency of contact and intensity of cognitive engagement with Islam. To measure deprivation, we chose two variables. Subjective relative deprivation is reflected in the survey item: "Compared with how others live in your country: Do you think you get your fair share, more than your fair share, somewhat less or very much less than your fair share?" Objective absolute deprivation is measured in the variable 'unemployment'. The presumed significance of an authoritarian personality structure was accounted for by surveying agreement with the items "We should be grateful for leaders who can tell us exactly what to do and how to do it" (authoritarianism) and "There is only one true religion" (religious dogmatism). Anomie as a possible individual disposition was covered by the item "Everything changes so quickly these days that I often have trouble deciding which are the right rules to follow" as its predictor. To control for general attitudes towards religion, we included the item "Religious symbols, such as crosses, should be forbidden in state schools", which indicates support for a strong separation of church and state and a critical stance towards religions. To survey the respondents' own religion, we used affiliation as a dummy variable,[18] frequency of church attendance as a measure of religious practice, and the item "I feel free to draw on teachings from various religious traditions" as a measure of syncretism. Finally, we also recorded relevant socio-demographic factors by surveying age and gender.[19] It should be said at this point that the results cannot be used to compare the situation directly in different countries as we cannot say to what degree the differences between them are statistically significant.

---

17  The individual regression models were calculated separately and gradually. Some indicators were excluded from all models calculated, including years of education (or for Germany, highest educational attainment), interpersonal trust ("There are only few people that can be trusted"), net household income and relative socioeconomic status (on a scale from 1=at the bottom to 7=at the top). We also ensured that correlations between the items included were not too high to allow for considering them separate indicators.

18  The reference category was "no confession".

19  A negative value in the beta coefficient indicates greater agreement with *negative* views of Muslims.

*Table 4: Factors Influencing Attitudes towards Muslims – OLS-Regression (beta-coefficient)*

| Attitudes towards Muslims[a] | D-West | D-East | DK | F | NL | P |
|---|---|---|---|---|---|---|
| There are too many foreigners living in my country. | -.297*** | -.322*** | -.413*** | -.241*** | -.379*** | |
| Contact with Muslims | .285*** | .153*** | .180*** | .180*** | .139*** | .176*** |
| Engagement with Islam | | | | .132*** | | .145** |
| Political attitude[b] | | -.112** | | | -.116*** | |
| Frequency of church attendance | .104** | | | | | .231*** |
| I feel free to draw on teachings from various religious traditions. | .126*** | | | .071* | | .118** |
| There is only one true religion. | -.123** | | | | -.087** | -.135** |
| We should be grateful for leaders who can tell us exactly what to do and how to do it. | | | .066* | | .106** | |
| Looking around the world, religions bring more conflict than peace. | -.123*** | -.115** | -.066* | -.135*** | -.089** | |
| Religious symbols, such as crosses, should be forbidden in state schools. | | | -.063* | | | .118** |
| Relative deprivation | | -.095* | | | | |
| Unemployment | -.080* | | | | | |
| I am proud of my nationality. | | -.074* | | .093** | .082* | |
| Confession: Catholic[c] | | | -.080** | -.067* | | |
| Confession: Non-Christian faith[c] | | .091* | | | | |
| Everything changes so quickly these days that I often have trouble deciding which are the right rules to follow. | | | -.066* | | | |
| Age | | | | -.088* | | -.113** |
| Gender[d] | | | | | -.089** | |
| R² | .320*** | .257*** | .279*** | .212*** | .252*** | .147*** |
| N | 596 | 606 | 776 | 771 | 813 | 518 |

Significance: ***p<.001; **p<.01; *p<.05
[a] Positive and negative beta-coefficients indicate the respective tendency in attitude towards Muslims the responses agree with, i.e. a negative coefficient indicates higher agreement with negative attitudes.
[b] On a scale from 1 (left) to 10 (right)
[c] Reference category: no confession
[d] Reference category: female

At first glance we notice two key factors that are identical in all countries (except Portugal): xenophobia is the strongest predictor in Germany, Denmark, France and the Netherlands, though the coefficient varies greatly between Denmark and France (cf. Table 4).

The second strongest influence in all countries surveyed is the frequency of personal contact, even without controlling for the type and valuation of these contacts.[20] Engaging with things that are perceived as different seems to make holding generalised negative attitudes more difficult. Active engagement with Islam as a religion, on the other hand, only seems to matter at all in France and Portugal. Personal contacts, even though they are much less consciously pursued at the cognitive level, appear to be better at reducing prejudice.[21]

While we find further relevant predictors in Germany, France and Portugal, this is not the case to the same extent in Denmark and the Netherlands. The only aspect that seems relevant in the Netherlands is that respondents who self-identify as left-wing tend towards greater tolerance. The influence of all other variables is not statistically highly significant. The positive coefficient between intolerance and xenophobia is also highest in the Netherlands and Denmark. Political orientation is a key factor in attitudes towards Muslims in East Germany as well.

Positive attitudes towards Muslims in Portugal are affected by different factors. Religion is especially influential. A similar correlation only exists in West Germany, where it is much weaker. Respondents who attended church regularly showed a more positive attitude towards Muslims. This is particularly interesting given that the findings by Allport/Ross (1967) suggest the opposite should happen.[22] As one would expect, a syncretic orientation, which requires a degree of openness towards other religions, also correlates with a positive view of Muslims.

Only in West Germany and Portugal can we show that devaluation of Muslims goes hand in hand with an authoritarian personality structure (dogmatism in religious matters). We also find a similar correlation with dogmatism in

---

20 We cannot check causal relationships on the basis of the data generated here. However, the meta-analysis of 501 surveys by Pettigrew & Tropp (2006) confirms the ability of contacts to reduce prejudice. Pettigrew, T. F. & Tropp, L. R. (2006) A Meta-Analytic Test of Intergroup Contact Theory. In: *Journal of Personality and Social Psychology*, 5, 751–783, 757–758.

21 Allport already pointed out that factually correct knowledge does not necessarily change attitudes (Allport (1971), 173). When a prejudice was factually countered, the related valuation shifted to the affective level (Ibid., 23).

22 These findings correspond to the results reached by Stefan Huber and Volkhard Krech (2009) where membership in a religious community showed up as an important factor in determining religious tolerance. Huber and Krech conclude that having a religious position has a positive impact on tolerance. Huber, S. & Krech, V. (2009) Das religiöse Feld zwischen Globalisierung und Regionalisierung: Vergleichende Perspektiven. In: Bertelsmann Stiftung (Ed.) *Woran glaubt die Welt? Analysen und Kommentare zum Religionsmonitor 2008*. Gütersloh: Verlag Bertelsmann Stiftung, 53–96, 74.

France, though it is much smaller. The Netherlands are the only country where the data show a strong effect of authoritarianism. A much weaker effect is found in Denmark, though it seems to be inverse, suggesting possible problems with the validity of this indicator. Altogether, we have found that personality structures do not seem to be of great importance for attitudes towards Muslims.[23] Critical positions towards religion in general tend to go together with negative attitudes towards Muslims in Germany and France. This correlation is also present in Denmark and the Netherlands, though it is noticeably less strong there. Support for secular principles only plays a role in Portugal, where it goes hand in hand with a more positive attitude towards Muslims. Given the continuing dominance of the church there, it is possible that the item regarding a ban on crosses in state schools was read as a criticism of Christian dominance and a plea for minority rights, which would include those of Muslims.[24]

Deprivation, a traditional predictor for intolerance, is almost insignificant in our findings. Only in the eastern part of Germany do we see a moderate influence, significant only at a very low level.[25]

The findings for the indicator of 'national pride' are very interesting. According to Weins (2004)[26], we would expect to find a positive correlation between national pride and xenophobia in countries with strongly exclusive citizenship laws. Countries with a liberal, open citizenship policy should not show such a correlation. Our findings confirm only one case of a significant, though small, positive correlation between national pride and negative attitudes towards Muslims in the eastern part of Germany. In the Netherlands and France, the correlation is negative. This suggests that national pride in these countries is more rooted in a patriotic affirmation of constitutional rights and democracy than ethnic nationalism.

---

23  This only refers to direct connections with the valuation of Muslims, not taking to account possible effects of interaction.

24  The hypothesis that supports for secular principles does not indicate a critical stance towards religion in Portugal is supported by the low bivariate correlation (after Pearson) of the compartmentalisation item with the item surveying general criticism of religion. It is a mere .07 and of low significance. Except for Denmark, where the correlation is similarly low (.09), all other countries surveyed show much higher values (between .13 and .42).

25  The reason for this remarkably low influence of deprivation is most likely found, at least partly, in how it was measured. While Rippl & Baier (2005) especially emphasise the importance of subjective collective deprivation, our model only measured subjective individual deprivation. Thus, this result also militates in favour of a stronger differentiation of the concept as advocated by the authors.

26  Weins, C. (2004) *Fremdenfeindliche Vorurteile in den Staaten der EU* Wiesbaden: Verlag für Sozialwissenschaften, 221.

## Summary

In conclusion, we can say that Germans both have a more homogeneous and more negative image of Islam and are more reserved in their attitude towards Muslims than their European neighbours. At the same time, it has become clear that we must distinguish between attitudes towards a religious community on the one hand and attitudes towards its members on the other: Islam is viewed more negatively in all countries surveyed than Muslims are. In Denmark and the Netherlands, the majority of people have a negative view of Islam while a majority also see Muslims positively. In regression analysis, we were able to confirm the importance of the contact hypothesis in all countries surveyed. People who have personal contacts with members of religious communities that they perceive as being foreign also tend to have more positive attitudes towards them. On the other hand, deprivation does not serve well as an explanation for negative attitudes towards Muslims. This result may be partly due to the reduced format of our survey, though. Religiosity appears to foster more positive attitudes, which suggests that there is a faultline between religious and secular positions. Finally, we must consider that 'Muslims' seem to be strongly associated with 'foreigners' in all countries surveyed.

*Gritt Klinkhammer*

# The Dialogos Project

## An Empirical Study of the Functioning and Impact of Christian-Muslim Dialogue Initiatives in Germany

## 1.  Introduction

What we in the following understand by the term 'interreligious dialogue projects' is a relatively recent phenomenon of the twentieth century. Systematic dialogue between Christians and Jews only began at the end of the Second World War at the instigation of the US government. By now, the *Gesellschaft für Jüdisch-Christliche Zusammenarbeit* has more than 80 separate active groups in Germany.[1] Christian-Muslim dialogue began at an international level following the Six-Day War[2] and received its greatest boost in the aftermath of the 9/11 terror attacks. The Dialogos project[3], a survey of interreligious dialogue initiatives in Germany, lists well over 200 separate Christian-Muslim and multi-religious dialogue initiatives.

Even a cursory glance at modern interreligious dialogue will reveal that its stated purpose has always been to defuse conflict and secure peace. Currently active dialogue initiatives often profess a variety of motives and aims in this spectrum such as "discovering and fostering shared values" (96%), "combating Islamophobia and prejudice" (92%), "shaping coexistence together" (85%), "understanding one's own religion better" (81%), "equality of all religious communities" (76%), "fostering social participation by migrants" (75%) or "strengthening religious interests vis-à-vis the state" (32%).[4]

Especially since 9/11, German policymakers have been embracing Christian-Muslim interreligious dialogue as an instrument to provide security and peace. Support of dialogue initiatives between Muslims and Christians was adopted by the programmes of several ministries (including the interior ministry and the ministry for family, youth, women's and social issues). The heightened expectations this created led to the question whether such initiatives were actually able to provide the benefits one hoped to gain from them. This led to the call for academic research to develop criteria to identify, foster and implement effective dialogue processes.

1   Braunwarth, E. (2011) *Interkulturelle Kooperation in Deutschland am Beispiel der Gesellschaften für christlich-jüdische Zusammenarbeit* München: Herbert Utz Verlag.
2   Sperber, J. (1999) *Dialog mit dem Islam* Göttingen: Vandenhoek & Ruprecht.
3   Klinkhammer, G. et al. (2011) *Interreligiöse und interkulturelle Dialoge mit MuslimInnen in Deutschland: eine quantitative und qualitative Studie* Bremen: Universität Bremen.
4   Ibid., 46–48.

## 2.    Interreligious Dialogue in the Perspective of the Dialogos Project

The term 'dialogue' comes from Greek philosophy where it denoted the consideration of philosophical problems in a conversational exchange of views to gain new insights (Socratic dialogue). Philosopher Hans-Georg Gadamer defined the dialogical situation as an opportunity for self-recognition by understanding dialogue as a reflexive learning process.[5] Martin Buber went further in viewing dialogue as a precondition of becoming human: "*Der Mensch wird am Du zum Ich*" (Man becomes I through You).[6]

This existential understanding of dialogue appears again and again in the self-descriptions of dialogue initiatives, e.g. when over 80 per cent of Christian-Muslim initiatives expect to improve not only their understanding of the respective other religion, but also their own. But how could such processes of self-recognition be rendered measurable? And how can they contribute to ensuring peace?

After all, dialogues are a common feature of life anywhere. The media are full of dialogues, often staged, on all kinds of issues. Especially in the public sphere, it seems that dialogues not only serve to negotiate options in a search for compromise, but are cathartic and apotropaeic rituals. To verbalise something, to enter into a conversation can be of more than mere symbolic significance; it can ritually signify the acceptance of a position or more generally, of the other party.

In order to generate a comparable sample, the Dialogos project had to limit its own study to a specific type of dialogue. It surveyed only instances in which Christians and Muslims met to form a 'group' for the specific purpose of interreligious dialogue. Such a 'social group' is defined by an immediate relationship with its members and a measure of stability over time.[7] The initiatives surveyed are mostly self-organised groups with varying degrees of formal structures. Their sizes varied, with 70 per cent of groups numbering between 10 and 39 regular participants.

The Dialogos project was able to study the functioning and impact of these dialogues through a structured quantitative and qualitative survey of the groups and their members.

### 2.1   How Dialogue Initiatives Function

A quantitative survey of organisers or chairpersons was used to ascertain how the surveyed initiatives functioned and augmented by participant observation

---

5   Gadamer, H.-G. (1960) *Wahrheit und Methode. Grundzüge einer philosophischen Hermeneutik* Tübingen: Mohr Siebeck.
6   Buber, M. (1923/1965) *Das dialogische Prinzip* Heidelberg: Schneider.
7   Neidhardt, F. (1979) Das innere System sozialer Gruppen. In: *KZSS*, 31(4), 639–660.

in 20 cases. The findings showed a broad spectrum of approaches in practice.[8] While 90 per cent of initiatives focus on conversational exchanges in face-to-face meetings (*Gesprächskreise*), many additionally visit places of worship, meditate or pray together, and jointly organise public information events, lectures, or other activities (peace prayers, celebrations etc.). Thematically, the variety is equally broad. Almost all initiatives report both discussing topics of religion, spirituality and theology as well as those concerning social policy and integration. Their method can be broadly summarised as follows:
- Teaching facts about other religions and cultures,
- Encountering other religions in dialogue with believers,
- Comparing different religious teachings and practices,
- Focusing on one religious teaching and practice in each session.[9]

"Learning more about their situation by talking to migrants" or "discussing questions regarding Muslim migrants and Islam in Germany" are considered important elements of their dialogical efforts by two thirds of respondents. One or the other is considered important in almost three quarters of the groups surveyed. The significance accorded to these aspects reflects the degree to which questions of social integration are today being addressed by and from a perspective of parties with specific religious affiliations.[10]

Addressing and resolving specific conflicts of interest ranks lowest among the aspects of dialogue work surveyed. Most likely, this is owed not least to the fact that entities other than civil society are responsible for making decisions in a large number of relevant cases (e.g. Islamic Religious Education, incorporation of religious organisations).[11]

The most common form of communication in the dialogue initiatives is face-to-face discussion, almost always moderated by a chairperson (this is often a rotating position) and accompanied by oral or written introductions to the topic of the session. About a third of initiatives surveyed have produced mutually agreed, written rules of conduct for these discussions.[12]

Interreligious dialogue initiatives often organise public discussions, prayer meetings or similar events, but in principle most of their dialogue groups are closed circles, with participants admitted only by their own request or by invitation. This appears a sensible solution, given that exchanges are not always harmonious and require a great deal of mutual trust. Nonetheless, almost all respondents considered the public perception of their efforts important and reported conducting public relations work and appearing in the local media on average once a year.

---

8   Klinkhammer et al. (2011), 65–85.
9   Ibid., 70.
10  Klinkhammer et al. (2011), 72.
11  Ibid., 73.
12  Ibid., 75.

Individual initiatives may not always be striving for public recognition, but participants do not view themselves as isolated. Most groups are organised at the local level and often report good contacts and a supportive attitude on the part of local authorities. [13] About half of them also participate in higher-level meetings organised by a number of Christian, Muslim and multi-confessional bodies (CIG, RfP, ACK, ICA, KCID, CIBEDO, DITIB et al.) where they exchange methods and ideas.[14]

## 3.    Measuring the Effectiveness of Dialogue Initiatives

In the following, effectiveness is measured by the interreligious dialogue initiatives' ability to support a peaceful social cooperation of the different involved religious groups. However, a measuring of the improvement of concrete local social cooperation and peaceful encounter only could be done by a long-term inquiry. The Dialogos Project did not have this possibility, but it collected self-assessments of the dialogue initiatives regarding goal attainment and measured concrete conditions and settings of the initiatives in order to value their contribution to the prevention of intergroup conflicts and to reducing prejudices.

The Dialogos project pursued three approaches to that end:

Firstly, it surveyed the initiatives' own perception of their impact. This instrument is inexact in that a quantitative survey cannot provide a differentiated understanding of the criteria the respondents applied in their judgement. Self-estimates in a field so loaded with normative expectations are also subject to normative bias in responses where the line between intent and reality becomes blurred.[15]

Further, we sought to produce a typology of initiatives through correlative analysis of their methods, goals, audience and surveyed attitudes, allowing us to draw conclusions about the impact of different approaches to dialogue. Interestingly, we found that dialogue efforts, while committed and varied, are currently too unspecific in its goals and audience orientation to generate statistically significant results in this regard.

Thirdly, we used concepts of social psychology to study the potential of dialogue initiatives to create positive social ties and reduce stereotypes, prejudice and intergroup conflict. I would now like to present key findings of this aspect of our research. As we will see, they are of great relevance to ensure a positive impact of future interreligious dialogue efforts.

---

13  Ibid., 85.
14  Ibid., 84.
15  The results can be found in the Dialogos study. They are largely positive [Klinkhammer et al. (2011), 46–50].

### 3.1   The Contribution of Dialogue Initiatives to Reducing Prejudice and Intergroup Conflict[16]

Reducing prejudice and fostering the peaceful coexistence of people from different religious backgrounds as well as the prevention of conflict are reported as central goals by most dialogue initiatives surveyed. We will now look at the utility of their efforts as a means to reduce prejudice and foster peaceful coexistence. To do this, we will look at the findings of the Dialogos project from the perspective of the current state of psychological research on prejudice, intergroup contacts and potentially positive contextual factors of these contacts.

Most approaches to improving intergroup relations discussed today refer to the theory of social identity proposed by Tajfel and Turner.[17] According to this, people identify themselves and others according to certain social groups (e. g. by gender, religion, football club etc.) and perceive others according to these categories (e.g. as a woman, Muslim or Chelsea supporter). Depending on the context, one of these group associations may supersede the others. Such social identities are important, among other things, to establish an individual's sense of self-worth. A strong identification with one group provides the individual with a sense that whatever happens to the group happens to itself.[18] A positive perception of the social group can thus contribute to a positive self-perception. This leads to the (mostly subconscious) motivation to gain a positive estimate of one's own group. This desire to have one's own social group contrast positively with others motivates people to represent other groups as comparatively worse both to themselves and others.[19] Alongside approaches that see the use of stereotypical ideas as a 'normal' cognitive shortcut that human brains use when processing information, prejudice and negative blanket judgements are also seen as emerging from this central function of social identities for the individual sense of self-worth. Persons who feel that their self-worth or social identities are materially or psychologically threatened tend to exhibit an increase in thoughts and actions devaluing other social groups.[20] The predominant view in the psychological study of prejudice is that any kind of contact between people from different social groups (intergroup contact) holds potential to positively influence their attitudes ("mere contact hypothesis").[21] However, this positive

16  The following results are primarily taken from the work of Tina Seibert in the course of the Dialogos project and include statistical data generated by her [Klinkhammer et al. (2011), chapter 4].

17  Tajfel, H. & Turner, J. C. (1986) The Social Identity theory of Intergroup Behaviour. In: S. Worchel & W. G. Austin (Eds.) *Psychology of Intergroup Behaviour* Chicago: Nelson Hall, 7–24.

18  Whitley, B. E. & Kite, M. E. (2010) *The Psychology of Prejudice and Discrimination* Belmont: Wadsworth.

19  Tajfel & Turner (1986).

20  Werth, L. & Mayer, J. (2008) *Sozialpsychologie* Berlin & Heidelberg: Spectrum.

21  Pettigrew, T. F. & Tropp, L. R. (2006) A Meta-Analytical Test of Intergroup Contact Theory. In: *Journal of Personality and Social Psychology*, 90, 753–781.

impact can be reinforced or hampered by contextual factors, even, under certain circumstances, becoming a liability for intergroup relations. Contact between strongly prejudiced individuals from different social groups, for example, could both reinforce their prejudice and burden future intergroup relations by producing a sense of threat in contact situations.[22] Interviews in the Dialogos project, in which experts – usually the organisers of dialogue initiatives – recall 'misadventures' (*Unglücke*) in dialogue lend reality to these concerns. Thus, the quest to identify positive contextual frameworks for intergroup contacts continues to be of great importance. Research into the ideal configuration of such contacts has a tradition of over 50 years in social psychology. The American psychologist Gordan Allport defined the conditions under which intergroup contacts would contribute to an improvement of intergroup relations as early as 1954. His 'contact hypothesis' has since been empirically validated multiple times, refined and expanded. The current consensus on conditions for successful intergroup contacts, inasmuch as it is relevant to interreligious dialogue, can be summarised as follows:

(1) There are no significant status differences between members of the different groups in the encounter.
(2) An explicit common goal is formulated and pursued cooperatively. This facilitates discovering common ground between participants from different groups.
(3) Contact between groups is supported by authorities and institutions.
(4) Contacts are voluntary, repeated, and take place over a longer period of time. There are opportunities to know each other personally, not just superficially. Contact is perceived as pleasant and reduces fears of the other.
(5) The interaction is perceived as positive (successful).[23]

These conditions overlap in many regards, some being dependent on each other or mutually reinforcing. However, as we will see, they also conflict with each other in some respects.

---

22 Pettigrew, T. F. (2008) Future Directions for Intergroup Contact Theory and Research. In: *International Journal of Intercultural Relations*, 32, 187–199.

23 especially Allport, G. (1954) *The Nature of Prejudice* Cambridge: Perseus Books; Stephan, W. G. (1985) Intergroup Relations. In: G. Lindsey & E. Aronson (Eds.) *Handbook of Social Psychology* New York: Random House, 599–658; Osbeck, L. M. et al. (1997) Similarity and Attraction among Majority and Minority Groups in a Multicultural Context. In: *International Journal of Intercultural Relations*, 21, 113–123; Armir, Y. (1969) Contact-Hypotheses in Ethnic Relations. In: *Psychology Bulletin*, 71, 319–342; Pettigrew & Tropp (2006); Pettigrew (2008); Brown, R. & M. Hewstone (2005) An Integrative Theory of Intergroup Contact. In: *Advances in Experimental Social Psychology*, 37, 255–343.

### 3.1.1 Equal Status of Dialogue Parties

Status differences can reinforce fears and insecurities in dialogue participants, which increase the danger of mutual devaluation in reaction. This problem has long been familiar in dialogue initiatives, where it is usually discussed under the heading of meeting "eye to eye" (*auf Augenhöhe*). This meeting "eye to eye", or at equal status, can manifest itself in a variety of ways. Inside organisations, it must be accounted for in allocating offices and tasks, but also in the educational and socioeconomic status and age of participants and in the numerical representation of the different groups. We have found that the initiatives surveyed often tended to involuntarily reproduce present social hierarchies within their structures e.g. by not taking the quantitative distribution of members of different groups or their educational status into account when trying to arrange "eye to eye" dialogue.

### 3.1.2 Formulating Common Goals and Finding Common Ground

Given that intergroup research shows formulating common ground strongly improves peaceful coexistence, the question whether a Christian-Muslim dialogue can be of any use to dissolve group boundaries is not a trivial one. By concentrating dialogue on different religious identities to the exclusion of other aspects, an imaginary boundary between Christians and Muslims is reaffirmed. The Dialogos study has found that an important factor in the emergence of conflicts in dialogue initiatives is a tendency of participants to ascribe differences to an imagined dichotomy of religious identities, thus moving conflicts to an essential, religious level. This is despite the fact that they often decided to participate in dialogue initiatives exactly in order to counteract stereotypes and achieve better understanding. Especially comparisons between religions, a common approach in interreligious dialogue, can backfire this way.

The role of dialogue initiatives that emphasise a common feature or goal beyond religious affiliation in their efforts is more unambiguously integrative, by contrast. These are e.g., interreligious dialogue groups of and for women whose encounter is defined less in terms of overcoming (seemingly natural) boundaries between religious traditions and more in terms of shared interests and needs, the common experience of 'womanhood' or common cause in fighting 'patriarchy'. The same applies to groups that dedicate themselves not to the question of "integrating Islam" – a perspective that practically institutionalises status differences for good – but rather to 'religion', 'peace' or 'spirituality'. Their group interest, too, is defined in terms of a shared goal such as giving religion a clearer, more vocal role in secular society.

### 3.1.3 Institutional Support for Dialogue

Though both the churches and the Islamic associations in Germany are supportive of Christian-Muslim dialogue, we frequently find a degree of tension between their positions and those of the dialogue initiatives themselves.[24] It is thus not surprising that many initiatives take a pointedly independent stance and pursue their own public relations efforts as they prefer not to be seen as arms of either the churches or the Islamic establishment.

In socio-psychological theory, acceptance and support by the authorities is an important factor for the success of intergroup contacts. Against this background, the establishment of the German Islam Conference (*Deutsche Islam Konferenz*) – despite all criticism levelled against it not least by independent dialogue initiatives – represents a vital symbolic acknowledgement and gesture of support for the interreligious effort of Christian-Muslim dialogue. Public funding for the staff and equipment needed for local dialogue efforts can equally serve to signal official approval and support, especially since lack of staff is noted as one of the main obstacles dialogue initiatives report having to overcome.[25]

### 3.1.4 Positive Emotions and Trust in Dialogue

It has long been assumed that combating prejudice was an effort mainly concentrated at the cognitive level, effected by providing information on the "other" group and counteracting stereotypical conceptions. Current research suggests, however, that the role of cognitive processes in changing attitudes is secondary to that of emotional and affective elements.[26] What is central is the reduction of fear and perceived threat and the development of empathy. Encounters allowing for a direct, individual exchange therefore are more relevant to this effort than factual education.

Single meetings are not usually enough to discover common ground and develop positive ties. A continuing, long-term contact is generally considered necessary. The findings of the Dialogos project bear this out in that it found a correlation between the regularity with which groups of people met to enter into dialogue and the reported level of trust and lower incidence of hostile encounters. The trust that is so often called for in interreligious dialogue is a resource that needs years of cultivation.

---

24  The relevant publication of the Evangelical Church in Germany [Evangelische Kirche Deutschland (2006) *Klarheit und gute Nachbarschaft. Christen und Muslime in Deutschland. Eine Handreichung des Rates der EKD*, EKD-Texte, 86] and the critical reception in many dialogue initiatives recorded in the survey show the intensity of such tensions.

25  Klinkhammer et al. (2011), 90–92.

26  Pettigrew (2008), 190.

It has emerged that dialogues should be organised with a view to the long term not least because almost half of non-Muslim participants reported first coming into contact with Muslims personally through their involvement.[27] On the one hand, this indicates that the initiatives are successful. On the other, the dearth of personal experience often impels participants to focus on whatever the news media, prompted by political discourses on integration or international conflicts, present as central. This media-induced perspective tends to focus on Islam as a problematic religion in need of change. Thus, personal dialogue can be overwhelmed by media discourse, turning the participants into representatives of their respective parties while creating little in the way of trust.

### 3.1.5 Self-Estimation of Impact and Range

Surveying the participants of dialogue initiatives showed that contact in these contexts is overwhelmingly perceived as pleasant and positive. Considering that 25 per cent of Christians and 86 per cent of Muslims active in interreligious dialogue report discrimination and perceived threats from persons of other religious or cultural backgrounds, this indicates that dialogue initiatives could ideally counteract such negative experiences in everyday life.

Findings of intergroup contact research further suggest that not only direct contact with persons of 'other' group affiliations contributes to reducing prejudice against these groups. Rather, positive contacts with members of the 'other' group can have an indirect positive effect on other members of the 'own' group who did not personally participate in the encounter. There is reason to believe, therefore, that such multiplier effects give dialogue initiatives an impact that reaches well beyond the circle of their immediate participants.

## 4.  Conclusion

The preconditions of potentially integrative and peace-affirming (conflict-preventing) effects in interreligious dialogue we have laid out here demonstrate just how complex and sensitive an endeavour a successful dialogue is. Not all forms of interreligious exchange appear effective or even desirable from this perspective. The complex situation which Muslim-Christian dialogue faces is not least owed to the social imbalances of German religious policy. In the absence of legal distinctions being made between religious communities, an encounter could define its own genuine questions and seek an open-ended discussion.

Though Christian-Muslim dialogue is currently burdened with expectations of its utility for integration and internal security by non-Muslim participants, it must be understood as more than an integrative social tool to improve govern-

---

27  Klinkhammer et al. (2011), 144.

ance.[28] We have found many dialogue initiatives are trying to escape precisely this definition by preserving their internal autonomy and/or defining themselves as critical observers of hierarchy – be it religious tradition, organised religion or government. The Dialogos project noted many instances in which such organisations acted autonomously and observed impacts that can legitimately be described as a dynamisation of religion religious practice. They tend to focus on independently chosen religious themes (e.g. monotheism, Abraham, creation, spirituality) and develop their own religious ritual to structure their activities (joint prayer, singing, religious services etc.). By concentrating on these self-selected focal points, they distance themselves from traditional, text-led interpretation and move towards constituting common ground.[29] Both Christian and Muslim participants reported again and again in interviews that interreligious dialogue to them was a place where they could reflect on their own religiosity.[30] Many explicitly welcome the opportunity to have new spiritual experiences. This dynamic effect on individual religiosity must not be ignored by a reductive focus on the integrative or normative functions of interreligious dialogue.

---

28  Tezcan, L. (2006) Interreligiöser Dialog und politische Religionen. In: *Aus Politik und Zeit-geschichte*, 28–29, 26–32, 26.
29  Klinkhammer et al. (2011), 193 ff.
30  Ibid.

*Alexander-Kenneth Nagel & Mehmet Kalender*

# The Many Faces of Dialogue

## Driving Forces for Participating in Interreligious Activities

### Introduction: Interreligious Communication as a Multi-Layered Phenomenon

On July 31st 2001, the following question was posted in the fatwa section of the Muslim internet portal Islamweb.net:

> "We are a Muslim community in Germany and have a mosque. In order to ameliorate the relationship with non-Muslims and show them the right view of Islam, we invite non-Muslim people to visit our mosque. They attend also the prayer to have an idea about Muslim spirituality. These visits are not welcome from all brothers in the mosque. [...] That's why the following questions: is it allowed to let non-Muslims enter the mosque? Are there any restrictions on such visits? Do women have to cover their heads? Is it allowed to invite groups of men and women together? Is there any restriction about the attendance of the prayer? Is there any difference between these issues in Muslim countries and in Europe where we live and where we have great interest at having good relationships with the society in which we live and that need our support to find the right way of Islam."[1]

At the core of this question lies a conflict within a mosque congregation: On the one hand, interreligious openness in its relation with the majority of society is emphasised, on the other, the presence of non-Muslims causes problems during prayers. It shows that interreligious events such as open mosque days take place inside a complex web of interests and expectations whose balance is a vital prerequisite for their continued success. That is why it is important both for a better academic understanding and a more successful practical implementation of these activities to understand the variety of driving forces behind them. This contribution represents an attempt to identify and categorise such impulses and motivations from findings of empirical research.

The idea that interreligious communication takes place at many levels simultaneously is not a new one. As early as 1991, the Pontifical Council on interreligious dialogue presented a document titled "Dialogue and Proclamation".[2] It not only lays out the theological justification for regarding dialogue as a task of the Catholic Church, but also distinguishes between four types of dialogue. Whereas the "dialogue of life" is focused on "human problems and preoccupa-

---

1   http://www.islamweb.net/emainpage/index.php?page=showfatwa&Option=FatwaId&Id=83119 (last accessed December 10, 2013)

2   http://www.vatican.va/roman_curia/pontifical_councils/interelg/documents/rc_pc_interelg_doc_19051991_dialogue-and-proclamatio_en.html (last accessed December 10, 2013)

tions", the "dialogue of action" aims at the "integral development and liberation of the peoples". By contrast, the "dialogue of theological exchange" refers to specialists deepening their understanding of their own religious tradition and the "dialogue of religious experience" denotes an encounter of people "rooted in their own religious traditions, [who] share their spiritual riches, for instance with regard to prayer and contemplation, faith and ways of searching for God or the Absolute".[3]

It is remarkable that these types of interreligious dialogue are regarded as equally important. As a sociologist of religion Levent Tezcan has pointed out that, in practice, the aspects of theological and practical interests in interreligious dialogue can be instrumentalised against each other: "In an interview, a Protestant representative responsible for dialogue with Islam carefully phrased the suspicion that the Muslims were not so much interested in "honest dialogue" as pursuing "concrete interests".[4] Tezcan describes how such mutual suspicions and the instrumentalisation of dialogue can corrode trust on all sides. While Christian representatives criticised the pragmatic attitude of their Muslim partners that made it difficult to arrive at a genuine exchange on matters of faith, many Muslims suspected that the Christian insistence on theological issues was a cover for missionary intent.[5] This clearly demonstrates that aside from actual intentions, assumed motivations can play an important role. Both an interest in theological exchange and a practical goal such as building a mosque or an Islamic cemetery may motivate parties in interreligious dialogue. According to Tezcan, though, the expectations and goals that the outside world brings into interreligious dialogue are at least as important. This is especially the case where government agencies support formalised contact between representatives of organised religions in the hope of furthering social integration.[6]

Tezcan views this mixing of levels as potentially problematic. It can lead to misunderstandings, as in the above case, or, where government is involved, may even undermine genuine understanding between the partners in dialogue. Gritt Klinkhammer et al. propose a less sceptical view on public-private collaboration in interreligious matters in their recently published study "Interreligiöse und interkulturelle Dialoge mit MuslimInnen in Deutschland" (Interreligious and Intercultural Dialogues with Muslims in Germany).[7] They distinguish four "directions of dialogical activity", namely sensitisation, cooperative problem-solving, empowerment, and theological discussion. Sensitisation aims to disseminate knowledge about and defuse prejudice against religious groups[8]

---

3   Ibid., § 42.
4   Tezcan, L. (2006) Interreligiöser Dialog und politische Religionen. In: *Aus Politik und Zeitgeschichte* (28/29), 26–32.
5   Ibid.
6   Ibid., 26.
7   Klinkhammer, G. et al. (2011) *Interreligiöse und interkulturelle Dialoge mit Muslimen in Deutschland. Eine quantitative und qualitative Evaluation* Bremen: self-published.
8   Ibid., 24.

while cooperative problem-solving focuses on resolving concrete difficulties (often of social integration) as a joint task of representatives of government and religious communities.[9] Empowerment describes the desire to mutually strengthen each other's resolve to pursue a goal[10], thus contributing to the mobilisation of resources, while theological discussions aim to explore common ground and the possibilities and limits of religious coexistence.[11]

Along with these general 'directions', the quantitative part of the study also surveyed concrete 'goals' and 'initial motivations' of dialogue initiatives. Many respondents mention neighbourly interest or global events such as the 9–11 attacks as an initial motivator, though practical challenges or personal experience of social conflict are also recorded.[12] Beyond these, three quarters of all initiatives identified with the global goals of "fostering shared values", "reducing prejudice", "shaping coexistence together", "understanding one's own religion better", "equality of all religious communities" and "fostering social participation by migrants".[13] This remarkable level of agreement on goals is indicative of the medley of overlapping motivations that underlie interreligious activities. Moreover, we can see how these categories are interrelated e.g. where global events create a local need for education or empowerment translates into claims for social equality and participation.

This overlap marks out the semantic field we will refer to as "driving forces for interreligious activities" in the following. It encompasses both the individual motivations of participants and the stated collective goals of groups and organisations engaged in interreligious dialogue as surveyed by Gritt Klinkhammer et al. When speaking of interests and goals, however, it is important to note that this does not mean we regard interreligious dialogue in a voluntaristic sense as an encounter of rational actors in full awareness of their goals and means. In order to avoid such oversimplification, we include the discursive and structural impulses that shape individual motives in our concept of 'driving forces'. Along with global political events, these include local or national incidents such as the opening (or closing) of places of worship, right-wing violence, or opportunity structures provided by government or charitable foundations.

The following analysis is based on empirical research carried out in the context of the North Rhine-Westphalian young researchers' group "Civic Potentials of Religious Communities". In a subproject on "Interreligious Activities and Religious Encounter in the Ruhr Area" we carried out a total of 26 participant observations in interreligious activities ranging from traditional public dialogue events through peace prayers and Iftar celebrations to school prayer services and

9   Ibid., 25.
10  Ibid., 26.
11  Ibid., 27.
12  Ibid., 43.
13  Ibid., 47.

football tournaments.[14] The observations were recorded in individual observer protocols and memos exchanged. We further conducted 17 semi-structured interviews with the hosts or organisers of these activities which were transcribed in full. This contribution presents the first steps towards a categorising analysis following the common approach of summarising, explication and structuring.[15]

While the abovementioned scholarly contributions concentrated primarily on Christian-Muslim dialogue, we deliberately tried to include other religious communities in our choice of events and interview partners. These comprise adherents of poly- or non-theistic religions such as Hindus and Buddhists, Baha'i and smaller Christian denominations such as the Old Catholic Church or the New Apostolic Church. This contribution will limit itself to a descriptive elaboration of our case, i.e. the identification and systematic categorisation of driving forces for interreligious activities. First, we will look at exogenous factors, namely the structures, expectations and events that can motivate such activities. In the following chapter, we will turn to endogenous factors, i.e. the goals and motivations of religious communities participating in interreligious activities. Here, we will distinguish between political, symbolic, dialogue-oriented and communitarian interests. In the conclusion part, we will summarise our key findings and outline a theoretical perspective on the link between endogenous and exogenous driving forces for interreligious activities.

## Impulses from Outside: Structures, Expectations, Events

Many of the interreligious activities in our sample were motivated by exogenous impulses, which include local opportunity structures, social expectation and single events. An example for the *structural* driving forces for interreligious activities is provided by the rising number of Muslim pupils in some urban schools. This demographic shift presents a challenge for the tradition of holding Christian services for new and graduating cohorts. A Protestant pastor explained: "There is a long tradition of the churches holding services for new pupils, and then the schools said it didn't really fit any more. Now they are taking in classes full of Muslim pupils and there is no Muslim representative there." In this case, the problem was solved by the pastor, who had long experience in Christian-Muslim cooperation and good contacts to local mosques. She organised a joint interreligious service at the school.

An example for the incentives and impulses that can arise from *local politics* is provided by an interreligious circle that has been organising joint peace prayers for Christians, Muslims, Jews and Baha'i for several years. The head

---

14  Nagel, A.-K. (2012) Vernetzte Vielfalt: Religionskontakt in interreligiösen Aktivitäten. In: Nagel, A. (Ed.) *Diesseits der Parallelgesellschaft. Neuere Studien zu religiösen Migrantengemeinden in Deutschland* Bielefeld: Transcript, 241–267.

15  Mayring, P. (2003) *Qualitative Inhaltsanalyse. Grundlagen und Techniken* Weinheim, Basel: Beltz, 58.

of the initiative recalls the last prayer taking place at a town hall: "Because the Peace Light by Leo Lebendig (an art project) was hanging there, they really asked us if we wanted to have our peace prayer there, together with the Peace Light of the Abrahamic faiths, in the town hall." The event took place by invitation and under the aegis of the local government, hosted by the mayor who also gave an opening speech. Thus, the political interest of joining the peace prayer and the Peace Light exhibition allowed the circle to make its efforts accessible to a much larger audience.

Along with such impulses and incentives, some respondents cited social or political *expectations* they felt they were facing as motivating their interreligious activities. This was particularly evident in the case of an unsalaried imam who is active in several interreligious groups and regards this commitment as a societal duty incumbent on all religious communities. Communities that abstained could expect to face harsh criticism: "How could the churches presume to say 'that doesn't concern me'? [...] We are an open society, and we need to demonstrate that, demonstrate it by setting an example, so we do not leave [...] the field to the demagogues." The "demagogues" (Scharfmacher) referred to here are right-wing populists such as the Pro NRW movement who use the opportunities of an open society to destabilise social peace. As a consequence, all religious communities are presented with the responsibility of actively and visibly furthering the cause of social cohesion.

This brings us to the role which individual *events* can play in triggering interreligious engagement. Such events need not be of global significance. Often, it is especially what happens at the local or regional level that impels people to become active. Many respondents stated that their activities came about in response to a conflict. The initial motivation then was to educate people in order to moderate local fault lines and defuse future conflicts. In one case, the chairman of a Muslim congregation reported: "Pro NRW was here, so we organised an interreligious service, a peace prayer at the mosque, as a counter-demonstration." These interreligious prayer meetings arose as an immediate response to social and political action directed against religious pluralism in general, and against one religious community in particular. Their participants see their activities as an expression of interreligious solidarity.

As in the findings of Klinkhammer et al. and Tezcan, the *9–11 attacks* are also often quoted as a trigger for interreligious activities by respondents in our study. Especially in Europe and North America, these events led to a rise in suspicion of Muslims and forced their communities to explain themselves. A Protestant pastor confirms: "Then, after 2001, the attacks in New York, this need for information came on strongly again." However, other global events also played a role in his work. He had earlier supported opening a Muslim section of the cemetery: "I was gone for a year. When I came back [...] nothing had happened. [...] Then something interesting happened, the Bosnian war started and the Bosnians suddenly had no country to go back to any more. [...] and they had an interest in making the cemetery happen right away. And we put it into action with their help." The new situation in the homeland of Bosnian immigrants led them to look more fully to their host country and develop the wish to build up an own religious infrastructure. It is remarkable in this case that the interest of a single immigrant community is sufficient to reactivate the negotiating process and establish a cemetery open not just to Bosnians, but to all Muslims.

## Impulses from the Inside: Political, Symbolic, Dialogue-Oriented and Communitarian Interests

Along with the exogenous impulses outlined above, there are a number of intrinsic driving forces for interreligious activities. We can distinguish political, symbolic, dialogue-oriented and communitarian interests here.

*Political interests* can be found where interreligious contact is used as a means to pursue concrete political goals. Our analysis indicates that particularly migrant communities who are still in the process of developing a religious infrastructure tend to regard religious and political dialogue as two sides of the same coin. A prominent example are Muslim communities planning to build a mosque or establish a cemetery and thus are in need of administrative assistance or symbolic affirmation.

A Protestant pastor who has been active in interreligious dialogue for almost 30 years explained: "[this support] is also expected, or hoped for, in solidarity between believers. The idea is: We finally need a fixed place to pray and teach in […] and you are Christians, you are also believers and know that you need a place to pray. […] Can you help us?" The expectation of political support is seen as deeply anchored in the nature of interreligious contact through empathy and solidarity between different religious traditions. Unlike the pastor quoted by Tezcan (s.a.), this respondent does not feel suspicious about 'concrete interests', but embraces the political dimension as a legitimate aspect of interreligious encounters.

In a similar vein, the imam of a mosque congregation stated: "The interests of the Muslims are part of dialogue work, of course. […] I would advise anyone who is building a mosque to start with a dialogue so as to have fewer problems." The political interests of mosque congregations, though not usually the sole aims of interreligious activities, are not only seen as legitimate, but as a matter of course. Even though it will more often be religious migrant communities facing practical problems in everyday life, the above mentioned imam emphasises the fundamental mutuality of interreligious solidarity: "When […] a church is closed, I'd say, we will take part in protesting, we will gladly do that. Yes, you could say it is a […] mutual support." This interreligious solidarity was realised e.g. in Duisburg-Marxloh, where a large Muslim community successfully protested against the closure of the neighbouring church.[16] The possibility of an interreligious alliance between dialogue-oriented communities in the face of perceived threats to religion (e.g. through church closures) is brought to the foreground here. As the example shows, it is not only small and migrant communities that enter into alliances of this kind to defend their interests.

While political interests can be directed towards specific projects arising from religious needs or requirements, respondents in our sample also often voiced the general wish to strengthen religion as a factor in an increasingly secular society. We termed this a *symbolic interest.* A Protestant pastor explained this regarding interreligious school services: "The parents and children are supposed to see that we [pastor, imam] are involved with them getting into school and leaving school." Above all, though, she considered it "important to somehow get the Divine in [into society] at all." This example indicates that the aim is not the teaching of specific tenets or the demonstration of religious distinctions, but the inter-traditional sacralisation of the secular social space that is public school.

While political interests need to be communicated to specific target groups, symbolic ones rely on a broad, public display of interreligious harmony. For example, the chairman of a Jewish congregation reported of interreligious events in a sports arena: "[At the final song 'We are the world',] the church president stood along with the bishop, and all were doing this [waving the arms in the air] that was a great sight, an image of connection. And that is more important, more accessible to the masses, than getting deeply into theology." The image of a religious community of values united across its different traditions is prominently presented here. The reference to being accessible to the masses stresses the desire for a broader impact.

Aside from strengthening religion in the abstract, there are efforts to use interreligious activities to strengthen the status of a particular religious community. We also group this kind of self-interested PR with symbolic interests. One Old Catholic priest interviewed sees his activities in a local Arbeitskreis Christlicher Kirchen (ACK, church cooperation group) primarily as a contribution to strengthening ecumenical cohesion: "We must speak with one voice on some matters, as Christians, and also present ourselves to the public as a church." Encounters with other religions are secondary to his view, taking place mainly in the context of a predominantly social neighbourhood project. Even where contact with other religious communities does take place, he stresses the importance of inter*confessional* exchanges. It is necessary for the Christian confessions to close ranks, "because the world needs it [...] because we have something to tell the world". The propagation of a Christian message is clearly in the foreground here, justified by the belief that Christianity is indispensable to the world. A priest in the New Apostolic church regarded the above

---

16 http://www.derwesten.de/region/kirchen-in-duisburg-muessen-schliessen-st-peter-in-marxloh-bleibt-id6268345.html (last accessed December 10, 2013).

mentioned neighbourhood meetings as one of the few opportunities to meet with other denominations. The New Apostolic church generally takes a critical stance towards ecumenical and interreligious efforts and does not participate in the *Arbeitskreis Christlicher Kirchen*. Hence, he considers his interreligious engagement primarily as an opportunity to represent his faith: "There, you could also present yourself a little and show, when the position was explained from the Catholic side and the Old Catholic or from the Protestants, what it is like from the New Apostolic point of view." Especially the encounter with other Christian confessions was important for as little as a few decades ago, the New Apostolic church was widely regarded with suspicion. Preparatory meetings for interreligious neighbourhood events were a good and low-threshold venue to reduce such fears: "Yes, just to show what we are like, that we don't, let's say, don't walk around with halos on our heads [...] that the others can see, we aren't from another planet, we are fellow humans, just like everybody else, only with the consciousness that we have a faith that we stand for, that we live and try to represent to others, too." As is the case in many Muslim communities (s.b.), education and public relations are seen as indivisible. Interreligious contact provides the forum to combat prejudice and improve the public image of one's own religious tradition.

Once again, the interest in good PR is not restricted to the marginal and contested, but also to the well-established denominations as the following statement by a Catholic priest demonstrates: "As the Catholic Church, we are also interested to ensure that people see us as an open community that accepts people and seeks to understand them." Given shrinking congregations and bad press, participation in interreligious activities may become a marker for openness and social responsibility through the advocacy for religious pluralism on the part of the Catholic Church.

Among the non-Christian religious communities, symbolic interests are especially pronounced among Muslim congregations. Unlike the established Christian churches, they often take a defensive stance against a perceived anti-Islamic prejudice and strive for acceptance and social recognition. Thus, the chairman of a small Muslim congregation reported: "We hold open mosque days to have a dialogue, to live better with the people, the neighbourhood. [...] If you know each other better, you can accept and respect each other." The invitation to an open mosque day is offered with the goal of symbolic recognition in mind. Acceptance will improve the community's standing in the neighbourhood.

Interestingly, we also have a representative of a German Buddhist community stating that the potential image gain for his tradition is the driving factor for his interreligious activities: "It was afterwards that it all changed, also through the work we did here. [We wanted to show] that we, too, are a real religion [...] and above all, that it is a problem, and it continues to be a problem today, that we aren't recognised as a religion." Once again the public recognition of a religious congregation is linked to its commitment to dialogue. In contrast to many Muslim communities, however, the primary goal is not to correct misconceptions or prejudice. The symbolic interest here is to present the non-theistic tradition of Buddhism as a 'real' religion which duly assumes an active role both in interreligious dialogue and public discourse.

The third pillar of intrinsic motivation is – what we call – *dialogue-oriented* interests. While in the case of symbolic interests, the desire for public presence and recognition is the central motivator, dialogue-oriented interest aims at shaping interreligious communication. In line with the above considerations of types of interreligious dialogue, we could identify two dominant trends representing different interests in interreligious dialogue in our sample. Theological dialogue on dogmatic questions is directed at discovering common ground or cultivating difference whereas the exchange about concrete matters of the religious conduct of life focuses on personal religious encounter and the reduction of prejudice (s.a.). The chairman of a dialogue initiative had this to say about the theological profile of its activities: "Well, we do see ourselves as an interreligious dialogue initiative that strives to, let's say, address social and theological questions, though I would see a certain focus in the theological field, and at least tries to look at them from both perspectives [Christian and Islamic] and to see, where is the common ground, where are the differences?" In this case, dogmatic and ethical issues are brought to the centre. The positions of religious traditions are related to each other, discussed, and often allowed to stand as equals.

One prominent interest in theological dialogue frequently appears to be exploring the historical family relationship – and thus the commonalities – among (primarily the Abrahamic) religions. This necessarily entails uncovering theological differences, as the chairman of another dialogue initiative reported: "We don't want the things that divide us to be […] swept under the rug, either […]. The significance of the person of Jesus in Christianity and Islam is fundamentally different. Those are two positions that cannot possibly be reconciled." An imam explained: "And, well, those differences do exist […] and we should experience that, too." Alongside the differences they cultivate and make explicit however, participants regularly emphasise the importance of the common ground they discovered as the following statement from a New Apostolic pastor illustrates: "That was the principle, in the end, too, and that is the point, that it is possible to find some common ground that we as Christians, and also people who adhere to Islam, that we share." In this case, finding common ground is primarily understood as a definitory exercise in order to clarify where one stands in a relationship.

As a matter of fact, this approach may easily exclude religious traditions outside the Abrahamic model (characterised by Abraham as a founding figure, monotheism, shared social ethics). One member of a German Buddhist community explained: "As a Buddhist, it can sometimes be […] difficult because there are lots of God-topics (laughs) like 'Grace of God' or what have you. That is so far removed, it has nothing to do with us, you see?" The example suggests that interreligious dialogues, for all the evident differences they explore, are often based on a more or less tacit theistic consensus that excludes some participants from the beginning.

Aside from theological exchanges, a dialogue on everyday questions of practical religiosity can likewise be subsumed under dialogue-oriented interests. Events of this type are often more popular and more accessible to laypeople. One organiser of evening dialogue events told us: "People should get together and talk about what they care about in their neighbourhood." Other groups hosting such events, too, regard them primarily as an "opportunity for neighbourly conversations". They frequently focus on dealing with specific situations with dialogue happening in a generally religious, but not specifically theological sphere. "We are no theologians. It is more about issues and arguments from our own lives", a Muslim woman who is active in interreligious dialogue explained. Along with personal experience, the media may be a prominent source of religious issues, such as headscarves: "That is brought up every now and then [...] there are questions [...]; like, is that required by Islam?" This is less a matter of theological education as an effort to deal with a sense of alienation that arises from visible differences in religious practice and lifestyles.

Last, but not least, *communitarian interests* are important motivators for interreligious activities. Their primary rationale is the desire to establish a more open, less prejudiced society where members of different religions can live together with rather than merely alongside each other. The creation of a sense of community primarily is effected through reducing fears, creating opportunities to become familiar, and promoting 'neighbourliness'. Visiting a mosque, for example, could be very important to 'reduce the sense of alienness'. The chairman of a mosque congregation pointed out that this was an important precondition of "getting closer to each other". Similarly, a spokeswoman of a Jewish congregation stated: "We wish to get to know each other and produce cooperation rather than separation." This was the path to "discover common ground". The pastor of a Protestant congregation records that they "[care about] meeting as neighbours, including neighbours that are interested in religion and religiously affiliated, not to define our differences, but to strengthen what unites us". This is to create a sense of community not solely on a religious basis, but also rooted in common humanity. Unlike with dialogue-oriented interests, the emphasis is less on the cognitive and more on the affective elements of coming to know each other, with the preferred instrument being not education, but direct human encounters.

The desire to maintain peace in the neighbourhood plays a significant role in these efforts to strengthen community ties. One member of a mosque congregation stated: "[Our goal is] to live together truly as neighbours in this city. This way, you can avert many things and simply foster peace." A more sobering, but similar assessment came from the priest of an Old Catholic congregation: "I just think it's positive that we keep in mind there are those living among us who are not Christian, but who have a different religion and that we respect their way of life and meet them, and once again: If you live together and do things together, the risk that you fight each other is reduced." Where the Muslim respondent emphasised the idea of living together, the Old Catholic rather stressed the importance of mutual tolerance as a means to defuse potential conflict.

Likewise, the priest of a Hindu temple regarded it as a religious duty to create a peaceful environment for his congregation: "We hold our peace prayers for all citizens, their health, happiness and peace [...] that is our duty." A member of a small Baha'i community, too, places interreligious community in a theological context: "Where representatives of different religions meet, [they have] one fundamental goal in common, to celebrate religion as such – the most important pillar for, you could say, the world's order. If you look at it from that perspective, you cannot but support all religions. [...] That is why the Baha'i support it, too." This corresponds closely to the symbolic interest of strengthening the public presence of religion in a secular society through interreligious activities. In this case, however, the community of religions goes beyond a PR exercise. As a "pillar of the world's order", it takes on soteriological qualities.

The reduction of prejudice, tied closely to educational and informative projects for dialogue-oriented interests (s.a.), becomes a key to the creation of a community under different premises. Encountering and coming to know the other from the perspective of communitarian interests requires not so much an exchange on theology and religious tenets as an experience of mutuality and respect. "If you don't engage with something, you don't have an idea in your head", the spokeswoman of a Jewish congregation explained. Likewise, the chairman of a Christian-Muslim dialogue group reported from his own experience: "[We find] fear and rejection with people who don't know anything about the others." Both statements envision as their goal a peaceful, pluralist mode of existence that presupposes a rapprochement at the human level, beyond the realm of theological positions. That is why, the above-mentioned chairman stated, it was "very wise, that there are invitations from the Muslim side to such big events [open mosque days], [...] because they show the real side of Islam."

This is also confirmed by a Muslim theologian who has been offering guided tours of her congregation's mosque for many years: "People initially come in with their questions and prejudices, and then, when you set things straight for them, I always got a positive reaction. They did not insist on their preconceived notions, but say 'right, we didn't know that, now we got it from the mouth of an expert', well, it is that way, I have had positive experiences with that." Beyond correcting prejudices and presenting one's own community, an open mosque day also aims to create the opportunity for direct encounters and positive experiences with the (religious and cultural) other. Through its strong presence in the media, Islam tends to be the focus of most interreligious activities of this kind. A Protestant pastor who heads a dialogue initiative said: "I think it's quite irritating that when they talk about Islam on television [...] you see the same pictures, long rows of men's behinds. That's just stereotypical, it explains nothing. But if you are there around prayer time [...] you feel something completely different from these stereotypes." Here, too, a strongly affective stance towards interreligious dialogue based on human proximity and shared experience is expressed. Exchanging knowledge is very much a secondary consideration.

## Conclusion and Prospects

Our intent with this contribution was to arrive at a better understanding of the driving forces that underlie participation in interreligious activities. From a religious studies perspective this endeavour is relevant since there has so far been rather little empirical research on interreligious contacts in modern immigration societies. Moreover, our analysis could gain practical value for participants in interreligious dialogue if they accept our findings as an invitation to consider the various motivations underlying their activities and thus secure the lasting commitment of the communities involved. Starting with extant studies of different types or trends of interreligious dialogue that adopted a primarily external perspective, we deliberately adopted a broader concept, linking the extrinsic and intrinsic driving forces for carrying out interreligious activities. This encompasses both the structures, expectations and events that can move participants to engage in dialogue from the outside and the various interests intrinsically motivating the religious communities involved in it.

Among the extrinsic factors, we count contextual ones such as local demographic and political *structures* (e.g. active support and involvement by local authorities) and their dynamics (e.g. religious pluralisation in an urban neighbourhood). As a matter of fact, these structures do not foster interreligious commitment 'objectively', but only as far as they become an issue in the local discourse. A more short-lived, but no less potent motivator were *events* such as religiously motivated or xenophobic attacks. It does not matter whether these were of global or local significance as long as they generated a certain level of presence in the media. Remarkably, throughout our sample, it is only conflictual events, perceived attacks on peace and cultural plurality, which motivate people to participate in interreligious activities. Finally, at a more discursive level, both given and assumed social *expectations* can underlie interreligious activities as well. Many respondents referred to a special responsibility for social cohesion that religious communities bore. As in our initial example, though, expectations can also grow out of discourses of endangerment and force parties to proactively participate in interreligious activities in order to escape suspicion.

By intrinsic motivation, we understand the interests and wishes that parties in interreligious activities connect with their participation. Where interreligious contact is sought out primarily to further concrete political goals, e.g. building a place of worship, we refer to *political interests*. It must be emphasised that, in contrast to Tezcan's observations, none of the respondents in our sample regarded such interests negatively. Political interests in the context of interreligious activities usually are religiously motivated even though their target group are political decision makers and processes. By contrast to political interests, we referred to the intent of improving the public image both of religion in general and one's own religious tradition in particular as *symbolic interests*. Where interreligious encounters are aimed more at education and mutual understanding, we refer to *dialogue-oriented interests*. Their goal is less to improve public perception or achieve specific goals, but instead to cognitively explore common ground and delineate differences. Where dialogue-oriented interests emphasise the acquisition of knowledge about each other, *communitarian interests* focus on the social capital of religion(s).[17] Interreligious exchange in this case is intended to build shared values and foster mutual trust.

It does not need emphasising that in practice these driving forces are closely intertwined rather than presenting themselves as distinct ideal types. Given the narrow scope of our survey and its limited sample size, it is equally clear that these findings cannot represent the final word, but rather must be understood as the beginning of a systematic, theoretically grounded typology of motivations for interreligious activity. Programmatically, we considered it important to combine an understanding of the motivations of participants based on action theory with a broader structural understanding of the environment interreligious communication occurs in.

This poses a theoretical challenge that can be delineated, but not explored in depth here: A synthetic typology of motivations for interreligious activities would require a theory on the link between exogenous and endogenous factors. In this regard, a sociology of knowledge perspective could argue that the objective or perceived change in religious structures towards pluralisation made interreligious interaction both evident and plausible.[18] A Neo-institutionalist focus would analyse interreligious activities as a space of legitimacy and empowerment: 'real religions' (s.a.) are supposed to be transparent and open to outside questions even though, as our initial example shows, this can create internal tension.[19] Finally, a rational-choice approach seeking the tie between external and internal impulses in the specific logics of the interreligious situation could equally present valuable insights.[20]

If this contribution has made one thing evident, it is that interreligious dialogue has many faces. As religious pluralism and awareness both of religion and religious difference grow, the significance of organised and structured forms of interreligious contact will increase. For participants in interreligious activities, this means they will need to understand their own expectations and aims, and

---

17  Kippenberg, H. G. (2006) Das Sozialkapital religiöser Gemeinschaften im Zeitalter der Globalisierung. In: G. Pfleiderer & E. W. Stegemann (Eds.) *Religion und Respekt. Beiträge zu einem spannungsreichen Verhältnis* Zürich: Theologischer Verlag, 245–271.

18  Berger, P. L. & Luckmann, T. (1990) *Die gesellschaftliche Konstruktion der Wirklichkeit. Eine Theorie der Wissenssoziologie* Frankfurt am Main: Fischer Taschenbuch Verlag.

19  Meyer, J. W. et al. (2005) Ontologie und Rationalisierung im Zurechnungssystem der westlichen Kultur. In: G. Krücken (Ed.) *Weltkultur. Wie die westlichen Prinzipien die Welt durchdringen* Frankfurt am Main: Suhrkamp, 17–46.

20  Esser, H. (1999) *Situationslogik und Handeln* Frankfurt am Main: Campus.

negotiate them with their partners. In this process, no goal can claim greater legitimacy per se. If religion has its *Sitz im Leben* (setting in life), why would you deny this to interreligious encounters? Where participants can view this complexity as an opportunity to better understand their goals and communicate on shared projects, it can become a source of strength for their work.

# Theology in the Plural:
# Interreligious and Dialogical Approaches

*Perry Schmidt-Leukel*

# Intercultural Theology as Interreligious Theology

## 1.    The Vision of an Interreligious Theology[1]

Theology needs visions. Its fundamental aim, I believe, is clear and remains valid: From its basis of faith in Divine revelation in the world, theology reflects on this faith through the instruments of reason. Theology thus provides faith with greater conceptual clarity, inquires openly about its possible truth without predetermining the outcome and precisely thereby heightens its credibility. But theology needs visions on how to fulfil this task convincingly and attractively under the prevailing conditions of its age – which means above all appropriate to the advance of human knowledge. If theology wishes to be a truly academic discipline, then like all other academic disciplines it must be characterised by genuine curiosity. The searching quest for truth, for a better and deeper understanding, is always exciting, unsettling and pioneering. This is what makes scientific research – and hence, potentially, theology too – attractive, even fascinating.

The vision outlined below grew and emerged with increasing clarity through the twentieth century. To name three prominent examples:

Missionary work, Ernst Troeltsch (1865–1923) writes in his final, posthumously published lecture in 1922, is inappropriate towards the great world religions. In encountering these, what we rather need is "agreement and understanding" ("Ausgleich und Verständigung"), even mutual (!) purification and deepening in the course of the continuous interior development of the religions.[2]

Thirty-nine years later, in 1961, Paul Tillich (1886–1965) re-addresses the same issue in his New York lectures "Christianity and the Encounter of World Religions". The appropriate attitude towards Judaism, Islam, Hinduism, Buddhism and Taoism cannot be the effort to 'convert' the other, but entering into a dialogue.[3] Yet what is the theological meaning and fruit of this dialogue? Tillich's answer initially remains vague. It becomes more concrete in his own

---

1    This contribution is a slightly edited and updated version of my inaugural lecture held at Münster University's Department of Protestant Theology on 20 January 2010 and was first published in German as: P. Schmidt-Leukel, Interkulturelle Theologie als interreligiöse Theologie. In: Evangelische Theologie 71 (2011) 4–16. Translated into English by Volker Bach.

2    Troeltsch, E. (1966) Die Stellung des Christentums unter den Weltreligionen. In: Id. *Der Historismus und seine Überwindung* Aalen: Scientia, 62–83, 80; also the debate in: R. Bernhardt & G. Pfleiderer (Eds.) (2004) *Christlicher Wahrheitsanspruch – historische Relativität. Auseinandersetzungen mit Ernst Troeltschs Absolutheitsschrift im Kontext heutiger Religionstheologie* Zürich: Theologischer Verlag.

3    Tillich, P. (1963) *Christianity and the Encounter of the World Religions* New York: Columbia University Press, 94 ff.

final lecture held in 1965, eleven days before his death. In it, he again addresses the relationship of Christianity towards other religions and regrets writing his Systematic Theology before he arrived at a better knowledge and deeper understanding of religious history, mainly through seminars held jointly with Mircea Eliade. In other words, his seminal Systematic Theology would have taken a different form had he written it with greater awareness of other religions. For the future of theology, in Tillich's own words, his hope is a "longer and more intensive interpenetration of systematic theology and religious history". Through this, the "structure of religious thought" could evolve in a way that might allow for a new manifestation of its core, what Tillich refers to as the "religion of the concrete spirit" ("Religion des konkreten Geistes"), i.e. the union of the sacramental, the prophetic and the mystical.[4]

The vision takes still clearer shape in the writings of Wilfred Cantwell Smith (1916–2000), like Tillich a faculty member of Harvard University. Since the 1980s, the idea of a 'world theology' or 'universal theology' was central to his work. "Theology is critical intellectualisation of (and for) faith, and of the world as known in faith; and what we seek is a theology that will interpret the history of our race in a way that will give intellectual expression to our faith, the faith of all of us, and to our modern perception of the world", as he wrote in 1981.[5] Future theology should therefore no longer be based on just one particular segment of human religious history – e.g. on the Judeo-Christian tradition – but, as he said in a lecture in 1984, on the religious history in its entirety.[6] Yet this basis of future theology will have to be mediated through an integration of the various religious perspectives from which different religions had interpreted parts of religious history so far. Only then and only in this manner can this desired form of theology give intellectual expression to "the faith of all of us".

In the following, I will point out why, in my view, the concept of an 'intercultural theology' must lead to this vision of a universal, or as I prefer to call it, an 'interreligious theology' and under which methodological principles this type of theology may be undertaken. To that end, we must first look briefly at the origins of 'intercultural theology'.

## 2.    From Intercultural to Interreligious Theology

The concept of an 'intercultural theology' emerged from the critical study of older concepts of how Christianity was to be inculturated. One example of these

---

4    Id. (1980) Die Bedeutung der Religionsgeschichte für den systematischen Theologen. In: M. Baumotte (Ed.) *Tillich-Auswahl, vol. 2: Die Zweideutigkeit des Lebens* Gütersloh: Gütersloher Verlagshaus, 288–300, 297.

5    Smith, W. C. (1989) *Towards a World Theology. Faith and the Comparative History of Religion* Maryknoll, N.Y.: Orbis (1. edition 1981), 125.

6    Smith, W. C. (1987) Theology and the World's Religious History. In: L. Swidler (Ed.) *Toward a Universal Theology of Religion* Maryknoll, N.Y.: Orbis, 51–85.

older conceptions is found in the instructions that the Roman Congregation *Propaganda Fidei* directed to the missionaries in China in 1659:

> "Do not regard it as your task and in no way coerce the peoples to change their customs, habits and usages unless they are clearly contrary to the faith and good custom. What could be more foolish than to bring France, Spain, Italy or another European country to China? Not these countries, but the faith is what you are to plant there, that faith which disregards or abolishes the customs and usages of no people but wishes to see them all guarded and protected."[7]

These instructions exemplify a concept of mission that has rightly been called the "core-and-shell model". In this, the culture of a people is viewed like the outer shell of a fruit while religion represents the core. The goal of missionary activity is to replace the old core, i.e. the non-Christian religion, with a new one, Christianity, while the shell remains untouched. This view of inculturation suffers from considerable problems. *Firstly,* it views non-Christian religions largely as negative. They can and shall be replaced by Christianity without any scruples. Should they contain anything good, this is fulfilled and surpassed by Christianity anyway so that their supersession is justified. I do not believe that this view of non-Christian religions can be supported by any historical facts. *Secondly*, the core-and-shell model assumes that religion and culture are cleanly separable. This is an unrealistic assumption both with regard to non-Christian religions and to Christianity. To be sure, culture and religion are not identical; major religions have spread over many cultures in the course of history, and many cultures are home to more than one religion. Nonetheless, the symbiotic relationship of culture and religion is so strong that a separation of the kind presumed by this model is simply impossible. Many aspects of culture are so strongly determined by a religion that its replacement would have far-reaching consequences. The same, conversely, is also true of religion, which is shaped to its core by cultural elements. What would be left of Christianity, to take one example, if it were stripped off its European, its Latin, its Hellenic and finally its Jewish cultural features? Or what would Buddhism look like once it had had its Japanese, Chinese, Tibetan and Indian elements removed? Religion and culture are inseparable, and this being the case, the missionary efforts of Christians in non-Christian cultures – despite all genuine efforts to inculturate the faith – effectively produced a conflict between the Western cultures that sent them and the cultures they were sent to, all the more since missionary work often took place in the context and under the protection of colonialism.

The realisation of the problems inherent in such conceptions of missionary work led to a re-evaluation or rather, reformulation of inculturation from which the idea of 'intercultural theology' was born in the 1970s. As Werner Ustorf

---

7    Kollbrunner, F. (1990) Die klassische Theorie: Akkommodation. In: G. Collet (Ed.) *Theologien der Dritten Welt. EATWOT als Herausforderung westlicher Theologie und Kirche* (NZM.S 37) Immensee, 133–141, 134 f.

demonstrated recently in a detailed study, the concept of 'intercultural theology' originated from the joint efforts of Hans-Jochen Margull, Walter Hollenweger and Richard Friedli.[8] The strong aversion towards colonial and hegemonial mentalities shared by these three scholars of mission studies led them to develop a new theological programme.[9] Similar efforts, though less clearly formulated, were also under way in the English-speaking world, where terminology shifted from 'inculturation' to 'interculturation' of religion.[10]

As Ustorf demonstrates, one of the central insights driving this development was that the wide variety of cultural and religious contexts had a "formative and continuing" impact on non-Western forms of Christianity.[11] This led to two normative conclusions at the theological level: *Firstly,* theology must always be aware of the cultural contexts that shape the concrete expression of religion without privileging or even absolutising one culture.[12] *Secondly*, it must remain conscious of the close symbiotic relationship between culture and religion and thus, in its form as an intercultural theology, open itself to becoming an 'interreligious theology', as Richard Friedli explicitly demanded.[13] Hence, the programme that its coiners associated with the term 'intercultural theology' was primarily designed to end the prevalent hegemonial understanding of mission-ary work in favour of a theological approach that takes into account the identity and value of other religions and cultures by listening to the religiously and culturally Other and learning from and with them.

This approach has had some impact. The German Bishops' Conference, for example, embraced in principle its key tenets in the document on mission "*Allen Völkern sein Heil*" (His Salvation unto All Nations) published in 2004. It states that mission does not aim at "the collision of a culturally neutral, 'pure' Christianity and a religion-free, 'pure' culture, but at an intercultural encounter of mutual giving and receiving, as well as change and purification".[14] Whether the document itself manages to do full justice to this insight is a different question, though.[15] To Hans Jochen Margull himself, 'intercultural theology' did not just mean a new understanding of missionary work, but its replace-ment by an alternative theological approach. Consequently, he stopped using

---

8   Ustorf, W (2008) The Cultural Origins of 'Intercultural Theology'. In: *Mission Studies*, 25, 229–251.
9   Ibid., 230.
10  Ibid., 232 f.
11  Ibid., 235.
12  Especially in Hollenweger; Ustorf (2008), 237.
13  Friedli, R. (1987) Interkulturelle Theologie. In: K. Müller & T. Sundermeier (Eds.) *Lexikon missionstheologischer Grundbegriffe* Berlin: Reimer Verlag, 181–185, 182.
14  Sekretariat der Deutschen Bischofskonferenz (Ed.) (2004) *Allen Völkern sein Heil. Die Mission der Weltkirche*, 23 (Die deutschen Bischöfe 76), September 2004, 42, translation Volker Bach.
15  Moerschbacher, M. (2006) Inkulturation – Voraussetzung oder Folge des Dialogs?. In: L. Bertsch et al. (Eds.) *Viele Wege – ein Ziel. Herausforderungen im Dialog der Religionen und Kulturen* (FS Georg Evers) Freiburg i.Br.: Herder, 126–138, 128.

the term 'mission' in his publications after 1970.[16] It is important to stress this point in view of the current tendency of using the term 'intercultural theology' as simply a new word for 'mission studies' ("Missionswissenschaft") without embracing the fundamental rethinking of mission that its creators intended. The 2005 declaration *Missionswissenschaft als Interkulturelle Theologie* (Mission Studies as Intercultural Theology) by the German Society for Mission Studies is not entirely innocent of this tendency.[17] Ustorf wrote that such tendencies could on occasion go far enough to rightly be called 'false advertising' ("Etikettenschwindel").[18]

If 'intercultural theology' is more than a pleasant and politically correct repackaging of traditional mission studies, then what is it? Ustorf summarises the intention of its creators as follows: "Intercultural theology does not think on behalf of others, but reflects its own premises in the presence of these others and, if things go well, together with them."[19] If the otherness of this 'other' is not exclusively and in a reductionist manner understood as merely cultural 'otherness' but is taken also and crucially as religious 'otherness', intercultural theology must of necessity be realised as interreligious theology. In this sense, Michael von Brück, already in his 1991 inaugural lecture in Munich, characterised intercultural theology as an "interreligious process of truth-seeking" that, on the one hand, "allows for concrete commitment" while at the same time "never comes to a stand-still".[20]

That intercultural theology, as it was intended by Margull and Friedli and concretised by von Brück and Ustorf, becomes interreligious theology not only by its own internal logic, but also in practice, can be seen in the more recent discussions within the most influential organisation of non-Western Christian theologians, the *Ecumenical Association of Third World Theologians* (EATWOT). Through the first decade of the 21st century, the EATWOT published five consultations under the programmatic title "Along the Many Paths of God" which aimed at constructively connecting theological insights from Liberation Theology, Pluralist Theology of Religions and interreligious dialogue.[21] The fifth and final volume of the series takes the step towards a "pluri-confessional theology that we could also call inter-religious or multi-religious, or (always paying attention to the nuances of the word) trans-religious."[22]

---

16 Ustorf (2008), 241.
17 Missionswissenschaft als Interkulturelle Theologie und ihr Verhältnis zur Religionswissenschaft. Available from: http://www.dgmw.org/Missionswissenschaft.pdf (last accessed December 10, 2013).
18 Ustorf (2008), 233.
19 Ustorf (2008), 244 f.
20 v. Brück, M. (1992) Religionswissenschaft und interkulturelle Theologie. In: *Evangelische Theologie*, 52, 245–261, 261, translation Volker Bach.
21 See the overview in: J. M. Vigil (Ed.) (2010) *Toward a Planetary Theology (Along the Many Paths of God V)* Montreal: Dunamis Publishers, 9–13; See also: Id. et al. (Eds.) (2008) *Along the Many Paths of God* Münster: LIT Verlag.
22 Vigil (Ed.) (2010), 8.

## 3. Principles of Interreligious Theology

This takes us back to the vision I initially outlined. But what exactly is interreligious theology to mean, and how can it be practiced? Interreligious theology proceeds from the positive assumption that theologically relevant truth is not only found in one's own tradition, but also in those of other religions. It is thus based not on a 'hermeneutics of suspicion' but on a 'hermeneutic benefit of doubt' or *'credit of trust'* ("Hermeneutik des Vertrauensvorschusses").[23] The justification for such theological confidence can be expressed in a variety of ways across different religious traditions. In Christianity, such confidence may be grounded in the assumption – well-supported by strong theological arguments – that revelation in the sense of divine self-communication is not limited to the people of the Judeo-Christian tradition. In Islam, such confidence can be based on the belief that the just and merciful God has sent His messengers to all peoples in the world (Surah 16:36), in Buddhism on the universal presence of the Buddha-nature manifesting itself in a variety of forms, etc.[24]

If this credit of trust is indeed theologically justified, then we need to look for and identify the truth as it is possibly testified to in other religious traditions. Ultimately, all truth – wherever and in whatever form it may be found – must be compatible. This follows from the fundamental intuition of the 'unity of reality' ("Einheit der Wirklichkeit")[25]. Faith in this *unity of reality* can thus be taken as the *second principle* of interreligious theology, following the theological credit of trust.

In practice, the task of interreligious theology is therefore to investigate the compatibility of different, at times even seemingly contradictory tenets of faith and pathways of religion. What appears an irreconcilable contradiction at first sight might, properly interpreted, turn out to be an ultimately compatible difference. It is in this context that Wilfred Cantwell Smith recommends to see apparent contradictions primarily as an "invitation to synthesis".[26] "To insist on seeing conflict whenever one finds, in fundamentally differing systems, two statements of which a person would not make both within one of those systems or in a third, is unduly embattled, beleaguered."[27] Here, interreligious theology

---

23  See also the work of Andreas Grünschloß on the interreligious importance of the hermeneutic "principle of charity", in: Grünschloß, A. (1999) *Der eigene und der fremde Glaube. Studien zur interreligiösen Fremdwahrnehmung in Islam, Hinduismus, Buddhismus und Christentum* Tübingen: Mohr Siebeck, 299 ff.

24  Some voices from non-Christian religions on the idea of an interreligious theology are found in Vigil (Ed.) (2010), [see. footnote 21].

25  See also v. Brück, M. (1986) *Einheit der Wirklichkeit* München: Kaiser. This work develops a pioneering example of a theology – referred to as "dialogical theology" – that draws on both Christian and Hindu sources.

26  Smith, W. C. (1975) Conflicting Truth-Claims: A Rejoinder. In: J. Hick (Ed.) *Truth and Dialogue. The Relationship between World Religions* London: Sheldon Press, 156–162, 160.

27  Ibid.

may also recur to the Jain principle of *anekāntavāda (non-one-sidedness)*: The belief that all things are multi-relational and interdependent has led the Jains to the assumption that any one thing comprises a hardly comprehensible multiplicity of aspects. As the truth of any given statement is relative to the aspect addressed, apparent contradictions may always be expected to possibly derive from a difference in aspect and might dissolve in a higher synthesis.[28] This question of eventual compatibility is above all what makes interreligious theology both attractive and theologically significant.[29] For an understanding of different perspectives can lead us not only to identify compatibility, but perhaps even to perceive complementarity. In concrete terms, insights from different religions can be mutually enriching in and through their very difference. The realisation that other religious traditions offer something genuinely new opens a perspective that, in the end, not only makes enriching, but even transformation of one's own belief a genuine theological option.

Although the two principles of theological credit of trust and unity of reality sufficiently describe the possibility and task of interreligious theology, two additional ones are needed which relate primarily to its practice. This can be illustrated by briefly attending to some weighty objections. They were offered by Edmund Chia, long-time executive secretary of interreligious dialogue to the Federation of Asian Bishops' Conferences, who personally expresses agreement with the project of an interreligious theology, but raises the following questions: Are the beliefs of the different religions not too disparate to be articulated in a single, all-encompassing theology? Will this not turn the space of 'inter-' into a no man's land so that it is a "theology that seems to belong to all but at the same time belongs to none"?[30] Have not differences even within each of the great religious traditions led to the fact that "people have been burned, wars have been waged, bombs set off, and people still crucify one another in the name of these theological differences"? Does this historical experience not make the dream of an interreligious theology appear completely illusory?[31]

This last question posed by Chia places interreligious theology in the tradition of ecumenical theology. But can we really say that ecumenism – inter-confessional theology, if you will – is illusory because people have in fact slaughtered each other over differences in their understanding of Christianity? Or isn't this rather an argument in favour of continued efforts to arrive at an ecumenical – and, analogously, an interreligious – theology? Yet what of Chia's question of

---

28  An effort to make apply this principle interreligiously is found in Drew, R. (2003) Reconsidering the Possibility of Pluralism. In: *JES*, 40(3), 245–266.

29  I have tried to exemplify this through the Christian affirmation and Buddhist rejection of divine creation in: Schmidt-Leukel, P. (2006) The Unbridgeable Gulf? Towards a Buddhist-Christian Theology of Creation. In: Id. (Ed.) *Buddhism, Christianity and the Question of Creation. Karmic or Divine?* Aldershot: Ashgate, 111–178.

30  Chia, E. K.–F. (2008) Is Interfaith Theology Possible? In: *Studies in Interreligious Dialogue*, 18, 112–117, 112.

31  Ibid., 113 f.

whether interreligious theology inhabits a theological no man's land? I believe that he himself provides the correct answer in saying that: "Interfaith Theology has to be done in an interfaith fashion."[32] This constitutes the *third principle* of interreligious theology.

To be truly interreligious, i.e. remain true to the principle of mutuality that the pioneers of intercultural theology valued so highly, and, as Smith phrases it, to give intellectual expression to the faith of all of us, interreligious theology must take place within an *interreligious discourse*. This does not exclude the possibility that individuals may make important contributions to interreligious theology on their own and from the particular perspective of their respective religious traditions. To a degree, this is unavoidable. Nonetheless, these contributions will always be dedicated to the overarching goal of integrating different perspectives. This does not put them in a theological or religious no man's land, but it does mean that they always and deliberately cross religious borders. As Smith puts it, interreligious theology is Christian, Muslim, Buddhist etc., but at the same time, it is more: it is, in his words, "Christian plus…", "Muslim plus…", "Buddhist plus…".[33] This 'plus' is exactly that effort to mediate between the insights of one's own tradition and those derived from other religious perspectives. That, in turn, means that interreligious learning processes hold the key to the methodology of practicing interreligious theology.

Interreligious theology, then, takes place in the context of a broadly understood interreligious colloquy. No one individual can synthesise all perspectives, which means it is impossible for any single person to produce something like a completed interreligious theology. Interreligious theology is necessarily not only a dialogical and or colloquial, but also an unfinished process. Otherwise, its results would be no more than the theological components of one or more newly emerging syncretic religions. I do not see any problems with syncretism in principle. All great religions are, after all, the product of syncretistic processes.[34] But any new syncretic religions will themselves need to be integrated into the ongoing process of interreligious theology and cannot in themselves be its goal. The process of integrating different perspectives, the acceptance of the invitation to synthesis, remains necessarily incomplete and open-ended. This does no more devalue the process of interreligious theology than the essential incompleteness of science devalues the progress of science. To quote Michael von Brück once more: Intercultural theology takes place as an "interreligious process of truth-seeking", that, on the one hand, "allows for concrete commitment" while on the other hand is "never comes to a stand-still".[35] This *processual, essentially incomplete nature* of interreligious theology is its *fourth principle*.

---

32  Ibid., 115.
33  Smith (1989), 125.
34  Schmidt-Leukel, P. (2009) *Transformation by Integration. How Inter-faith Encounter Changes Christianity* London: SCM Press, 67–89.
35  v. Brück (1986), 261.

## 4.     Interreligious Theology: "not yet, and yet already"

I am convinced that the future of theology is in the vision of an interreligious theology as presented here – a future that, in fact, has already begun. Interreligious theology is already part of our world; it is already practised.

The first instance to be noted here are the forms of intercultural theology in which Christian theology enters into a *dialogue with other religions* not only on a purely ethical, social, political or simply pragmatic level, but in an effort to learn from their beliefs and practices. Interreligious theology is realised in all forms of interreligious dialogue in which Christianity takes its non-Christian partners and their religious traditions seriously as a source of theological understanding. One good example of this is found in the work of Lynn de Silva (1919–1982).[36] De Silva was a Methodist minister in Sri Lanka and initially dedicated himself to the inculturation of the Gospel into the Buddhist culture of his home country. Being aware of the indivisibility of culture and religion, he tried to represent the Gospel in a way that would make it intelligible to Buddhists as an answer to their own faith. De Silva operated on the assumption that Buddhism incorporated existential questions that would find their redeeming solution in Christianity. In trying to put this concept into practice, though, he increasingly found that Buddhism had its own good answers to its own questions. As a result, de Silva's understanding of the Christian message began to transform in the light of his better understanding of these Buddhist answers.[37] Sadly, his early death abruptly ended this fascinating development, but his path remains exemplary for the necessary transition from intercultural to interreligious theology.

Another field in which interreligious theology is already being practised is so-called "*comparative theology*".[38] Unlike the older discipline of "comparative religion", "comparative theology" goes beyond the level of merely phenomenological comparisons. It rather seeks to compare individual religious ideas, teachings, figures, motives, practices, etc. with the explicit expectation of gaining theological insight. It does not exclude the question of truth from the comparative method, but rather uses interreligious comparison as a means of theological truth finding. Thus, the Comparative Theology Group of the Amer-

---

36 On Lynn A. de Silva see Schmidt-Leukel, P. (1992) "*Den Löwen brüllen hören...*". *Zur Hermeneutik eines christlichen Verständnisses der buddhistischen Heilsbotschaft* Paderborn: Schöningh, 185–202; Id. (2009) *Transformation by Integration* London: SCM Press, 107–123. For a German translation of some of his work see: De Silva, L.A. (1998) *Mit Buddha und Christus auf dem Weg (Theologien der Dritten Welt 24)* Freiburg i.Br.: Herder.

37 See especially his posthumously published essay: (1982) Buddhism and Christianity Relativised. In: *Dialogue N.S.*, 9, 43–72. German translation in: De Silva (1998), 148–184.

38 See the recent introduction: Clooney, F. X. (2010) *Comparative Theology. Deep Learning Across Religious Borders* Chichester: Wiley-Blackwell; R. Bernhardt & K. v. Stosch (Eds.) (2009) *Komparative Theologie. Interreligiöse Vergleiche als Weg der Religionstheologie* Zürich: TVZ.

ican Academy of Religion deliberately chose the designation "interreligious theology" for this approach.[39]

Some representatives of "comparative theology", in particular James Fredericks, have declared it an alternative to the "theology of religions".[40] This position, though, is indefensible if "comparative theology" is to be and remain a form of genuine theology.[41] For any theological comparison will automatically lead to questions whose answers have immediate implications for the theology of religions: "Is the knowledge of the Divine that other religions attest true knowledge of the Divine? Are their intermediaries of salvation truly such intermediaries, indeed, might they too be incarnations of the Logos, although in different forms? How do non-Christian conceptions of salvation relate to Christian ones, and what does this mean for the concrete question whether and how salvation is possible within and outside Christianity?" and so on. Carrying out their comparisons, comparative theologians will sooner or later come up against such questions and thus enter a field where it becomes inevitable to opt for one of three basic positions of a theology of religions, i.e. exclusivism, inclusivism, or pluralism.

Above all, interreligious theology is already being practiced in an area of theological studies that, so far, has only been entered by a few pioneering scholars: The reconstruction of *systematic theology from an interreligious perspective*. This is what Paul Tillich, as mentioned above, had been wishing for his own Systematic Theology. To briefly quote a few examples: The Anglican theologian and religious studies scholar Ninian Smart together with the Orthodox theologian Steven Kontantine published a *Christian Systematic Theology in a World Context* in 1991.[42] In Germany, Hans-Martin Barth published in 2001 his Dogmatics presenting "Protestant Faith in the Context of the World Religions".[43] While intercultural theology, interreligious dialogue and comparative theology usually proceed bilaterally, correlating the Christian faith with one specific other, these systematic approaches try to multilaterally combine various individual dialogical-comparative efforts. As Smart and Konstantine write: "Hitherto, Christian theologies have been mostly Eurocentric, and though there have in recent times grown up traditions of Asian, African, Latin American and other theologies, these

39  *Statement for the Comparative Theology Group for the AAR*, Nr. II.1. www.aarweb.org/upfiles/PUCS2007/AARPU145/CTGroupAAR.doc (last accessed December 10, 2013).

40  Fredericks, J. (1999) *Faith among Faiths: Christian Theology and Non-Christian Religions* New York: Paulist Press; Similarly in v. Stosch, K. (2002) Komparative Theologie – ein Ausweg aus dem Grunddilemma jeder Theologie der Religionen? In: *ZKTh*, 124, 294–311.

41  Schmidt-Leukel, P. (2009) *Transformation by Integration* London: SCM Press, 90–104; Id. (2005) *Gott ohne Grenzen. Eine christliche und pluralistische Theologie der Religionen* Gütersloh: Gütersloher Verlagshaus, 87–95.

42  Smart, N. & Konstantine, S. (1991) *Christian Systematic Theology in a World Context* London: Marshall Pickering.

43  Barth, H.-M. (2001) *Dogmatik. Evangelischer Glaube im Kontext der Weltreligionen. Ein Lehrbuch* Gütersloh: Gütersloher Verlagshaus.

have often neglected the whole-world context, and the reflection of that in religious studies."[44] Hans-Martin Barth takes a similarly broad approach in relating individual Christian themes to Judaism, Islam, Hinduism and Buddhism, posing the question "what both sides may respectively be able to gain thereby".[45]

Both Smart & Konstantine and Barth expect the reconstruction of Christian systematic theology in an interreligious context to lead to changes in theological thinking. This is even more explicit in the four volumes published by the former Oxford Systematic Theologian Keith Ward, *Religion and Revelation* (1994), *Religion and Creation* (1996), *Religion and Human Nature* (1998), and *Religion and Community* (2000).[46] In these volumes, he places a particular emphasis on constitutively integrating a self-critical reflection on Christianity with complementary insights gained from other religions into the development of systematic theology.[47] The list could be expanded by a number of more specific works such as John Hick's sketch of an interreligious eschatology[48], or Wilfred Cantwell Smith's interreligious study of the concept of Scripture.[49] The field waiting to be researched is immense: Interreligious theology, as Claude Geffré has recently remarked, is not just another new particular area within theology, but concerns "all the great tractates of a dogmatic theology", indeed, it is "a dimension coextensive with the entirety of theology".[50] Should theology choose to embrace this insight, it would mean radical change throughout the discipline.

There is yet another field in which interreligious theology is already being practised, though usually in a rather non-academic way. A number of sociological surveys have shown that the phenomenon of *multi-religious identity formation*, religious bricolage and hybridisation, is spreading. The international survey *Religionsmonitor 2008* found that 22% of German respondents agreed with the statement "For my own life I draw on the teachings of different religious traditions". In Indonesia, the corresponding figure was 23%, in Great Britain 27%, in the United States 32%, in India 71%.[51] One remarkable detail is that in Germany, 22% of Catholics and 25% of Protestants agreed. That means that here the process of multi-religious identity formation already involves nearly a quarter of

---

44  Smart & Konstantine (1991), 17.

45  Barth (2008), 8, *"was gegebenenfalls beide Seiten dabei zu gewinnen vermögen"*, translation Volker Bach.

46  Ward, K. (1994) *Religion and Revelation. A Theology of Revelation in the World's Religions* Oxford: University Press; Id. (1996) *Religion and Creation* Oxford: University Press; Id. (1998) *Religion and Human Nature* Oxford: University Press; Id. (2000) *Religion and Community* Oxford: University Press.

47  Id. (2000), 341.

48  Hick, J. (1990) *Death and Eternal Life* Basingstoke: Macmillan (1st ed. 1976).

49  Smith, W. C. (1993) *What is Scripture? A Comparative Approach* London: SCM Press.

50  Geffré, C. (2007) Unterwegs zu einer 'interreligiösen Theologie'. In: *ZMR*, 91, 16–28, 26. *"alle großen Traktate einer dogmatischen Theologie" betrifft, ja "um eine Dimension, die der ganzen Theologie koextensiv ist"*, translation Volker Bach.

51  Bertelsmann Stiftung (Ed.) (2009) *Woran glaubt die Welt? Analysen und Kommentare zum Religionsmonitor 2008* Gütersloh: Verlag Bertelsmann Stiftung. Data included on CD.

church members. I believe this development is, in principle, a good thing.[52] It is good when people open themselves to what they perceive as true, helpful and holy, even if it comes from a different religious tradition. It would be less good if anything foreign were rejected just because of being foreign. But academic theology has so far offered people who draw on a variety of religious traditions in their spiritual lives little in the way of active support or guidance. This could well entail something like the practical dimension of interreligious theology. In any case, the trend towards multi-religious identities to me appears to emphasise once again the importance and necessity of an interreligious theology.[53]

Among those who profess multi-religious identities, we also find some individuals who reflect their hybrid identity theologically at the highest academic level. This is true e.g. of Raimundo Panikkar (1918–2010), Julia Ching (1934–2001), Bettina Bäumer or Sallie King. Their theological writings often grew from the need to render an existentially experienced and lived interreligious existence rationally intelligible through the development of an interreligious theology. Paul Knitter's latest book *Without Buddha I Could not be a Christian* is a particularly good example. In it, he not only autobiographically reveals the existential components of interreligious learning processes, but also demonstrates how these necessarily lead to the emergence of a new – an interreligious – theology.[54] Jeannine Hill Fletcher argues that the specific feature of a feminist theology of religions might become the reflection of religiously hybrid identity formation – precisely because of its emphasis on 'embodied' theology.[55]

The various paths along which interreligious theology is currently emerging seem to support the assumption that this is where the future of theology lies. Interreligious theology does not turn theology into a no man's land, but it does turn it into an exciting new territory. Facing the emerging questions and challenges openly and creatively implies exactly the kind of inquisitive spirit that makes theology – like any form of science – such a fascinating enterprise.

---

52  Schmidt-Leukel, P. (2009) *Transformation by Integration* London: SCM Press, 46–66; Id. (2008) Multireligiöse Identität. Anmerkungen aus pluralistischer Sicht. In: R. Bernhardt & P. Schmidt-Leukel (Eds.) *Multiple religiöse Identität. Aus verschiedenen religiösen Traditionen schöpfen* Zürich: TVZ, 243–265.

53  On the recent theological discourse on multi-religious identity see the abovementioned essay collection as well as C. Cornille (Ed.) (2002) *Many Mansions? Multiple Religious Belonging and Christian Identity* Maryknoll: Orbis.

54  Knitter, P. (2009) *Without Buddha I Could not be a Christian* Oxford: Oneworld Publications.

55  Hill Fletcher, J. (2008) Feminisms: Syncretism, Symbiosis, Synergetic Dance. In: A. Race & P. M. Hedges (Eds.) *Christian Approaches to Other Faiths* London: SCM Press, 136–154; Id. (2005) *Monopoly on Salvation? A Feminist Approach to Religious Pluralism* New York – London: Continuum; Kalsky, M. (2008) Religiöse Flexibilität. Eine Antwort auf kulturelle und religiöse Vielfalt. In: R. Berhardt & P. Schmidt-Leukel (Eds.) *Multiple religiöse Identität* [see note 52], 219–242.

*Wolfram Weisse*

# Dialogue from a Christian and Muslim Perspective
Early Visions of a Dialogical Theology

## 1. Introduction

Religions are nowadays playing an increasingly important role in European societies, both in dialogue between people of different faiths and in the context of social tension and conflict. This is apparent both in academia and in the public arena. More and more scholars who formerly were not involved in the field of religion are taking up this topic. An outstanding example is Jürgen Habermas. For decades he refused to take religion into account within his thinking of communication. For a couple of years now he has been writing more and more on religion and its function for mutual understanding. Jürgen Habermas regards religious tolerance as "the pacemaker for multiculturalism, correctly understood, and for the equal coexistence of different cultural forms of life within a democratic polity". [1] And even in France, where the system of laicité has been dominant since more than 100 years with a strict separation of church resp. religion and state, there is a new tendency: religion is coming back "dans la sphère publique". [2]

An important question today is how religions in their diversity can be a resource for coexistence rather than becoming a pattern of strict separation. To this end, it is not enough to strive for a peaceful existence of people of different language, culture and religion alongside each other; more than ever, we need to move towards recognition of the other. Is such an endeavour linked with the danger, to loose one's own identity? I would like to indicate an answer to this question referring to three approaches: that of the Jewish philosopher of Eastern European origin Emmanuel Lévinas who taught at the Sorbonne in France, that of the Protestant philosopher Paul Ricœur who taught as well at the Sorbonne, and that of the Catholic theologian and educational researcher Helmut Peukert.

Emmanuel Lévinas emphasises that all our ethics are based on our relation to the other, the neighbour. Responsibility for the other – "pour autrui" – is directed to the neighbour, both in the spatial and spiritual sense. According to Lévinas, this responsibility is unlimited and cannot be understood as a due to be paid. It reaches to the core of the self: "Et c'est là la subjectivité du moi". [3]

---

1  Habermas, J. (2008) *Between Naturalism and Religion. Philosophical Essays* Cambridge, UK: Polity Press, 257.

2  Willaime, J.-P. (2008) *Le retour du religieux dans la sphère publique. Vers uns laicité de reconnaissance et de dialogue*, Lyon: Olivétan.

3  Lévinas, E. (1993) Penser Dieu à partir de l'éthique, in: Id. *Dieu, la Mort et le Temps,* ed. J. Rolland, Paris: Grasset, 157.

Thus, responsibility for the other is the prerequisite for subjectivity. The self can only be discovered, developed and shaped through the other – the neighbour.

Paul Ricœur laid the foundations of a dual demand: to both accept the other in his/her otherness and to recognise oneself as an acting and responsible subject, to achieve mutual recognition and reassurance in one's own identity. He suggests a relational approach as the quest for identity cannot be followed by protectively shutting out others, but only in relation to them.[4]

The Catholic theologian and educator Helmut Peukert warns that "the attempt to desperately be oneself can become the attempt to embrace one's own power".[5] He sets the Christian tradition against this vision of identity-through-might. According to Peukert identity "is not the defence of an achieved completeness, but a hopeful, eager expectation of the gift of integrity to the other and, only through this, also to oneself".[6]

These three positions destroy the simplistic view of the self as a unique whole to which an individual can lay proprietorial claim. Identity is not a cut-and-dried package of traditions and habits, but an unending desire dependent upon grace, one in which the self cannot take shape without the other. Therefore, these approaches have far-reaching consequences both for the individual and society. It is here that religious pluralism, too, needs to be taken into account: If recognition of the other is a necessary pole for recognition of the self and acceptance in social life, a plurality of religions offers the opportunity to practice this mutual recognition.

Many questions are linked with this presupposition. In the following contribution I would like to focus on the role of theologies in this process with the following focus:

Is dialogue with other religions from a theological perspective a threat of its own religious identity, is it superfluous, a trendy luxury or even an inadequate adaptation to contemporary developments? Or is dialogue a theological requirement, grounded in the heart of theology?

We need thorough analyses in order to be able to answer these questions. In this contribution I would like to evoke the remembrance of two theologians, one Christian, one Muslim, who could be considered as pioneers for basic theological reflections on dialogue with other religions, or better: with people of other religions. Both lived in the same time in Germany, but I doubt that they met and had an exchange, although their thoughts seem to me very close to each other. Maybe this contribution enables a hidden conversation between them and serves to go back and get impulses from these theologians with regard to an experience-based concept of interreligious dialogue

---

4   Ricœur, P. (2006) *Wege der Anerkennung. Erkennen, Wiedererkennen, Anerkanntsein*, Frankfurt am Main: Suhrkamp.

5   Peukert, Helmut (2005) Identität, in: Eicher, P. (Ed.). *Neues Handbuch theologischer Grundbegriffe*, Bd. 2, München, 184–192, citation 190.

6   Ibid.,191.

To this day, efforts persist to define and contrast the typical and distinguishing characteristics of Islam, Christianity, Judaism, Hinduism, Buddhism etc. Such an attempt may have its merits, but it will invariably suffer from the severe disadvantage of neglecting each religion's internal diversity. The historical and geographic varieties that exist inside religions tend to be neglected in such classifying approaches. The result, even among well-informed and well-meaning individuals, is a tendency to ascribe certain specific characteristics to religions that can reinforce stereotyping and prejudice.

I would thus plead for a closer study of the conditions under which dialogue can be made a success. There are a number of approaches in theology, Islamic studies, and education today that are trying to do this. I will concentrate on two theological concepts, that of the Christian theologian Hans Jochen Margull, and that of the Islamic theologian Abdoldjavad Falaturi. One can easily find strident opposing voices to both approaches, of course. There were and are Christian and Muslim theologians who favour a strict separation from and condemnation of all religions except their own. However, for an effort towards a dialogical theology, I believe Margull and Falaturi remain important guides.[7]

## 2.    Theological Concepts of Dialogue

### Hans Jochen Margull

Hans Jochen Margull (1925–1982) was active in the Ecumenical Council of churches in Geneva for some time before accepting the Chair of Ecumenical and Missionary Studies at Hamburg University, where he remained until the end of his life in 1982.

His approach is shaped by three underlying assumptions: The first is that he regards religions as historical artefacts whose future form is subject to change. In this, he rejects a fundamental understanding of religion as an ahistorical, unchanging body of beliefs and forms.[8] The second assumption concerns the validity of religious claims to absolute truth and the tension between particular viewpoints and absolutist demands. Margull assumed that the irreducible truth claim of any religion was at heart an absolutist statement, and that it was defensible at the level of a subjective certainty that salvation was possible. He took a strong position against deriving any objective claims from absolute truth, especially since these would have to, in actual fact, compete with those of

---

7   See also Weisse, Wolfram: *"Christlich-islamischer Dialog – Möglichkeiten und Grenzen"*. Presentation on 2 February 2006 at the NEK synod in Rendsburg. http://www.nordelbien. de/download/synode_2006_1/Top1_2Weisse.pdf Last accessed 26.11.2013.

8   Margull, H.J. (1992) Zeugnis und Dialog. Ausgewählte Schriften mit Einführungen von Th. Ahrens, L. Engel, E. Kamphausen, I. Lembke, W. Ustorf, W. Weiße und J. Wietzke. In: *Perspektiven der Weltmission 13*, Ammersbek bei Hamburg: Verlag an der Lottbek, 270.

other religions as particular, not universal religions.[9] The third addresses the expression of "vulnerability" (*Verwundbarkeit*). In the course of dialogue, the insight is gained that Christianity – like all other world religions – is merely a particular element. This represents a painful slight to the Christian self-image. However, the pain it causes is no greater or different than the one it causes any other religion.

Against this background, Margull formulates the following priorities for dialogue:

1. *An Encounter of Equals*: To Margull, interreligious dialogue meant the meeting of and exchange with people of equal standing and different religious backgrounds. Following Martin Buber, he viewed it as both a precondition and fundamental fact of such encounters that "nothing less and nothing more painful than equality and respect is the precondition for true dialogue".[10] This must find expression in the terminology used. Instead of speaking of a dialogue *with* other religions (implying the primacy of your own), he insisted on speaking of dialogue *between* people of different religious traditions as the central feature.

2. *Christian identity is dialogical, not monological:* Margull rejected the idea of an exclusive Christian identity that shuts out the word and its religions as a "donjon of monologue". People from different religious traditions should "be involved in our theological thought from the very beginning".[11] Thus, the encounter and dialogue with adherents of other faiths is not a more or less desirable addition or even a threat to the development of a Christian identity, but an indispensable piece of its core.

3. *The common features of people, not the differences of religions, are a key:* From his own experience, Margull concluded that the central perspective of dialogue should never be on the differences in religious traditions, but on an awareness of human commonalities which the Jewish and Christian traditions see rooted in our shared createdness in God's image. He did not view the doctrinal constructions of other faiths as important, but the personal encounters with individual adherents. The claim to self-determination in each individual could never be superseded by the doctrinal requirements of formal religious affiliation.

4. *Interreligious dialogue does not foster syncretism:* His concrete experience allowed Margull to dismiss the frequently voiced concern that interreligious dialogue would lead to a syncretistic unitary world faith or intended to do so.

5. *Dialogue and silence*: Dialogue does not mean incessant talk; it includes silences. Especially for European and North American Christians, the historical dominance of their faith dictates a degree of reticence in their encounters with people from other religions: "Dialogue for us [Western Christians,

---

9   Ibid., 303.
10  Ibid., 310.
11  Ibid., 323–27.

W.W.] first of all means to listen long and thoroughly, because we especially have to combat the stigma of being poor listeners."[12]

6. *Theology is not founded on the possession of truth, but emerges in dialogue:* In this approach, the development of a Christian identity is impossible in isolation or even by referring solely to the church. Ecumenical theology in Margull's sense proceeds from the assumption that God's promise is to all humanity, regardless of their beliefs. Sustaining Christianity, or any other religion, by reference to truth in a timeless doctrine is not a viable approach. Rather, from this perspective dialogue is an indispensable process that allows us to develop our own identity not through the exclusion of other people and their religious and philosophical beliefs, but through encounters with them.

Interreligious Dialogue: Encounter of People in Respect and Equality

The decisive starting point for dialogue consists, according to Margull's experiences, not in the differences of the particular religious traditions but in the common grounds of the people, since all mankind are an image of God.[13] Decisive for him were the *personal* encounters with other believers, for example within the field of Buddhism:

> "My knowledge of the multiple forms in the profound field what I simplified called Buddhism, is definitely much more limited than my respect for a couple of people which *we* call Buddhist rather they themselves."[14]

In his dialogical endeavours the notions of "encounter of people"[15] and encounter-like dialogue[16] are at the very centre. People should not be classified from outside, even not by their formal adherence to a particular religion. The theological reflections should rather intend "to focus on the human beings who are not necessarily defined by one of our already defined religions. Nevertheless they can be understood – in keeping their peculiarity and freedom – within the structure of a religious tradition".[17] Following Buber, Margull demands as a precondition for the objective "living mutuality" the "simple experience that nothing less – and maybe nothing more causing grief – than equality and respect are the preconditions for *real* dialogue".[18] Therefore, he rejects the concept of a dialogue *with* the other religions, in particular since this concept in its tendency draws on the superiority or at least dominance of one's own position. Margull

---

12  Ibid., 287.
13  Ibid., 313 f.
14  Ibid., 273.
15  Ibid., 288.
16  Ibid., 305.
17  Ibid., 310.
18  Ibid.

demands a Christian understanding of the dialogue *between* the *persons* belong-ing to different traditions.[19]

The immediate cause for dialogue is often in fields of societal conflict.[20] It has its limits which can induce silence, silence in dialogue.[21] There are op-portune and inopportune times for dialogue. Despite high objectives, dialogue sometimes cannot go beyond a basic respect of the 'other'.[22] These limits are distressing but not fundamental limitations. His experiences allowed Margull to invalidate the widespread fears with regard to syncretism and uniform global religion as a result of interreligious dialogue. Syncretism is not the result of such encounters but the product of prejudice.[23] When Christian people take, for example, an interest in Buddhism, it cannot be explained in the frame of syncretism, but it occurs, generally, out of frustration about the Church.[24] And the idea of a uniform global religion never appeared in the processes of interre-ligious dialogue.[25]

Margull sees interreligious dialogue as an "expectant and obliging talk at an open encounter of people of different religious backgrounds with equal rights".[26] The fundamental preconditions for dialogue appear thus to be ex-tremely ambitious.

Margull underlines the necessity – grounded in our past history – to give precedence to the others and to stay voluntarily in the background. He refutes the notion of a narrow Christian identity which fades out world and world-reli-gions as a "circular tower of monologue".[27] It cannot be at stake to understand the 'other' from our centre but "to understand the other as he understands him-self". This phrase represents – in acknowledgement of the difficulties and limi-tations to understand the other from the centre of the other – the brief formula of the "ethos of dialogue".[28] People of other traditions should "from the beginning participate in our theological reflections"[29], they should "became a substantial part of our reflections on faith."[30]

Encounter and dialogue are thus central parts, even the heart of theologiz-ing. They are not merely luxury which one may afford or not or which could be justified by a united religious front against secularism.[31]

---

19  Ibid., 309 f.
20  Ibid., 259.
21  Ibid., 340.
22  Ibid., 335.
23  Ibid., 361
24  Ibid., 281.
25  Ibid., 225.
26  Ibid., 297.
27  Ibid., 362.
28  Ibid., 339.
29  Ibid., 327.
30  Ibid., 323.
31  Ibid., 289.

The tolerance in the initiation of dialogue[32] and the dialogical events on which Margull reflects are neither ignorant toleration nor limitless acceptance but approaching each other with questions and counter-questions about one's own person and tradition from the perspective of other religions, and vice versa. This initiates a process of mutual understanding, of speaking up mutually for the respective other; a process which enriches, demands – and wounds.

Dialogue thus moves into the centre of theology and of theological processes, it becomes constitutive for Christian self-understanding which considers truth not as (its sole) possession, which restricts the search for truth not to its own tradition but regards itself as depending on the questions and answers of people of other religious convictions. Dialogue becomes indispensable for one's own self-understanding.

## Abdoldjavad Falaturi

Professor Abdoldjavad Falaturi (1926–1996) is one of the most well-known Muslim scholars. He worked in Cologne for a considerable time, e.g. collaborating with Udo Tworuschka on a series of German books on Islam. His plan to establish an Islamic academy in Hamburg was cut short by his death in 1996.

Falaturi views two factors as necessary for any dialogue: Firstly, all participants must make the effort "to understand the other approximately the way they understand themselves and feel their own religiosity".[33] Secondly, each participant should enable the other to "be understood and empathised with by the other in the way they see and feel themselves in their religious consciousness".[34] He develops six points that he considers necessary for successful dialogue:

1. *Overcoming absolutist claims*: The most important condition for a successful dialogue is to "distance oneself from the insistence on the exclusive possession of truth". Anyone who thinks himself in sole possession of the truth and all others as erring makes success impossible. "The idea of limiting salvation to the adherents of your own faith while assigning condemnation to all others is no more than a monoperspectival limitation of divine love and charity, an egocentric attempt to coerce God. Assigning heaven and hell to groups of people, or rather, arrogating the function of gatekeeper there shows a naive idea of the relationship between man and God".[35]

2. *A self-critical stance and the awareness of imperfection*: Openness towards the "truth of the other" (Wahrheit des anderen) for dialogue means the "willingness to take a distanced and self-critical approach to the tenets of one's

---

32  Ibid., 353.

33  Falaturi, A. (1996a) Hermeneutik des Dialoges aus islamischer Sicht. In: Id. *Der Islam im Dialog. Aufsätze von Professor Abdoldjavad Falaturi*, 5th extended ed., Hamburg: Islamwissenschaftliche Akademie Verlag, pp. 156–172, 156.

34  Ibid., 157.

35  Ibid.

own faith and the courage to admit to weaknesses and errors in the history of one's own religion. Muslims, Buddhists, Christians and Jews need to admit not living 100% by the tenets of their faiths because their own strength does not allow it. This mutual admission is necessary to ensure than any errant behaviour by one party is not understood by others as the standard practice of his faith". [36]

3. *Equality and Respect*: A precondition of these first two – most important – requirements for dialogue is a partnership of equals among the parties. Where this is not the case, arrogance and preachiness result. Successful dialogue requires the respect and recognition of the opposite party in their unabridged identity.

4. *Readiness to learn from the other and reflect quotidian problems*: Falaturi sees another requirement in the readiness and even eagerness "to learn from the partner not only in their positive values, but also in their handling of everyday problems and the solutions they apply".[37]

5. *Mutual responsibility for an undivided humanity*: Dialogue must be understood as a means to peace. What is needed is "the conviction of both partners in dialogue about a mutual responsibility for the world and all people, regardless of their differences".[38] This may be hard to live up to, but he regards it as absolutely necessary.

6. *The creation of a new theology on both sides*: A phenomenology of religions has contributed little to mutual understanding in Christian-Muslim dialogue. Falaturi argues that "one thing will most likely be helpful: the creation of a new theology on both sides based on mutual understanding of the other's self-understanding. In the long run, neither Christians nor Muslims will be able to avoid this if they are serious about dialogue in this sense".[39]

## Difficulties and Misuse of Dialogue

Falaturi looked at the difficulties with dialogue, such as the differences between Christian and Islamic approaches to Christology. He further provides an impressive 11-point list of circumstances under which dialogue is only used as a means of creating legitimacy, purely for show: mutual scepticism, negative views of the other, arrogance, prejudice, perceptions of inferiority or hostility and proselytizing intentions are all listed as obstacles to real dialogue. This kind of sham dialogue (Scheindialog) is commonly undertaken "when extreme events such as current political events related to violence (revolution, the Gulf War, local wars, radicalism etc.) provide the occasion to roll out a series of meetings without showing any interest in the complete situation surrounding

---

36  Ibid., 158.
37  Ibid., 158 f.
38  Ibid., 159.
39  Ibid., 171.

the event in question, and to engage in dialogue in order to highlight certain aspects of doctrine, history and beliefs that can be used to paint an exaggerated and hateful image of the other party's religion and culture – which happens particularly often to be Islam". [40] This sounds like a valid criticism of an event that Falaturi himself did not live to see, the attacks of 11th September 2001 and the conclusions commonly drawn about Islam in their wake.

## Dialogue as Encounter with Focus on a Common Ethics

Falaturi clearly points towards the foundation of the Qur'an which – for all extant differences – advocates dialogue and a common effort of Muslims, Christians and Jews. He counsels that "from this perspective, Christians, Muslims and Jews of genuine good will are well advised to let their encounters in any situation and at any level be guided by their shared and common root of love and charity that is at the heart of the relationship of humans to God and God to humans, and to use this basis to foster an emotional bond with the aim of meeting their shared responsibility for the world and everyone in it in a spirit of peace and unity".[41]

## 3.   Conclusion

These are clear theological bases for a dialogue on which, at heart, Margull and Falaturi are in agreement. The possibility of a dialogue, as we have seen in the concepts of both, depends on certain preconditions: renunciation of absolute objective truth claims, mutual respect, equality, openness, the willingness to understand the other from their own perspective and not to assign one's own interpretations, no expectations of perfection, and hope for a further development of a theology in service to humanity and peace.

Both do not see their religious identity threatened by entering into dialogue with others, and for both, dialogue is central for theological reasons, not as a mere accommodation of contemporary societal developments. On the contrary, dialogue is a key element in their project of developing a new theological thinking – a "new theology" (Falaturi) based on a growing mutual understanding.

Both Hans Jochen Margull and Abdoldjavad Falaturi
- regard dialogue as theologically necessary, even as a precondition for the development of theologies, at least in the Christian and Muslim tradition,
- reject the supposition of an identity through exclusion of others, but stress the necessity to encounter others in order to develop and form one's own identity,
- refer to their tradition in a way that embraces the current realities of life,

---

40  Ibid., 161.
41  Ibid., 171 f.

- insist that dialogue should not be restricted to experts but involve the lay adherents of the different religions, too,
- regard it as important to focus on people's understanding of their religion, rather than restricting dialogue to the systematics or dogmatics of religions,
- focus on dialogue between people of different faiths, not between religious systems,
- see it as necessary to include all human beings in a dialogue, not only those who consider themselves religious,
- regard the encounter of different people in daily life as an important dimension of dialogue, and
- see the development of dialogue in theologies as a key challenge to serve humanity and focus on central ethical issues.

Remembering the basic ideas of Hans Jochen Margull and Abdoldjavad Falaturi can encourage us to develop a new theology of dialogue that is

- based on the sources of different religions,
- shaped by a deep academic conversation that highlights commonalities without ignoring differences,
- linked to the diverse experiences of people with their religious self-understanding,
- relevant for people with their diverse backgrounds in a plural society and
- contributing to a form of coexistence in which people in all their differences are aware of their respective backgrounds and respect each other.

# Dialogue in Jewish Thinking

*Ephraim Meir*

# Building Stones for an Interreligious Dialogue and Theology

All religions are about something that transcends everyday, empirical perception: they are windows to an Ultimate Reality. This fact gives us the rationale for the realisation of an interreligious religiosity and the construction of an intercultural theology.[1]

## Cultural Changes

Theologies are traditionally intellectual reflections upon denominational attitudes and ideas. In the past, theologians claimed to be in sole possession of the truth. However, during the last decennia in Western Europe radical changes have taken place on cultural, social, and religious levels. Contacts with different cultures and religions have become quite normal and foreign religions have quickly become what Wolfram Weisse calls 'neighbour religions'.[2] Given this situation, an interreligious religiosity and a pluralisation of theologies are far from being solely an intellectual pastime; they have become a necessity. This necessity cannot be reduced to the need for an 'oecumenical' attitude: this term is too Christian. In the following I offer building stones for an inter-cultural, inter-religious encounter and for the construction of a 'trans-different' theology. Such encounters and theologies are no longer optional or voluntary, a nice hobby; in the present constellation of our interlinked societies they have become inevitable.

---

1   Hick, J. (1980) *God Has Many Names: Britain's New Religious Pluralism* London and Basingstoke: Macmillan; Eck, D. (2011) *A New Religious America: How a "Christian Country" Has Become the World's Most Religiously Diverse Nation* San Francisco: Harper; Knitter, P. F. (2008) Doing Theology Interreligiously: Union and the Legacy of Paul Tillich. In: *Crosscurrents*, 61, 117–132; Schmidt-Leukel, P. (2012) Religious Pluralism and the Need for an Interreligious Theology. In: S. Sugirtharajah (Ed.) *Religious Pluralism and the Modern World: An Ongoing Engagement with John Hick* Birmingham, UK: Palgrave Macmillan, 19–33; Weisse, W. (2009) Religious Education as Encounter with Neighbor Religions. In: S. Miedema (Ed.) *Religious Education as Encounter: A Tribute to John M. Hull* Muenster: Waxmann, 111–128. Weisse refers to Hans-Jochen Margull and Abdold-javad Falaturi as pioneers who laid a theological basis for an interreligious dialogue in Germany. In the United States the influential Christian theologian Paul Tillich contributed to the construction of a dialogical theology. In his article, Knitter writes on "the legacy of Tillich", for whom religious diversity was seen as God's will. He formulates Tillich's standpoint pointedly: "[…] to be religious today means to be religious interreligiously".

2   See the title of Weisse's article "Religious Education as Encounter with Neighbor Religions". Here Weisse uses the term in reference to Klöker, M. & Tworuschka, U. (1994) *Religionen in Deutschland. Kirchen, Glaubensgemeinschaften, Sekten* München: Olzog.

## Religion and the Ineffable

Since people of different religions desire access to the Ultimate Reality that in the end escapes any grasp, one has to admit that one's own religion is only one single attempt to discuss what is ultimately ineffable, which is deliberated on in a mosaic or kaleidoscope of approaches. What is beyond anyone's comprehension cannot be accessed in a monologic manner. Others organise their lives around a Higher Reality as well. Their religious acts and thoughts may be relevant for one's own religious life.

In the process of opening up the traditional theologies to what other theologies have to say about the Ineffable, one gradually becomes conscious that one's own religious identity is intimately linked to the religious identity of other persons: one knows oneself only through the other.

## Positioning Oneself in Dialogue with the Other

In the praxis of interreligious dialogue in the cities of the world, one's own religious position is often challenged by another. In multicultural towns, different reactions to such a challenge are possible. One may, in an exclusivist view, maintain that the entire truth is in one's own religion and that consequently, all the others are wrong. Such a view is less and less common, although one should not underestimate the growing power of fundamentalists who still proclaim it, protecting and defending their own tenets of faith against a threatening outside world. We also find inclusivists, who will admit certain truths in the other religions, but remain convinced that the whole truth nevertheless lies in their own religion. Pluralists admit that all sincerely search for the truth about Ultimate Reality. In my own view, being a religious inclusivist or a religious pluralist is not enough. Present multicultural societies demand an interreligious religiosity and theology, an openness to what others have to say about Ultimate Reality, which all religious people strive for without finally reaching it.

In the interreligious encounter one may feel threatened or forced to take a defensive position. In this case, one sticks to absolute truth claims, denying truth in the approach of others to what transcends daily life. With a different attitude, one may try to strengthen one's own viewpoint in interaction with the other, without denying that he too searches for what is ineffable. In a further step in the direction of an interreligious religiosity, one may confirm the other in his search for truth, sincerely desiring that he make progress in his own way towards the Higher Reality.

In dialogue there is frequently a shift of the boundaries of one's own tradition in the search for truth. One may become influenced or inspired by others. Eventually one combines a set of cultures and integrates elements from different lifestyles in order to realise one's own personal religiosity. Mixed forms of religiosity are not infrequent today. One may revive one's own religion, reinterpret it, or even re-imagine it. One finally may look for an all-inclusive 'new we' where nobody hurts or disturbs the other but instead all gladly accept other lifestyles.[3]

## Dialogue as Successful Meeting

If interreligious dialogue is a specific way of being in dialogue, we have to reflect upon the essence of dialogue. Dialogue or genuine conversation exists when one allows his own monologue to be interrupted by the other. In one of his *War Notebooks*, Lévinas makes the following remark: "Do I interrupt you? – No. Meaning: one always interrupts."[4] Being in dialogue means allowing the other to interrupt your own thoughts. Eminent examples of such dialogue as a chain of interruptions are to be found in the Talmudic tradition, where people discuss together and reach conclusions on the basis of rational positions, with preservation of every deviating opinion. Although in the Talmud decisions are made, the opinions that are not accepted are never blotted out and the names of the people who are involved in the ongoing dialogue are always mentioned. The Talmudic discussions are therefore exemplary of meeting successfully.

An authentic dialogue leads to a situation in which one is challenged by the other; one does not know a priori what will come out of the conversation. In a real conversation, one is forced to review one's own earlier positions and (elements of) traditional views. One may have things to say about one's own way to the Transcendent, without 'teaching' or 'preaching'. Above all, others may have things to say about the Ineffable that one has not heard before and that could be of relevance for one's own position.

## Presuppositions for Dialogue

The multicultural and complex religious situation in Western Europe and in other parts of the world demands a reflection on the presuppositions of a real interreligious dialogue. In the following I will spell out some of these presuppositions.

The teaching of three Jewish masters of thought come to my mind. I consider their ideas on dialogue to be highly inspirational for present day interreligious dialogue and for the construction of a growing theology in the plural. These

---

3   Kalsky, M. (2007) Embracing Diversity. Reflections on the Transformation of Christian Identity. In: *Studies in Interreligious Dialogue*, 221–231; Id. (forthcoming) Multiple Religious Identities and the Logic of Diversity. In: F. Fällmand & Y. Xusheng (Eds.) *The Challenge of Multiple Identities: Sino-European Perspectives on Religion and Society* New York: Peter Lang.

4   Lévinas, E. (2009) *Carnets de captivité suivi de Écrits sur la captivité et Notes philosophiques diverses* Paris: Bernard Grasset/IMEC, 83. "Je vous interromps? – Non. C'est-à-dire on interrompt toujours."

masters are Martin Mordechai Buber, Emmanuel Lévinas, and Abraham Joshua Heschel. What is common to the thoughts of these three towering spiritual persons is that they do not concentrate upon contents or dogmatic elements in religions. They are not interested in creeds as such, but in faith, and in approaches to the Absolute. They favour a novel attitude that allows people to listen carefully to others, who also organise their lives around what is beyond pure reason. The Ineffable, beyond the boundaries of pure reason, always remains beyond our grasp. Yet, these three masters highlight that the *noumenon* of Higher Reality may be approached in the mystery of inter-subjective meeting.

Further, Buber, Heschel, and Lévinas remind us that all religions have the function of creating holy peace. Holy wars were commonplace in the past. Holy peace is our goal in the present. In the meeting with others, one should not be naïve: hatred and biased ideas are still present. However, according to the three thinkers I have chosen in order to discuss dialogue, all religions will have to save humankind from its own destruction, and all religions have the task of saving the human soul.

## The Relevance of Presence in Martin Buber

Buber's philosophy as written down in *I and Thou* conceives of the dialogue with other human beings as leading to the uncovering of a depth, in which one receives a glimpse of the eternal Thou.[5] If one relates holistically to the other, not in a partial or objectifying manner, one overcomes the traditional subject-object scheme and enters into a meeting with another subject. The I becomes I-you in relation to the other: in the relationship, the I becomes an I committed to the other in pure presence. This I as I-you is to be distinguished from an I as I-it , who is relating to the other in a partial way, using, classifying, and objectifying him. Buber was concerned about the steady growth of I-it and he wanted to promote the emergence of I-you, of what he calls the 'between-man' (*Zwischenmensch*). Eventually, a mutuality may come into being, changing the relationship (*Beziehung*) into a meeting (*Begegnung*).

Buber did not immediately apply his dialogical thought to the interreligious dialogue for the simple reason that he was more interested in religiosity than in religions. However, the third part of his *I and Thou* points to the necessity of religions, which all create "a new form of God in the world" to the degree that they relate to their living source and force, the ever present Thou.[6] Human beings may not always be present, for it occurs that I am present and make the other present or that the other makes me present and that I am less present. There is also the Divine gift to human beings who may be present to each other.

---

5    Buber, M. (1970) *I and Thou* trans. Walter Kaufmann, New York: Charles Scribner's Sons, 113.
6    Ibid., 166.

But only the eternal Thou is always present and therefore He is the ontological ground for human existence.

One may learn from Buber that one really meets another human being only when one is present for the other, making him present without preconceived ideas, without classifying and objectifying, and without functionalising or admonishing him. Such an attitude and the realisation of the "between-man" are cornerstones for the realisation of interreligious meetings and theologies.

## Emmanuel Lévinas' Concept of Difference

Lévinas had a quite different philosophy than Buber. He did not have the intention of correcting him, but rather he started with the idea of the Infinite in the finite other.[7] He focused upon an aspect of the relationship that might be of utmost importance for a sound understanding of the interreligious dialogue. Lévinas made it clear that relationship is only possible on the basis of the recognition of the exteriority and alterity of the other, without expecting reciprocity. The infinite demand from the other urges me to respond. Like Gilles Deleuze,[8] Lévinas wrote about absolute difference that is never to be neutralised. In his view, difference is not opposed to sameness, which would put both terms in a common overarching category. In Lévinas' ethical metaphysics, difference – alterity or exteriority – is the main constituent of any relationship. In other words: I am only relating to the other's difference in respect for him, in obedience to

---

7   Lévinas, E. (1969) *Totality and Infinity: An Essay on Exteriority* trans. Alphonso Lingis, Pittsburgh: Duquesne University Press, 68–69: "One may however, ask if the thou-saying does not place the other in a reciprocal relation, and if this reciprocity is primordial. On the other hand, the I-Thou relation in Buber retains a formal character: it can unite man to things as much as man to man. The I-Thou formalism does not determine any concrete structure. The I-Thou is an event, a shock, a comprehension, but does not enable us to account for (except as an aberration, a fall, or a sickness) a life other than friendship: economy, the search for happiness, the representational relation with things. They remain, in a sort of disdainful spiritualism, unexplored and unexplained. This work does not have the ridiculous pretension of 'correcting' Buber on these points. It is placed in a different perspective, by starting with the idea of the Infinite".

8   Deleuze, G. (2009) *Difference and Repetition* trans. Paul Patton, London/New York: Continuum. In this work, first published in 1968, Deleuze pleaded for "a thought without images" (*une pensée sans images*) (208). In his critique of the "I think" which implies a conceiving, judging, imagining, remembering, and perceiving I, "difference is crucified" (174). In the representing I, "only that which is identical, similar, analogous or opposed can be considered different: difference becomes an object of representation always in relation to a conceived identity, a judged analogy, an imagined opposition or a perceived similitude". Deleuze's "thought without images" is not a representing, recognizing, and reproducing thought, in which difference is finally neutralised. His "thought without images" and his effort to write about difference as that which "is not and cannot be thought in itself, so long as it is subject of the requirements of representation" (330) run parallel to Lévinas' explicitly ethical reflections on an alterity that resists a mastering, totalizing thought and provokes the exposition of the I to the other, in responsibility.

the infinite, ethical demand, "Thou shalt not kill", coming from his naked face. Lévinas's insight made it possible to think about God in terms of Infinity, urging us to act and to answer the other's call. This is of extreme importance in the construction of a future dialogical theology. It seems to me that a pluralistic, or better, interreligious theology is more than a science. It is first of all wisdom that discusses a prescriptive or normative element: the uniqueness of every human being who asks to be listened to, honored, and respected.

It is not enough to respect differences between human beings when it comes to interreligious meetings. Lévinas taught us that what really makes a difference in the meeting is the ethical, non-indifferent response to the alterity of the other, who is never to be neutralised by my own totality. Exclusivists, but also inclusivists, totalise the other. Pluralists are liberal, their adagio is "live and let live". In itself the pluralist, liberal position is good, but still far removed from the position of the dialogical person who finds his own uniqueness in the response to the appeal and challenge coming from the other.

## Heschel's "No religion is an Island"

In his famous 1965 lecture "No Religion Is an Island", the influential neo-hassidic thinker Abraham Joshua Heschel formulated some basic thoughts that are of great importance for interreligious dialogue.[9] Heschel considers that what is needed in the dialogue between religions is reverence and humility. Although, like Franz Rosenzweig, Heschel concentrated mainly upon the Jewish-Christian dialogue, one may understand his prophetic words on dialogue in reference to other religions and worldviews as well. His voice remains of crucial importance for the theory and praxis of present day interreligious dialogue.

In "No Religion Is an Island" Heschel writes, parallel to Buber, that religion is not an end in itself, but is a means; religion becomes idolatrous if it becomes an end. God the Creator and the Lord of history is above all, and therefore "to equate religion and God is idolatry".[10] Heschel warned that one should not confuse religions with God Himself: God as perfect reality is not religion, which is our imperfect understanding of the ineffable reality. It is a fact that

---

9  Heschel, A. J. (1966) No Religion is an Island. In: *Union Seminary Quarterly Review*, 21 (2), 117–134. Heschel's inaugural lecture as Harry Emerson Fosdick Visiting Professor at Union Theology Seminary, New York, was reprinted in: H. Kasimow & B. Sherwin (Eds.) (1991) *No Religion Is an Island: Abraham Joshua Heschel and Interreligious Dialogue* New York: Orbis, 3–22 and in: S. Heschel (Ed.) (1996) *Moral Grandeur and Spiritual Audacity: Essays by Abraham Joshua Heschel* New York: Farrar, Straus and Giroux, 235–250. With his thoughts on theopaschism, on a suffering God, Heschel inspired Christian theologians such as Juergen Moltmann and Eberhard Juengel. Heschel, S. (2007) The Revival of Theopaschism in Post-World War II Theology. In: H. Pedaya & E. Meir (Eds.) *Judaism, Topics, Fragments, Faces, Identities. Jubilee Volume in Honor of Rivka Horwitz* Beer-Sheva: Ben-Gurion University Press, 69–86.

10 Heschel (1966), 243.

many in the past and even in the present are ready to be killed for their faith. On another level, there were and are people, ready to kill for it. Putting a separation between religions as houses of God and God Himself as did Heschel prevents one from absolutising one's own religion. In his depth-theology, Heschel made his listening and reading public sensitive to the Divine by developing a sense of indebtedness, wonder, and mystery in them. For him, respect for the faith of the other was more than a political or social imperative, it was the demand that follows from the fact that God is greater than religion and that each theology is finally rooted in what he called 'depth theology', which provides a common ground for all religious people.[11]

In a world in which a new materialism and empiricism function as contemporary glamorous religions with hotels and malls as new temples, these words are a real remedy. There is more than what the eyes see and than what one may possess. Religions in Heschel's view have a soteriological function in that they fight against lack of solidarity, indifference, poverty, and injustice. Heschel's own fight for the human rights of blacks in the United States and his courageous anti-Vietnam War position were the result of his deep religious engagement. Like Buber and Lévinas, he was unable to perceive of a relationship with God without a relationship with other human beings.

## Interreligious Learning

A growing 'theology in the plural' revolutionises our thoughts. We are no longer talking solely about religions living side-by-side as 'sons' of the one Father-King, as was the case in Lessing's well-known ring parable.[12] There are more than three religions; there are world religions with millions of followers and there are numerous small, regional religions with few adherents. All religions are, in Heschel's words, "the will of God". The anthropological consequence of this is well formulated by Paul Knitter of the Union Theological Seminary in New York, who writes that "to be religious today means to be religious interreligiously".[13]

---

11  For an account of Heschel's contribution to the interreligious dialogue see inter alia Kaplan, E. K. (2009) 'Seeking God's Will together': Heschel's Depth Theology as Common Ground. In: S. Krajewski & A. Lipszyc (Eds.) *Abraham Joshua Heschel: Philosophy, Theology and Interreligious Dialogue* (Juedische Kultur 21) Wiesbaden: Harrassowitz, 188–195; Kasimow, H. (2009) Heschel's View of Religious Diversity. In: Krajewski & Lipszyc, 196–201.

12  The poet-philosopher Gotthold Ephraim Lessing supported liberal positions such as that of Hermann Samuel Reimarus in his struggle against the dogmatic parson Goeze. Lessing told his famous parable of the three rings in *Nathan the Wise,* which appeared in 1779.

13  Knitter (2008), 117.

## Translation, Untranslatability, Difference and Trans-Difference

I have mentioned that diversity in approaching the Ultimate is not only to be tolerated, it is to be celebrated. In different religions, one may frequently hear the claim that only its adherents can understand what a particular religion is about: only Jews understand Judaism, only Christians understand Christianity, and so on. I do not agree with this standpoint, since I believe that communication between people is possible and, therefore, notions and ideas belonging to one religion are to a certain extent comparable to and translatable into terms and ideas of other religions. True, one has to be careful, since the same words may have different meanings in different religions. I also admit that there are untranslatable elements in one's own religion. Yet, the uniqueness of each and every human being does not prevent the lofty possibility of communication. On the contrary: it is the uniqueness and alterity of every person that makes possible what I call a 'trans-different' attitude in which one affirms *and* transcends differences.[14] As Perry Schmidt-Leukel aptly remarked in the Hamburg *Academy of World Religions*, from the perspective of reaching out to others, a Muslim may say to a Buddhist that Buddha is a prophet and a Buddhist may say that Mohammed is an enlightened person, a Bodhisattva. It is this openness and readiness to understand the others in one's own terms and also to translate one's own words into words understandable to the other, that make it possible that both are starting to listen to each other. Franz Rosenzweig was a master of translation. To his beloved Gritli Rosenstock-Huessy, a Christian woman, he explained that for a Jewish family, Shabbat evening is something extraordinary; Shabbat evening, he writes, is a kind of family festival (*Familienfest*), like an anniversary.[15] Franz made the singularly Jewish language understandable to Gritli. This was possible because of their openness to each other in trans-difference. Rosenzweig developed an entire hermeneutical method in order to explain his own world in Gritli's words. He invited her, for instance, to wish him "a good year" on Rosh Hashanah.[16] To his cousin Hans Ehrenberg, who converted to Christianity, he explained the specific Jewish reality of learning Talmud together, of '*lernen*': he designated it as a "sacrament".[17] *Lernen* is of course not a sacrament, but by translating it into terms that his cousin could understand, Rosenzweig's explanation of this particular Jewish reality points to

14  Meir, E. (2011) *Quo vadis, religio*? Religion as Terror and Violence or as Contribution to Civilisation. A Plea for Trans-Difference. In: Id. *Identity Dialogically Constructed* (Jerusalemer Texte 4) Nordhausen: Traugott Bautz, 10–27.

15  Rühle, I. & Mayer, R. (Eds.) (2002) *Franz Rosenzweig: Die "Gritli"-Briefe. Briefe an Margrit Rosenstock-Huessy* with a preface of Rafael Rosenzweig, Tübingen: Bilam Verlag, 568 f.; Meir, E. (2006) *Letters of Love: Franz Rosenzweig's Spiritual Biography and Oeuvre in Light of the Gritli Letters* New York: Peter Lang, 16.

16  Rühle & Mayer (2002), 657.

17  Rosenzweig, R. & Rosenzweig-Scheinmann, E. (Eds.) (1979) *Briefe und Tagebücher. 2. Band. 1918–1929* (Franz Rosenzweig. Der Mensch und sein Werk. Gesammelte Schriften I), in collaboration with Bernhard Casper, Haag: Martinus Nijhoff, 728.

a readiness to create a common, trans-different world. The art of translating and the readiness to share a common world, with all the differences that exist within it, is crucial in interreligious dialogue.

## Admitting Negative Points, Adopting Maximum Interpretations, Making Changes

All religions have verses and sayings that do not contribute to dialogue between religions. It is not difficult to find passages in various religious texts that hurt the outsider. This is a stumbling block to dialogue. Yet, there is always the possibility of reinterpreting those passages in a dialogical way.

In order to open up specific terms and to promote dialogue, one may adopt a strategy such as that of Yusef Whagid, for instance, who gives the broadest possible interpretation to classical Islamic categories such as *umma*, *ijtihad*, and *shura*, interpreted respectively as human community, juridical discussion, and dialogue. In his *Conceptions of Islamic Education*[18] he offers a refined way of combining religion, issues of democratic citizenship, and cosmopolitism, and opts for a maximalist Islamic education in South Africa.[19] By widening specific concepts in his maximalist interpretation, Waghid succeeds in showing the compatibility of Islam with modern values and the relevance of Islam for modern society. For Waghid, Islamic education in a maximal approach means that one actively reaches a dialogical exchange of meaning-making. He is conscious that in some Muslim communities indoctrination, ready-made answers, and uncritical listening is the norm, and talking back, questioning, and relating to the views of others is not looked upon favourably. For him, however, recognition of the presence of the other, with whom I may disagree, and the connection to him, is the prerequisite for any education. His anti-parochial view and his opening up of the particular to the universal are exemplary for all religions that seek to become relevant in the promotion of respect for human life, responsible action, and democracy.

Sometimes, as Luther has said, it will be necessary to take certain terms "to the bath", in order to purify them from connotations that are unfavourable to interreligious dialogue. It is important to keep in mind that no religion remains the same throughout the course of history. Many changes occurred. Different approaches to Ultimate Reality are subject to historical changes. If one accepts the historical conditions of different religions, one may develop a greater flexibility in order to make courageous changes in one's own religion. Participating in a living tradition is not only preserving it, but also renewing it and eventually criticising it. It was Buber's ethical sensitivity and his dialogical understanding

---

18  Waghid, Y. (2001) *Conceptions of Islamic Education. Pedagogical Framings* (Global Studies in Education, 3), New York: Peter Lang, 15–33.

19  In South Africa, there is a minority of Muslims, about 2 millions, who represent 2% of the population.

of the Bible that prompted him in a conversation with the orthodox Jew Markus Cohn to disapprove of Samuel's killing of Agag the Amalekite (1 Sam. 15). Presented with the dilemma of choosing between God and the Bible, he chose God. He adopted an anti-bibliolatric standpoint and favoured King Saul, who spared the life of Agag over the prophet Samuel, who killed the prince of the Amalekites. Buber sincerely believed that the prophet Samuel misunderstood God.[20]

One still may construct a theology or intellectual reflection on one's own faith, but the time has come to construct a theology of the faith of all.[21] Conversions remain possible, but lesser changes should also be conceivable.[22] In dialogue, the limitation of one's view will become clear and – in the best case scenario – one will develop the virtue of humility.


## A New We?[23]


A radical strategy is followed by Manuela Kalsky, who proposes not to reinterpret traditions, but to re-imagine them. In her opinion, one has to take into account the 'opacity of the other', not merely to pin him down to a past, whatever that may be, but to stimulate his sense of belonging. In order to create a 'new we', one should accept from the start that there are always differences. In Kalsky's view, one counters the desire for a well-defined, nationalistic identity that quickly becomes xenophobic through the recognition of individually constructed (eventually "hybrid" or mixed) identities that all belong to a 'new we'.

In Dutch society, Kalsky proposes to replace a 'logic of unity' by a 'logic of diversity', in which differences are perceived not as a threat, but as contributing to a 'new we' that invites people of all types to develop a sense of belonging.

---

20  Friedman, M. (1991) *Encounter on the Narrow Ridge. A Life of Martin Buber* New York: Paragon House, 287–288.

21  Smith, W. C. (1989) *Towards a World Theology* Mayknoll, NY: Orbis, 125: "Theology is critical intellectualisation of (and for) faith, and of the world as known in faith; and what we seek is a theology that will interpret the history of our race in a way that will give intellectual expression to our faith, the faith of all of us, and to our modern perception of the world."

22  Hick, J. (1980) *God Has Many Names: Britain's New Religious Pluralism* London and Basingstoke: Macmillan, 85: "[I]nter-religious dialogue undertaken just like that, as two (or more) people bearing mutual witness to their own faith, each in the firm conviction that his is the final truth and in hope of converting the other, can only result either in conversion or in hardening of differences –occasionally the former but more often the latter. In order for dialogue to be mutually fruitful, lesser changes than total conversion must be possible and must be hoped for on both (or all) sides."

23  See note 3 and Kalsky's online web project http://www.nieuwwij.nl/ ("*New We*"), last accessed December 10, 2013.

## Radical Otherness, Differences, and Trans-Difference

An interreligious theology serves the dialogue between people, who remain different. Frequently, one objects to a theology in the plural that it does not take into account one's specificity. However, as Schmidt-Leukel communicated to me in a private correspondence, differences may be compatible in the interreligious dialogue and theology, and the question is therefore how one interprets these differences.

As I mentioned previously, in my eyes, there is a radical difference in every human being, which adds to the interreligious dialogue an eminently ethical dimension. It is the ethical demand of the other, who wants to be taken seriously in his approach to the unutterable, which makes dialogue truly human.

Something new can be learned from the other in his approach of the Divine. Additionally, if I do not open myself up to the other's understanding of the Ultimate, I may miss an aspect of religiosity that is relevant to my own religious life. The standpoint of supremacy in which – God willing – all would have to be like myself is absurd. Such a standpoint is totalising and hurts the uniqueness of every other person. The diversity of human beings as well as one's own self-understanding demand that we leave behind a narrow confessionalism that does not contribute to an intercultural and interreligious dialogue concerning what touches the depth of our human existence.

## Three Final Remarks

It seems to me that one of the main problems in the interreligious dialogue is that one is perceived of or perceives the other as a representative and not as a unique person who has his own specific way of approaching what is beyond pure reason. In the construction of one's (religious) identity, one is not merely a representative of some grand narrative. One is always a unique person, called upon to participate with other unique persons in the dialogue about what ultimately surpasses the boundaries of pure reason. Human beings are more than institutions; they do not have to sacrifice themselves to institutions, although institutions are not necessarily negative entities. One is first of all a human being and concrete, never a mere representative.

Secondly, dialogical theology is not a kind of syncretism or another name for a unifying global religion. As I have noted, interreligious theology takes into account diversity, but does not limit itself to multiculturalism, in which one exists alongside another. Dialogical theology is rather the intellectual account of true intercultural and interreligious meetings.

Finally, dialogue between religions is necessary in order to establish an enduring peace between people, races, and nations. If one knows and appreciates the other's religion, a basis is formed for a coexistence that cannot be left to an elite of intellectuals or to economists and politicians.

# Dialogue in Christianity

*Reinhold Bernhardt*

# Jesus Christ as a Stumbling Block in Interreligious Dialogue?

"Dialogue in Christianity" – the title of this section of the present volume – is somewhat ambiguous. It can mean "*inter*religious dialogue as practiced by Christians". But it also can mean: "*intra-Christian* dialogue on interreligious encounter". Such an understanding leads us towards what is called the 'theology of religions'.

'Theology of religions' is an intra-Christian endeavour addressing theoretical conditions required for the possibility of interreligious dialogue. It explores the Christian self-understanding vis-à-vis other religious traditions and reflects on the transformations of that self-understanding as a result of the encounter. Thus it goes hand in hand with the practice of interreligious dialogue and is as controversial within Christianity as the project of interreligious dialogue itself.

Interreligious encounters are not exclusively and probably not even primarily regulated by the *theological* mind-set of the Christian dialogue-partner. *Psychological, social* and *cultural* conditions are at least equally important factors which shape the motivations and expectations, the view of one's own and of the other's religiosity and the style of communication. But the way the dialogue-partners approach and understand the contents and the truth-claims of their faith-traditions also influences their attitudes towards the religious other.

In the following considerations on Christology and on the understanding of 'truth' in the Christian faith, I will suggest interpretations which, while intended to be fully in accordance with main strands of the theological tradition, lay the foundations for a sincere encounter with adherents of other faith-traditions.

## 1.  Christology and Interreligious Dialogue

At the theological level it matters a lot if – for example – the Christian understands Jesus Christ primarily as the universal Logos of God, which "was in the beginning with God" (John 1:1) and which "was the true Light, which lighteth every man that cometh into the world" (John 1:9) or if he/she focusses on Paul's proclamation of the "word of the cross and the resurrection" as decisive for the justification of the believers. A Christology which derives from a Johannine universalism will likely pave the way for interreligious dialogue more effectively than a Christology which proceeds from the Pauline 'staurocentrism' (centrality of the cross). That may explain why Protestants with their emphasis on the theology of the apostle of Paul tend to be more hesitant to dispose their faith in mutual openness to believers of other faith-traditions.

To be prepared for such a dialogical openness not only requires openheartedness at a psychological level, but also a theological mind-set which supports (or at least does not suppress) such an attitude. In most cases that mind-set is not brought into conscious awareness in terms of an elaborated theological system. It functions more implicitly than explicitly. Nevertheless it shapes a persons' attitude towards adherents of other religious traditions.

That applies to both branches of Christology: the interpretation of the *person* of Jesus Christ ("who was/is he?") and the determination of his *soteriological relevance* ("what did he do in favour of humankind?"). The first question traditionally was answered by the doctrine of the 'two natures' of Jesus Christ, the second question by the doctrine of his 'three offices'.

The doctrine of the 'three offices' can be illustrated by referring to different christological-soteriological approaches: When the Enlightenment writer Gotthold Ephraim Lessing understands Jesus as a teacher of humanism, his 'Jesuology' is focused on the proclamation of Jesus as it is reported in the Gospels, which means on the '*prophetic* office'. When secondly the theologians of a 'Protestant orthodoxy' – following the biblical Epistle to the Hebrews – stress the significance of Jesus' self-sacrifice on the cross for the redemption of humanity, they claim the '*priestly* office' to be central. And when, thirdly, Eastern ('Orthodox') and Indian Christians worship Christ as the ruler over the whole cosmos – drawing on the 'cosmic Christology' of the biblical Epistles to the Colossians and the Ephesians – they emphasise the '*kingly* office'.

The three 'offices' must never be entirely separated, but every interpretation of the soteriological relevance of Jesus Christ tends to approach one vertex of the triangle and be at greater distance from the others. This way of 'locating' soteriology can have an impact of the believer's attitude towards non-Christians. Each preference nurtures a specific disposition towards interreligious encounter. Stressing the *proclamation* of Jesus which is centred on the reign of God as a reign of justice and grace tends to lead into a dialogue with other theistic and even non-theistic religions on ethical questions. Stressing the salvific *sacrifice* of Jesus as vicarious atonement, on the other hand, may prepare for a dialogue on the question of redemption, but will produce a more mission-oriented communication intending to proclaim the good news of the salvation in Jesus Christ alone. Stressing the cosmic *rule* of the exalted Christ can lead to a dialogue on eschatological issues and inviting adherents of other faiths to be partners on the pilgrimage to that (common?) end of history.

Obviously it is not possible or useful to correlate a dialogical attitude unilaterally to specific christological-soteriological concepts while assuming that others lead into apologetic or missionary patterns of communication. However, those concepts can display tendencies towards one or the other direction. They can influence the agenda of an interreligious encounter inasmuch as they determine the thinking and the behaviour of the Christian partner.

I will now turn to the interpretation of the *person* of Jesus Christ and its consequences for interreligious encounters. In this part of my contribution, I will discuss the question whether claiming Jesus Christ to be 'vere Deus' – as the doctrine of the 'two natures' of Jesus Christ teaches – will make an interreligious encounter impossible or turn it into a one-way communication aimed at proclaiming this divine truth and converting the dialogue partner. Does the designation of Jesus Christ as "true God" necessarily entail an exclusivist attitude toward non-Christian religions?

Through these reflections, I hope to build a bridge for a theological dialogue between the adherents of different religious traditions. As far as I can see there is something like a structural analogy between all religions which refer to a transcendent reality manifesting in the world. They all focus in different ways on the mediation between two levels of reality: divine and human, supernatural and natural, eternal and historical. In the central symbols of mediations, the two 'natures' approach closely without mingling.

- According to Islamic understanding, the written Qur'an is a copy of the heavenly Qur'an. Thus the Divine has appeared in history, the revelation used historic means, had historical occasions and requires historical explication and application. Of course, most Muslims are not inclined to regard the written Qur'an as historic in origin and thus in nature, but it mediates between God and humanity.
- According to Mahayana Buddhism the 'Nirmana-kaya' (transformation body) is the manifestation of the 'Dharma-kaya' (body of enlightenment). Some scholars of Buddhism take this as an analogy to the concept of 'incarnation'[1] which expresses the in-historisation of the divine word. I will leave open the question whether it is possible not only to speak of a 'revelation' but of an 'incarnation' of dharma in Buddhism. This would certainly be an analogical mode of speaking. However, a kind of mediation of the dharma into history is obviously assumed at least in Mahayana Buddhism. Another way of applying the doctrine of the two natures analogously refers to the teaching that the Buddha-nature impersonates itself in humans.

According to Christian theology the 'logos asarkos' (the universal divine nature of Christ) is incarnated in human nature as the 'logos ensarkos' (the human logos). The question how to understand the relation between the two 'natures' is crucial for Christology, for theology in general, and as a consequence also for theology of religions. Even within Protestantism the ways of relating the Divine and the human nature differ. While the Lutheran tradition emphasises that the logos *has become* a human being, the reformed tradition claims that in Jesus Christ the logos performed an "*assumption* of the flesh". As a consequence, Lutheran theology focused more clearly on Jesus Christ as the one and only self-mediation of God, while reformed theologians like Zwingli were open to thinking that God could have manifested his spirit outside the revelation in Christ, for example in Greek philosophers.

---

1   Schmidt-Leukel, P. (2009) *Transformation by Integration. How Inter-faith Encounter changes Christianity* London: SCM, 124 ff.

If God's *logos* has become flesh in the person of Jesus Christ alone – if the title "vere Deus" can be applied uniquely to him – then there can be no salvific relation to the Divine which is *not* mediated through him. It should follow that the religion which bears his name and mediates this unique relationship between the Divine and the human is the *true* religion. Does not such a truth-claim inevitably devalue the truth-claims put forth by other faith traditions?

John Hick has spelled out the problem clearly: "If Jesus was literally God incarnate, and if it is by his death alone that men can be saved, and by their response to him alone that they can appropriate that salvation, then the only doorway to eternal life is the Christian faith. It would follow from this that the large majority of the human race so far have not been saved. But is it credible that the loving God and Father of all men has decreed that only those who have been born within one particular thread of human history shall be saved?"[2]

I will here seek to explore a way of christological thinking that does not inevitably lead to such a christocentric soteriological exclusivism.

## 2.    Two Natures as Two Relations – Revelation as Representation

My first suggestion is to understand Christ's twofold nature not in an essentialist manner, but as two relations. Thus it is not to be understood as an ontological co-existence of two incompatible forms of being: the being of God on the one hand and the being of the human on the other. It makes more sense to understand 'vere Deus' as the recognition of the intensity which permeated Jesus' relation with God, the intensity of relationship that binds him with God. A relational interpretation of the 'vere Deus' allows us to stress not only the unity, but also the difference between the divine and the human nature, between the human being and God. Jesus distinguished himself clearly from God, as is apparent in a number of New Testament passages. He was clearly most conscious of his one-ness with God, but at the same time he rejected any attempts to assign divine titles to him. Rather, he repeatedly directed attention away from himself and towards the Father, to whom alone all honour and glory are due (John 8:50). This polarity between oneness and differentness corresponds to a distinction which is significant for the theology of religions: the distinction between God as the Revealer and the self-communication of God (the revelation).

In fully realizing this distinction, in fully acknowledging that the God "who dwells in unapproachable light" (I Tim 6:16) remains an unfathomable mystery *even in his revelation,* it becomes possible to believe, and to expect, that God has revealed himself in other historical instances and experiences as well. God's revelation in Christ does not exhaust *God's* being – which is inexhaustible. Jesus Christ 'reflects' and presents – *re*presents – God. In this way, a salvific relation

---

2    Hick, J. (1977) *The Myth of God Incarnate* Philadelphia, PA: Westminster, 180.

to God becomes possible for his adherents in the encounter with Christ, but that does not mean that there can be no *self-presentation,* no *self-representation* of God *extra Christum* (beyond Christ). Just as a *human* being's 'self-revelations' cannot exhaust the mystery of his person, so too *God's* own self-revelation in Christ does not exhaust his *being.* This enduring difference between the revealer and the revelation was already recognised by Thomas Aquinas: "Though the divine nature in the Person of the Son was wholly united with the Son's human nature, nevertheless this could not encompass, could not incorporate, as it were, the entirety of the power of the Divinity."[3]

Thus my second suggestion is to take the idea of 'representation' as Christology's central concept. In acknowledging that the being of God is inexhaustible and thus transcends any and all revelations, we can assume that God might also engage symbolic appearances of other religions to represent his presence. In acknowledging this, a powerful theological motivation for an open encounter with the followers of other faith-forms emerges. Indeed, it may well turn out that God's call will be heard precisely from 'over there' – from 'foreign parts', as it were.

I dare not say that there are divine revelations equal in value to the revelation in Christ. Like adherents of other faith traditions, Christians cannot take up an epistemological stand- und viewpoint that would allow them to make such a statement. The biblical testimony is wholly centred on Christ. For Christians, phenomena of other religious traditions can be seen as rays of the divine light which – according to the Christian faith – shines in Christ only in the 'Christ-perspective'. But if Christ does indeed embody the universal 'Word', the *logos* of creation and salvation, it then follows that this 'Word', expressing and representing God's mighty presence, extends *beyond* the Christian tradition.

I am hesitant to address the non-Christian religions as 'ways to salvation'. From what perspective could one make such a judgement? This would require adopting the absolutist perspective of an omniscient observer. The same applies for the claim that Christianity alone is the way to salvation. Just as it is an irresponsible, almost ideological, generalisation to describe Christianity as the only true religion, so it is an equally nonsensical prejudice, because it is so utterly abstract, simply to regard all religions side by side as ways to salvation.

By contrast, it seems meaningful and justified to me to suppose that God could find ways to human beings and human beings could find ways to God in each of the great religions, ways which transform and transcend and save their lives. It makes a considerable difference whether we say that the religions are ways to salvation or that there are ways to salvation *in* the religions. The latter statement takes account of the fact that religions also encompass disastrous paths. It also takes the limitations of our perspectives seriously. As an empirical judgement, it holds only "as far as we can see". And thirdly, this judgement is hypothetical. It has to demonstrate its truth in the encounter with concrete

---

3   STh III, 10, 1, ad. 2.

religious phenomena. The assumption that there can be ways to salvation *in* the religions is not meant to be a theological judgement but a theological proviso which reminds the consciousness of the Christian that God's ways for his creation are ultimately unfathomable. This does not call the unique Christian path to God into question, merely the claim that it is the only way.

Let us now return to the theological interpretation of Jesus Christ. The idea of representation seems to me to be particularly suited as the key concept of a Christology which holds fast to the divinity of Christ while not limiting divine revelation to Christ alone. It allows us to understand and speak of Jesus Christ in a personal and relational mode, both as the representative of God amid human beings and as the representative of authentic humanity. No claim to exclusivity is inherent in this. A Christology which develops out of this concept of representation might indeed bring about the kind of theologically grounded openness which would, in dialogue, open the way for the work of defining and configuring a relationship to other religions.

I am using the term 'representation' in the sense of 'making present': Jesus made present the Presence of God. He embodied this presence so intensely that he was called the 'image of the invisible God' (Col 1:15; cf. II Cor 4:4). Because Jesus was 'inhabited' by God, suffused with God's Spirit, he embodied 'God-presence' and conveyed it to those who became his followers. As a person who lived – utterly and totally – through the relationship with God, he personified authentically human being: wholly open for and receptive to the God who is the ground of Creation.

In this light then, representation means more than serving as the 'delegate' for another, more than acting and speaking in the name of one who is himself absent. No, precisely in representation we find the expression of that which the concept of revelation is meant to express: that is, not a communication from a God who himself is not present, but on the contrary, the mode of and vehicle of his presence, of his effective *Being-Here*.[4]

The concept of representation has a number of advantages:

(a) In contrast to the long-standing tendency to emphasise the divine nature of Christ while underplaying the human nature, the representational model allows a conception of the personhood of Jesus in which we can recognise both relationships equally.

(b) Whereas the classical 'dual-nature' Christology has emphatically stressed the idea of 'union' of the two natures, the representational model allows us to envision a union in differentness.

(c) The model of participation of being, as formulated in Chalcedon, allows virtually no room for anything other than an exclusivist Christology – that is: God's Word, equal in nature to God himself, has in Christ (and only in Christ) become united with human nature. In contrast, the representational

---

4   On the concept of *representation* see: Schaede, S. (2004) *Stellvertretung: Begriffsgeschicht-liche Studien zur Soteriologie* Tübingen: Mohr Siebeck, 171–238.

model, makes room for the distinction between that which is represented and the "event" of representation – in other words, between the symbolised content and the act of symbolisation, – we could say: between the Christ-content and the Christ-event.

Now what is it that is 'represented' in Jesus Christ? As I understand the New Testament testimony, this 'what' is God's all-embracing and unconditional grace and attentiveness. Wolfgang Pfüller defines the Christ-content as "limitless, self-offering love in radically trusting confidence in God and in the coming of God's kingdom"[5]; Hans Kessler understands the Christ-content as "true human being – human being entirely in accord with God's being".[6] This Christ-content becomes real in the Christ-event, but is not restricted to it; rather, it exists before the event, drawing it onward, and extends beyond it. The event 'represents' the communion between God and the human being which God has initiated and thereby makes it available.

The Christ-content is universal and extends beyond the Christ-event. Were it to be linked exclusively to the Christ-event, it would forfeit its universal significance. The historical representation in Jesus points to a reality which precedes the particular representation – while still being genuinely revealed in and by it.

With his well-known expression, "Jesus is the Christ, but Christ is not (only) Jesus"[7], Raimon Panikkar wants to distinguish the transhistorical reality of the cosmic Christ from the historical reality of Jesus of Nazareth *without* cutting them off from each other.[8] The 'Christ-reality' is to be de-historicised, as it were, no longer tied exclusively to a single historical instance. For Panikkar, this is not to "deny its historical facticity, but simply to no longer make its particular historicity equal to its reality".[9] Reality is 'more' than a series of events in history, and Christ-reality extends beyond the Christ-event. According to Panikkar, only in distinguishing them can we do justice to the universal dimension of 'Christ'. The universal dimension must be realised ever anew – in other words, it must become an 'event' once more: over and over again, in the most varied cultural and religious contexts, once again releasing its life-transforming

5    Pfüller, W. (2001) *Die Bedeutung Jesu im interreligiösen Horizont: Überlegungen zu einer religiösen Theorie in christlicher Perspektive* [Theologie 41] Münster: Lit, 208.

6    Kessler, H. (1995) Christologie. In: T. Schneider (Ed.) *Handbuch der Dogmatik* Düsseldorf: Patmos, vol. I, 392 ff.

7    Panikkar, R. (1981) *The Unknown Christ of Hinduism: Towards an Ecumenical Christophany* Bangalore.

8    For further discussion of this see also: von Sinner, R. (2003) *Reden vom dreieinigen Gott in Brasilien und Indien. Grundzüge einer ökumenischen Hermeneutik im Dialog mit Leonardo Boff und Raimon Panikkar* Tübingen: Mohr Siebeck, 302 ff.; Valluvassery, C. (2001) *Christus im Kontext und Kontext in Christus. Chalcedon und indische Christologie bei Raimon Panikkar und Samuel Rayan* Münster et al.: Lit, 142 ff.; Nitsche, B. (2008) *Gott – Welt – Mensch. Raimon Panikkars Gottesdenken – Paradigma für eine Theologie in interreligiöser Perspektive* Zürich: TVZ, 379–483, esp. 401 ff.

9    Panikkar, R. (1993) *Trinität. Über das Zentrum menschlicher Erfahrung* München: Kösel, 13.

power. Historical concreteness and universality by no means exclude each other; rather, they condition one another.The representational Christology which I prefer unites the Christ-reality with the Christ-event, but does not limit the former to the latter. That approach allows us to retain the truth claim inherent in the Christian Creed while not necessarily entailing the automatic rejection of the truth claims made by other religions.

The question of mediating the dimensions of the Divine and of the human could be an interesting topic for interreligious dialogue. Is there an assumed difference between the *content* of revelation and the *event* or historical *medium* in which the Divine is manifested or manifesting not only in the Christian faith, but also in other spiritual traditions? If the Divine is assumed to be wholly and totally present in the religious medium, what does that mean for assessing the truth-claims of other faith traditions for which this medium is not the normative core of the manifestation of the Divine?

## 3.    Truth-Claims of the Christian Faith

The distinction which I propose to make between the *content,* the *event,* and the historical *medium* of revelation has consequences for the understanding of religious truth claims, for claiming the truth of one own religious tenets and for relating it to truth claims of other religious traditions. With the following reflections, we turn from Christology as an issue of material dogmatics to the question of religious truth claims which is located at the more fundamental level of philosophical prolegomena of a theology of religions.

What does 'truth' mean in the Christian faith?

The certainty faith gives is not knowledge about facts of salvation that can be formulated as objective statements or dogma. Rather, it is existential trust in God as mediated by Jesus Christ and empowered by the Spirit of God. Understood that way, the truth of the Christian faith has nothing to do with religious imperialism. It has nothing to do with a sense of superiority which denies the truth of other certainties. It is a certainty, instead, which is existential. And an existential certainty exists in and with the people who live in it. It is not 'ab-solute', which means 'separated' from its bearer. It can never claim to be an *exclusive* expression of the one universal truth.

This (biblical) understanding of truth has enormous implications for the encounter with adherents of other Christian confessions, of other religions, or with people holding a non-religious view of the world. If Christians remain conscious that they do not simply possess the truth of God, but point to it as to a mystery which has been revealed – but revealed as a mystery – they will not restrict this truth to the media of their religion. They are entitled to believe in that truth as an authentic and fully salvific self-representation of God. But they have come to understand and formulate it through the specific route of their tradition and their history, and the sources from which they know this tradition and history. They cannot therefore claim those media to be the immediate truth of God.

It is precisely this difference between God's truth, which is too high for the believers to ever attain, and their sense of certainty of truth which is a reaching-out towards God's truth, which can open their minds for other religions' perspectives. The certainty of truth to which the believers refer does not have its basis or centre in itself, but points to something beyond and in this sense makes itself relative. This certainty is an expression of a truth which "passeth all understanding" (Php 4:7) and that includes all *religious* understanding. It is higher than any religious consciousness or religious practice. It includes the religious Other. According to Christian understanding, Muslims are also made in the image of God, just as in Islamic understanding, Christians carry a genuine revelation of God.

An understanding of the truth-claims of the Christian faith as personal and existential witnesses to the divine truth which exceeds religious understanding enables Christians to allow space for other certainties of the truth beside theirs. As personal truths about faith, love and hope, they can never be absolute, though for those who confess them they are unconditionally valid. These truths are bound to the persons, or the fellowships, of those who believe, love and hope, and thus even within the same religious tradition can be lived out in more or less different ways. With this consciousness, we can arrive at a fundamental acknowledgement of the different certainties there are in faith. And thus we act not simply out of an Enlightenment requirement to be tolerant. Our attitude grows from the insight formulated here about the nature of religious certainty.

Openness to dialogue requires a calm confidence in the foundations of one's own certainty of the truth, which also acknowledges how religious truth as personal certainty is, in the final analysis, always relative. Only a person who rests calmly in the truth they have understood and experienced can risk emptying themselves in order to understand the persons they are encountering in terms of the ground of the *other's* being. If there is uncertainty in faith, if there is fear of losing one's own grasp of the truth, or if there is a lack of trust in the truth of God which always lies beyond us, then a need to secure one's own religious identity through setting limits on contact can develop. Therefore, strengthening one's own certainty in faith is a prerequisite for openness to adherents of other faiths.

An open encounter between different certainties of religious truth includes the possibility that the certainties one takes into the encounter will be seriously questioned and could indeed be changed and expanded. The tradition held by others may come to appear in a new light, but so may one's own. This experience can be challenging, even perturbing, but it can also give the horizons of one's own faith and one's reflections on it a breadth and depth they did not have before.

I draw some conclusions from this understanding of the truth claims of the Christian faith.

1. The claim to *exclusiveness*, to being the sole truth, holds *within* this faith. It is part of the unconditional certainty about the truth for Christians. But as such, it remains related to faith and the confessional expressions of faith. That means that to say "Christ alone (solus Christus) is the way to God", "no man cometh unto the Father, but by him" (Joh 14:6) is to say something about the Christian's confession of Christ. It is not to state a universal abstract truth 'about', but a personal testimony 'to'. True as it is that God's self-event in Jesus Christ holds good not only for Christians, but for all men and women, it is also true that only to Christians does the fullness of the Spirit of God disclose itself solely in Christ. Of course this avenue is potentially open to all men and women, but those who do not take it need not necessarily be on the wrong path.

2. The claims to *universality* and *finality* are not to be related to the reality of Christianity as a religion within history, including the teaching of Jesus Christ. In them, attention is drawn to the eschatological dimension of God's revelation. They are and remain promise. Referring to Joachim Jeremias, Joseph Ratzinger points out that "in Jesus' own message universalism is … pure promise, as in the Old Testament".[10] Theo Sundermeier points out that in Paul, universalism belongs in the doxologies.[11] We are still on the way to a comprehensive realisation of the reality of God; it is provisionally given to us only as a hope, a pledge.

Understood this way, the claim to universality and finality, and even the claim to exclusiveness, can be retained as an expression of the Christian certainty of faith without lapsing into an absolutist attitude. It then contributes to expressing the proprium of the Christian faith without the need to repudiate the particular features of other forms of faith.

The Christian claim to absoluteness has its real place not in dialogue, but in praise of God, in doxology. Believers can and may speak in the superlatives of devotion in praise of the majesty of the Creator, his creative and reconciling presence in the human world and his promise of a new heaven and a new earth. Language must go to its limits – and sometimes even beyond – in order to hint at the ineffable.

However, this terminology must not be confused with the factual language of the intellect which is used to describe or explain reality as it is. This is not the cool prose of reason, but the passionate poetry of the heart. It is not a report, but devotional language, an expression of the absoluteness of God. For that is all that the 'claim to absoluteness' can mean: that we do not claim absoluteness

10  Ratzinger, J. (1967) Das Problem der Absolutheit des christlichen Heilsweges. In: W. Böld (Ed.) *Kirche in der außerchristlichen Welt* Regensburg: Pustet, 26 f.

11  Sundermeier, T. (1991) Evangelisation und die "Wahrheit der Religionen". In: R. Bernhardt (Ed.) *Horizontüberschreitung. Die Pluralistische Theologie der Religionen* Gütersloh: Gütersloher Verlagshaus, 184.

for our faith, but rather that the Absolute – God himself – lays claim to us as to his whole creation.

## 4.   Epilogue

The preceding reflections on the understanding of Jesus Christ and on religious truth claims are not to be understood as an adaption (or even submission) to the assumed needs of an interreligious dialogue. I have merely been pursuing the question what kind of Christological approaches and which understanding of the truth of the Christian faith could be compatible with such an endeavour. Obviously, there are forms of Christology and concepts of truth which would not permit this – such as, for example, the substance-centred view of the Incarnation which sees Jesus Christ as literally embodying the hypostatic union of the divine with the human physis. This approach ends in a theological exclusivism; that means in understanding the truth of Christian faith in terms of exclusive epistemological and soteriological truth claims.

Interreligious relationships characterised by mutual respect and esteem find their foundation primarily not in *theological* motives, but in motives reflecting the *pragmatic* interests of coexistence. Afterwards, the task of theological reflection is to test whether and to what extent this position is 'thinkable', i.e. whether and to what extent it can be exegetically and systematic-theologically backed up. We then may have an answer to questions which confront the thoughtful believer: questions which arise out of our new situation in which perceptions, interpretations, and evaluations of cultural and interreligious 'givens' are undergoing change.

This is a theological reflection upon religious efforts to explore ways of thinking which will adequately take into account changing demands and requirements and yet will not abandon the normative content of the Christian tradition. In order to approach a theological conception of dialogical relationships towards other religions, it is not necessary to develop a speculative 'bird's-eye view' theory. Within the Christian tradition, there is enough potential for creating such a conception. Pope Benedict XVI rightly asked: "Must we really invent a theory as to how God can make salvation available without demolishing the whole edifice of Christ's uniqueness? Isn't it perhaps more important to grasp this uniqueness from the *inside*, as it were, so as to become conscious of the breadth and scope of its radiance – without having to define each and every point individually?"[12] Theology of religions is an undertaking which "doesn't have to make a judgement here and now concerning the eternity-value of the religions – that is a burdensome question which can actually be answered only by the World-Judge"[13]. Theology of religions does, then, not start from the question

---

12  Benedikt XVI. (2005) *Glaube – Wahrheit – Toleranz* Freiburg/Br. et al.: Herder, 44, translation from German.

13  Ibid., 16.

of "the truth" in the religions in general, but rather with the truth-convictions of the Christian faith.

By taking these certainties of truth as a starting-point, theology of religions would be able to show how a spirit of openness towards adherents of other faiths becomes theologically possible – openness in delineating and clarifying, shaping and developing the relationships among the religions. Specifically, this openness occurs when we truly comprehend the 'opening' made by God in the first place: theologically, this opening is called 'revelation'. It consists in the expectation that occurrences of God's grace are also to be found in non-Christian understandings of human relationship to God.

*Manuela Kalsky*

# In Search of a 'New We' Connecting the Differences

## A Multimedia Contribution to a Paradigm Shift in Interreligious Dialogue

A religious upswing is notable worldwide. Even Europe does not represent merely a small secular island surrounded by a huge religious ocean, but is experiencing its own religious revival. In the Netherlands, one of the most secular countries in Europe, a certain helplessness regarding this unexpected emergence of religion can be observed, resulting in a desperate quest for a religious identity of one's own.

Under the impact of secularisation, but above all of individualisation, the Netherlands has undergone a radical transformation of religious identity.[1] The so-called 'pillarisation' of Dutch society[2] has come to an end and the process of decentralisation is still going on. Not only the churches as institutions are under pressure. Political parties, trade unions and other associations are losing members too. The Dutch have become vocal citizens and will no longer be told what or how they have to believe. As a matter of fact a lot of people turned their backs on the Christian churches during the last century. While in the early 20th century 98 per cent of the population belonged to a church, nowadays only 40 per cent of the Dutch citizens feel connected to a church. The number of church members is constantly declining and many young people in the Netherlands today have no idea what Christianity is about.

On the other hand nearly sixty per cent of the Dutch people still claim to be a believer, but only four out of ten people who state this are referring to the traditional Christian faith. The remainder falls into the category: "unaffiliated spirituals". These new believers are patching together their own religion from the wisdom sayings of different traditions. According to surveys, 75 per cent of the Dutch people are convinced that this is the way forward for religion in the future.[3] But it is not only a large number of the Dutch citizens who don't want to take part of a religious community in the classical sense anymore. This trend can be seen all over Europe today. In general, Europeans don't want to

---

1  Nissen, P. (2012) The Holistic Revolution. Contemporary Transformations of Religiosity in the Netherlands. In: M. Kalsky & P. Nissen (Eds.) *A Glance in the Mirror. Dutch and Polish Religious Cultures* Münster: Lit Verlag, 23–37.

2  For a short information about the 'verzuiling'-structure of Dutch society: http://www.encyclopedia.com/doc/1O88-pillarization.html (last accessed December 12, 2013). See also: Thung, M. A. et al. (1982) Dutch Pillarisation on the Move? Political Destabilisation and Religious Change. In: *West European Politics*, 5 (2), 17–148.

3  Bernts, T. et al. (2007) *God in Nederland: 1996–2006* Kampen: Ten Have.

represent a religious group anymore. They prefer to represent just themselves, or perhaps two or three others around them.[4]

On the other hand the Dutch observe with trepidation Muslim solidarity and their sense of a religious 'we', feared because of the events of 9/11 and subsequent terrorist attacks by Islamic extremists. Suddenly Dutch people realise that they themselves no longer have a comparable sense of common identity to counter it. What do we actually believe in, and are we still proud of our country and our own culture? These are frequently asked questions. In the demarcation from others – above all from Islam – there has been a recurrence of national feeling, a desire for a well-defined identity and pride in the achievements of Dutch history, which was laid down in a cultural canon that children have to learn at school.

## Hybrid Identities

When Princess Maxima in September 2007 gave a speech during the presentation of the report of the Scientific Council for Government Policy (WRR) on Dutch identity, in which she confessed with a twist that – even after seven years of living in the Netherlands – she still had not found the Dutch identity, a scandal was born.[5] With her plea against segregation and in favour of embracing the power of diversity at that moment in Dutch history she went a step too far. The same applied to the content of the report. The members of the Scientific Council recommended shifting the debate from national identity to processes of identification with the Netherlands. According to them it would be better to focus on a forward-looking policy strategy than on a static and well-defined concept of the Dutch identity, which never existed as such in real life.

Eventually the WRR report could not turn the tide. Their recommendation to give room to cultural and religious diversity by stimulating mutual encounters and permitting dual nationalities was ignored. The uncertainty among the Dutch population in the midst of Europeanisation, migration, loss of stable group relations and the current economic crisis still stirs up national consciousness under the motto: one passport – proud to be Dutch! This approach resulted in a political inward-oriented gaze, which disregards the fact that the histories of many Dutch people originated elsewhere. They have their roots in Turkey,

---

4   Kalsky, M. (2010) Die Dialogfähigkeit des Christentums in der pluralen Gesellschaft. In: S. J. Lederhilger (Ed.) *Den Himmel offen lassen. Der christliche Glaube in der Herausforderung des wissenschaftlichen Weltbildes* Frankfurt a. M.: Peter Lang Verlag, 92–111; *Religionsmonitor 2008*, Gütersloh 2007; L. Halman et al. (Eds.) (2005) *Atlas of European Values* Leiden: Brill.

5   'Máxima: Nederlandse identiteit nog niet ontdekt'. In: *NCRV-archief 25-9-2007*: http://vorige.nrc.nl/article1846825.ece; Wetenschappelijke Raad voor het Regeringsbeleid (2007) *Identificatie met Nederland* WRR-rapport 79, Den Haag/Amsterdam: Amsterdam University Press.

Greece, China, North and South America, Asia, Africa and so on. Their cultural and religious legacy will also determine the future of the Netherlands.

There are Asian, African and oriental-looking young women and men in the Netherlands who, as soon as they open their mouth, exhibit an unmistakable local Amsterdam accent, as though their ancestors had never lived anywhere else than in the Jordaan district, the heart of the old city of Amsterdam. They are migrant children who have grown up bi-culturally and/or bi-religiously and who are now, as the second or third generation of migrants, bearers of a hybrid identity.

## Blurring Boundaries

This whole development is no longer strictly a matter of intercultural or in-terreligious dialogue, in which representatives of different religions exchange commonalities and differences in their understanding of Buddha, Krishna, Mohammed and Jesus. Here, different cultures and religions melt into one another in one and the same person. This is not the result of an inter-subjective dialogue but of an intra-subjective dialogue and of internal loyalties towards several cultures and religious traditions, which are directly related with that specific person. People like these embody a multi-cultural and a multi-religious identity.

A few years ago, a book with interviews was published, entitled *Let's make love – 27 impossible love relationships.*[6] It contains reports by bicultural and bi-religious couples about the problems and opportunities of multicultural and multi-religious relationships. The story of Susan und Yahya stayed with me for a long time. She is a Danish Jew and he is a Muslim from Morocco. They met at a pantomime training course in Amsterdam. Like many other couples who embark on what looks like an 'impossible love', Susan and Yahya experienced hostilities from the community – their relatives, friends and acquaintances – that made things hard for them. They have to deal not only with personal differences, but are forced to take on the burden of the entire political situation in the Middle East. They are not willing to give up their love because of the Israeli-Palestinian conflict, however, and with the help of their pantomimes, which they perform with and for children, they strive to eliminate stereotypes that typecast the enemy. They have given their daughter a Jewish-Arab name: Blume Yamina. They consider her a sign of hope in the midst of a hopeless war and intend to raise their child biculturally and bireligiously in order to give her the best of both traditions. A contribution to peace between the peoples, under the slogan: the *Jewslims* are coming!

While this initiative is primarily an individual action, it is also a political statement and an example of the situation young people are facing in a glo-

---

6   A. de Groot & F. van der Linden (Eds.) (2008) *Let's make love – 27 onmogelijke liefdes* Antwerpen/Amsterdam: Uitgeverij Contact.

balised world. Cultural and religious identities of the future generations are becoming much more hybrid – if they aren't already. The citizens of Europe are developing multiple religious identities in everyday life through their encounters with people of other religions and through the information flow on Internet. These identities no longer conform to the law of purity and unity. Boundaries are blurring and identities are becoming fluid. The insight of postcolonial thinkers that there is always 'an other' in 'the other' has made clear that the dualist separation between rulers and ruled, colonisers and colonised, is an over-simplified analysis of the real power relations. The role we play in life is far from clear.[7]

This observation of multiplicity in daily life also applies to the religious sphere. Religions, too, are not clearly defined entities. They cannot be tidily sorted into clearly defined categories. All religious traditions are products of intercultural and interreligious processes. As soon as there are alternatives to the cultural rules and to the basic values of a society, new identities are constructed.[8] The purity of a truth or doctrine of faith yields in practice to the mixing of different religious truths, even when this is generally rejected as syncretism in official theological and ecclesiastical circles.[9] However, when a normative tradition is no longer the rule, but rather a religious *bricolage* constructed out of the elements of different religious traditions, then one can ask whether the existing concept of interreligious dialogue is still suitable.

## Transreligious Encounters

Of course the relation between people of different religious and non-religious views of life should still be one of mutual understanding. I have my doubts, however, whether the term 'interreligious dialogue' is still the proper expression for what should happen in the encounter between people with different religious and cultural backgrounds, though the term strongly suggests a verbal relationship with each other. Yet the encounter should not primarily be about discussion of one's own religious convictions and the central truths of a certain normative tradition, but rather about the establishment of mutual trust and understanding. In this sense the word 'interreligious dialogue' points too strongly to the cognitive aspect of the encounter and too little to the ordinary life of

---

7    Kalsky, M. (2007) Embracing Diversity. In*: Studies in Interreligious Dialogue*, 17 (2), 221–231, 224–226.

8    von Brück, M. (2008) Identität und Widerspruch. Bemerkungen zu einer Theologie multipler religiöser Identität. In: R. Bernhardt & P. Schmidt-Leukel (Eds.) *Multiple religiöse Identität* Zürich: TVZ, 291–328, 313.

9    On the concept of syncretisme see: Bernhardt, R. (2008) Synkretismus als Deutungskategorie multireligiöser Identitätsbildung. In: Id. & P. Schmidt-Leukel (Eds.) *Multiple religiöse Identität*, 267–290.

individuals and their embodied practices of lived religion.[10] How do we create a common 'we' in our immediate environment? A 'we' that does not immediately produce a 'they' by excluding others; a 'new we' that makes cultural and religious differences fruitful and enables a more relational and holistic view of what 'the good life for all' could be; a we in which we learn to see through the eyes of the others and are thus in a position to expand our own limited view with the other's perspective in personal relationships.

In other words: fruitful interrelatedness begins not with communicating one's own (dogmatic) belief, but with sharing (religious) experiences and stories out of everyday life with each other. It is an exchange of knowledge of heart and mind, of feelings and thoughts, of stories and art-expressions to get to know more about 'the other' and to become aware of one's own prejudices. The American theologian Paul Knitter, who has been active in interreligious dialogue for many years, has come to the conclusion that dialogue with people of other faiths works best in interreligious cooperation. To him not the exchange of beliefs is the basis of this collaboration, but the ethical inspired actions that arise from these beliefs. From this shared engagement – in the case of Knitter peace missions in conflict areas – friendships between Hindus, Buddhists and Christians developed. Knitter wrote: "Acting, struggling, and suffering together for the cause of peace or justice make for special friendships. But such friendships, because they were between religious people, also bear their religious, dialogue fruits."[11]

Nowadays, in our network society[12] these bonds of friendships can be found in a new way on the World Wide Web. In less than three years more than 350 million Facebookers have come up, searching for connection with each other, in a quest for a new sense of belonging – crossing cultural and religious borders in less than three years time.[13] Network societies produce network religions. In this sense Internet facilitates the ongoing processes of negotiation and change of religion and religious identities.[14]

---

10  McGuire, M. B. (2008) *Lived Religion: Faith and Practice in Everyday Life* Oxford: University Press.

11  Knitter, P. (2002) *Introducing Theologies of Religions* New York/Maryknoll: Orbis Books, 244; Hunt, M. E. (1992) *Fierce Tenderness. A Feminist Theology of Friendship* New York: Crossroad Publishing Company.

12  See Manuel Castells systematic theory of the information society and the new social and economic developments brought by the Internet and the 'new economy': Castells, M. (1996) *The Rise of the Network Society* Oxford: Blackwell Publishers.

13  Levitt, P. (2007) Redefining the Boundaries of Belonging. The Transnationalisation of Religious Life. In: N. T. Ammerman (Ed.) *Everyday Religion. Observing Modern Religious Lives* Oxford: University Press, 103–120.

14  Campbell, H. A. (2012) Understanding the Relationship between Religion Online and Offline in a Networked Society. In: *Journal of the American Academy of Religion*, 80 (1), 64–93.

## From unity to Multiplicity

Europe today is facing the challenge of a paradigm shift, from a mindset of unity to a mindset of multiplicity. The nostalgic attempts to recreate a long-gone European culture of nation states, based on unity of language, territory and religion, will have to be replaced by a concept of culture integrating multiple identities.[15]

The hermeneutical and epistemological key for what is important in life and faith today lies in the experiences of people who live and survive in a multi-ethnic and multi-religious society. Multiplicity calls for communication. This means we have to intensify dialogue and forge connectedness where at present we still fearfully avoid one another. There is an urgent need to find answers to the problems and challenges for the common future of Europe, such as: how can we create a peaceful and just society that enables people to live together in a multi-ethnic Europe? How can prejudice against and fear of other faiths be dismantled without denying the problems that arise when people from different cultures and religions live together? How can we help ourselves and our society to benefit from the fruits of cultural and religious differences in order to guarantee *the good life for all*?

## Transformations of Religious Identity

These questions have been the focus of the multidisciplinary research programmes at the Dominican Study Centre for Theology and Society (DSTS) over the last ten years.[16] During this period the transformation of religious identity in the Netherlands was our main research topic. The aim of the research centre of the Dutch Dominicans is to offer theological reflection on religion-related issues which are currently important in society. Theology at the DSTS is not solely seen as an academic activity, but also as an everyday practical enterprise. Therefore the research programmes at the DSTS do not only have an intra-theological but rather an inter-disciplinary orientation. Sociological, religious, cultural-philosophical and literary studies are incorporated. Our aim is to take the signs of the times seriously and to reflect on them theologically. This contextual approach calls for an inductive way of doing theology. The hermeneutical and epistemological setting for contemporary theology is not to be found in theology itself but rather in the day-to-day life experiences of ordinary people. In the Netherlands people live in a multi-ethnic society with a mix of

---

15  Kalsky, M. (2006) Wahrheit in Begegnung. Die Transformation christlicher Identität angesichts kultureller und religiöser Pluralität. In: *Christian Identity I / Christliche Identität I* Forum Mission, Jahrbuch Band 2/2006, Luzern: Brunner Verlag, 29–52.

16  The Dominican Study Center was founded in 1988 by the Dutch Dominicans. Visit www.dsts.nl (last accessed December 10, 2013) for more information and recent publications.

non-believers and religious or spiritually orientated believers. In Amsterdam, people with 180 different nationalities live together with all the positive and negative consequences that this pluralism entails. Because of this multiplicity of ethnic and (non) religious backgrounds, the focus of the work at the DSTS is not the re-interpretation of traditional theological-dogmatic Christian concepts but rather the questions that directly concern people's life and faith. How do people experience their daily encounters with people of other religions or non-believers? What are their own religious experiences like? And how has their religious identity changed during the course of their life?

In the past fifteen years the Dutch mentality towards dissenters has changed a lot. Three years after the events of 9/11, the Dutch filmmaker Theo van Gogh was murdered in the streets of Amsterdam by a young radicalised Muslim, born and bred in the Netherlands. It was a big shock for the Dutch people, who were very proud of their open and tolerant society and their way of dealing with 'the other'. After this murder, fear of political Islam and fundamentalist Muslims increased and Dutch society became more closed and inward-oriented. Suddenly the Muslim neighbour became a possible 'enemy' and a growing gap developed between 'us' and 'them', with all the related tensions. It became very obvious that people didn't know much about the religion of the other. Stereotypes of '*the* Islam' as a monolithic and very static religious system set the tone, even in the serious press. Therefore the researchers at the DSTS decided to put the focus of their research on the diversity within the various religions itself. And, even more important, they wanted to know whether people – as a result of living within a multi-religious society, as the Netherlands is today – are developing multiple religious belongings. In Asian countries it is not so strange to be a Christian and a Buddhist at the same time, and perhaps even a Hindu.[17] In an originally Christian country, however, this 'syncretist' behaviour of nearly 40 per cent of the Dutch citizens, the 'unbound spirituals', is something new.

## The Gender of the 'Unbound Spirituals'

Also in Dutch society, changes do not occur without internal and external tensions. Some people feel threatened by the loss of clearly defined identities and hark back to tradition in their need for security, while others see the dissolution of fixed identities and imposed cultural and religious roles as a liberation from oppressive structures. People are searching for meaning and values in their lives, for something that is able to offer them direction and wisdom within a non-institutional framework.

---

17 Phan, P. C. (2004) *Being Religious Interreligiously. Asian Perspectives on Interfaith Dialoque* New York: Maryknoll; C. Cornille (Ed.) (2002) *Many Mansions? Multiple Religious Belonging and Christian Identity* New York: Maryknoll; A. Sharma & K. M. Dugan (Eds.) (1999) *A Dome of Many Colors. Studies in Religious Pluralism, Identity, and Unity* Harrisburg: Bloomsbury T&T Clark.

The *Religionsmonitor* of the Bertelsmann Stiftung, developed by religious scientists, sociologists, psychologists and theologians confirms this trend. In a representative survey, 21.000 people from all the continents and world religions were asked about their views on the world and the meaning of life, their religious practices and notions of God. The researchers do notice a spiritual dynamic in all the secularised cultures, which is no longer affiliated with the official churches. Another common element of this spirituality is that God or the divine can be imagined as a person as well as energy or a power inside the world that makes it possible to live one's life in a holistic way.[18]

Especially women seem to be attracted by a holistic spirituality.[19] The sociologists Paul Heelas and Linda Woodhead come to the same conclusion in their empirical research on 'holistic spirituality' in Kendal, a small city in Great Britain. 80 per cent of the participants of those spiritual activities are women and 78 per cent of groups are led or facilitated by women.[20] It is evident that these women show traces of what the Canadian philosopher Charles Taylor called "the subjective turn of modern culture".[21] Interestingly he does not speak of an 'individualistic turn' because, as Heelas and Woodhead underline in their research, individualisation should not be equated simply with individualism. Although the individual and his/her associated personal experience is the prevalent authority and source of meaning in his or her life, this does not automatically suggest that this individual is egocentric and atomistic. In their research Heelas and Woodhead demonstrate that even when women place an emphasis on their 'being an individual' or 'a subject' they still refer to the whole and consider themselves as an 'individual-in-relation' rather than an 'individual-in-isolation'.[22] Their spiritual quest does not necessarily turn them into egocentric individuals, since their (religious) identity is formed in conversation with and in direct relation to other people.

A recently published research of the university of Tilburg confirms that the alleged selfishness of the 'unbound spirituals' in the Netherlands is based on prejudices. The researchers indicate that one of the motivations to participate in courses on spirituality at Christian spiritual centres has to do with the longing for temporary connection to others, besides the hope that the course will contribute to their spiritual growth. Already the study by Van den Brink (2012) into contemporary idealism in the Netherlands showed that values such as "to help one's neighbour" and "civic engagement" score high. Incidentally, also in the

---

18  Zulehner, P. M. (2007) Spirituelle Dynamik in säkularen Kulturen? Deutschland – Österreich – Schweiz. In: *Religionsmonitor 2008* Gütersloher Verlagshaus, 152–154; Huber, S. (2007) Analysen zur religiösen Praxis. Ein Blick in die Schweiz. In: *Religionsmonitor 2008*, 163.

19  Table 4 in: *Religionsmonitor* 2008, 176.

20  P. Helaas & L. Woodhead (Eds.) (2005) *The Spiritual Revolution* Oxford: Blackwell, 94 ff.

21  Taylor, C. (1991) *The Ethics of Authenticity* Cambridge, MA: Harvard University Press, 26.

22  Heelas & Woodhead (2005), 1–11.

Tilburg research 75 per cent of the visitors were female.[23] In their explanation of this phenomenon, they refer to Eeva Sointu and Linda Woodhead, who explain the attractiveness of a holistic spirituality to women as follows:

> "... we suggest that at the current time many holistic spiritualities capture and enable women's desire to move away from traditional roles ascribed to feminine subjects. More specifically, holistic spiritualities can be seen to relate to one of the key dilemmas facing women today, which Beck and Beck-Gernsheim characterise as the dilemma between 'living life for oneself' and 'living life for others'."[24]

Holism in their view is not only attractive to women because of the assumption that there is a spiritual dimension to life and nature, but also because this spiritual dimension connects the individual to others. Both authors conclude: "... the 'whole' to which the individual belongs is not the spirit of 'nature' so much as the web of personal relationships that make up everyday life."[25] With this holistic spirituality women conquer transcendence, the sacred that was forbidden for women to enter. In a way holistic spirituality combines a sense of openness to the future and 'a room for one's own' with the traditional immanent role of women in daily life as being-for-others.[26]

It seems to me that a case can be made for the assertion that the secular and religious feminist movement is one of the causes that religion in the 21st century has become more personal, more daily-life-orientated and more free from the authority of theological and ecclesiastical institutions. The subject increasingly becomes the final authority in assessing what should and should not be justified in a religious sense. Religious traditions thus become an open legacy of diverse meanings and values, from which one can borrow freely in order to give meaning and direction to one's life.[27]

## The Multimedia Projects of the DSTS

Internet plays an important role in gaining access to previously closed religious strongholds – whether we like it or not. The rapid advancing digitalisation of Dutch society led to the decision to connect the DSTS research programmes

---

23  Pieper, J. et al. (2013) Bezoekers van christelijke spirituele centra in Nederland. In: K. de Groot et al. (Eds.) *Zelf zorgen voor je ziel. De actualiteit van christelijke spirituele centra* (Utrechtse Studies 17), Almere: Parthenon, 76–81.

24  Sointu, E. & Woodhead, L. (2008) Spirituality, Gender, and Expressive Selfhood. In: *Journal for the Scientific Study of Religion* 47 (2), 259–276, 260–261; Beck, U. & Beck-Gernsheim, E. (2002) *Individualisation, Institutionalized Individualism and its Social and Political Consequences* London: Sage, 54–84.

25  Sointu & Woodhead (2008), 267.

26  Ibid., 270.

27  See for the genderspecific aspects of religious identity: Strahm, D. (2007) Christliche Identität in einer pluralistischen Gesellschaft – eine Spurensuche aus feministischer Perspektive. In: *Christliche Identität II*, Forum Mission, Jahrbuch 3/2007, 105 ff.

to multimedia websites. The first website the DSTS established focused on the interreligious dialogue in the Netherlands and the rise of multiple religious belonging.

## a) Reliflex.nl – religious flexibility

See trailer: http://www.youtube.com/watch?v=AMWoWvdOjIk
(last accessed December 10, 2013)

On the multimedia website Reliflex.nl, six portraits of Dutch people from different religious traditions were exhibited – Kaouthar Darmoni (Islam/Sufism), Ton Lathouwers (Buddhism), Jan Lagas (Baha'i), Narsingh Balwantsingh (Hinduism), Petra Katzenstein (Judaism) and Annemiek Schrijver (Christianity). The format of Reliflex was founded on the insight that interreligious dialogue is not an encounter of 'religions' but one of flesh-and-blood people. Thus the portraits of these six persons were situated amid their daily reality. Their personal history was central, their relationships, their social context and the choices they had made with respect to their religion. With the help of their stories and the added background information on the website in the shape of articles, weblogs and interviews with experts, the visitor could get more information about present-day (inter)religious questions on sacred texts, emancipation, fundamentalism, religious education of children, circumcision, mixed marriage – and in what way the religion in question played a part in the life of the interviewed people. From the practical day-to-day living with religion it became clear that religious traditions are no static and monolithic entities, but are in themselves flexible in nature. The internal diversity in opinions and traditions was larger than outsiders usually think. And the internal diversity of voices and views did not stop at the religious traditions in question.

Three of the six persons who were portrayed on Reliflex drew the ingredients for their religious identity no longer from one religious tradition only, but from two or three.

The Dutch Zen master Ton Lathouwers – emeritus professor of Slavonic literature at Leuven University and founder of Maha Karuna Ch'an – appeared to be rooted in the Catholic Christian tradition *and* the Chinese Zen tradition. Also Annemiek Schrijver, a Dutch TV presenter, feels at home in two religious traditions: the Protestant Christian tradition and, under guidance of her spiritual teacher Rinpoche, Tibetan Buddhism. Elements from both traditions feed her daily life and teach her how to enrich her spirituality. Kaouthar Darmoni, born and bred in Tunisia, fled to Europe to escape her father who was increasingly influenced by Wahhabism, making the atmosphere in the family more and more fundamentalist. She ended up in the Netherlands and married Gerard, a non-practising Catholic who calls himself secular. They have a son whom they are raising bi-culturally. As a sign of this hybridity they gave him a name which is both western and eastern: Sacha-Shams. On the doorpost at their home's entrance, following the Jewish custom, they have affixed a *mezuzah* and a statue of Mary is welcoming you on entering. "A double protection", Darmoni explains in the interview, laughing. The sacred texts of the various religious traditions are flanking each other in the bookcase and she deliberately takes her son to a synagogue, mosque, church and temple to familiarise him with the different religious practices in a Dutch society which grows ever more multicultural and multireligious.

Next to the portraits one could find articles so as to go more deeply into the information provided by the portrait, and, moreover, weblogs, columns and audios with well-known Dutch people, men and women, on the theme of the week. A permanent element of the website was a self-test of one's religious flexibility. Next to the portrait there was another video each week in which two young Muslims asked young people about their experiences, impressions and views on intercultural and interreligious topics, such as: What do you think about fundamentalism? What do you believe? What gives direction to your life? Are you religious? What do you think of the fact that people are inspired by different religious traditions, is this multiple religious belonging an issue in your life as well? The visitors of Reliflex.nl were invited to respond to the content on the site.

Hetty Zock, professor of religion/philosophy and mental health at Groningen University, remarks rightly that the persons who are featured on Reliflex are highly educated and that such a conscious cultivation of religious multivocality requires a high level of self-awareness and self-reflection. Zock was one of the twelve scholars who were connected to the Reliflex project and who did research into the usability of the concept of 'religious flexibility'. Her critical remarks notwithstanding, in her contribution to the book *Buigzame gelovigen* ('Flexible believers'), which combined the results of the Reliflex research, she comes to the conclusion that the only way to live together in a constructive way within a culturally and religiously diverse society lies in the promotion of people's ability to reflect, which means taking on the 'me' position, in which one reflects on internal and external dialogues and is attentive to possible asymmetry and conflict of interests.[28]

Our aim with Reliflex.nl was to acquaint the general public with ideas and views concerning multiple religious identity and religious hybridism and to show that religious traditions are not static monolithic blocks, but rather lively and flexible. By picturing a personal story, and hence the practical day-to-day living of concrete religious people, the website enabled the visitors to put their own story next to what they saw and heard there. In this way, similarities and differences with the story of their own life and faith came to light. The added background information on the site served to enlarge the knowledge about the various religious traditions. One person functioned as an example of the religious transformation that is going on in society. By using the new media we created a platform where everyday life and scientific insights met and stimulated visitors to form an opinion of their own and exchange their views with others. Reliflex collected living material for the study of shifting identities – from a mindset of *either/or* to a *both/and* approach.

Apart from the infotainment content, which was also used in schools, the site also had a research section. We invited twelve scholars from different disciplines – sociology, philosophy, theology, culture, literature, religion and religious psychology to reflect upon the usefulness of the concept of religious flexibility. What are the chances and the limits of religious flexibility in a dynamic society? Can religious flexibility make a contribution to a better interreligious communication? For a month, each scholar had to write a weblog on Reliflex in which they described the development of their insights. The idea was to create a kind of a laboratory of scholars by which the visitors of Reliflex could gain new insights. At the end of the project each of the scholars wrote an article in a book they published together: *Flexible Believers. Essays on religious flexibility.*[29]

After this first internet project, which put the individual and the new phenomenon of multiple religious identity building in the Netherlands at the centre, we decided to ask the question about how to find social cohesion in a highly individualised and at the same time multicultural and multireligious society. How can we create a peaceful and just society that allows for people to live together in a multi-ethnic Europe? How can prejudice against and fear of people with other faiths be dismantled without denying the problems that arise when people from different cultures and religions live together? How can we help our society to benefit from the fruits of cultural and religious differences in order to guarantee *the good life for all*? In short: What is needed for a 'new we' that binds people together and makes differences fruitful?

---

28  Zock, H. (2008) Het dialogische zelf. Identiteit als dialoog tussen collectieve stemmen. In: C. D. van Troostwijk et al. (Eds.) *Buigzame gelovigen. Essays over religieuze flexibiliteit* Amsterdam: Boom, 74–83.

29  C. D. van Troostwijk et al. (Eds.) (2008) *Buigzame gelovigen. Essays over religieuze flexibiliteit*, Amsterdam: Boom.

## b) Nieuwwij.nl – a new We in the Netherlands

These questions indicate the direction of the present research programme of the Dominican Study Centre entitled 'In search for a new we in the Netherlands'.[30] Once again a multimedia website was built, this time supported by the Dutch Ministry of Housing, Spatial Planning and the Environment (VROM). This website project on interreligious and intercultural communication started on 1 December 2008, and with 25.000 unique visitors a month, by now this site has become one of the most visited sites in the field of religion, culture and spirituality in the Netherlands.

What kind of *We* do we have now and what kind of *We* do we need in the future? How can the gap between *us* and *them* be bridged? How can we find a 'new we' which takes diversity in a variety of guises (gender, age, race, religion, etc.) serious and doesn't automatically draw the border towards 'them' by aiming at exclusive unity? Which ingredients are needed for a new we that is able to value differences positively and connect them in a serious and at the same time flexible way together with all those who aim for the good life for all?

See trailer: http://www.nieuwwij.nl/index.php?pageID=26
(last accessed December 10, 2013)

---

30 The research programme on a new we in the Netherlands started in 2009 and will run until the summer of 2013.

The project *We* uses the slogan *Let's connect the differences* and allows (young) people with different cultural and religious backgrounds to work together. The philosophy behind this slogan is that differences must be faced before we can build something new together.

Accepting diversity means learning to think 'in plural', a difficult change of the familiar western mindset. After all, not only the concept of culture of the modern age is modelled after the idea of (national) unity. In Christianity, as well, unity is a central notion. 'We are all one in Jesus Christ', Paul states in order to strengthen the cohesive powers of the first Christian communities. But in the name of that same unity, those who had a different interpretation of faith than those of power in the church, were declared heretics. Unity is not only a uniting concept, but often also a violent one. But can a community be based on diversity? Is it possible not to put truths in the forefront as a uniting element, but instead embark on a common search? Is a truth thinkable, which arises through or in encounter and provides room for people with multiple or other religious identities?

Project *We* is not about giving answers in the first place but about asking questions. It aims at picturing the creativity and energy of people in the neighbourhoods of towns and villages and stimulating their ability to find their own solutions, making new common initiatives possible on a small scale. The project wants to stimulate people to take their responsibility and to show their strength instead of taking on the part of the victim. The 'Generation Y' video team, for instance, pictures projects and people who are still working on this 'new we', making them accessible to a wider Dutch-speaking audience.

Without denying that living amid all those differences entails problems, project *We* focuses on the positive developments in an increasingly plural country. By doing this, *We* wants to motivate people to work on shaping their own lives and society in a constructive and creative way – for words and images are not innocent. They are not only a reflection of reality; but they are also creating reality themselves.

Instead of fostering fear and cynicism, project *We* wants to promote the development of a common culture, in which mutual differences are made fruitful. The right to 'be different' is an achievement within liberal democracy. The struggle about the question which values should be defining society, is part of this democratic process. The debate on this question, in my view, must not be seen as a problem but as a privilege, for in an open society which strives for individual emancipation as a human right, there will always be conflicts of interest. The common ground is that people comply with the law, with the rules that are laid down in the Constitution.

## Connecting Differences

As long as diversity is associated with loss of identity and relativism of values, and the convictions of 'the other' are seen as a threat to one's own identity, there will be no room for a new we. Mutual acceptance and equality, while retaining and respecting the differences, are indispensable ingredients for the development of new sustainable connections. This is why we chose the motto '*We* – connects the differences'. It underlines the necessity not to downplay differences in favour of common things in the search for mutual connections. *We* advocates facing the differences and making them fruitful – moving away from the *either/or* thinking and searching beyond the prejudices and with an open mind for an *and/and* approach.

How can we conquer fear for the other? How can we connect without having to become the same? It is not the search for a big new *We* which takes centre stage, but rather the existence – side by side and mingled – of small 'we's', dependent on mutual communication and making connections. There is no ready-made recipe for a new we on the site. There are, however, inspiring ideas, conversations, information and opinions about what is needed for it. The *We* team is asking people in the street, in neighbourhoods, young people, people with little education and highly educated, well-known and less-known Dutch people. People and their initiatives come into the picture. And also the sceptics get a voice. Project *We* aims at mutual communication. It wants to promote the exchange of visions on what is valuable and what could give direction to a new '*We-land*'[31], to which all Dutch can contribute and where they can feel at home.

Breaking down prejudice by encounters, promoting knowledge about and providing inspiration from the various religious traditions, and stimulating communication about them with a view to creating a peaceful and just society: this is what project *We* aims at. It is the longing for new ways of connectedness.

A theology which takes the signs of the times seriously and seeks for God's salvation amid 'the messiness' of our daily life must give room to multiplicity.[32] Multiplicity not only in one's own Christian circle – no matter how important and relevant this may be – but in particular in the sense of giving room to the voices of the religious and spiritual stranger in our midst.

The burning question is: Will I allow this? Will I allow that this other interrupts my own narrative and disrupts my peace? That he or she exposes the assumptions in my thinking and acting, and questions my complacency? Do I have the courage to have my own limited view on the world expanded, mean-

---

31  B. Brandsma & M. Kalsky (Red.) (2008) *W!J-land. Voorbij de bindingsangst* Ten Have.

32  Egnell, Z. H. (2009) The Messiness of Actual Existence. Feminist Contributions to Theology of Religions. In: A. Esser, et al. (Eds.) *Feminist Approaches to Interreligious Dialogue, Journal of the European Society of Women in Theological Research*, 17, 13–27, 25 f.; Schneider, L. C. (2008) *Beyond Monotheism. A Theology of Multiplicity* London/New York: Routledge; C. Keller & L. C. Schneider (Eds.) (2011) *Polydoxy. Theology of Multiplicity and Relation* London/New York: Routledge.

ing I may have to face things I would rather not see? In short: do I make the other into an alter ego, into the projection of my own desires or do I sustain the opaque unicity of every human being? Together with Emmanuel Levinas I would plead for the latter: no practice of 'egology', not determining the other from my own ego and reducing them to myself, but letting myself be surprised by the opacity of the other. For the Heidelberg theologian and missiologist Theo Sundermeier, who lived and worked in Africa for many years and who is an expert in the field of intercultural communication, wonder is the beginning of all hermeneutics. He writes:

> "In wonder, I am open for the little, the humble, and in this I discover otherness, beauty, multiplicity. He who is moved by wonder, is capable of enduring dissonance with resignation and will not look for harmony too easily. For the dissonant, as well, belongs to the fullness of life." [33]

Today, doing theology in a Dominican way means going to the virtual marketplace, where people meet each other in very different ways, playing with identities, narratives, imagination and desires and where God can be found in many spiritual guises. The game of theology has changed. The (non)religious other becomes a *locus theologicus*. One of the consequences is that the slogan 'unity in diversity' should be replaced by 'diversity in search of connections', searching for a new we. Or, better, searching for small *we's* which are able to connect in a network which does not cherish the desire for Oneness but instead strives to make the differences fruitful in order to build a society in which all can feel at home.

Whoever thinks that this is a Utopian and naive idealism, is mistaken. It is the reality of the twenty-first century. The century in which the neo-liberal market thinking within a nation state – and the related excesses of egocentric wealth accumulation at the expense of both the majority of humankind and the earth's natural resources – is running into its limits. Making new and just connections on a global scale and developing a spirituality of the good life for all is not the hobby of a 'leftist church', but an urgent necessity. Perhaps it is about time to have the project *We* look beyond the borders of the Netherlands, under the motto: Looking for a new *We* in Europe connecting the differences.

---

33 Sundermeier, T. (1996) *Den Fremden verstehen. Eine praktische Hermeneutik* Göttingen: Vandenhoeck & Ruprecht, 184 f. (transl. MK).

*Julia Ipgrave*

# Inter Religious Relations and the English Model of Church Establishment in Nation and Parish[1]

This article will view inter religious engagement in England through a specifically Church of England perspective and explore the way the very particular type of church establishment we have in England influences relations between peoples of different faiths. What I present here is the product of research on the smallest scale, the findings of six interviews conducted over two weeks with Church of England clergy working at different levels of the interface between church establishment and England's multi-cultural society. Those who kindly agreed to share their perspectives with me are the Secretary for Inter Religious Affairs for the Church of England and to the Archbishop of Canterbury, his predecessor the Inter Religious Affairs Adviser to the Church of England and the Archbishop of Canterbury; the Bishop of Leicester who is the lead bishop in the House of Lords and Diocesan bishop of the English city with the highest proportion of religious minorities; the Bishop of Kingston who is Chair of the Southwark Diocesan Board of Education and Chair of the Christian Muslim Forum; the Director of the Contextual Theology Centre, base of the Eastern London Near Neighbours project (of which more later), and the Co-ordinator of the Eastern London Near Neighbours project. I have also used several of the key Church of England documents which relate to my question and in which some of the participants themselves have had a hand. This is not the result of a detailed, sustained piece of research therefore, but an opportunity to present a particular model of inter religious relating, and raise some questions for consideration. The comments I recorded in the interviews have not been checked against other perspectives as what is presented here is essentially an insider's account. I am indeed writing as an insider myself being an Anglican and wife of a Church of England clergyman.

The paper will be in three parts – the first characterising the English church establishment in relation to other faiths, the second describing a shift in the nature of inter faith involvement over the last ten years or so and the place of the established Church in these, and the third outlining some of the issues for the Church of England's inter faith involvement that were raised by the interviewees.

---

1 This article follows the Church of England conventions by using 'inter faith' and 'inter religious' rather than 'interfaith' and 'interreligious'. Behind this convention is a concern to respect the distinctness of the different faith traditions and avoid the impression of syncretic or pluralist theologies of religions.

# 1.    Nature of the English Church Establishment

## Queen's Speech and Community Centres

I shall follow the advice of one of the interviewees by beginning this paper with the Queen. In February 2012, in her diamond jubilee year, Queen Elizabeth addressed a gathering of the British leaders of nine major religions gathered at Lambeth Palace, home of the Archbishop of Canterbury. She wanted, she said, to 'pay tribute to the particular mission of Christianity and the general value of faith in this country'. She described the religious traditions as both 'sources of a rich cultural heritage' and 'contemporary families of faith' providing 'critical guidance for the way we live our lives, and for the way in which we treat each other'. She then went on to say:

> Here at Lambeth Palace we should remind ourselves of the significant position of the Church of England in our nation's life. The concept of our established Church is occasionally misunderstood and, I believe, commonly under-appreciated. Its role is not to defend Anglicanism to the exclusion of other religions. Instead, the Church has a duty to protect the free practice of all faiths in this country.
> It certainly provides an identity and spiritual dimension for its own many adherents. But also, gently and assuredly, the Church of England has created an environment for other faith communities and indeed people of no faith to live freely. Woven into the fabric of this country, the Church has helped to build a better society – more and more in active co-operation for the common good with those of other faiths.[2]

And she ended

> … Prince Philip and I wish to send our good wishes, through you, to each of your communities, in the hope that – with the assurance of the protection of our established Church – you will continue to flourish and display strength and vision in your relations with each other and the rest of society.[3]

In this statement the Queen, as both Head of State and Supreme Governor[4] of the Church of England set out the role of the established[5] Church in relation to other faiths:

---

2    HM Queen Elizabeth II (2012) *The Queen's speech at Lambeth Palace, 15 February 2012* The Official Website of the British Monarchy. Available from: http://www.royal.gov.uk/ LatestNewsandDiary/Speechesandarticles/2012/TheQueensspeechatLambethpalace15 February2012.aspx (last accessed December 10, 2013).

3    Ibid.

4    The role of 'Supreme Governor' does not involve a spiritual headship but rather the sovereign is 'supreme Ordinary and visitor'. He/she has powers to grant licences and dispensations and significant patronage rights including the appointment of bishops and archbishops. Hill, M. (2007) *Ecclesiastical Law (Third Edition)* Oxford: Oxford University Press, 12–13.

5    'Establishment' means very different things in different national contexts. The Church of England is not a department of government; it is neither funded nor controlled by the government. Ibid., 11.

- To protect the free practice of all faiths in this country[6] …
- To create an environment for other faith communities and people of no faith to live freely …
- To co-operate actively with other faiths for the common good …
- To offer protection to other faiths so they might flourish …

I was told by one who was present at this gathering that what was particularly significant was not just what the Queen said but that the leaders of nine faith communities were standing in front of her nodding in agreement as she spoke.

That is establishment at one level. I now offer a different example shared with me by one of my interviewees who had previously been vicar of a parish church engaged in a number of social projects in a predominantly Muslim area of Birmingham. The city council approached the church's community project asking to work in partnership to convert the church hall into an expanded children's centre. During the building works the children's groups, run and attended by Muslim women dressed in *hijab* and *niqab,* were invited to move into the church itself. The women's response was very positive both because the church was the biggest building in the neighbourhood and because they appreciated its religious character (complete with massive cross) as 'one where faith is taken seriously', and 'better than a secular space devoid of religious symbolism'. It is an example of Church collaboration with the public sector for the good of the wider community, of the Church being rich in resources (it had the building and the space) from which others could benefit, of hospitality to those of other faiths, of those of other faiths feeling sheltered under the religious character of the Church.

In these two examples we have instances of what the Bishop of Leicester terms 'high establishment' and 'earthed establishment'. 'High establishment' relates to the level of the Queen, the presence ex officio of bishops in the upper parliamentary chamber, the House of Lords, and various other Church links at the level of state and nation, while 'earthed establishment' concerns how the Church works on the ground in the cities and local communities.

## High Establishment

*The Queen*

The Queen's interest in inter religious affairs has already been noted. Two of those interviewed observed how the Queen's televised Christmas Day speeches to the nation were becoming increasingly Christian (she talks about the significance of Jesus' birth) and multi-faith, (she is photographed at 'other'-faith

---

or multi-faith events). The Bishop of Leicester reported how the Queen had chosen that city for the start of her Jubilee tour of the country. In the communications between city, diocese and Buckingham Palace it was made clear that she wished to begin her tour with the image of herself among people from a variety of faiths. The service she attended in Leicester Cathedral that day (the Church of England as host) included readings from major world faiths. Even where the Queen is not herself present she has a role in inter religious relations. One of those interviewed recalled how at the church in East London where he had formerly been vicar the local London Cockneys and Bangladeshi community came together to celebrate her Golden Jubilee with a fun day in the church grounds culminating in a service in the church at which each of the faith groups and other groups placed an object on the table to say something important about who they were and how they saw their role in the community.[7]

## The Bishops in the Lords

The Queen is widely popular and generally perceived to be a focus of unity. The position of the bishops in the House of Lords is less prominent in public thinking and, where it is discussed, is more controversial. The interviews took place at a time of discussion and consultation about reform of the House of Lords in which the bishops' presence in the chamber was a subject of debate. Opponents (including, vociferously, the British Humanist Association and National Secular Society) view it as an anachronism in a liberal democracy and what they perceive to be an increasingly 'secular' (by which they usually understand atheist) world; they also raise the argument of unjust privilege to one faith in a religiously plural society. The draft parliamentary bill that emerged from this process of consultation had proposed that, though the number of bishops in the House of Lords be reduced from 26 to 12, their presence be retained and in the same proportion to the reduced size of a reformed House of Lords. In the end the bill was withdrawn, but, for the theme of this paper, it is interesting that those of other faiths wanted the presence of bishops retained. The support of the Abrahamic faiths in particular was noted by the interviewees and their concern that such a reform might lead to the disestablishment of the Church of England. The government minister presenting the bill explained, 'I think that there is a fair degree of consensus among other faiths that they want that faith representation to continue so that is why we have proposed it'.[8] That the bishops acted as a voice for all faiths in Parliament was valued by other faith leaders. The

---

7  This was paralleled at the Lambeth gathering reported above where the religious leaders had each displayed for her inspection an item of significance to them.

8  UK Parliament (2011a) *Draft House of Lords Reform Bill – Joint Committee on the Draft House of Lords Reform Bill 4 Appointments, Bishops and Ministers*. Available from: http://www.publications.parliament.uk/pa/jt201012/jtselect/jtdraftref/284/28406.htm (last accessed December 10, 2013).

Muslim Council of Britain opposed the reduction in the number of bishops on the grounds that it would further reduce the 'voice for the spiritual and moral dimension in formulating new law or influencing public policy'.[9]

The then Chief Rabbi, Lord Sacks, in his own submission on Lords reform put it like this:

> Disestablishment would be a significant retreat from the notion that we share any values and beliefs at all. And that would be a path to more, not fewer, tensions. Establishment secures a central place for spirituality in the public square. This benefits all faiths not just Christianity.[10]

A theme that came out of several of the interviews was that of 'mild establishment'. The Bishop of Leicester stated that

> if [church establishment] was from a strong privileged and powerful position it might be a problem but it is low key and understated.

He explained that the draft bill was not about giving the Church of England status above others or privileging it, but it lays responsibility on the Church to ensure it speaks in public to government taking full account of other faiths.

The Bishop of Kingston likewise said:

> A mild establishment is a good environment for multi faith conversation – better than secular.

The very same point was made by Muslim commentator Tariq Modood writing in the Political Quarterly several years ago:

> The minimal nature of the Anglican Establishment, its proven openness to other denominations and faiths seeking public space, and the fact that its very existence is an ongoing acknowledgement of the public character of religion, are all reasons why it may be far less intimidating to the minority faiths than a triumphal secularism.[11]

---

9   In a submission to the Reform Bill Joint Committee prepared 23 April 2012. UK Parliament (2011b) *Draft House of Lords Reform Bill – Joint Committee: Muslim Council of Britain.* Available from: http://www.publications.parliament.uk/pa/jt201012/jtselect/jtdraftref/284/284iii69.htm (last accessed December 10, 2013).

10  In a submission to the Reform Bill Joint Committee prepared 23 April 2012. UK Parliament (2011c) *Draft House of Lords Reform Bill – Joint Committee Muslim Council of Britain: Chief Rabbi, Lord Sacks.* Available from: http://www.publications.parliament.uk/pa/jt201012/jtselect/jtdraftref/284/284iii85.htm (last accessed December 10, 2013).

11  Modood, T. (1994) Establishment, Multiculturalism, and British Citizenship. In: *Political Quarterly*, 65, 53–73, 53.

*Role as Convenor*

The interviewees described the established Church's role as convenor of gatherings of leaders and representatives of other faiths; this might be for dialogue with each other leader-to-leader and theologian-to-theologian, not just at a national but also at an international level. The position of Archbishop of Canterbury within the wider Anglican Communion often presents occasion for international inter faith dialogue, for example the *Building Bridges* seminars[12] between Christians and Muslims and dialogue with the Chief Rabbinate of Israel and with al-Azhar. Nationally the Church of England has been instrumental in the establishment of bi-lateral inter faith dialogue forums – the Council of Christians and Jews, Christian Muslim Forum, Hindu Christian Forum and work towards a Sikh Christian Forum. Such activity has very often percolated down to the local diocesan level with the Church's involvement with city or regional inter faith forums.

In addition to inter faith dialogue the Church of England is de facto convenor of most religious leadership statements vis à vis the public, so there are what were described as 'endless meetings' at Lambeth Palace on a variety of subjects such as the environment, ethics and economics, or education, each of which produces joint public statements. The former Archbishop of Canterbury, Rowan Williams, was particularly interested in convening meetings of young people of different faiths around some of these issues as in the conference at Lambeth Palace in 2009 when thirty Christian and Muslim young people spent the day with the archbishop and scholars from both faiths to compose a statement urging long-term action for Climate Change which they then took to the United Nations Climate Change Conference in Copenhagen.

Again this role of convenor is replicated at local level and the Inter Religious Adviser could name a number of diocesan bishops who were active in bringing together religious leaders and making statements on areas of key concern in their localities. The position of the Church meant bishops were also able to bring into such meetings leaders of the local councils or, at a national level, government ministers, in this way acting as a channel for the voices of smaller or more marginalised religious communities to be heard in the civic and political sphere. The ability of the archbishop to include the general secretary of the Muslim Council of Britain at a meeting attended by government ministers after a cooling of relations between the government and this body was an example of the Church's brokering role.

A phrase that was used for the Church's involvement with other faiths by more than one of the interviewees was 'holding the ring' as in overseeing and taking responsibility for meetings between people of different faiths. The for-

---

12  Which generated a series of publications eg Ipgrave, M. (Ed.) (2008) *Building a Better Bridge: Muslims, Christians, and the Common Good* Washington DC: Georgetown University Press.

mer Inter Religious Affairs Adviser was keen to emphasise that the Church's role went beyond 'holding the ring' to showing the world that religions can work together for the common good. It is, he says, 'a pro-active approach to reducing the secular misconception of religion and demonstrate that it is not a problem to do these things together'.

## Earthed Establishment

### Meso (Civic) level

We now move from 'high establishment' to 'earthed establishment' the roots of which are in the local parishes. Before we reach these roots however there is an intermediary meso level of engagement – the level of city, town, of area and diocese – between the established Church and other religions. I was told that this level of engagement between faiths has often been the strongest. It has already been mentioned how the inter faith convening – the dialogues and public statements – noted at the high level are replicated at diocesan and local authority level and supported by local inter faith advisers. It is also facilitated by the traditional close engagement of the Church at the civic level, the strong links between councils and Anglican churches demonstrated publicly in civic services, memorial services and celebrations, hosted in churches and cathedrals, and taking place outside the public eye in discussions and consultations on local affairs including those relating to the relationships and concerns of other faith communities. The Church has often been able to draw leaders from other faiths into these existing relationships; it is, I was told, 'about local networks and stories' and being well placed for 'building connectivity'. Key events in the life of the city or borough and of the diocese are both marked by church services in which are present and prominently placed both members of the council wearing their chains of office and representatives of other faiths.[13] The relationships are more than ceremonial – relations are in place when faith groups meet local crisis or difficulty. *Presence and Engagement*, the Church's 2005 report on local level engagement with other faiths – a report in which the former Inter Religious Affairs Adviser had considerable input – speaks of, 'a stable degree of confidence in the Church of England by other Faith communities', a confidence that 'has been strengthened by a range of local and diocesan actions in support of other Faith communities at times of stress and tension and in relation to particular issues of concern. Such issues have included for example, the presence in communities of racist or other extremist organisations, issues of immigration and asylum, the disturbances in the northern towns and the consequences of

13  Mayors' chaplains are more often than not Christian and the role of chaplaincy generally in state institutions such as the Armed Forces and the Prison Service is formally the responsibility of the Church of England, drawing in other faiths as needed.

the military action in Iraq'.[14] As a recent example I was told that Anglicans had been at the heart of the civic response to the propaganda and the planned march by the ultra right English Defence League (EDL) in Tower Hamlets, a predominantly Bangladeshi and Muslim area of London. The Church of England Area Dean and rector of a local church had been proactive in visiting mosques and consulting with faith leaders, offering reassurance and calming fears at a time when the EDL was using the language of Christian identity to stir up fears of an Islamic takeover of Britain. As he stated:

> The language of the EDL builds upon fears and ignorance to suggest that Muslims are a threat, and the values of a multicultural society are misguided. They portray Tower Hamlets as an Islamic Republic that seeks to remove liberal and Christian values. None of this is true – and local people should stand together to make this clear.[15]

Much earlier, with the Muslim protests against Salman Rushdie's *Satanic Verses*, when the political left and liberal consensus failed the Muslim protestors and the whole corpus of the media turned against them, it was, as Tariq Modood has observed, only the Anglicans and inter faith fora who 'tried to moderate the hostility against the angry Muslims', and 'tried to create the space where Muslims could state their case without being vilified'.[16]

*Micro (Parish) Level*

And now to the parishes – at one level establishment means bishops in the House of Lords and at another it means the parish system whereby the Church has (just about) maintained a presence – a church building and a clergy household – in every community, and a church school in many parishes also. Central to its ethos – an ethos backed by law – is the idea that the Church has a duty of care for all, the 'cure of souls' within the parish whatever their religion or whether or not they have a religion at all. My interviewees stressed that the fact that the Church of England is *not* a membership church is central to its understanding of its relations with people of other faiths. One of the peculiarities of this status is that the church wardens (senior lay officials of the church) can be elected by anyone who lives in the parish[17] – so even in the former parish of

---

14  General Synod of the Church of England (2005) *Presence & Engagement: the churches' task in a multi faith society* (GS 1577). Available from: http://www.churchofengland.org/media/1259044/gs1577.pdf (last accessed December 10, 2013), 11.

15  Cited in Sulaiman, T. (2011) Don't let the preachers of hate and extremism divide us. In: *East End Life* August 8, 2011. Available from: http://www.towerhamlets.gov.uk/news__events/east_end_life/8_august/%E2%80%9Cdon%E2%80%99t_let_the_preachers_of_ha.aspx (last accessed December 10, 2013).

16  Modood, T. (2006) British Muslims and the Politics of Multi-culturalism. In: Id. et al. (Eds.) *Multiculturalism, Muslims and Citizenship: A European Approach* Abingdon: Routledge, 42.

17  *Churchwardens Measure* (2001), para 5.1.

one interviewee with a 65% Muslim population, all were entitled to vote. The parish church has a responsibility to, a duty of support and service for, people of other faiths. This is the 'presence' and 'engagement' in the title of the document referred to earlier. It is also the basis for the church community project and children's centre described at the beginning of this paper. As the Secretary for Inter Religious Affairs said, it is about 'staying in there' even in areas where Christians are a tiny minority and at times of financial difficulties for the Church. There is a wide variety in the response of individual Church of England priests and their congregations to this duty of service to the neighbourhood but involvement in community activity outside the immediate membership and collaborating with other groups on local projects is an expectation; because of the Church's networks, and also, importantly because of its buildings in each locality, the Anglican church often has a leading or hosting role in these projects – as one of my interviewees said, 'community organising runs with the grain of the Anglican soul'.

The *Presence and Engagement* report of 2005 identified parishes across the country with significant populations from other faiths in some cases where other faiths predominated. It portrayed the 900 parishes in such places as 'a remarkable and valuable asset' that had not as yet been fully appreciated or tapped:

> This value lies precisely in their continuing faithful presence in places from which many others have now fled; and in their continued loving engagement with the issues that face people of all Faiths in some of the toughest and yet most vibrant neighbourhoods of our country. As a result of this commitment, there is a depth of knowledge and experience which is quite unparalleled in any other part of society.[18]

As well as these assets of commitment, knowledge and experience – and of buildings – there are also administrative support structures for this level of engagement. The publication of the Church's *Faith in the City* report in 1985[19] was the key to a new phase in the fulfilment of this duty of service. It did not give much explicit attention to the place and role of other faith communities, it nevertheless gave impetus through the formation of the Inner Cities Religious Council and work of the Church Urban Fund, to a rapidly growing range of initiatives and responses to changing local circumstances and working in the most deprived areas of England, including these multi-faith communities.

These are the assets that are now being put to use in the new government-funded Near Neighbours project that is governed as a charity by the Archbishops' Council and the Church Urban Fund and uses Church of England

18　General Synod of the Church of England (2005) *Presence & Engagement: the churches' task in a multi faith society* (GS 1577). Available from: http://www.churchofengland.org/media/1259044/gs1577.pdf (last accessed December 10, 2013), 74.

19　Archbishop of Canterbury's Commission on Urban Priority Areas (1985) *Faith in the City: a Call for Action by Church and Nation* London: Church House Publishing.

networks to support a multiplicity of local level initiatives that bring together people of different faiths in service to the common good. As the project website states:

> The infrastructure is already in place through the Church, the Church Urban Fund and their partners to deliver this new initiative within local communities, so the money goes where it is needed without creating new layers of administration.[20]

## Schools

This concept of responsibility for wider community was described as 'part of the mindset of the Church of England' and applies to schools as well as to other areas of interaction. At parish level local clergy are very often governors in schools that are not church schools and invited in regularly to lead collective worship. In addition, through a mix of historical accident and pragmatism, there are a large number of Church of England schools (a third of the total of primary schools and a growing number of secondary schools). The Bishop of Kingston was clear that Church of England schools are not confessional – not designed to nurture children into Anglicanism or even primarily to educate children of Anglican families (although school admissions policies often reserve places for these). It is not just parallel to, but part of, the parish system with parish church and church school tending to work as partners. In Bradford, a city where more than elsewhere in England, the segregation of communities has become an issue, a combination of places for Anglican children and places for other children from the neighbourhood means that the Church of England schools are some of the relatively few in the inner city that are multi-religious and multi-ethnic. The 2001 church commissioned report on Church of England schools, *The Way Ahead,* found church schools where the school population was majority or even wholly of another faith, primarily Muslim or Sikh:

> We find that, in these cases, the schools are respectful of the faith of parents, but nevertheless offer the children an experience of the Christian faith, both through the everyday life of the school and through inclusive forms of worship. The advice to us was that parents welcome the opportunity to send their children to a faith school where there is belief in God.[21]

Two of the interviewees observed from their experience in parishes that Muslim families were often happy to send their children to Church of England schools as places where religion is taken seriously. In the combination of hospitality towards other faiths and appreciation by those of other faiths of the religious character of these institutions it is a parallel situation to the case of the Bir-

---

20  http://www.cuf.org.uk/near-neighbours/about (last accessed December 10, 2013).
21  Church Schools Review Group (2001) *The Way Ahead: Church of England Schools in the New Millennium* (GS 1406) London: Church House Publishing, 16.

mingham children's centre reported earlier in this article. One of the benefits of the arrangement is the opportunity it gives for the Church through its schools to build up positive relations with the families of other faiths whom it serves.

In education too, the Church has proved the gatekeeper, or rather opener of doors, for other faith communities. The existence of Church schools, however inclusive their admissions, meant that eventually schools for other faiths (in 1997 Muslim schools) had, just as a question of social justice, to be permitted. Being a well-established and integral part of the education system, as compared with Islamic schools, for example, the Church sometimes acts as adviser and consultant. The Bishop of Kingston recalls being visited by the director of a Muslim education institute who wanted to learn from church schools lessons for the organisation of his own.

## 2.    Models of Inter Religious Engagement

Having given a flavour of the nature of the English church establishment I now consider some of the different models of organisation for inter religious engagement that have been employed in recent years leading to the current Near Neighbours programme. Behind the changes of approach my interviewees identified a shift in understanding of inter faith from one where other faiths were considered as fairly recent arrivals and the emphasis was on hospitality – welcoming the stranger – through a concern for equality between faiths to the position today where the Church views people of other faiths as fellow citizens and is more confident about the distinctive role it can play in facilitating inter religious collaboration on that basis. There is increasing focus on the neighbourhood and parish level of inter religious co-operation, a level at which, according to the Bishop of Leicester, the Church had been rather slower to become engaged.

The Near Neighbours co-ordinator put his project in the context of inter faith initiatives that had gone before and charted a move from special interest dialogue groups through community consultation to neighbourhood action. The first stage of which he spoke involved local and national inter faith networks and fora where Christians in general and Anglicans in particular often had a large part to play – an observation substantiated by the large number of Christian clergy and lay leaders given as contacts in the Inter Faith Network directory for inter faith organisations. Other faith members of these fora may well be on the margins of their own faith communities and the character is often that of a special interest group for people who enjoy being together. Over the last 20 years these local inter faith groups have done valuable work; they have ensured a multi-religious presence at events and celebrations at the civic level and presented public examples of inter religious friendship but they have been less engaged with the grassroots of the respective communities. During the last Labour government such groups were given one-off grants by the Community

Development Foundation[22] to employ co-ordinators for inter faith activities. Some of the inter faith groups carried out useful projects in the community while the funding was there, but their outputs were patchy. After three years funding dried up and in several cases attendance at forum meetings began to decline.

The Labour government worked with local councils to set up faith fora for consultation on key community issues such as procedures in the case of a pandemic, or to obtain faith group input on its Community Strategy for promoting and improving the economic, social and environmental well-being of their areas, and contributing to the achievement of sustainable development in the UK. Based on his own experiences of such meetings, my informant described this pattern as problematic. There were so many constituencies involved that it proved difficult to find people to represent the faith groups and congregations or who were in a position to make a decision if they did attend, and the discussions sometimes became 'bogged down and boring'. The Labour government had wanted to co-ordinate inter faith activity and to be even-handed in its approach, but the Church of England inter religious affairs adviser was aware that the Church was in a good position to lead on inter religious relations having quite sophisticated networks of inter faith officers and chaplains in hospitals, further and higher education institutions, with the forces and in prisons, as well as the parish structures and experience of the Church Urban Fund. It also had a history of working with other faiths. When the new Coalition government arrived (2010) with its 'Big Society' agenda and interest in local community action, he approached the Department for Community and Local Government with a proposal for a Church-co-ordinated inter faith project and was granted £5 million funding for three years for the Near Neighbours programme.[23]

The Near Neighbours programme is delivered through the Church Urban Fund using the Church's local networks and is based locally at four centres in areas of religious diversity, one in eastern London, one in Leicester, a third in Birmingham and the fourth in Bradford. The emphasis is essentially on the local and the focus is social action. The idea is to bring together people and groups who are near neighbours in communities that are diverse, so they can get to know each other better, build up sustainable relationships and collaborate on initiatives that improve the local neighbourhood in which they live. It is more what is known as 'side-by-side' than 'face-to-face' inter faith engagement.

Near Neighbours sets out its two key objectives as follows:

1. Social interaction – to develop positive relationships in multi-faith areas i.e. to help people from different faiths get to know and understand each other better.

---

22  An enterprise based in Cambridge commissioned by the government to administer the Faiths Capacity Building Fund.

23  Near Neighbours Press Release (2011) *Eric Pickles Officially Launches £5m Near Neighbours Programme* Mon 14 November 2011. Available from: http://www.cuf.org.uk/near-neighbours/press-release/14Nov2011 (last accessed Dezember 12, 2013).

2. Social action – to encourage people of different faiths, or no faith, to come together for initiatives that improve their local neighbourhood.[24]

Small grants are awarded to a multiplicity of neighbourhood projects involving local people from different faith communities. Applications are usually given to the local Anglican priest[25] who delivers them to the programme co-ordinator along with his or her own comment, using local knowledge, on the value and feasibility of what is being proposed. These priests are then likely to pay a visit to the projects where applications have been successful to show interest and give encouragement. Examples of the kind of project include a soup kitchen for homeless people set up by an Islamic group and local church in the church hall in Leicester; an initiative in Birmingham that brings together members from the African Caribbean and Somali community (two groups between whom there has been a lot of tension) to work on gardening projects to beautify their neighbourhood; a ten-week course in Waltham Forest, London, training people of different faiths to act as mentors for teenagers in local schools.

## 3.   Issues

I end this paper by highlighting four of the issues that emerged during the interviews and that might form the basis for future discussion.

### The Language of Faith

The first issue is one of terminology. Problems were identified by three of the interviewees with the development of the language of 'faith' (as in 'inter faith', 'faith communities', 'faith schools' or 'faith sector') which is widely used in the public sector and media. The word, I was told, has been overworked and now carries a number of meanings quite removed from its significance when used by churches, mosque communities and others. When employed in public discourse it has a tendency towards homogenisation. It is used to hold together concepts, actions and groups that are not in fact alike as though faith were a product and the 'faith communities' just brands of the same. The use of the term 'faith' makes it possible for people from a diversity of communities to be lumped together in an undifferentiated whole and separated out from 'mainstream' society. It is also associated with minority ethnic groups and the issues associated with minority status, and recently it has been linked to national se-

---

24 'Near Neighbours in a Nutshell' on the Near Neighbours website. Available from: http://www.cuf.org.uk/near-neighbours/about (last accessed December 10, 2013).

25 This pattern is not universal across the Near Neighbours projects. Those in East London often go straight to the programme co-ordinator. They do, though, as a rule need the support or at least consent of the Parish Church Council.

curity concerns. To use the term 'faith community' for the Church transforms it into a minority group with which society has dealings rather than it being an integral part of that society in its many aspects. It is for such reasons that alternative terminology is increasingly being used in the Church, the previous title of Inter Faith Adviser being changed to Inter Religious Affairs adviser; the Church avoiding the commonly-used terminology of 'faith schools' for its own Church schools, the terms 'presence' and 'engagement' being used for the Church's relations with those of other religions. 'Near Neighbours', too, is a useful term because it implies proximity and shared space (no one is left on the outside) but does not exclude difference and for those acquainted with scripture has a recognisably Christian reference.

## The Language of Equality

The language of faith causes problems and so too does the language of equalities; in fact the two were seen as related. The homogenising use of the term 'faith' was presented as an illustration of public authorities' reluctance to allow for difference in the public sphere; differentiating between religious groupings runs counter to the equalities agenda. Both present and former inter religious affairs advisers spoke of the inclination of Tony Blair's Labour government to treat different religions as though they should all relate to each other on a level playing field, to make the government the convenor and neutral broker in religious affairs gathering all faiths around the table on an equal basis. It had been Church policy to oppose Downing Street ideas of a multi-religious advisory group at senior level as something that would be difficult to achieve on a practical level and would not reflect a reality where only 7% of the population were of non-Christian faiths and where, as one Church document states:

> The former dominance of Christian (and especially Anglican) norms in society places the Christian churches in a particular relationship to other faith communities which is not one of simple equivalence in the present.[26]

I was told that this was why other religions accept the Church of England's established role, 'they don't want a secular state and there can't be a multi-religious constitutional settlement. It is the core reason it works'.

The interviewees saw Near Neighbours as a breakthrough, a sign of the different position taken by the new Coalition government towards religion and of the trust placed by that government in the Church of England to safeguard and promote the interests of those of other religions.[27] Some responses from people

---

26  General Synod of the Church of England (2010) *Sharing the Gospel of Salvation* (GS Misc 956). Available from: http://www.churchofengland.org/media/39745/gsmisc956.pdf (last accessed December 10, 2013), 9.

27  http://www.cuf.org.uk/near-neighbours/news/press-releases (last accessed December 11, 2013).

of other religions to the launch of the Near Neighbours programme echoed the Church's understanding: one Muslim spokesperson spoke of the chance it gave for:

> Christian and Muslim leaders to develop a dynamic spirit of open-mindedness, cooperation and friendship through meeting, working and learning together and for local Muslim communities to learn from the greater professionalism in the churches[28]

and another of the scheme 'providing minorities protection under the wing of the Church of England'.[29]

## Privilege

If the Church accepts a differentiated role in inter religious relations, is there a danger that its dealings with its religious neighbours might be tarnished with the brush of imperialism? This was a question that exercised some of the interviewees. They recognised the privileged position of the Church of England. Although the Queen is enormously popular across communities it is nevertheless the case that the monarch and supreme governor of the Church is at the top of a social hierarchy – it is a top-down relationship. Although the clergy themselves may live in the poorer areas of the inner city and council estate they tend to live in the biggest house in those places. Their educational background is frequently more advantaged than that of the majority of their parishioners in Near Neighbours areas, for example.

There is also the concern that closeness to the government at local and national level can constrain their freedom to criticise? One noted how the local Roman Catholic priest had, unlike him, not been in the least bothered about upsetting the council in an ecumenical and inter religious Living Wage campaign in which they were both engaged. The current inter religious adviser recorded his mixed feelings when Archbishop Rowan published a leading article constituting an outspoken attack on the government's policies in the *New Statesman*.[30] His dominant reaction was dismay that the Archbishop should be upsetting the government at a time when the Church was involved in negotiations to land the Near Neighbours grant but at the same time there was a feeling that as a result 'we could look our Muslim neighbours in the face'. Another spoke of the Church's 'agonistic' notion of its political role, 'push, pull, compromise is the nature of it'.

---

28  Dr Musharraf Hussain, Director of the Karimia Institute. Available from: http://www.cuf. org.uk/near-neighbours/press-releases/15Feb2011 (last accessed December 11, 2013).

29  O'Toole (2012) Faith and the Coalition: A New Confidence to "Do God"?. In: *Muslim Participation in Contemporary Governance Working Paper*, No. 3, Centre for the Study of Ethnicity and Citizenship university of Bristol, 5.

30  Williams, R. (2011) The government needs to know how afraid people are. In: *New Statesman 9th June 2011.*

## Christian Mission

A fourth issue was less one of other people's perspectives of the Church of England than one of its own self understanding. As an interviewee said:

> It is easy for the Church of England to hold the ring for everyone else, but do we have a voice in the circle ourselves? Are we so scared of being tribal that we don't have anything else to say at all?

Are the interests of (Anglican) Christianity lost in the promotion of the interests of those of other religions? Is it not the mission of the Church rather to bring the Gospel to non-Christians than to ensure that their non-Christian faiths flourish under its protection? These concerns have been expressed at different levels, for example, in a private member's motion on the uniqueness of Christianity in Britain in the Church's General Synod, a motion that led to a detailed response in the report *Sharing the Gospel of Salvation* (2010).[31] It was found in the reaction of one parishioner of the Birmingham church to opening up the premises as a children's centre for Muslim families; 'If we were Baptists instead of Church of England we could set up a stall outside the mosque on Friday and hand out Christian tracts'. The then vicar posed himself the question, 'Do we have anything to say except that we are welcoming?' He was concerned to find a way to articulate that Christian ethos without proselytising or taking advantage of the established position, and so he commissioned a mosaic for the entrance to the new community centre that portrayed the Fruits of the Spirit – Christian but not exclusive. During monthly staff training days for all the centre's volunteers and leaders (a group where Christians were in the minority) he included a slot on ethos where they looked at an issue such as the grievance procedure, forgiveness, gossip and backbiting, and shared perspectives as a Christian organisation on these issues using the Scriptures and inviting other members of the group to share from their faith perspective whether Muslim, Sikh or Hindu. He explained: 'in this way we wanted to articulate our faith in terms other people can identify with and speak to from their own traditions'.

The interviewees knew that people of the Church who engaged in these inter religious activities needed theological assurance that they were doing what God wanted them to do, the reassurance that they were being faithful (the fact that the Birmingham Near Neighbours' centre has been called *The Faithful Neighbourhood Centre* is a reflection of this). They were aware of the concern of some that they might be conceding too much, watering down their faith in their dialogue and engagement with people of other faiths. In this respect universalist and pluralist theologies such as those of John Hick and Alan Race were deemed unhelpful; they seemed to promise a 'slippery slope to relativism'. There is no

---

31 General Synod of the Church of England (2010) *Sharing the Gospel of Salvation* (GS Misc 956). Available from: http://www.churchofengland.org/media/39745/gsmisc956.pdf (last accessed December 11, 2013)

shortage of high level Christian theology of religions and inter faith dialogue but in the document *Presence and Engagement,* and more particularly in the later document *Generous Love* a developed Trinitarian theology was set out for Anglicans engaged in inter religious relations, and a series of Bible studies (*'Encouraging Reading'* and *'Hospitality of the Heart'*) has been produced that can be used at parish level. 'Presence' is related to incarnational theology and 'engagement' to Pentecostal theology – the ways in which the Spirit is calling churches and individuals to engage with new diversities.[32] A fuller quote from *Generous Love* gives the tenor of this theological underpinning of inter religious activity:

> Our commitment to be a stable presence in each place, to sanctify the life of the local community through prayer and witness, and in so doing to learn to value more deeply and share more widely the treasure entrusted to us, is a response to the incarnational logic that lies at the heart of the Christian story. The presence which we are living is that of the Body of Christ: the presence of the God who expresses himself in our midst in body language, by living a life, dying a death, and rising to a new life. Through his cross and resurrection, Jesus gives us forgiveness, healing and new life, and shapes us into a community which offers these blessings to our neighbours in a pattern of gracious and generous discipleship.[33]

The practical theology of mission of John Milbank and others who make the life of the Church central to the calling of evangelism, has also had an impact in the Church's inter religious activity and is seen as helping to overcome the difficulty of translating between languages of faith. As the document *Sharing the Gospel of Salvation* states:

> It makes example – the example of the Church as a whole, as well as of individual Christians – the shared vocabulary through which the Christian story may become known.[34]

Thus engagement with one's non-Christian neighbour in action for the good of community can be a way of expressing one's Christian identity and faith in unity with the different identity and faith of one's neighbours.

---

32  General Synod of the Church of England (2005) *Presence & Engagement: the churches' task in a multi faith society* (GS 1577). Available from: http://www.churchofengland.org/media/1259044/gs1577.pdf (last accessed December 11, 2013), 5.

33  The Network for Inter Faith Concerns (NIFCON) of the Anglican Communion (2008) *Generous Love: the truth of the Gospel and the call to dialogue: An Anglican theology of inter faith relations* London: The Anglican Consultative Council, 10.

34  General Synod of the Church of England (2010) *Sharing the Gospel of Salvation* (GS Misc 956). Available from: http://www.churchofengland.org/media/39745/gsmisc956.pdf (last accessed December 11, 2013), 13.

# Dialogue in Islam

*Katajun Amirpur*

## "Straight Paths"

Thoughts on a Theology of Dialogue[1]

Both Christianity and Judaism know a tradition of a theology of dialogue. You will be familiar with its representatives, people such as Martin Buber, Paul Knitter and John Hick. In the Islamic world, there have been relatively few such approaches among Muslim intellectuals. All the more, it becomes incumbent on Islamic theology in Germany to develop them.

The reason for this relative rarity of dialogical approaches among Muslims is most likely historical: As an established majority religion, it was not felt necessary to develop them until very recently. At the height of Islamic civilisation, neither Christianity nor Judaism seemed to offer a credible challenge. The terms of coexistence could be dictated from a position of strength. Unless I am much mistaken, it was also the minority religion that made the offer of dialogue between Judaism and Christianity first and produced the first approaches. Obviously, if you are in the stronger position, you have to have the need for dialogue pointed out to you. The weaker party will be much more immediately aware of this. That is why Islam as a majority religion did not produce much in the way of dialogical approaches. It has to be said, though, that coexistence, living dialogue, generally was a success nonetheless. In its heyday, Islamic civilisation was tolerant and could bear ambiguity, non-conformism and pluralism well. Jews and Christians under Islamic rule profited from this. Later on, Christianity and Judaism posed too great a challenge for Islam. Under colonial conditions, Islam was in a position so inferior that it made initiating or having a dialogue impossible. Impotence and foreign determination are not conducive to a theology of dialogue, either.

Circumstances and views have changed today. Both sides, whether they find themselves in the stronger or weaker position, share the insight that dialogue has to take place. This is as true for the Christian majority religion vis-à-vis Islam here in Germany as it is for e.g. Islam as the majority religion vis-à-vis Christian and Jewish minorities. Voices advocating the acceptance of religious pluralism and dialogical relations between the branches of the Abrahamic family are increasingly heard in the discourse of Islamic scholars. They include

---

1   Inaugural Lecture for the Chair of Islamic Studies and Theology at the Academy of World Religions of Hamburg University on 18 October 2011. (Translated from German into English by Volker Bach).

Mohammed Arkoun who sadly died last year[2], Hasan Askari[3], Mahmoud Ayoub[4], Ali Asghar Engineer[5], Farid Esack[6], Seyyed Hossein Nasr[7], Mahmut Aydın[8] and Abdulaziz Sachedina[9], to name but a few of the most familiar representatives.

The theological foundation of an Islamic pluralism is based on three Qur'anic pillars. First, the affirmation that salvation is possible for all those who live virtuously and righteously, even if they are not Muslims (Surahs 2,62; 2,112; 2,213; 20,112). Second, the conviction that God has not abandoned any people without revelation or prophetic guidance (Surahs 5,19; 5,48; 10,47; 14,4; 35,24). Third, the belief in a divine transcendence that surpasses all possibility of human expression (Surahs 17,43; 37,180; 112,4).

2    Arkoun, M. (1998) Rethinking Islam Today. In: C. Kurzman (Ed.) *Liberal Islam. A Sourcebook* New York: Oxford University Press, 205–221; Id. (2002) *The Unthought in Contemporary Islamic Thought* London: Saqi; Id. (1999) *Der Islam. Annäherung an eine Religion* Heidelberg: Palmyra; Id. (2005) *Humanisme et Islam. Combats et propositions* Paris: Vrin.

3    Askari, H. (1982) *Islam in a Plural World* Birmingham: Selly Oak Colleges; Id. & J. Hick (Eds.) (1985) *The Experience of Religious Diversity* Aldershot/Brookfield: Gower; Id. & J. Avery (Eds.) (1991) *Towards a Spiritual Humanism. A Muslim-Humanist Dialogue* Leeds: Seven Mirrors; Id. (2002) Die theologischen und anthropologischen Herausforderungen an den interreligiösen Dialog. In: R. Kirste et al. (Eds.) *Neue Herausforderungen für den interreligiösen Dialog* (RIG 7), Balve: Zimmermann, 11–30.

4    Ayoub, M. (1997) Islam and Pluralism. In: *Encounters. Journal of Inter-Cultural Pespectives*, 3, 103–118; Id. (2000) Islam and the Challenge of Religious Pluralism. In: *Global Dialogue*, 2 (1), 53–64; Id. (2004) Christian-Muslim Dialogue. Goals and Obstacles. In: *The Muslim World*, 94, 313–319; Id. (2007) *A Muslim View of Christianity. Essays on Dialogue* Maryknoll: Orbis.

5    Engineer, A. (2004) *Islam. Challenges in Twenty-first Century* New Dehli: Gyan Pub. House; Id. (2005) Islam and Pluralism. In: P. Knitter (Ed.) *The Myth of Religious Superiority. A Multifaith Exploration* Maryknoll: Orbis, 211–219; Id. (2005) *On Developing Theology of Peace in Islam* New Delhi: Sterling; Id. (2007) *Islam in Contemporary World* New Delhi: New Dawn.

6    Esack, F. (1997) *The Qur'an. Liberation and Pluralism. An Islamic Perspective in Interreligious Solidarity against Oppression* Oxford: Oneworld; Id. (1999) *On Being a Muslim. Findung a Religious Path in the World Today* Oxford: Oneworld.

7    Nasr, S. H. (1993) *Ideal und Wirklichkeit des Islam* München: Diederichs; Id. (1998) *Islamic-Christian Dialogue. Problems and Obstacles to be Pondered and Overcome* Washington D.C.: Georgetown University; Id. (1999) Religion, Globality, and Universality. In: A. Sharma & K. M. Dugan (Eds.) *A Dome of Many Colours. Studies in Religious Pluralism, Identity and Unity* Harrisburg: Trinity, 152–178; Id. (2007) *The Garden of Truth. The Vision and Practice of Sufism* San Francisco: Harper. See also: Aslan, A. (1998) *Religious Pluralism in Christian and Islamic Philosophy. The Thought of John Hick and Seyyed Hossein Nasr* Richmond: Curzon; L. Hahn et al. (Eds.) (2001) *The Philosophy of Seyyed Hossein Nasr* Chicago: Open Court.

8    Aydın, M. (2000) Is there only One Way to God? A Muslim View. In: *Studies in Interreligious Dialogue*, 10, 148–159. Id. (2001) Religious Pluralism. A Challenge for Muslims – A Theological Imagination. In: *JES*, 38, 330–352.

9    Sachedina, A. (1999) *The Qur'an on Religious Pluralism* Washington D.C.: Georgetown University; Id. (2001) *The Roots of Democratic Pluralism* Oxford: University Press.

I would now like to begin by giving you an example how a theology of dialogue is emerging in the Islamic world and then address Europe and speak about strategies through which I hope to achieve one here. I also would like to note in advance that personally, I believe a dialogical theology holds great potential if we read the founding texts of the Islamic faith again from that perspective.

The example for greater openness towards other religions I would first like to address comes from Iran. This is a country where Islamic law applies in many areas of life and where, based on this law, Jews and Christians enjoy some civil rights, but are not legally the equals of Muslims. They do have rights: they have their own hospitals, retirement homes and schools, can learn and speak their own languages, have places of worship and even send their own representatives to parliament. However, they do not enjoy legal equality. They cannot, for example, be elected to the presidency or hold many other offices in government and especially the military.

Thus, you cannot but call Iran a divided society, and hardliners in the Islamic Republic regard exactly this as the realisation of a divinely ordained system. Take, for example, the influential cleric Ayatollah Mesbah Yazdi. He heads a school that many leading Iranian statesmen graduated from and is considered a mentor of the current president, Mahmud Ahmadinejad, whose anti-Semitic tirades have drawn worldwide attention. In his book *The Political Theory of Islam*, Mesbah Yazdi writes that future political leaders need to internalise the fact that:

> In a democracy such as the one some people advocate today, all members of society have equal access to government offices. If Iran were such a democracy, that would mean a Jew could become president of the country. All people would be equal and we would no longer have first and second class citizens.[10]

He concludes:

> We must either become humanist or remain Allahist.[11]

That is a position on the question of dialogue that you can take, and that – let's not ignore the facts here – some people do take. The other, opposite position is the one I would now like to introduce you to. It was voiced by a man who – this is another reason I have chosen to present this particular case – has long lived and worked in Hamburg, by Mohammad Mojtahed Shabestari. Born in 1936 in Iran, he came to Hamburg from Ghom/Iran in 1968 to head the Islamic Centre near the Aussenalster. During his tenure there, he not only attended to the daily

---

10  Mesbah Yazdi, M. T. *Nazariye-ye siyasi-ye eslam* (The Political Theory of Islam). The first edition was published in 2000. This essay quotes from the version published on Mesbah Yazdi's website: http://mesbahyazdi.org/farsi/?./lib/nazariye2/ch04.htm (accessed October 25, 2011) (Trsl. from Farsi by Katajun Amirpur, trsl into English by Volker Bach).

11  http://mesbahyazdi.org/farsi/?./lib/nazariye1/ch14.htm (accessed October 25, 2011)(Trsl. from Farsi by Katajun Amirpur, trsl. into English by Volker Bach).

routine of the Centre – marriages, divorces and burials – but also fostered Islamic-Christian dialogue. Much later, he spoke of this dialogue in an interview:

> Back then we Christians, Muslims and Jews sat together in the sessions of interreli-
> gious dialogue. It was new to us Muslims, and something of an event. For me, it was
> especially impressive and I learned through these encounters that it is not enough to
> study the sources or read about the others, but that personal meetings are richer and
> teach you more.[12]

Shabestari came to know Professor Hans Jochen Margull (d. 1982), Protestant theologian and Professor of Ecumenical Relations at Hamburg University,
during his stay. Shabestari's personal relationship with him is so worth emphasising because it demonstrates how important interpersonal exchange and
dialogue are in developing a theology aimed at tolerance.

Margull assumed that the indivisible truth claim of each religion contained
an absolute. At the level of a subjective certainty of the possibility of salvation,
he regarded this absolute claim as justified. Objective claims to absolute truth,
on the other hand, were unacceptable to him, especially since their particular
nature was demonstrated by the competing claims of different religions.

We find this motif taken up again by Shabestari in his argument for granting
legal equality to Iran's Christians and Jews, a step he considers indispensable. You will recall that we are now entering the territory of a discourse in
which leading scholars argue against such equal status. To counter their claims,
Shabestari has written an essay titled Human Rights and the Understanding of
Religions (*Die Menschenrechte und das Verständnis der Religionen*). His main
argument is that the reasons which motivated Muslims to create an unequal
system in the past no longer apply today.

To support his position, Shabestari studied the historical relationship between the three revealed religions. He makes the three-step argument that this
is related to the progress of human rights:

1. The views that Jews, Christians and Muslims had of each other in the past
   were based on religious beliefs. Adherents of all three faiths tended to see
   the others either as enemies or as misguided.
2. These convictions were expressed in social structures. The assumption that
   adherents of other religions did not share their pre-eminent proximity to
   God dictated that they should not hold pre-eminent positions in society, ce-
   menting a second-class status for them. In addition:

> It might seem that convictions conducive to violence and the consequent injustices
> were created and put into practice by only a few adherents of these religions. However,
> it is undeniably true that the texts of all three revealed religions, Judaism, Christian-

---

12  Interview with Mohammad Mojtahed Shabestari (Pt 1): "Der Islam ist eine Religion, kein
    politisches Programm". Internet portal Qantara 2008. http://de.qantara.de/inhalt/interview-
    mit-mohammad-mojtahed-shabestari-teil-1-der-islam-ist-eine-religion-kein (last accessed
    December 10, 2013) (trsl. into English by Volker Bach).

ity and Islam, contain passages that, unless interpreted correctly, will lead to such convictions. In Jewish religious texts, it is stated that only the Jews are the Chosen People closer to God than the rest of mankind. In Christian texts, this proximity is the privilege of the Christian faithful, and in the religious texts of Islam it is reserved for those who follow the religion of Muhammad.[13]

Shabestari does not want to reinterpret the holy texts. He merely aims to explain where this argumentation went wrong, namely in the inability of believers to separate two different issues: proximity to God and legal rights within a society. They had transferred the premise of one conclusion to another. The objects, though, are entirely different ones, Shabestari argues, and their premises must not be confused.

He explains that the proximity of a human to God touches on the spiritual bliss of an individual beyond this life, while human rights touch upon the co-existence of humans in this life. The first concerns the vertically structured relationship between God and humanity which cannot be subject to human will shaping it, whereas the second concerns a horizontally structured human relationship. Unlike the relationship with God, which is not subject to human interference, the relationships among humans are shaped by them – and are unrelated to questions of religion. They are located beyond the religious sphere.

The result of mingling the two spheres was that the horizontal, social relationships came to mirror the vertical relationship between God and humanity. The power structures of society were designed according to an ideology that arose from this mirror image. This takes Shabestari to his final step, the conclusion:

> In the present age, our situation is entirely different. Today, the fact that philosophy and science have been embraced as independent sources of knowledge and the developments of critical, legal, moral and political philosophy have allowed adherents of the three religions to rightly and clearly separate the fundamental human rights that are at the heart of all human relationships from the question of the relation between a person and God. Today, we can thus believe that God censures and reproves nonbelievers in the Hebrew Bible, the New Testament and the Qur'an, but at the same time holds all people – believers and nonbelievers – responsible for granting everyone the same rights in their relationships with other humans, allowing for no exceptions.[14]

With these arguments, Shabestari can justify how the same rights can apply to the adherents of all different religions in a modern society. He thus proposes a secular stance by the state. This may be interesting for a country whose political system is based on Islam, but it is less exciting when applied to Germany. Nonetheless it shows that a theology of dialogue and tolerance is emerging in

---

13  Shabestari, M. (2000) *Naqdi bar qera'at-e rasmi az din* (A Criticism of the Official Interpretation of Religion), Teheran: Tarh-e Naw, 313. (Trsl. from Farsi by Katajun Amirpur, trsl. into English by Volker Bach).
14  Ibid., 316–317. (Trsl. from Farsi by Katajun Amirpur, trsl. into English by Volker Bach).

the Islamic world. Shabestari is taking the first step towards a full acceptance of nonbelievers. A secular view of other religions is, I believe, the first precondition for dialogue.

In addition we must not forget that in order to take root in Europe, a modern Islamic theology must find reassurance in the Islamic world. It cannot emerge here in isolation from it, but needs to be able to refer to connection points and examples. Otherwise, what we are developing here would be a lost cause of no international significance. That is why we need to stay able to relate to the international debate, to connect with what is called *Nouandishi-ye dini* in Farsi and can only be rendered with the rather complex circumlocution of new thought or Newthinking in religious terms.

Beyond this, the example of Shabestari was to show, as I said, how important dialogue between theologies and theologians is. Shabestari profited greatly from his stay in Hamburg, where he learned German and studied Protestant theological works. His perspective on those is more than fascinating. He has, for example, drawn parallels between the thought of Paul Tillich that God is what "concerns us unconditionally" (*uns unbedingt angeht*) and Islamic mysticism, especially that of Ibn 'Arabi (d. 1240), the greatest hermeneuticist the Islamic world ever produced. To Ibn 'Arabi, the word of God has such an overpowering effect on an addressee that his critical faculty of reflection is interrupted. He cannot think, except mystically of God. In that sense, Ibn 'Arabi, too, sees God as what concerns us unconditionally.

This is where Shabestari begins his quest for a new understanding of revelation, which he believes the Islamic world is in need of for reasons I cannot discuss in detail here. Let it be enough to say the wish was born from his experience with the fundamentalism of the Islamic Republic of Iran and its totalitarian view of God. In Shabestari's view, it must be replaced with a relationship of the I and the You. In this, he follows Tillich's criticism of the reification of God that has made a being, and thus an object, of Him. At the heart of this new theology, the *'elm-e kalam-e jadid* he wishes the Islamic world to arrive at, must be faith as the religious experience between an individual and God. This is radically different from the official line preached in Iran, and very close to Tillich.

So much for the approaches from the Islamic world, where the subject is still a new one, and an example of a productive Christian-Muslim dialogue in the case of Shabestari's modern theology. In the light of this it appears to me that the modern Islamic theology emerging here could profit greatly from a close cooperation with Christian theology.

And besides of that, I see a great deal of potential for a dialogical theology if you go and look at the founding texts of Islamic theology anew, reading them from this perspective. I would like to give two examples for this. The opening Surah of the Qur'an reads: *ihdina as-sirata al-mustaqim* – guide us on the right path. This means, of course, the one right path, in the singular, the Islamic one, to God. Naturally, Islam makes the assumption here that the Islamic path to God is the right one. All monotheistic religions believe that only they can guide the faithful on the right path while the others cannot. Christianity too shares this absolute truth claim. Anything else would reveal an odd view of oneself, to tell the truth. It would be strange to say that I believe in a certain religion, but am not really sure whether it is true after all.

That is why the Qur'an speaks of the one, the Islamic way. And yet it also says other things. Even in the Qur'an, we read of several paths. It says the prophets follow a right, straight path, not the right, straight one. That is the case for example in Surah 16,120–121: I quote the translation by Arthur J. Arberry.

> Surely, Abraham was a nation
> obedient unto God, a man of pure faith
> and no idolater,
> showing thankfulness for His blessings;
> He chose him, and He guided him
> to a straight path.

Or Surah 36,3–4, where Muhammad is addressed:

> thou art truly among the Envoys
> on a straight path;

You can read these Surahs to mean that God has designed this plurality, that it is desired and part of his work. And a very important person for the Islamic world has read them in exactly that sense before: Maulana Jalaleddin Rumi (d. 1273 in Konya), who is considered among the highest authorities in both Turkey and Iran. His tomb continues to attract pilgrims to this day.

Maulana Jami, who was born in what is Afghanistan today, refers to Rumi's main work, the Mathnavi, as the Qur'an in the Persian tongue, *Qor'an be zaban-e parsi.* That is a rather heretical turn of phrase. To put it less provocatively, the Mathnavi is a Qur'an commentary, and a mystical one. It represents a spiritual act of grasping the inner meaning of the Qur'an. Alongside this inner meaning, *batin*, there is an outward meaning, *zahir*, which is open to everyone. There is a long tradition of hermeneutical commentaries by Sufis such as Rumi who had reached the inner meaning. The Mathnavi is certainly the most influential one of these works. You could go so far as to call it the most important Qur'an commentary of all for Iranians, but also many Turks. It is certainly the best known and most famous of Rumi's works, not least because it has been interpreted by many Persian musicians. Mohammad Reza Shajarian, Iran's most famous classical singer, who is considered the voice of the Iranian people by many, mostly performs his works. Rumi's fame has also spread to the West. Translations of the Mathnavi were bestsellers in the United States during the 1990s. The movement he founded, the whirling dervishes of Konya, enjoys considerable popularity here, too.

I will now present a story from the Mathnavi in the translation by Reynold A. Nicholson:

The elephant was in a dark house: some Hindús had brought it for exhibition.
In order to see it, many people were going, every one, into that darkness.
As seeing it with the eye was impossible, (each one) was feeling it in the dark
with the palm of his hand.
The hand of one fell on its trunk: he said, "This creature is like a water-pipe."
The hand of another touched its ear: to him it appeared to be like a fan.
Since another handled its leg, he said, "I found the elephant's shape to be
like a pillar."
Another laid his hand on its back: he said, "Truly, this elephant was like a throne."
Similarly, whenever any one heard (a description of the elephant), he understood
(it only in respect of) the part that he had touched.
On account of the (diverse) place (object) of view, their statements differed:
one man entitled it "dál", another "alif'".
If there had been a candle in each one's hand,
the difference would have gone out of their words.[15]

One thought the elephant a drainpipe, the second a column, the third a throne. That is how different our understanding of the same thing can be. Rumi ponders further that, had these people held a candle, their differences would have vanished. They would have recognised what really was in front of them. But in the dark chamber of nature, our recognition of the truth – symbolised by the elephant – must remain fragmentary. We all hold a part of it in our hand, but nobody owns the whole. Admitting that our knowledge is deficient should be enough to teach us a degree of humility. And tolerance, openness for pluralism and dialogue are nothing other than the fruit of the tree of humility. This humility is the most important lesson we should draw from Rumi's poem.

Abdoldjavad Falaturi is a familiar name in Hamburg. This Islamic cleric and scholar who died in 1996 must certainly be viewed as the most interesting Muslim thinker in Germany on matters of Christian-Islamic dialogue. Falaturi once said that the most important precondition for an interreligious dialogue was "to distance oneself from the insistence on possession of an exclusive truth".[16] If you think yourself in possession of the truth and see everyone else as erring, you destroy any basis for true dialogue.

The idea of limiting salvation to the adherents of your own faith while assigning condemnation to all others is no more than a monoperspectival limitation of divine love and charity, an egocentric attempt to coerce God. Assigning heaven and hell to groups

---

15  Nicholson, R. A. (1930) *The Mathnawí of Jalálu'ddín Rúmí* London: Luzac, vol. IV, Book III, Beyt 1259 f.

16  Falaturi, A. (1996) Hermeneutik des Dialoges aus islamischer Sicht. In: Id. (Ed.) *Der Islam im Dialog* (5th expanded edition) Hamburg: Islamwissenschaftliche Akademie, 156–172, 157. Quoted after: Weiße, Wolfram: *"Christlich-islamischer Dialog – Möglichkeiten und Grenzen"*. Presentation on 2 February 2006 at the NEK synod in Rendsburg. http://www.nordelbien.de/download/synode_2006_1/Top1_2Weisse.pdf, last accessed 11 December 2013.

of people, or rather, arrogating the function of gatekeeper there shows a naive idea of the relationship between man and God.[17]

I am sure he was thinking of Rumi, who once said:

> From the place (object) of view, O (thou who art the) kernel of Existence,
> there arises the difference between the true believer and the Zoroastrian and the Jew.[18]

What he meant by this is: The difference between the three is not one on right and wrong or true and false, but only one of different perspectives. These are not the perspectives of the adherents, but of the prophets. The truth was one, but the three prophets viewed it from different perspectives, or rather, it appeared to them in its glory and brightness in three perspectives, which is why they presented three different religions. Therefore, differences between the three religions are owed not solely to different social circumstance or the fact that one religion degenerated and was replaced by another. Rather, the different manifestations of God in the world have created the religious laws differently, just as they did nature.

The Jewish philosopher Hermann Levin Goldschmidt has designated dialogics as an opposite to dialectics in his work *Philosophie als Dialogik.* According to him, antagonism is a fundamental and productive tension that cannot be resolved in any form of higher synthesis. Two (and very likely more than two) opposing positions must be tolerated, contend with each other productively, and be recognised in their equal importance. I believe that this comes very close to what Rumi wanted to say about the different perspectives of the Jew, the Christian and the Zoroastrian.

I would like to quote you another story from the Mathnavi of Rumi. It tells of Moses and the herdsman. In it, the prophet reproaches a herdsman for addressing God in loving, but foolish terms. God, in turn, reproaches Moses. This is once more the translation by Nicholson, abridged by me.

> Moses saw a shepherd on the way, who was saying, "O God
> who choosest (whom Thou wilt),
> Where art Thou, that I may become Thy servant and sew
> Thy shoes and comb Thy head?
> That I may wash Thy clothes and kill Thy lice and bring
> milk to Thee, O worshipful One;
> …
> Moses said, "Man, to whom is this (addressed)?"
> He answered, "To that One who created us; by whom this
> earth and sky were brought to sight."
> "Hark !" said Moses, "you have become very backsliding (depraved);
> indeed you have not become a Moslem, you have become an infidel.
> What babble is this? what blasphemy and raving?

---

17  Ibid. (trsl. into English by Volker Bach).
18  Nicholson, (1930) Book III, Beyt 1258.

...
The stench of your blasphemy has made the (whole) world stinking:
your blasphemy has turned the silk robe of religion into rags.
...
If you know that God is the Judge, how is it right for you
(to indulge in) this doting talk and familiarity?
...
Are the body and (its) needs among the attributes of the Lord of glory?
(Only) he that is waxing and growing drinks milk: (only) he that has need of feet
puts on shoes.
And if these words (of yours) are (meant) for His servant,
...
(The words) He begat not, He was not begotten are appropriate to Him:
He is the Creator of begetter and begotten."
...
He (the shepherd) said, "O Moses, thou hast closed my mouth
and thou hast burned my soul with repentance."
He rent his garment and heaved a sigh, and hastily turned
his head towards the desert and went (his way).
A revelation came to Moses from God —"Thou hast parted My servant from Me.
Didst thou come (as a prophet) to unite, or didst thou come to sever?
...
of (all) things the most hateful to Me is divorce.
I have bestowed on every one a (special) way of acting
...
I did not ordain (Divine worship) that I might make any profit;
nay, but that I might do a kindness to (My) servants.
In the Hindoos the idiom of Hind (India) is praiseworthy;
in the Sindians the idiom of Sind is praiseworthy.
I am not sanctified by their glorification (of Me);
'tis they that become sanctified and pearl-scattering (pure and radiant).
I look not at the tongue and the speech;
...
I gaze into the heart (to see) whether it be lowly, though the words uttered be not lowly,
Because the heart is the substance, speech (only) the accident;
...
The religion of Love is apart from all religions:
for lovers, the (only) religion and creed is – God."[19]

Moses immediately regrets his harshness and starts looking for the herdsman,
but he has by now risen to a much higher spiritual level.

This story, too, tells us of several ways to God, the right ways. Just like the
way Moses uses, the herdsman's way is also right. Love and commitment of
religious practice are much more important than the quote-unquote 'correct'
belief. Different manifestations of the one Divine may have been granted to
different people, but it is still the one God.

---

19  Nicholson, R. A. (1926) *The Mathnawí of Jalálu'ddín Rúmí* London: Luzac, vol. II, Book
    II, Beyt 1720–1770.

Our understanding of HIM, the one God, is of necessity limited and approx-imate, just as that of the herdsman. What Rumi is saying here is that God does not listen to our prayers because they do Him justice or because the supplicant sees Him as He really is, but because God is kind. We were granted permission to pray to him with our limited, anthropocentric understanding because we would be unable to free ourselves from it entirely anyway, because we are too limited to comprehend God – and because God is kind.

Just as individuals develop different approaches to God or different readings of a religious text – let us just think of the myriad interpretations of the Qur'an, mystical and rational, to only name two main thrusts – so may religions. Per-haps this pluralism is something desired? That is how I read Rumi, and I believe it is how he read the Qur'an.

This approach reminds me of what the British religious philosopher John Hick (d. 2012) represents in Christian dialogical theology today. Hick is read rather widely in the Islamic world. He is mentioned, for example, in the writ-ings of the Iranian religious philosopher Abdulkarim Soroush, one of the most important Iranian intellectuals alive today, who has been referred to as the 'John Hick of Iran', but has also come to the attention of the establishment. In 2005, Hick was invited to present his ideas at a meeting organised by the Tehran *Anjoman-e hekmat va falsafe* (The Society of Wisdom and Philosophy) on the topic of the dialogue of cultures.

John Hick advocates the position that different religions can be true and lead to salvation – a position referred to as theological pluralism. Soroush quotes Hick's book *Disputed Questions in Theology and the Philosophy of Religion*, in which the author asks questions that impressed him greatly. These questions were: Why should my Muslim and Jewish friends be less an object of God's love than I? Does He truly love them less than me, the Christian? What did I do that they did not? Were there fewer saints of good people among Muslims and Jews than among Christians? Have they sinned more than we have?[20]

Hick comes to the conclusion that the truth of religious tenets is not a deci-sive theological factor. He sees this rather in their practical function of leading to salvation. This, Hick argues, is possible to the same high degree for a variety of rites and beliefs. According to him, the core of all religions is a transcendent being he calls "The Real". In all historical religions, this is represented inad-equately, which is the root of differences in religious traditions. The various human interpretations of 'the Real' go back to specific human cultural and in-dividual ideas.

Soroush finds this concept in the verse of the Persian poet Foroughi Bastami (d. 1857) who wrote:

---

20  Soroush, A. (1999) *Saratha-ye mostaqim* (Rechte Wege), Teheran, 20.

You appear to me in thousandfold glory so that I may adore you with a thousand eyes.
Ba sad hezar jelve b'run amadi ke man/ba sad hezar dide tamasha konam tora.[21]

The type of reception that Soroush is attempting here is a very important aspect
of cultural transfer. I call it framing. He translates a modern idea, that of John
Hick, into a traditional thought. The anthropologist Sally Engle Merry referred
to this as *vernacularisation,* rendering in the local language, in connection with
human rights. Framing the idea as a familiar Islamic concept allows people to
accept it as their own. It is important for another reason in this particular case:
only if such ideas are embraced as native – a process the philosopher Seyla
Benhabib called iteration – will the suspicion of Western paternalism surrounding them be dispelled.

The case of John Hick I quoted also provides us with an example for the
circulation of ideas in the other direction: To explain his concept that other
religions are different, but equally valid answers of the same eternal reality we
call God, Hick turns to none else than Jalaleddin Rumi. He quotes:

The lamps are different but the Light is the same; it comes from beyond.
In sefal-o in pelite digar ast/lik nurash nist digar z' an sar ast.[22]

Hick explains that religious pluralism is not – as has long been assumed – a
product of the Enlightenment era, but was already developed by Rumi and Ibn
'Arabi in the 13th and by the Indian scholars Kabir and Nanak in the 15th century.[23] He is most likely referring to the words of Ibn 'Arabi:

I will no longer say to one whose religion is different from mine: My religion is better
than yours. For my heart is ready to take any form, to be a pasture for gazelles, a
monastery for monks, a temple for idols, the Kaaba for one who has made a vow, the
tablets of the Torah, the scrolls of the Qur'an. To me, there is but the religion of love.
Wherever its ascent takes me will be my creed and my faith.[24]

My approach within a modern dialogical theology would be to seek ideas of
a theology of dialogue and plurality in the texts of Islam itself. These works,
Rumi being the best example, have value and meaning to the people. In the
terms of Islamic discourse, they carry conviction. That is to say readers will

---

21  Quoted after Ibid., 22. (Trsl. from Farsi by Katajun Amirpur, trsl into English by Volker
    Bach).
22  Hick, J. (2005) *Religious Pluralism and Islam.* Lecture delivered to the Institute for Islamic
    Culture and Thought, Tehran, in February 2005. http://www.johnhick.org.uk/article11.pdf,
    p. 11. (last accessed 11 December 2013).
23  Ibid., 15.
24  Ibn Arabi (1966) *Tarjuman al-ashwaq* Beirut: Dar Sadir, 43 f., quoted after: Ayoub, M.
    (1992) Das Wort und der Weg. Des Menschen Suche nach Gott in der islamischen My-
    stik. In: A. Bsteh (Ed.) *Hören auf sein Wort. Der Mensch als Hörer des Wortes Gottes in
    christlicher und islamischer Überlieferung* (Beiträge zur Religionstheologie 7), Mödling:
    St. Gabriel, 167–187, 186. (Trsl. into English by Volker Bach).

assume something Rumi says is true. As an aside, this power stems not so much for any particular authoritarian mindset of the Muslim world, but largely from the beauty of his language. Rumi's poetry is almost magical, and the conviction that something that is beautiful must be true is not limited to the Orient. Truth is beauty, beauty is truth.

To get back to the main point, my intention is to offer a new reading, or to give new currency to an old one, as I would by helping Rumi's interpretation come to light again. At this point I should probably address the objection that the outcome would be only an eclectic interpretation. To that I can only say: I do not know if the mode of reading the Qur'an I am proposing is indeed the right one. *Wa allahu a'lam*. God knows better. This is the formula with which classical Qur'an commentaries traditionally ended. Their style was similar to the *Midrash*: First, the relevant Surah was mentioned. The interpretation of that Surah according to authorities A, B and C followed. On occasion, dozens of commentators were found worth repeating. Often, their views of one and the same Surah could differ completely. All of it closed with the sentence: *Wa allahu a'lam* – which meant: In the end, God alone knows.

Of course it is true that my reading may be determined and prejudiced by a certain interest, that I may be putting together my own personal version of Islam. That may be, but I am doing so with good intentions, and in Islamic tradition, *niyya* counts. What is certainly true is that religions are less determined by what their sacred texts say and more by what people take from them. These are basic principles of hermeneutics that nobody can simply nullify. The idea that, as Gadamer puts it, a certain interest and pre-understanding prejudice a certain reading is neither a new idea nor was it ever viewed as unnatural in the Islamic world. The first Imam of the Shi'a said what has become the guiding principle of Shi'ite exegesis:

> The Qur'an is writing hidden between two book covers. It does not speak. It requires an interpreter, and in truth, it is people that make it speak.[25]

25 Abi Talib, 'Ali ibn (1972) *Nahj al-balagha*, edited and interpreted by 'Ali Naqi Feiz ol-Eslam, sermon 125, 386, Teheran. (Trsl. from Farsi by Katajun Amirpur, trsl. into English by Volker Bach).

*Mahmoud Ayoub*

# Religious Pluralism and the Qur'an[1]

## Introductory Remarks

Religious diversity is as old as human history. From ancient cave dwellers to the societies of the great empires of China, India, Iran, Egypt and Babylon, religion as the human quest for the divine manifested itself in a variety of languages, devotional practices, myths and rituals. In reality, in these and myriad other cultures, religion has been the fountainhead of civilisation.[2]

Religion may also be regarded, at least in its literary, artistic and philosophical manifestations, as the product of culture. Thus the plurality and diversity of religions is a reflection of the plurality and diversity of cultures and civilisations. In this essay, I will first define pluralism religiously and philosophically. I will then attempt to contextualise it within the history of the civilisations of the Middle East. I will finally discuss religious pluralism in the Qur'an. I am convinced that the Qur'anic worldview, with its emphasis on the diversity of human racial and cultural identities and man's innate capacity to know and have faith in God, recognises the diverse religions of humankind as divinely preordained ways to this ultimate goal.[3]

## What is Pluralism?

In its lexical usage, pluralism signifies plurality, as opposed to singularity. Plurality, moreover, implies difference, and hence diversity. Theologically, the expression religious pluralism must be distinguished from religious exclusivism on the one hand, and religious inclusivism on the other. While the proponents of these two rival ideologies to religious pluralism affirm it as a religious phenomenon, they in fact negate, or at least, seek to render it theologically meaningless.

---

1   Reproduced with written permission from the copyrights holder of the International Institute of Islamic Thought (IIIT), first appeared in the book *Contemporary Approaches to the Quran and Sunnah* edited by Prof. Mahmoud Ayoub. This essay has appeared in different forms in the following publications:
    • (1997) Islam and Pluralism. In: *Encounters*, 3 (2), 103–118.
    • (2000) Islam and the Challenge of Religious Pluralism. In: *Global Dialogue*, 2 (1), 53–64.
    • (2002) Religious Pluralism and The Challenges of Inclusivism, Exclusivism and Globalism: An Islamic Perspective. In: T. Sumartana et al. (Eds.) *Commitment of Faiths: Identity, Plurality and Gender* Yogyakarta, Indonesia: Institute of DIAN/Interfidei.
2   For the role of religion in the rise of human civilisations, see: McNeill, W. H. (1991) *The Rise of the West: A History of the Human Community* Chicago: University of Chicago Press.
3   This capacity is called in the Qur'an "*fitrat Allah*", God's pure creation. See Q. 30:30, to which we shall return later in this discussion.

Exclusivism denotes the view that the truth, and consequently the way to salvation, is only one. It is furthermore limited to only one true religion, and is the prerogative of one and only one faith-community. Exclusivism has moral, theological and philosophical implications. Philosophically, it confines the truth to one belief and value system; while morally and theologically, it ultimately condemns all other faith-communities to manifest error in this world and to perdition in the world to come.

In the three Middle Eastern, or so-called Abrahamic religious traditions, exclusivism, in one form or another, remains a fundamental tenet. In the Jewish tradition it is expressed in the doctrine of the chosen people, with its moral, political and theological implications. To be sure, ancient prophets spoke against an exclusivist nationalism that abhorred other nations and condemned them to a state of total insignificance in the sight of God. Jewish exclusivism has remained largely an exclusivism of indifference to what may be termed gentile religions and belief-systems.

The well-known exclusivist Christian doctrine formulated by the North African theologian Cyprian in the third century, "salus extra ecclesiam non est" (outside the Church there is no salvation)[4] characterised the theology of the Catholic Church at least till the Second Vatican Council. But the Vatican Council adopted an inclusivist theology which denied real validity to religions other than Christianity, as we shall presently see.

The Qur'anic assertion, "Anyone who desires a faith other than *islam*, it shall not be accepted of him; and in the hereafter he shall be among the losers,"[5] expresses an exclusivist view of religion, but only if the term *islam* is taken narrowly to refer to Islam as an institutionalised religion. If, however, it is taken to signify a human attitude of total submission (*islam*) to God, then we are talking not about religious institutions, but about an ideal relationship between God and human beings that transcends all religions, including Islam.[6]

The opposite of exclusivism is inclusivism. Inclusivism is a modern and mainly Western humanistic Christian theological concept which takes many forms. One of these forms is the belief that even though my religion is the only way to salvation, moral women and men of good conscience, even if they be atheists, will attain salvation by being anonymous members of my faith-community.

4   See *Encyclopedia of Religion* Mircea Eliade editor in chief, Macmillan Publishers, Electronic Edition produced by Infobases Inc, Provo, Utah. SV Cyprian. For a modern Protestant defense of Christian exclusivism, see: Plantinga, A. (1999) Pluralism: A Defense of Religious Exclusivism. In: K. Meeker & P. Quinn (Eds.) *The Philosophical Challenge of Religious Diversity* New York: Oxford University Press, 172–192.

5   Q. 3:85. See also v. 19; and: Ayoub, M. (1992) *The Qur'an and Its Interpreters vol. 2* [hereafter Ayoub Qur'an] Albany: State University of New York Press, 56, 66, 240–243 for the views of Qur'an commentators of these verses.

6   For a good study of the term Islam in the Qur'an and exegetical tradition, see: Smith, J. (1975) *An historical and semantic study of the term "islām" as seen in a sequence of Quran commentaries* Published by Scholars Press for Harvard Theological Review.

The well-known German theologian Karl Rahner (1904–1984) coined the term "anonymous Christians" to formulate a theology of Christian inclusivist salvation.[7] He echoed in this the Second Vatican Council declarations *Nostra aetate* and the Dogmatic Constitution on the Church *(lumen gentium)*. The Constitution states:

Those also can attain to everlasting salvation who, through no fault of their own, do not know the gospel of Christ or his Church, yet sincerely seek God and, moved by grace, strive by their deeds to do his will as it is known to them through the dictate of conscience.[8]

Rahner argued for the validity of his theology of universal salvation through the atoning death of Christ on the ground that it is in virtual agreement with the theology of Vatican II. But while Vatican II presupposes faith in God, however erroneous such faith may be, Rahner made everlasting salvation available to all decent men and women of good conscience, even if they are atheists. It must be observed that his theology of salvation ultimately goes against the Christian doctrine of original sin and the need for redemption and atonement through faith in the cross of Christ.

Religious pluralism, as has already been observed, is the recognition of the multiplicity and diversity of religions as a natural or divinely willed phenomenon. Yet if religious pluralism is to serve as a meaningful framework of constructive dialogue among the followers of the various religions, all religions, or at least all theistic religions, must be recognised as legitimate ways to the Truth or Ultimate Reality. It must be further agreed that the followers of every religion have the right to regard their own faith as the true one for them. Since, moreover, the need for everlasting salvation in some form is common to at least all the major religions, no one way should be privileged as the only way to salvation.

It may be argued that acceptance of the equal validity of all the major religions would ultimately lead to religious relativism, or the relativity of the Truth. Some have therefore posited a super-religion as a unifying spiritual vision of all religions. This view is, in the final analysis, another form of inclusivism, which reduces all religions to one imaginary ideal faith.[9] That God spoke to every community or nation in its own language, through a long list of prophets and sages, is frequently asserted in the Qur'an and the New Testament.[10] All the major religions hold that the Truth is One, and it transcends human understand-

---

7   Rahner developed his idea into an elaborate theology of salvation through the cross of Christ. See his *Theological Investigations*, particularly *vols 14* and *16*, both available in English translations.

8   *Dogmatic Constitution on the Church no. 16.*

9   See for a penetrating study of the different approaches to religious pluralism, as well as the issue of religious relativism: Hick, J. (2005) *An Interpretation of Religion* New Haven and London: Yale University Press.

10  See for example: Q. 10:47, 4:41 and 16:36; and Acts 2:1–11, I Tm 2:4 and Heb. 1:1 ff.

ing. Yet since the goal of all religions is to seek the Truth, they must all be ways
to that goal, for "to God do we belong, and to Him we shall return". (2,156).

## Religious Pluralism in Ancient Iran and the Mediterranean Basin

The period from the eighth to the third century BCE can be regarded as the
axial age in religious and philosophical creativity in greatly separated areas
around the then known world.[11] It witnessed the rise of Chinese philosophy in
its Taoist, Confucianist and other forms. In India, during this period of spiritual
growth, the great sages of the Upanishads formulated an enduring mystical mo-
nistic philosophy which supplanted the somewhat crude Vedic religion. In India
too the Buddha "set the wheel of dharma turning" with his moral philosophy
of suffering and salvation, and challenged the vast Hindu pantheon with its
authoritarian priesthood.

Ancient Israel saw the rise of the prophetic movement with its messianic
hopes and ideas of universal salvation. Voices like those of Amos, Mica, Jeremiah and others called for social justice and the worship of YHWH as the
sovereign Lord of all nations.

The first man of authority to recognise and promote religious pluralism was
Cyrus the great, founder of the Persian Empire in the fifth century BCE. Cyrus
founded an empire that stretched from Iran to Central Asia to Egypt, Iraq, Syr-
ia-Palestine, and even into Europe. This great imperial domain was unrivaled
until the rise of the Muslim empire following the death of the Prophet Muhammad, and especially after the phenomenal expansion of CE 711.

Cyrus sought to honor all the deities of his realm. He allowed his foreign
subjects to return to their lands, worship their gods and pray for his success and
prosperity. He thus gave permission to the Judean exiles to return to Judea and
rebuild the Jerusalem Temple of YHWH their God. This earned him the honor
of being called by the author of II Isaiah YHWH's servant or messiah.[12]

The next empire builder was Alexander the Great [BCE 356–323]. Alexander was not only a great conqueror, but also a philosopher. According to
classical Islamic hagiography, he was even a prophet.[13]

Alexander may be regarded as the father of the classical civilisations of
Judaism, Christianity and Islam. With Alexander we witness a conscious at-

---

11  This notion was first introduced by Karl Jaspers (1953) in his *Origin and Goal of History*
New Haven: Yale University Press. For a good discussion of this important period in the
development of human civilisation and Islam's place in this development, see: Hodgson, M.
(1974) *The Venture of Islam: Conscience and History in a World Civilisation* Chicago and
London: University of Chicago Press, vol. 1.

12  *The Cambridge History of Iran: Vol. 2 (1985), The Median and Achaemenian Periods* Cambridge: Cambridge University Press; Isaiah 44:27–28, 45:1–3, 12–14; also II Chronicles
36:21–23; Ezra, 1:1–9, 3:6–8, 5:12–17, 6:2–4.

13  Muslim hagiography identified Alexander with the prophetic figure *dhū al-qarnayn* of Q.
18:83–98.

tempt to impose a single civilisation framework on at least the Mediterranean basin, including western Europe, the Middle East and north Africa. This was the Hellenistic civilisation, with its rich religious and philosophical heritage, in particular its Platonic and Aristotelian philosophical and scientific worldview.

Within this Hellenistic framework, the Mithraic mystery cult, as well as the inherently dualistic worldview of the religions of ancient Iran, which was expressed in the eternal struggle between good and evil, light and darkness, became a powerful Gnostic movement which threatened and deeply influenced early Christianity. The influence of these Gnostic philosophies on all three monotheistic religions of the Middle East is undeniable. Less significant in the long run were the mysteries of Isis and Osiris in Egypt, and the Delphic and other Greek mysteries which flourished during this culturally and religiously formative period of Western civilisation.

It may be argued that the axial age, mentioned above, culminated with Alexander the Great. With Alexander we see the beginning of a civilisational synthesis which began with the rise of Christianity and Manichaeism and culminated with Islam. Therefore, the period from Alexander to Muhammad may be viewed as another seminal epoch in the formative history of the civilisations of Judaism, Christianity and Islam.

Jesus and Paul rejected the particularistic Jewish faith to which they both belonged. The new universalistic faith which they founded constituted a sharp contrast with the traditional narrow Jewish view of religion and culture. From the beginning, moreover, Christianity challenged, and soon supplanted, Greek wisdom and Egyptian religiosity.

Christianity did not eliminate Greek philosophy, but absorbed it as the framework of its own theology. As for Hellenised Egyptian and other mystery cults, they survived in Christian hagiography and popular piety. Both Egypt and the East, most likely Iran, are represented in the account of the nativity of Jesus. For instance, the wise men of the East who came seeking the divine child, the new king, are believed to have been Magian or Zoroastrian priests. This account was meant to affirm that the humble child, placed in a lowly manger, was Christ the King.[14]

Religion has always been associated with power and humility. In Christ the King who was laid in a humble manger, the reconciliation was finally achieved between the two warring Egyptian gods Horus and Seth, represented by the ox and the donkey respectively. Through this Hellenistic synthesis, moreover, Christianity rendered the universalistic vision of the ancient Hebrew prophets a message of salvation for all of humankind.

It is noteworthy that the first post-Christian religious authority to recognise the plurality and unity of religions was another Iranian, Mani the Babylonian prophet. Mani, who presented yet another vision of the unity of all religions in the third century CE, failed to actualise this vision in a new religious system.

---

14  Matt 2:1–12.

He failed because Manichaeism, which was yet another Iranian dualistic faith, denied the unity of the creation under one sovereign, all-powerful and wise God. This unity of creation under a supreme divine being was essentially the message of Zarathustra, the prophet of ancient Zoroastrianism, of which Manichaeism was a later corruption. This message was also propagated by many Greek sages, particularly Plotinus. It may in fact be argued from an Islamic point of view that Plotinus, with his mystical faith in the One Divine source of Being, was the prophet between Jesus and Muhammad. This is not to say, however, that Mani's explanation of good and evil was quickly forgotten. On the contrary, Manichaeism exerted a deep and lasting influence on the religious thought and piety of Europe and the Middle East.

Mani proclaimed a universal religion of light and salvation. He sought to present himself as the final messenger of God and his religion as a synthesis of Zoroastrianism, Buddhism and Christianity. Yet ironically this great religious genius had a tragic end, and his religion came to be regarded as a great heresy by both Christian and Muslim theologians and heresiographers.[15]

## Religious Pluralism in the Qur'an

Among all the scriptures of the theistic religions the Qur'an is unique in that it sets its worldview within the context of divine Oneness and human diversity, including the plurality of religions. Furthermore, it regards religious diversity as one of the signs (*ayat*) of God, second in importance to the "creation of the heavens and earth".[16] The Qur'an does not directly and categorically deny the validity and truth of any religion. Rather it is concerned with individuals and nations and their faith (*Imam*), or rejection of faith (*kufr*) in God, witnessing (*shahadah*) to His Oneness (*tawhid*) and acceptance of humankind's accountability before Him on the Day of Judgment.

The Qur'an presents its view of religious pluralism in a somewhat progressive manner. In a preliminary statement it simply enumerates the religions known to the Prophet's listeners and leaves the question of their truth for God to judge on the Day of Resurrection. It states: "Surely those who have accepted faith [that is the Muslims], those who are Jews, the Sabaeans, the Christians, the Magians and those who have associated other gods with God, God will judge among them on the Day of Resurrection. God is witness over all things".[17] It should be observed that the verse under consideration first lists the legitimate religions and then mentions those who associate other beings or things with the worship of God alone as people without a legitimate religion.

---

15  See for a quick reference on Mani's life and death and his religion, *Encyclopedia of Religion* sv Mani.

16  30,22. See also 2:213 and 5:48.

17  22,17.

The Qur'an lays down four basic principles, which are necessary for the truth-claim of any religion. The first is that a true religion must be enshrined in a divinely revealed scripture or sacred law (*shari'a*). Secondly, it must affirm God's absolute Oneness (*tawhid*). Thirdly, it must profess active faith in God and the last day. Finally, it should foster righteous living (*ihsan*). On the basis of these four principles, the Qur'an affirms the truth of the faith of Muslims, Jews, Christians and Sabaeans.[18]

It is to be observed that although a scripture or divinely revealed book is of the utmost importance for the truth of a religion, it is not the sole criterion by which a religious community is to be judged. While the Jews, Christians and Muslims are people of the Book, the Sabaeans may not have had a scripture. Nor is it clear that they were true monotheists, as they are reported to have venerated the stars. They did acknowledge a divine creator, on the basis of which the Qur'an includes them among the people of faith in God. Hence, it may phenomenologically be concluded that the Sabaean faith may spiritually prefigure the truth in the non-prophetic wisdom religions, such as Hinduism, Buddhism and the religions of China and Japan.

It may be further argued that the Qur'an affirms faith in any book that God has or may have revealed.[19] This means that, like the plurality of religions, the plurality of scriptures is open ended. The Zoroastrians, for instance, under Muslim rule collected an impressive canon of sacred books, which they claimed goes back to their ancient prophetic sages.[20]

It is noteworthy that the Prophet himself bestowed on them the status of the people of the Book in his command: "Follow in dealing with them the Sunnah (practice) of the people of the Book."[21] Likewise, the famous young Umayyad general Muhammad b. al-Qasim extended this status to the Hindus, following his conquest of the Indus Valley in 711.

The Qur'an claims to have been revealed as a book confirming all previous scriptures, but particularly the Torah, the Psalms and the Gospel. Thus the scriptural requirement is understood, and therefore omitted in the following crucial verse for our discussion. The three remaining principles are affirmed, where the Qur'an transcends all religious affiliations: "Surely those who have faith [that is the Muslims], the Jews, the Christians and the Sabaeans; whoever accepts faith in God and the last day and performs good deeds, those shall have their reward

18  Ayoub, M. (2007) *A Muslim View of Christianity: Essays on Dialogue* New York: Orbis, 17–30. For a more detailed discussion of these four principles from a comparative religion point of view, consult my original lecture, on which this essay is largely based, in the IIIT archives, summer 2008.

19  Rahman, F. (1994) *Major Themes of the Qur'an* Minneapolis: Bibliothica Islamica, 162.

20  Muller, M. (Ed.) (1897) *Sacred Books of the East, vol. 47 "Pahlavi Texts, vol. 5 of 5. Marvels of Zoroastrianism"* Oxford: Oxford University Press.

21  Majd al-din Abu al-Sa'ada al-Mubarak b. Muhammad b. al-Athir al-Jazari (1403 A.H.) *Jami' al-usul fi ahadith al-rasul* 'Abd al-Qādir al-Arna'ūṭ (Ed.) Beirut: Dār al-fikr, *vol. 2,* 660, h. 1161.

with their Lord; no fear shall come upon them, nor will they grieve."[22] This verse is of decisive importance for several reasons. First, it occurs twice in the Qur'an at the beginning and near the end of the Prophet's career in Madinah, as Surah 2 was the first major Surah to be revealed in Madinah and Surah 5 was revealed before Surah 9, which was the last major Surah sent down to the Prophet. It must therefore be conclusively argued that this verse could not be abrogated, as many classical and modern jurists and Qur'an commentators have held. This is because abrogation applies only to legislative verses and this is a narrative verse.

The verse under discussion is important also because it does not limit faith and its rewards to the people of the book. It has already been observed that the Sabaeans may not have had a sacred scripture.[23] Yet they are included among those who shall have the reward of their faith with God. The identity of the Sabaeans has been under debate. Shahrastani, in his book *al-Milal wal-nihal* presents two sects of the Sabaeans.[24] These are the religious Sabaeans of Iraq and the philosophical Sabaeans of Harran in northern Syria. While the religious Sabaeans, with whom we are here concerned, acknowledged one divine creator, they probably did not have a sacred book and they venerated the stars, as did the Babylonians before them. Yet they are included among the people of faith in God.

A close hermeneutical analysis of this verse would reveal two further points. The first is that both the plurality of religions and scriptures are open ended, and closely related. Even though the Qur'an limits the designation "people of the Book" to the Jews and Christians, it speaks of an unspecified number of prophets and messengers who were sent by God as guides and warners to every nation or community. On the basis of this Qur'anic assertion, Muslims, as we have already observed, extended this designation to Zoroastrians and even Hindus. Any other community that could lay credible claim to a sacred scripture would have been included. The second point is that the assertion, "whoever has faith in God and the last day and performs good deeds" provides a universal criterion of divine favour, independent of any religious identity.

According to the principles outlined above, religious affiliation in itself is no guarantee for the attainment of Paradise. The scriptural religions are important frameworks of legal and social identities, but they must be lived within a higher sphere of sincere faith and righteous works. God addresses Muslims and the people of the Book with the warning: "It is not in accordance with your [Muslims] wishes, nor the wishes of the people of the Book; rather, whoever does evil, he will be recompensed for it, nor will he find for himself any friend or helper against God. And, anyone who performs righteous deeds – be he male

---

22  2,62 and 5,69.

23  See for a *tafsir* discussion of the religious identity of the Sabaeans: Ayoub, M. (1984) *Qur'an, vol. 1,* Albany: State University of New York Press, 109–110.

24  Shahrastani's two-volume famous heresiographical work exists in many editions. See the chapter on the Sabaeans in the first volume.

or female – and is a person of faith, those will enter the Garden [of Paradise] and they will not be wronged in the least".[25] Thus we see that the criterion for acceptance with God is neither religious identity, nor class or gender but faith and good deeds.

The plurality of religions and scriptures arises ultimately from the great number of prophets and messengers who followed one another, from Adam to Muhammad, in a great universal procession. Relying on the Qur'anic assertion, "There is no community (*ummah*) but that a warner was sent to it,[26] later Islamic tradition puts the number of prophets at one hundred and twenty-four thousand. The Qur'an further asserts that God did not send a messenger to a community except in its own language, in order that he may elucidate for them God's commands and prohibitions.[27]

Human history, according to this Qur'anic worldview, is prophetic history. Prophetic history is in reality the history of divine guidance of humankind to God through the mission of His prophets and messengers. Divine guidance, moreover, is promised to a heedless humanity that must be reminded again and again of its primordial covenant with God.

God tells us in the noble Qur'an that in primordial time, when humankind were still in the realm of potentiality, called by tradition "the world of atoms" (*'alam al-dharr*), God took out of the loins of the children of Adam their progeny and made them witness over themselves. He said, "Am I not your Lord?" they said, "Yes, we hear and we witness." God then warned humanity, "lest you say on the Day of Resurrection we were heedless of this…"[28] The human part of this primordial divine covenant is to affirm in word and deed the sovereign Lordship of the One God. God's part is to guide humankind out of the darkness of heedlessness (*ghaflah*) into the light of faith in Him.

God first renewed this covenant with Adam and his spouse, after they lost the bliss of Paradise through man's first act of heedlessness, first in His saying, "Their shall come from me to you guidance; and whoever follows my guidance, no fear shall come upon them nor will they grieve".[29] God then renewed this covenant with every prophet until the coming of the last Prophet, Muḥammad, may God's peace and blessing be upon him.

The Qur'an presents religion as such under two distinct, but also interrelated, dimensions. The first is institutionalised religions, such as Islam, Christianity and Judaism. These are the frame work of the laws and rituals of worship which give their followers their legal and social identity as Jews, Christians and

25  4,123–24. This is a cardinal principle of the Qur'an; see for example, 2,177, where faith in God, His revelations and prophets and human virtues such as generosity, steadfastness and keeping one's covenants are given as true signs of righteousness.

26  35,24; see also 40,78, where the plurality of faiths is clearly asserted.

27  14,4; see also 10,47.

28  7,172.

29  2,38. For the story of Adam's sin and God's forgiveness, see: Ayoub (1984) *Qur'an, vol. 1,* 83–93.

Muslims. All three traditions should ideally constitute what the Qur'an calls, "*millat abikum ibrahim* (the religion of your father Abraham)", who called all his children *muslims*. Institutionalised human religions are the necessary vehicle and framework of the inner dimension which they represent.

The Qur'an calls this inner dimension the *fitrah*, or original creation of God of all His human creatures. The Qur'an identifies this divine original creation with the "straight (*qayyim*) religion: "Set [O Muhammad] your face straight towards God, a man of pure faith *(hanifan)*, for this is God's original creation *(fitrah)* upon which He created humankind; there is no altering of God's creation."[30]

This divine pure creation is the innate capacity to know God and have faith in Him, with which every human being is born. This means that every child is born pure, like Adam before he sinned, and is thus ready to affirm anew the divine primordial covenant of "Am I not your Lord?" This innate capacity to know God is realised through human unaided reason, as was the case with Abraham who took first the luminous star to be his Lord, then when it set, he said, "I love not those that set. He then turned to the moon, and when it set, he exclaimed, "if my Lord guides me not, I shall surely be one of those who had gone astray". He finally took the sun to be his God, but when it set he realised that the sun is not God. Then, in an outburst of adoration, he cried out, "I turn my face towards Him who created the heavens and the earth, a man of pure faith, nor will I be one of the associators (*mushrikin*) ".[31]

This Qur'anic two-dimensional view of religion in no way implies dichotomy or duality. Rather institutionalised religion is itself legislated by God as the instrument for the realisation of the inner dimension of faith and righteous living. God says in the Qur'an:

"To everyone of you we have appointed a [sacred] law and a course to follow. For, had God so wished, He would have made you all one community. Rather He wished to try you by means of what He had given you; who among you is of the best action. Compete therefore with one another as if in a race in the performance of good deeds. To God shall be your return, and He will inform you concerning the things in which you had differed."[32]

This verse first stipulates that the exoteric dimension of religion should mirror its inner dimension through the performance of good deeds. Secondly, differences among God's laws which He appointed for different peoples should be respected, and should not lead to conflicts. Finally, the truth concerning these

---

30  30,30. The Prophet is said to have asserted that every child is born upon this divine *fitrah*, and then his parents bring him or her up a Jew, a Christian, or a Magian. M. Shakir Ahmad (Ed.) (1995/1416) *Ahmad b. Hanbal, Musnad Ibn Hanbal* Cairo: Dar al-Hadith, vol. 7, 33, h. 7182.

31  6,76–79. This human capacity to know God by the unaided reason has been recognized by both ancient and classical philosophers and theologians. It is called by Muslim theologians "the way of the Friend (Khalil) of God," that is Abraham.

32  5,48. This is a recurrent theme of the Qur'an.

different divine dispensations will be known only on the Day of Judgment when God will inform all faith-communities of all their religious differences. To paraphrase St. Paul, here we see things through a glass darkly, but then we shall see things as they are.[33] Here we must avoid turning our religious differences into religious conflicts through dialogue in humility and the desire for better understanding. But then God, the absolute Truth (*al-haqq*) will manifest the truth, all the truth.

The Qur'an not only acknowledges religious diversity and plurality, it also lays down the principles that should govern interreligious relations. It first calls for respect and protection of all places of worship. God says: "Had God not repelled some people by means of others, synagogues and churches, mosques and monasteries in which God's name is mentioned, would have been demolished."[34] The Prophet himself applied this principle by allowing the delegation of the Christians of Najran to pray in his mosque. He went even further by calling them and the Muslims to "just word of common ascent" between the two communities.[35] It took the Muslims fourteen centuries to renew this call, and for some Christians and Jews to listen.

The Qur'an enjoins Muslims to dialogue with Jews and Christians in the fairest manner. It sets forth both the etiquette and theology of dialogue: "Do not debate with the people of the Book save in the fairest manner, except those among them who do wrong; and say to them 'we accept faith in that which was sent down to us [that is the Qur'an] and that which was sent down to you [that is the Torah and the Gospel]. Our God and your God is one, and to Him we are submitters (*muslims*).[36]

What then is the ultimate goal of interfaith dialogue from the point of view of the Qur'an? The following few conclusions will, it is hoped, suggest some tentative answers.


## Concluding Remarks

It may be first concluded from the preceding discussion that, neither the Qur'an nor the Prophetic tradition demands of Jews and Christians that they give up their religious identity and become Muslims unless they freely choose to do so. The basis of this religious freedom in Islam is the categorical Qur'anic assertion (2,256), "there is no compulsion in religion". This is a categorical command, not a statement of fact.

Secondly, the Qur'an and Prophetic tradition only enjoined Muslims as well as the followers of other faiths to engage in meaningful dialogue, cooperation

---

33 I Cor. 13,12
34 22,40, see also 24,36.
35 3,61–64, and Ayoub (1992) *Qur'an, vol. 2*, 187–208.
36 29,46, see also 49,13, which calls upon all the peoples and tribes of humankind to get to know one another through dialogue.

and agreement on basic principles. This is what the Qur'an calls "a just word of common ascent", between the Muslims and the people of the Book to worship no one except God and not "take one another as lords beside God".[37] This important call to a unity of faith across the diversity of religions is far more relevant to our time than it was to the time of the Prophet and his people. It goes far beyond the issue of whether Christians actually worship their monks or not. One of the Companions of the Prophet, 'Adi b. Hatim who was formerly a Christian, said to the Prophet: "But the Jews and the Christians do not worship their Rabbis and their monks." The Prophet said, "Do not they legislate for them and they accept their legislation?" This is tantamount to worshipping them.[38] This is because worship in Islam is obedience and if one obeys anyone other than God it is as though one worships him instead of God.

It is important in this regard to observe that Karaism, a movement within Judaism which arose after Islam, may be regarded as an answer to this call. The Karaite movement continues to this day to call other Jews to return to the law of God as revealed in the Torah, and rejects Rabbinic Judaism. It is with this Rabbinic Judaism that the Qur'an was concerned and with which the Muslim community has been struggling ever since.

Judaism, as it has been observed for nearly 2,000 years, is Rabbinic Judaism. Although Rabbinic Judaism is continuous with biblical religion, the latter has been completely superseded by the former. This is perhaps the reason behind the Qur'anic call for the people of the Torah to judge by what God has revealed in it. For the same reason, the Qur'an calls upon the people of the Gospel to judge by what God has revealed in it.[39]

To the extent that Eastern Christians, more than other peoples, at least at the time of the revelation of the Qur'an, tried to harmonise their faith in God with moral living and humility before Him, they are considered to be the "nearest in amity" to Muslims.[40] This special relation with the Christians does not close the door to dialogue with other religious communities. In fact, the legal designation of *Ahl al-Kitab* (peoples of the Book) has been quite fluid. It came to include more and more communities as Muslims came to know more and more religious traditions.

To conclude: what then is the challenge that the Qur'an presents to us today? The challenge is this, that we all have faith in God and compete with one an-

---

37  3,64. It is significant that this call to dialogue follows the only heated debate which the Prophet had with the Christians. This debate is alluded to in the Mubahalah, or imprecation verse, 3:61. Ayoub (1992) *Qur'an, vol. 2,* 188–202, 206.

38  Ibid., 205–207.

39  5,44, 47.

40  The piety and humility of these Christians is touchingly described in the Qur'an 5:82–5. See also my article (1997) Nearest in Amity: Christians in the Qur'an and contemporary exegetical tradition. In: *Journal of Islam and Christian-Muslim Relations,* 8 (2), 145–164. Or in my book (2007) *A Muslim View of Christianity: Essays on Dialogue* New York: Orbis, 187–208.

other in righteous works. It follows from this challenge that all people of faith respect one another and that they believe in all of God's revelations.

The Qur'an presents the followers of all three monotheistic religions not only with a great challenge, but with a great promise as well. The promise is this:

Were the people of the Book to abide by the Torah, the Gospel and that which was sent down to them from their lord [i.e. the Qur'an], they would be nourished with provisions from above them and from beneath their feet.[41]

---

41 5,65–6. This means that they would eat of the bounties of the sky through rain and the rich yield of the earth.

*Mahmut Aydın*

# Islam and Interfaith Dialogue

## Qur'anic Teaching of the Religious Other

As is well-known, the issue of living together with 'the other' already started to be one of the most important problems of humanity from the controversy between Cain and Abel whose story is told by both the Bible and the Qur'an. This problem has become very complicated in our time. On the one hand strengthening efforts to constitutional state, supremacy of the law, democracy and human rights have given positive results in some part of the world, on the other hand some arbitrary administrations, dictatorships, violations of human rights and abusing or misusing religious beliefs have continued to lead to conflicts, exploitations, oppressions, persecutions, wars and genocides in other parts of the world. All these positive and negative developments directly concern all of us, they have been occurring in our global world, which has become a 'global village' in which followers of different faiths, cultures and civilisations easily get in contact with each other because of rapid technological developments and means of communications. Furthermore our contemporary intercommunicating and interdependent universe has made us aware, more clearly but also more painfully than ever before, of the multiplicity of different religions and cultures. Thus the presence, power and richness of 'the others' have vigorously entered our own awareness. Because of these developments the issue of living together with the other has become an important problem which we need to overcome by developing new models that urge us to be more tolerant and more open to others by accepting them as they accept themselves and respecting their otherness. In short, living together with the other in peace, which has been an existential problem, is a common destiny of mankind. This factual reality should not be underestimated in the mutual relationships between human beings and between human beings and nature.

In this paper I would like to deal with the issue of living together with the other within the context of the Qur'an's dialogue with Jews and Christians and then I extend my findings to all non-Muslims. There are two main reasons of my starting with the Qur'anic teaching. The first is that Muslims must regulate their relationship in the light of the Qur'anic teaching because it is the centre of the Muslim faith. So, one of the most influential factors which affect Muslims' relationship with the others is the Qur'an. Since it is central in determining Muslim attitudes, it is important to know what it says about other faiths. The second is that it seems to us that a more positive and a more open Muslim attitude towards the others can only be achieved by hearing from Muslims more of the Qur'an than of the historic formulations of Islam. In this paper I am hoping to answer clearly the question of how Muslims should live with the religious other within the context of mutual understanding and mutual respect in our dialogue age in the light of the Qur'anic teaching.

## General Qur'anic Attitude Towards the 'Other'

The Qur'an, the foundation on which the institutionalised religion of the Prophet Muhammad – the religion of Islam – is based includes a number of very positive statements towards those whose faiths, like that of Islam, centres on the one and only God especially in its Meccan surahs/chapters. By taking these positive and tolerant statements into account we can say that religious diversity is a factual reality, which is acknowledged by the Qur'an itself, as it teaches us that it is God himself who permits that there is more than one religious community in the world. If God willed otherwise, He would have made humankind as a single community. The Qur'an underlines[1] this essential principle of God's will several times as follows: "… If God had so willed, He could surely have made you all one single community …" (Q, 5: 48) "And had your Sustainer so willed, He could surely have made all mankind one single community" (Q, 11:118), "… had God so willed, He could surely have made you all one single community" (Q, 16:93), "… had God so willed, He could surely have made all one single community" (Q, 42:8).

Just after all these Qur'anic statements, in which the diversity of human communities is acknowledged, the main purpose of this diversity in the divine scheme of things is clearly stated as follows: "… but (He willed it otherwise) in order to test you by means of what He has vouchsafed unto you" (Q, 5:48); "but (He willed it otherwise and so) they continue to hold divergent views" (Q, 11:118); "God lets go astray him that wills (to go astray) and guides aright him that wills (to be guided)" (Q, 16:93); "He admits unto His Grace him that wills (to be admitted)" (Q, 42:8). As is seen from these and other similar verses, while the Qur'an on the one hand is acknowledging the factual reality of religious diversity and expressing clearly its main objectives, on the other hand it explains human accountability with regard to this diversity as follows: "… and you will surely be called to account for all that you ever did" (Q, 16:93); "… the evildoers shall have none to protect them and none to succour them (on Judgment Day)" (Q, 42:8).

It is true that the Qur'an also says that all humankind were once one single community (Q, 2:213; 10:19). But it does not specify the time of such primal religious unity among humans except to say that it existed in the past. Yet the Qur'an recognises the divergent human views that have appeared in history by God's will and that have eventually led to religious pluralism. God's decree in this regard was to permit such differences, for the Qur'an says "…And had

---

1 For the translations of the Qur'anic verses we used Muhammad Asad's *The Message of Qur'an: Translated and Explained,* Gibraltar: Dar Al-Andalus, 1984.

it not been for a decree that had already gone forth from your Sustainer, all their differences would indeed have been settled (from the outset)" (Q, 10:19). God's design was rather to guide humankind in their religious plurality by sending them prophets with clear divine revelations. The Qur'an further says: "… whereupon God raised up the prophets as heralds of glad tidings and as warners, and through them bestowed revelation from on high, setting forth the truth, so that it might decide between people with regard to all on which they had come to hold divergent views" (Q, 2:213).

Thus, although human beings have been divided into diverse religious communities, they have not been left without divine guidance. Addressing the various communities, the Qur'an says: "Unto every one of you We appointed a different law and way of life" (Q, 5:48); and similarly "for every community faces a direction of its own, of which He is the focal point" (Q, 2:148). And immediately following these statements in these two verses there is a command addressed to all the communities, which says "Vie then with one another in doing good works" (Q, 5:48). 'Divine guidance' in the Qur'an is constitutive of God's purpose in creating human beings. There is in the world "for those who reflect", a moral purpose – a purpose which will be fulfilled in the Day of Judgment. Concerning this issue the Qur'an states as follows: "Consider the human self, and how it is formed in accordance with what it is meant to be? And how it is imbued with moral failings as well as with consciousness of God" (Q, 91:7–8). According to this verse for human beings in order to attain the purpose for which they are created, they need to be adequately guided. Moreover God has already endowed human beings with the necessary cognition and volition to further their comprehension of the purpose for which they are created and to realise it by using their knowledge.

After this general introduction to the teaching of the Qur'an concerning the religious diversity and God's purpose for it, I would like to move on to explain what would be a Muslim's attitude towards people of other faiths within the context of its teaching in the light of its dialogue with Jews and Christians. By doing this, first of all I would like to highlight the issue of God's covenant with Jews, Christians and Muslims and then I will draw some conclusions from this examination in order to apply them to all non-Muslims.

When we look at the Qur'an we can easily see that it bases its relationship with people of other faiths (the people of the book, i.e. Jews, Christians and others) on the concept of 'covenant'. As is well-known, God has made a 'Core Covenant' with all human beings. According to this covenant, human beings have promised God to obey His orders and to observe regularly His commandments. Within the context of this core covenant now first of all I would move to examine in which way Jews, Christians and others have kept their promise to God. By doing this I will try to show how the Qur'an rejects all kinds of privileges which Jews and Christians have argued for themselves because of God's special covenant with them. In the last stage, too, I will discuss what kinds of works/deeds human beings need to do in order to attain salvation without looking at which faith they belong to.

## Qur'an's Response to Jewish and Christian Understanding of the Covenant

The Qur'an underlines that Jewish people have been trying to justify their exploitation and oppression of the poor by arguing that they were not like any other people, since according to Jewish belief, God made a covenant with them which has given them a special status in His sight. Because of this exclusivist claim, Jewish people have argued that they have always had a special and privileged status in the sight of God. The Qur'an challenges this Jewish claim as follows: "Say: 'O you who follow the Jewish faith! If you claim that you (alone) are close to God, to the exclusion of all other people, then you should be longing for death – if what you say is true'" (Q, 62:6). Furthermore the Qur'an reports that because of God's covenant with them, the Jews were being arrogant towards those who had no revealed book by claiming that they do not have any ethical responsibility towards them. "Among the followers of earlier revelations there is many (a one) who, if you entrust him with…a tiny gold coin, will not restore it to you unless you keep standing over him. This is an outcome of their assertion: 'No blame can attach to us for anything that we may do with regard to these unlettered folk.' So, they tell a lie about God, being well aware that it is a lie." (Q, 3:75).

Moreover according to the Qur'an Jewish people were claiming that they were in some special status and superior to all other human beings because of God's covenant with Abraham, Jacob, his sons and Moses. Even they had called themselves "sons of God" and "His beloved ones". "Both the Jews and the Christians say 'We are God's children, and His beloved ones.' Say: 'Why then does He cause you to suffer for your sins?' Nay you are but human beings of His creating. He forgives whom he wills and He causes to suffer whom he wills…" (Q, 5:18). The Jewish people also believed that the Covenant had given them special privileges that had not been accorded to any other people. For example they claimed that the Paradise was only for the Jews and not for any other people. "If an afterlife with God is to be for you alone, to the exclusion of all other people, then you should long for death." (Q, 2:94). And further they claim, "… None shall ever enter paradise unless he be a Jew …" (Q, 2:211). After monopolising afterlife and paradise for themselves, Jews also argued that if they go to the Hell, the fire will touch them for no longer than a limited number of days (Q, 3:24). The Qur'an informs us that the Jewish people have indulged in the vanities of this world and continued to commit sin by claiming that whatever they do shall be forgiven by God in one way or another (Q, 7:169).

As we have observed up to now, according to the Qur'anic teaching the Jews claimed that they have been granted a special status by God because of His covenant with them. They argued that non-Jews and their religions have nothing true to stand upon and for that reason they will not be acceptable to God. And they claim that "the Christians have no valid ground for their beliefs" (Q, 2:113) and "none shall ever enter paradise unless he be a Jew or "a Christian" (Q, 2:111). Upon their claim that the Creator has made a special covenant with them the Jews have advanced these exclusivist claims and clearly announced that they will not accept any revelation apart from their own one. "…when they are told 'Believe in what God has bestowed from on high' they reply, 'We believe only in what has been bestowed on us', and they deny the truth of everything else, although it be a truth confirming the one already in their possession" (Q, 2:91). Furthermore the Qur'an informs that the Jews have argued that they do not have any moral obligation to be just against non-Jews by claiming that their special Covenant with God has bestowed them a special relationship with Him. "…no blame can attach to us (for anything that we may do) with regard to these unlettered folk…" (Q, 3:75).

When we take into account Qur'anic critiques of the exclusivist Jewish understanding of the Covenant we can say that most of the Jews have tried to justify their exploitation of non-Jews by arguing that they have had a special place and some privileges in the sight of God. They have underlined that they are superior to other people and for that reason not others but only they will be acceptable to God and thus go to Paradise.

The Qur'an informs us that just like the Jews, Christians, too, have argued that they are sons of God and his beloved ones because of God's special covenant with Jesus Christ (Q, 5:18). According to the Qur'an the Christians' attitude towards people of other faiths and their religions is similar to that of the Jews as we have observed above. They claimed that the Jews have nothing to stand upon (Q, 2:111); that unless one become a Christian, he/she will not be rightly guided (Q, 2:135); and that no one shall enter the Paradise unless he/she is a Christian (2,111). Most important of all, they argued that their covenant with God requires them to believe in the following issues concerning the nature of God: (1) God is the third of a Trinity (Q, 5:73; 4:171). (2) God is the Christ, Son of Mary (Q, 5:17, 72; 9:31). (3) Jesus and Mary are two Gods beside God (Q, 5:116) and (4) The Christ is God's son (Q, 9:39; 2:116). As is well-known, Christians have always believed that Jesus is the only conduit between God and humanity. He is the only Son of God and the only Saviour, since they regard him as the Way, the Truth and the Life as is expressed in the Gospel of John (John 14:6).

As we have seen up to now the Qur'an underlines that Jews and Christians have argued that they possess some privileges because of God's special covenant with them; they have claimed that they are superior to other people and they can be unjust to them because of their privileged position in the sight of God. Furthermore the Qur'an maintains that Jews and Christians have been those people who have not obeyed the necessities of their covenant with God (Q, 3:77). The Qur'an also states that there were some religious men among

Jews and Christians "who distort the Bible with their tongues, so as to make you think that (what they say) is from the Bible, while it is not from the Bible; and who say, 'this is from God', the while it is not from God: and thus do they tell a lie about God, being well aware (that it is a lie)" (Q, 3:78).

After expressing the Qur'an's rejection of the superiority and privilege claims of the Jews and the Christians because of God's special covenant with them, now I would like to move on to the Qur'anic understanding of the covenant.

## Qur'anic Understanding of the Covenant

The Qur'an emphasises the universality of God's guidance by considering humanity as one community/*ummah* unlike the above exclusivist claims of the Jews and Christians, "…all mankind were once but one single community, and only later did they begin to hold divergent views. And had it not been for a decree that had already gone forth from your Sustainer, all their differences would indeed have been settled from the outset" (Q, 10:19).

As is seen from this verse, universal guidance of God was transferred to the whole mankind through God's agents (prophets) without making any distinction. Since, unlike the Jews' and Christians' claims, according to the Qur'an, God has not made his covenant only with one nation or a number of nations or communities but the whole mankind by sending prophets to each nation or community. In chapter 7 verse 172 the Qur'an states that when God creates a human being, He asks him/her "Am I not your Lord", he/she answers "Yes, of course". According to this verse God takes our promise that we are programmed by Him to believe in and worship Him alone by making a covenant with each of us one by one. So, God calls his servants whom He has taken a promise that they worship only Him to behave "in accordance with the natural disposition which God has instilled into man" (Q, 30:30). Parallel to this Qur'anic statement the Prophet Muhammad underlines that "Every child is born with an innate capacity for *submission to God,* i.e. *islam*; it is her/his *parents* that Christianise, Judaise or Magianise her/him, as an animal delivers a perfect baby animal. Do you find it mutilated?"[2] As we have seen up to now, the diversity of religions is designed by God Himself. For that reason religious plurality is our destiny and we need to live our lives in accordance with the necessities of this diversity. So, "the intrinsic principle in Islam is pluralism, not exclusivism or inclusivism".[3]

The universality of God's plan of salvation, the inclusion of God's divine guidance of all mankind and the fact that His covenant does not only apply to one nation or community but to all mankind indicate that all people are equal in the sight of God and all religious communities have equal rights and respon-

---

2    Al-Bukhari, *Sahih al-Bukhari Janâ'îz, No* 80.

3    Atay, R. (1999) *Religions Pluralism and Islam: A Critical Examination of John Hick's Pluralistic Hypothesis* (unpublished PhD thesis, St. Andrews University), 219.

sibilities in His plan of salvation. Because of this factual reality, according to the Qur'anic teaching, none of the community has the right to claim that it has a special and privileged position in relation to God.

The Qur'an sometimes refers to God's covenant with all mankind as *mithaq* (putting trust in someone) or *'ahd* (stipulation), but at other times, the conditions of this covenant are stated in terms of the commands given by God to the Jews, Christians, Muslims and other religious communities. According to the Qur'an God's universal covenant with all mankind mainly consists of God's main demands from his servants in the following issues.[4]

I) Theologically
- To serve and worship none but God only.[5]
- To not ascribe to God anything but truth only.[6]
- To proclaim and explain God's revelation to people as it is without hiding or concealing anything from it.[7]
- To believe in all the prophets and support them without making any separation.[8]
- To observe prayers regularly[9] or to be constant in prayer.

II) Socially
- To behave in the best manner and kindly to parents, relatives, orphans, the poor and all people.[10]
- To not kill anybody, to not harm any living things, to not spread corruption on earth and to not cause any corruption or conflict.[11]
- To be forgiving[12] and to call to do what is right and to forbid to do what is wrong.[13]
- To help the poor by paying alms/poor due and to give to charity.[14]
- To stay away from usury and to not devour other people's possessions.[15]

III) Desirable Attitudes
- To worship God only and to stay away from all kinds of vain/useless things.[16]

4   Hamilton, E. (1990) The Qur'anic Dialogue with Jews and Christians. In: *The Chicago Theological Seminary Register*, LXXX (3), 24–38.
5   *Qur'an*, 98,5; 2,83; 17,2.
6   *Qur'an*, 2,256; 16,36; 7,169.
7   *Qur'an*, 3,187.
8   *Qur'an*, 5,13; 3,81.
9   *Qur'an*, 98,5; 5,13; 2,83.
10  *Qur'an*, 2,83,177.
11  *Qur'an*, 5,32.
12  *Qur'an*, 5,45
13  *Qur'an*, 3,104,110; 5,79; 7,157,199.
14  *Qur'an*, 98,5; 2,83.
15  *Qur'an*, 4,61.
16  *Qur'an*, 98,5.

- To not corrupt religion/faith with superstitions and to not be divided there-in.[17]
- To hold fast to that which God has given.[18]
- To be sincere to the promises which were given to God at the time of the covenant with Him.[19]

IV) *Promises and Threats*
- The evil deeds of those who remember their covenant with God and fulfil/observe God's commandments will be forgiven by God and then they will be rewarded with Paradise. Those who do not remain loyal to God's covenant and thus do not observe His orders will be punished in hell because of their perversions.[20]

According to the Qur'an these essential, irrevocable and universal principles have been informed to all the communities through the prophets from Adam to the Prophet Muhammad, since they are the main points of God's covenant not only for Muslims but also all other religious communities. For that reason the Qur'an emphasises that this universal covenant of God must be accepted by all people whichever religious tradition they belong to. To this understanding, whether one is a Jew or a Christian or a Muslim or adherent to other religions, he/she needs to observe the following main principles to his/her life in order to be acceptable to God and be saved. (1) To believe in the oneness of God (2) To believe that God communicates with human beings through his messengers and revelations which were given to them. (3) To accept one's absolute dependence on and gratitude to God. (4) To eradicate all kinds of tyrannies and oppressions in familial and social relationships by exercising kindness and justice and by respecting every human being's right to a full life. (5) To eliminate all kinds of economic exploitation by supporting the poor and the weak, by not taking usury and refraining from amassing wealth through deceptive means.

This covenant, which is made not with a particular nation or community but all nations and communities, can be called 'the Core Covenant' because it contains the most essential conditions for an acceptable relationship between God and human being as well as between one human being and another. As we have observed above, the Jews and the Christians claimed that God made this 'Core Covenant' not with others but only with them. But the Qur'an underlines that God made it with Adam and Eve long before, when He said to them "… there shall, none the less, most certainly come unto you guidance from Me: and those who follow My guidance need have no fear, and neither shall have grieve" (Q, 2:38) Moreover the Qur'an informs us that God raised a messenger in every nation to proclaim "Serve God and shun false Gods" (Q, 16:36) and

---

17  *Qur'an*, 42,13.
18  *Qur'an*, 2,63. 93; 7,171.
19  *Qur'an*, 2,93; 7,171.
20  *Qur'an*, 5,12.

to warn, "that those who do evil will be punished, and to give good tidings that those who do good will be rewarded" (Q, 18:56; 22:50–51). "Indeed God bestowed a favour upon the believers when he raised up in their midst an apostle from among themselves, to convey His messages unto them, and to cause them to grow in purity, and to impart onto them the divine writ as well as wisdom – whereas before that they were indeed most obviously lost in error" (Q, 3:164).

After reminding human beings of this fact, God explains why he did this with these statements: "We sent all these apostles as heralds of glad tidings and as warners, so that men might have no excuse before God after the coming of these apostles" (Q, 4:165). "...had we destroyed them by means of a chastisement ere this (divine writ was revealed), they would indeed be justified to say on Judgment day: 'Our Sustainer! If only You had sent an apostle unto us, we would have followed your messages rather than be humiliated and disgraced in the Hereafter'" (Q, 20:134).

When God gives his covenant through his messenger to a community who is unaware of it or has forgotten or corrupted it, then that community incurs certain responsibilities with regard to the fulfilment of the necessities of the Covenant, since at that time it becomes incumbent upon the people of that community to decide whether to accept or reject the Covenant, to continue to follow or give up their old ways. It is they who must decide whether or not to seek God's help, for the Qur'an underlines that "God does not change men's condition unless they change their inner selves..." (Q,13:11). Therefore the addressees of that Covenant are held morally responsible for either accepting or rejecting God's message. If they decide to accept the Covenant, they are obliged to observe all its commandments without making any distinction between them (Q, 2:85; Q, 5:14).

Moreover, if those people accept the Covenant they must accept the responsibility to continually keep it, because if they break the Covenant, God will choose another community/a group of people in their stead (Q, 6:84); if they forget God, He will forget them also because God is not bound to those who abandon his Covenant (Q, 2:24; 6:89; 9:67).

After maintaining that those whom God makes a covenant with t are under the responsibility of fulfilling its requirements, the Qur'an points out that those who accept the covenant and keep it by observing its commandments are not the same as those who do not accept it or accept it without fulfilling its requirements. Since while the former ones will be rewarded by God the latter ones will be punished in the Hereafter. Moreover the Qur'an emphasises that each person is responsible for his/her good and evil deeds and no one can bear the signs of punishment for another but only for himself/herself, nor does anyone have the power to intercede on behalf of another before God for either the forgiveness of sins or the removal of punishment. "Those people have passed away; unto them shall be accounted what they have earned, and unto you what you have earned; and you will not be judged on the strength of what they did" (Q, 2:141).

The Qur'an states that God takes a promise from those whom he has made his covenant with, not only to fulfil the necessities of that covenant but also to believe in and support other messengers who confirm that covenant which they hold. "God accepted, through the prophets, this solemn pledge (from the followers of earlier revelation), 'if, after all the revelation and the wisdom which I have vouchsafed unto you, there comes to you an apostle confirming the truth already in your possession, you must believe in him and succour him'…" (Q, 3:81). This verse clearly indicates that every message which each prophet conveyed to his community confirmed the messages of other prophets who came to different communities, since the Qur'an states that all the revelations emanate from a single source, namely "the Mother of the Book" (Q, 43:4; 13:39) and "the Hidden Book" (Q, 56:78). That is why the Qur'an invites the Prophet Muhammad and his followers to believe in the prophethood of previous prophets such as Noah, Abraham, Moses and Jesus. Since God's religion and the prophethood are indivisible. For that reason it does not matter which faith we belong to, it is incumbent on all of us to believe in all the messengers without making any distinction among them.[21] For that reason, just as "the Prophet Muhammad and his followers believe in all the prophets and their teachings, all people must also and equally believe in him"[22], since disbelief in Muhammad would be equivalent to disbelief in all the prophets.

After maintaining the fact that God made the same universal Core Covenant not only with a particular nation or community but all the nations and for that reason all people are under the responsibility of this Covenant, the Qur'an underlines that no community is superior to others because of God's Covenant with itself, since according to the Qur'anic teaching, superiority of one nation or a community can only be attained by the fulfilment of the necessities of the Covenant. In other words, according to the Qur'an one community or nation is distinct prophetically from the other, not covenantly. "… all (true) guidance is God's guidance, consisting in one's being granted revelation such as you have been granted …" (Q. 3:73). It seems to me that this emphasis of the Qur'an is a response to the exclusivist beliefs of the Jews and the Christians who have argued that their own faiths are unique and superior to the others and that for this reason they alone will attain salvation in the Hereafter because of God's special Covenant with each of them.

Moreover in chapter 2 verses 111 and 113 the Qur'an first of all condemns this sort of exclusive claim of the Jews and the Christians and then reminds not only them, but also those Muslims who make such exclusive claims, for salvation or liberation cannot be achieved by mere claims but only by true belief and right actions. In chapter 4 verse 123–124 the Qur'an makes clear who will be

---

21  Rahman, F. (1986) A Muslim Response: Christian Particularity and the Faith of Islam. In: D. G. Dawe & J. B. Carman (Eds.) *Christian Faith in a Religiously Plural World*, Maryknoll: Orbis Books, 71.

22  Id. (1989) The People of the Book and the Diversity of Religions. In: P. J. Griffiths (Ed.) *Christianity through Non-Christian Eyes*, Maryknoll: Orbis Books, 104.

attaining God's salvation: "it may not accord with your wishful thinking – nor with the wishful thinking of the followers of earlier revelation – that he who does evil shall be required for it, and find none to protect him from God, and none to bring him succour, whereas anyone – be it man or woman – who does whatever he can of good deeds and is a believer withal, shall enter paradise, and shall not be wronged by as much as (would fill) the groove of a date-stone" (Q, 4:123). With this clear statement the Qur'an underlines that religious patriotism which limits being a chosen nation/community or being acceptable to God only with its own followers, has no value in the realm of God.

It is in the context of this Core Covenant, which the Prophet Muhammad believed God had made with all nations through his messengers, that the Qur'anic discussion with the Jews and Christians took place; it was in terms of this Core Covenant that the Qur'an evaluates the beliefs and behaviours of Jews and Christians; and it was this Covenant to which the Prophet wanted the Jews and Christians to return. Moreover the primary concern of the Prophet Muhammad was not that Jews and Christians must observe his teaching but that they return to the Core Covenant and correct their own false beliefs in the light of his warnings. "If the followers of the Bible would but attain to true faith and God-consciousness, We should indeed efface their previous bad deeds and indeed bring them into gardens of bliss; and if they would but truly observe the Torah and the Gospel and all the revelation that has been bestowed from on high upon them by their Sustainer, they would indeed partake of all the blessings of heaven and earth..." (Q, 5:65–66).

The Qur'an on the one hand warns Jews and Christians and those whom God made the covenant with that unless they return to the core covenant and follow the terms of the prophetic codes that their prophets had given them, they cannot attain salvation. "O followers of the Bible! You have no valid ground for your beliefs, unless you truly observe the Torah and the Gospel, and all that has been bestowed from on high upon you by your Sustainer" (5,68). On the other hand it underlines that there have been those people among the people of the book who hold fast to the Core Covenant and fulfil its requirements. According to the Qur'an this sort of people look at the message of the Prophet Muhammad (the Qur'an) with sympathy, "... when they come to understand what has been bestowed from on high upon this Apostle, you can see that their eyes overflow with tears, because they recognise something of its truth, and they say 'O our Sustainer, We do believe; make us one then with all who bear witness to the truth. How could we fail to believe in God and in whatever truth has come unto us, when we so fervently desire that our Sustainer count us among the righteous?'" (Q, 5:83–84).

As is seen from these Qur'anic verses, all Jews and Christians are not the same with regard to their attitudes to God's covenant and to those are not from themselves. Since besides those people among them who claim that they are superior to the others and have a special favour in God's eye thanks to God's special Covenant with themselves, there are also those people who understand their covenant with God not exclusively but inclusively by observing the following points. (1) They believe in God and worship him alone; (2) They believe in the Hereafter; (3) They enjoin to others to do what is right and good and forbid them to do what is wrong and bad; (4) They always do righteous deeds and (5) They try to advance what is true, good and useful in other religions by acknowledging them. In this point I would like to stress that if those Jews and Christians who fulfilled the above points within the context of their Covenant with God, were not satisfied with merely acknowledging the message of the Prophet Muhammad but also wanted to be his followers, then the Prophet Muhammad would only be pleased to see them as his *ummah* (community). When we look at the time of the Prophet Muhammad, there were such kind of Jews and Christians who not only acknowledged that Muhammad was a prophet but also followed his teaching by leaving aside their own ones. However, when we look at the Qur'an and the words of the Prophet Muhammad (*hadith*) we can see that neither the Qur'an nor the Prophet himself insisted or even implied that Jews, Christians and others who have these sort of positive features must be 'Muslim' in the sense that they need to follow the teaching of the Prophet Muhammad, or in other words the institutionalised religion of the Prophet Muhammad by putting aside their own faiths. The Qur'an mentions two main duties of the Prophet Muhammad: The first one was to call both those who acknowledged God as Creator but adopted secondary deities besides Him in order to reach out to Him and those who were unaware of the oneness of God to worship only God by making known to them the absolute Oneness and the Unity of God. The second one was to correct those peoples' beliefs who God made his covenant with and gave them divine messages through his prophets but they distorted them by overstepping the bounds of truth in their beliefs. The renowned ecumenical theologian Hans Küng realised this function of Muhammad by accepting him as a "prophetic corrective" and "prophetic warner" for Christians in order to inform them that "the one incomparable God has to stand in the absolute centre of faith; That associating with him any other Gods or Goddesses is out of the question; That faith and life, orthodoxy and orthopraxy, belong together everywhere, including politics".[23] At this point I would like to remind you that those Jews and Christians whose beliefs the Prophet Muhammad wanted to correct were not those who were holding fast to the Core Covenant and observing its orders but those who argued that they were superior to other people by claiming that God made a special Covenant only with them and so they had some privileges in the sight of God.

---

23 Küng, H. (1993) *Christianity and World Religions: Paths to Dialogue,* Maryknoll: Orbis Books, 129.

## Evaluation

When we take into account what we have said up to now concerning the Qur'an's response to the Jews' and Christians' claims to certain privileges and a special favour in the sight of God because of His special Covenant with them and its teaching of the Covenant, we can say the following as a conclusion.

The Qur'an rejects totally every kind of *a priori* exclusive claims concerning the relationship between human beings and God and salvation – and related to it all kinds of superiority and election or chosenness claims, because one of the main objectives of the Qur'anic message is to affirm religious pluralism and to include all people in God's plan of salvation. And while doing this it presents us the conditions of acceptability to God, namely believing in God and the Hereafter, and performing righteousness (Q, 2:62; 5:69). In the course of time, this universal message of God has been narrowed by different religious communities by claiming that only their own religion is right and acceptable to God. For example, in chapter 2 verse 111 and 113 the Qur'an condemns Jews and Christians who make exclusive claims about the uniqueness of their own religion by emphasising the fact that to be acceptable to God is not based on claims alone, but on genuine faith and good action, "… everyone who surrenders his whole being unto God, and is a doer of good withal, shall have his reward with his Sustainer; and all such need to have no fear and neither shall they grieve" (2,129). So, this Qur'anic rejection of all notions of exclusivism concerning the superiority of one religion over others teaches all of us not to absolutise our way as the one and only way to God by excluding the others. Moreover, in chapter 2 verse 124 God clearly opposes all sorts of chosenness and superiority claims by this answer to Abraham's question, "… when his Sustainer tried Abraham by His commandments and the latter fulfilled them, He said: 'Behold, I shall make you a leader of men', Abraham asked: 'And will you make leaders of my offspring as well?, God answered: 'My covenant does not embrace the evildoers'" (Q, 2:124). It seems to me that this verse also reminds those Jews who claim that they are descendants of Abraham and for that reason they are superior to others, unless they hold fast to their covenant and fulfil its necessities, God's covenant does not include them. Moreover, according to this verse, all those who do not observe the main principles of God's Core Covenant and do not treat others justly are outside of God's promise. Similarly, after referring to previous prophets and their communities, the Qur'an warns the Muslims as follows: "… those people have passed away; unto them shall be accounted what they have earned, and unto you, what you have earned, and you will not be judged on the strength of what they did" (Q, 2:134).

After reminding all of us that no community or no people is superior to others and has some privileges in the sight of God because of their Covenant with God or their own revelation or prophet, and after indicating that salvation cannot be attained by mere claims but only through faith and righteous deeds, the Qur'an points out that there can be those kinds of people who can be accept-able to God and thus attain salvation in every religious tradition:

> The believers, the Jews, the Christians and the Sabians – whoever believes in God and
> the Last Day and does what is good – shall receive their reward from their Lord. They
> shall have nothing to fear and they shall not grieve (Q, 2:62).
> Surely, the believers, the Jews, the Sabians and the Christians – whoever believes in
> God and the Last Day and does good deeds – shall all have nothing to fear and they
> shall not grieve (Q, 5:69).

These verses, one revealed at the beginning and the other at the end of the Prophet Muhammad's Medinan career, clearly inform us that there are three minimum conditions of being acceptable to God: (i) to believe in one God; (2) to believe in the Hereafter; and (3) to do good deeds. So, if someone fulfils these three conditions in his/her life fully, without looking at which religious tradition he/she belongs to, we can say that he/she can go to Paradise. Unfortunately, as Fazlur Rahman underlines, the vast majority of Muslim commentators exercise themselves fruitlessly in order to avoid having to admit this obvious meaning of these verses. Because of the wholesale approach of these commentators, the obvious meaning of these verses has been either manipulated or reduced to a few people who lived in the time of the Prophet Muhammad, or they have simply been abrogated.[24] M. Ayoub gives the following response to these com-mentators: When the Prophet arrived at Medina, verse 2.62 was revealed as a guidance to deal with "Jewish Tribes of Medina and the Christian community of Najran".[25] Later on, it is "repeated verbatim in the last but one major chapter to be revealed to the Prophet before his death".[26] Neither the repetition, nor the timing of the verses is discussed by those who abrogated these verses. Ayoub points out that there are important implications of this fact to weaken the claims of abrogation. Suppose the first one, 2.62, was abrogated, then the second one, 5.69, still stands. If it was abrogated already, why was it necessary to repeat it? That the second revelation is close to the end of the prophethood of Muhammad makes it very unlikely that it is abrogated. So, as Ayoub concludes, "neither the words nor the purport of these two identical verses was abrogated".[27]

As we have seen up to now, the Qur'an clearly and openly declares that salvation or being acceptable to God can be achieved not by being a member of a particular religious tradition or community but only by holding fast to God's Core Covenant and fulfilling its necessities as it is required. So, according to this understanding, divine guidance and salvation, which can be attained as a result, cannot be monopolised by any faith or religious community, because it is a gain which can be obtained not by belonging to any religious community

---

24  Rahman (1986), 75.
25  Ayoub, M. (1997) Islam and Pluralism. In: *Encounters* 3/2, 114.
26  Ibid., 113.
27  Ibid.

but by believing in God and the Hereafter and being a faithful believer. Because of this fact in the Qur'anic teaching, neither Muslims nor the followers of any other religious tradition can claim that they are elected by God and that for this reason only they can go to Paradise.[28]

By taking this point into account we can conclude that if the Qur'an strongly rejects the election and superiority of any people to the detriment of others and recognises goodness among the other religious communities such as Jews, Christians and Sabians because of their belief in God and the Hereafter, then surely in good logic the Muslim community can only be one community among others. It seems to us that concerning the problem of the plurality of world communities, the Qur'an gives the following clear and definite response: "… Unto every one of you have we appointed a different law and way of life. And if God had so willed, He could surely have made you all one single community; but He willed it otherwise in order to test you by means of what He has vouchsafed unto you …" (5,48).

The Qur'an emphasises that God has made us not a single nation but different communities and gave us different ways of life not to fight but to compete with one another in doing good works in order to attain His will. As we can see from this verse, the reason of God's sending different books (messages) is not to negate each other's orders but to confirm each other's messages.

As it is seen from this verse, the differences between religious communities should not be used as a tool to create enmity and conflicts between followers of different religious communities. On the contrary, they should be seen as an opportunity in order to compete with adherents of different faiths in doing good works for establishing a better world in which all people can live peacefully. We need to acknowledge and accept religious differences as they are without leaving them aside or underestimating them, since they are the result of the will of God. So what we need to do – as Muslims, Christians, Jews and members of other religious communities – is to hold fast to God's guidance as it is expressed in our sacred books in the light of our Covenant with Him and then to try not to be a slave of our desires, blind ambitions and caprices in our relationships with each other.

In conclusion, in the light of the above explanation of the Qur'anic verses concerning the religious other, it is obvious that the Qur'an provides us Muslims with the very basis of a theology of interfaith relations that regards religious pluralism as a divinely ordained system of human co-existence. In order to develop this, Muslim scholars should re-read the related Qur'anic material in light of the multifaith context by investigating them with an openness for new meanings and nuances.[29]

---

28  Rahman, F. (2000) *Major Themes of the Qur'an* (translated into Turkish by Alparslan Açıkgenç) Ankara: Ankara Okulu, 243–244; Lakhassi, A. (1998) The Qur'an and the Other. In: L. Swidler (Ed.) *Theoria – Praxis: How Jews, Christians and Muslims Can Together Move From Theory to Practice* Leuven: Peeters, 108–109.

29  *Qur'an*, 5,12.

# Dialogue in Hinduism

*Anantanand Rambachan*

# The Nature and Authority of Scripture

## Implications for Hindu-Christian Dialogue

In a thoughtful series of reflections on the future of Hindu-Christian Dialogue, Klaus Klostermaier observes that there are "few Hindus who are interested in (contemporary) Christian theology, and there are fewer still who have a desire to enter into dialogue with their Christian counterparts".[1] Others have noted that, with few notable exceptions, the initiatives for dialogue, in recent times, have been from the Christian side.[2] In an earlier study, I suggested, briefly, a few possible reasons for this lack of interest on the Hindu side. The memories of colonialism and its association with aggressive Christian missionary activity, misrepresentation of other religions, and the lack of genuine interest in the study and understanding of these traditions are not easily erased. There are still barriers of mistrust to overcome.[3] I interpreted this lack of interest, also, as a reflection of certain popular Hindu attitudes towards religious pluralism. The famous Rig Veda text, "One is the Truth, the sages speak of it differently", (I.64.46) is often employed to explain away doctrinal differences as merely semantic ones. The point of this text, as its context makes quite clear, is not really to dismiss the significance of the different ways in which we speak of the One or to see these ways as equally valid. The text is really a comment on the limited nature of human language. Such language must by nature be diverse in its attempts to describe that which is One and finally indescribable. The text, however, is widely cited in ways that seem to make interreligious dialogue redundant.

Klostermaier laments the trend in contemporary Christianity and Hinduism "to dismiss the intellectual approach to religion as irrelevant and to cultivate only its emotional and pragmatic sides". Arguing that intellectuals and scholars must be allowed to play a more vital and central role in the development of these traditions, Klostermaier affirms that Hindu-Christian dialogue "must recover the intellectual substance of Hinduism and Christianity and must contribute actively to the ongoing search for truth/reality in all spheres of life. The intellectual dimension of life has not lost its importance in our time."[4]

The loss of intellectual vigour in contemporary Hinduism is a matter of deep concern and the causes are many and complex. There are also serious impli-

1   Klostermaier, K. (1989) The Future of Hindu-Christian Dialogue. In: H. Coward (Ed.) *Hindu Christian Dialogue* Maryknoll: Orbis Books, 265.

2   Coward, H. (1988) Hindu-Christian Dialogue: A Review. In: *Hindu-Christian Studies Bulletin*, 1, 1–5.

3   Rambachan, A. (1989) Religious Pluralism: A Hindu Perspective. In: *Current Dialogue*, 17, 25–27.

4   Klostermaier (1989), 269.

cations for the Hindu interest in dialogue with Christians and for the nature
of such dialogue. In this article, I want to identify what I perceive to be one
major cause for the erosion of intellectual life in Hinduism and its divorce from
spirituality. I wish to reflect also on the significance of this for Hindu-Christian
dialogue.

It is my contention that the decline in the significance of Vedic exegesis and
the reinterpretation of the authority of the Vedas in contemporary times *vis-à-vis*
personal experience are connected closely with the weakening of scholarship
in Hinduism and its lack of interest in vigorous dialogue with Christianity. It is
not possible, here, to describe in detail and to trace the historical roots of this
process of reinterpretation and I have already attempted this elsewhere.[5] I will,
however, highlight some of the salient and relevant historical developments and
draw attention to their significance for Hindu-Christian dialogue.

The Western impact on India in the eighteenth century had far reaching
implications for almost every aspect of Indian life and served as a catalyst for
the cultivation of attitudes of rational inquiry and criticism. The earliest Hindu
reformer to reflect the impact of the West in his thinking about Hinduism is the
Brahmo Samaj leader, Rammohun Roy (1774–1833). While Roy's attitude to
the authority of the Vedas had an element of ambiguity about it, even among
his own followers, it is quite clear that his approach to the texts was different
from orthodox Purva Mimamsa exegetes or from the Advaita Vedanta interpreter Shankara (ca. 8th CE). Roy applied the extrascriptural criterion of 'true'
religion in his evaluation of the worth of any text, including the Vedas. He did
not see religious truth as being limited to the texts of the Vedas or see the Vedas
as being indispensable for our knowledge of God. The texts themselves, and not
only their interpretations, he argued, must be subject to rational analysis.

What I perceive as a watershed in the attitude of contemporary Hindu interpreters to the authority of the Vedas occurred under the leadership of Roy's
successor, Debendranath Tagore (1817–1905). The change was initiated as a
consequence of a debate sparked by the conversion to Christianity of Umesh
Chandra Sarkar and his wife. Sarkar was a student at Alexander Duff's school,
and there was vigorous opposition to the school. Duff responded with a challenge to the doctrines of the Brahmo Samaj, questioning, in particular, the belief in Vedic infallibility.[6] The Samaj initially defended the doctrine, but this
stirred a great degree of unease in its ranks. In an effort to resolve this issue,
Debendranath Tagore sent four *brahmin* youths to Benares to study the Vedas.
His own visit to the city in 1847 was partly in pursuit of the same inquiry.
Finally, the doctrine of Vedic infallibility was abolished in 1850.[7] Perhaps

---

5   Rambachan, A. (1994) *The Limits of Scripture: Vivekananda's Reinterpretation of the Au-
    thority of the Vedas* Honolulu: University of Hawaii Press. See Chapter 1.
6   Sastri, S. (1974) *History of the Brahmo Samaj* Calcutta: Brahmo Samaj, 2nd ed., 63.
7   It is unfortunate that there are no records of the details of the argument on both sides. Such
    records would have clarified the concerns of the Brahmo Samaj about the authority of the
    Vedas.

the main reason for Tagore's rejection of the doctrine of infallibility was his refusal to accept passages in the Upanishads affirming the identity of *atman* and *brahman.* He chose to see *brahman* as lord and regulator of the universe and to see the *atman* as dependent on *brahman* for its existence.[8]

From that time onwards, the non-authoritative status of any text became enshrined in the creed of the Brahmo Samaj. Nature and intuition took the place of scripture as twin sources of knowledge. The basis of Brahmoism became "the pure heart filled with the light of intuitive knowledge". Tagore himself became increasingly reliant on personal intuition as his authority and the notion of divine command *(adesha)* assumed a significant role in his life.

Tagore's successor to the leadership of the Brahmo Samaj, the charismatic Keshub Chandra Sen (1838–1884), rejoiced in the rejection of Vedic infallibility. He saw it as a grand step in the evolution of the Samaj and its embrace of monotheism which "was not confined to Hindoo books, to the scriptures of their own countrymen, but was to be found in human nature in all the races and tribes and nations of the world".[9] Keshub propagated a general theory of revelation in which he included nature, history – by which he means "great men" – and inspiration. He clearly emphasised inspiration, as the most direct and significant form of revelation. He described it as "the direct breathing-in of God's spirit – which infuses an altogether new life into the soul, and exalts it above all that is earthly and impure. It is more powerful, being God's direct and immediate action on the human soul while revelation made through physical nature and biography is indirect and mediate".[10]

Sen went much further than Tagore in his denunciation of what he regarded to be doctrine and dogma and his unfavourable comparison of these with "fire of inspiration". Doctrine and dogma that relate to intellectual cognition, reasoning and logical thought were cold and lifeless and had nothing to do with the attainment of salvation. Sen spoke of direct perception as the only reliable, conclusive and self-evident means of gaining spiritual knowledge and saw this perception as affirmed in the Upanishads. He further explained: "No expression is more frequently used in the *Upanishads* than the 'perception' of God *(darshan)*. It appears that Hindu sages, not content with intellectual conceptions of the Almighty or abstract contemplation of certain Divine attributes, sought earnestly and indeed successfully, to behold the Supreme Spirit directly and to apprehend Him as a distinct and vivid reality in their inner consciousness."[11] Towards the end of his life, Sen, like Debendranath Tagore before him,

---

8   Das, S.K. (1974) *The Shadow of the Cross: Christianity and Hinduism in a Colonial Context* Delhi: Munshiram Manoharlal, 70–71.

9   Sen, K.C. (1904) The Living God in England and India. In: *Discourses and Writings* Calcutta: Brahmo Tract Society, 149.

10  Id. (1870) Great Men. In: S.D. Collet (Ed.) *Lectures and Tracts by Keshub Chunder Sen* London: Strahan, 88.

11  Sen, K.C. (1904) Primitive Faith and Modern Speculations. In: *Discourses and Writings* Calcutta: Brahmo Tract Society, 46.

gave increasing prominence to the authority of divine command *(adesha)* and claimed to have received a special revelation and dispensation from God. The significance of scriptural revelation was reduced by his claim that the texts of this New Dispensation (Nava-Vidhan) included "the whole of science, physical, metaphysical and moral and also the science of religion".

At the time of Keshub's death in 1884, the centre of religious attention in Calcutta had already shifted to Ramakrishna (1836–1886) who had taken up residence in the Kali temple at Dakshineshwar. Primarily through Vivekananda and the Ramakrishna Mission founded in 1897, Ramakrishna, like the Brahmo Samaj, has exerted significant influence on the character of contemporary Hindu attitudes to scriptural authority. While Ramakrishna's background was different from that of the Brahmo Samaj leaders in that he was virtually unexposed to Westernising influences, he concurred with them in his disdain for scripture and in his championing of personal experience.

Ramakrishna possessed a deep aversion to formal learning and education. Learned persons were likened by him to kites and vultures, which soar to great heights in the sky but whose eyes are forever focused on the decaying carcasses below. They were also described as similar to foolish people in an orchard, who count the leaves and fruit and argue to estimate their value instead of plucking and relishing the juicy fruit. Reason and the intellectual life received little attention or recognition in his teachings.

Ramakrishna confessed scepticism about the value of scriptural study. The scriptures are diluted, containing, as he puts it, a "mixture of sand and sugar", difficult to distinguish and separate. They are of no use in conveying the feeling of God: "This feeling is something very different from book-learning. Books, scriptures, and science appear as mere dirt and straw after the realisation of God." Similar to K.C. Sen, the direct vision of God was the main theme of Ramakrishna's instruction. It was the only form of verification: "But seeing is far better than hearing. Then all doubts disappear. It is true that many things are recorded in the scripture; but all these are useless without the direct realisation of God."[12]

Swami Vivekananda (1863–1902), the foremost disciple of Ramakrishna has, more than any other Hindu in recent times, influenced the popular understanding of Hinduism in India and abroad. There is very little in modern Hindu, particularly Vedanta, apologetic writing which does not carry the imprint of Vivekananda's influence. His attitude to scriptural authority was shaped by the teachings of Ramakrishna, but also by the stand of the Brahmo Samaj in whose circles he was active as a youth. He developed the suggestions and outlines from these sources into an elaborate rejection of the necessity for scripture.

Vivekananda followed his teacher, Ramakrishna, in attributing a low value to scriptures and in upholding the supremacy of personal experience. The ad-

---

12 Gupta, M. (1977) *The Gospel of Ramakrishna* trans. Swami Nikhilananda, New York: Ramakrishna-Vedanta Center, 543, 645 f., 476.

equacy of scriptures is compared to the utility of a map to a traveller, before visiting a country.[13] The map, according to Vivekananda, can create only curiosity for first-hand knowledge of the place and can communicate only a vague conception of its reality. Maps are in no way equivalent to the direct knowledge of the country, gathered by actually being there.

Vivekananda understands the Vedas to be records of the spiritual discoveries of others and the methods by which such discoveries have been made. These findings, however, have no validity unless each person personally rediscovers them:

> There are certain religious facts which, as in external science, have to be perceived and upon them religion will be built. Of course, the extreme claim that you must believe every dogma of a religion is degrading to the human mind. The man who asks you to believe everything, degrades himself, and, if you believe, degrades you too. The sages of the world have only the right to tell us that they have analyzed their minds and have found these facts, and if we do the same we shall also believe, and not before. That is all there is in religion. *(CW,* 2:163).

The proof of the truth of the Vedas is the direct knowledge of the individual, not the fact of its embodiment in any text. The individual must verify the text and this verification is likened to ordinary direct perception.

> The proof, therefore, of the *Vedas* is just the same as the proof of this table before me, *pratyaksha,* direct perception. This I see with the senses, and the truths of spirituality we also see in a superconscious state of the human soul. (*CW,* 3:253).

The imperative, therefore, for Vivekananda, is that everyone should become a *rishi.* The chief characteristic of *rishi* status is the possibility of a direct apprehension of truth. The possibility and requirement of every individual to become a *rishi* is one of the important points of contrast that Vivekananda emphasised between Hinduism and other religious traditions. In the latter, he claims, insight is limited to a few select individuals through whom truth is made available to the many. "Truth came to Jesus of Nazareth, and we must all obey him. But the truth came to the *rishis* of India – the *mantra-drashtas,* the seers of thought – and will come to all *rishis* in the future, not to talkers, not to book-swallowers, not to scholars, not to philologists, but to seers of thought" (*CW,* 3:283). Vivekananda often asserted that only in becoming a *rishi* does one understand the scripture properly. His argument appears to be that these texts, being products and records of direct perception, were not written for the intellect, or for understanding through a process of rational inquiry and analysis. They become meaningful only when one has lifted oneself to the same heights of perception. At that point, however, they are useful only to the extent that they confirm what

---

13  *The Complete Works of Swami Vivekananda (CW),* (1964–1971), 8 vols, Calcutta: Advaita Ashrama, 1, 185 f. (Documentation is hereafter given in the text).

one has known directly (*CW,* 4, 165, 7:85, 89). An opinion, like this, seems to deprive the scriptures from having even the preliminary worth of a map.

Vivekananda describes scriptural analysis as intellectual opium eating (see *CW,* 1:45, 4:168). Scripture is specified by him as unsatisfactory theoretical religion and hence included among the non-essentials of religion. Among other non-essentials, he listed doctrines, dogmas, rituals, temples, images and forms.

S. Wesley Ariarajah reminds us of four different types of interreligious dialogue, each with its unique contribution to make.[14] *Dialogue of life* is an encounter that takes place in the course of everyday life among people of different traditions who live in the same community. There is no conscious or explicit articulation and exchange of religious belief. Such explicit exchange of beliefs and perspectives is a characteristic of the *dialogue of discourse.* In the *dialogue of spirituality*, participants seek "to go beyond words to encounter the other at the level of the heart". It attracts those "who feel that the essential unity of humanity cannot be expressed in words, but must be celebrated in worship and meditation". Finally, the *dialogue of action* is characterised by cooperation among people of different faiths for the attainment of desirable ends of their common existence such as peace, justice, protection of the environment, human rights etc.

While acknowledging the various forms of interreligious dialogue, it appears to me that the *dialogue of discourse* will continue to be one of its necessary and vital forms. While not prominent in the other forms, it seems to be implied in them. The sharing of thought and reflection, the understanding of the scope and limits of reason and language in other traditions, and the mutual enrichment which comes from exposure to each other's wisdom *(jnana)* are facets of dialogue which, if engaged in with commitment, humility and a passion for truth, can never become 'ivory tower' intellectualism. Such dialogue needs to find a prominent place in the meeting of Hinduism and Christianity.

The decline of intellectual vigour in any tradition through the denigration of reason and the intellect will be reflected in the quality of its interest in other traditions and in the kind of interreligious dialogue in which it desires to engage. The championing in contemporary Hinduism of personal experience over the authority of scripture, which I have briefly traced in this essay, has contributed to the divorce of scholarship from spirituality. Examples of scholarship without religious commitment and religious commitment lacking the self-critical insights of scholarship abound. Their creative combination in modern Hinduism is rare. The disconnection between scholarship and spirituality in Hinduism limits the quality of the Hindu dialogue with Christianity. The dialogue of discourse is most enriching when it occurs among participants whose lives reflect the integration of both.

The divorce to which I am referring can be illustrated by highlighting the classic approach of Shankara or Ramanuja (ca. 11th CE). For Shankara, the

---

14  Ariarajah, S. W. (1993) Pluralism and Harmony. In: *Current Dialogue,* 25, 17–19.

Vedas are the definitive and unique source of our knowledge of *brahman*, the gain of which leads to the discovery of liberation *(moksha).* The Vedas are a valid source of knowledge in the form of words *(shabda-pramana),* and liberating knowledge depends on the proper comprehension of the meaning of these words. Scriptural learning and exegesis therefore, become very important along with such disciplines as grammar and etymology that aid interpretation. Proper principles for arriving at the meaning of the text are important.[15]

The acceptance of the Vedas as an authoritative source of knowledge did not mean the abandonment of a very important role for reason. Reason is important for deciding between different interpretations of passages and for reconciling conflicting ones. Reason also plays an important role in assessing and responding to rival views. Shankara obviously takes differences of doctrine very seriously, and in responding to the claims of rival systems which do not accept the authority of the Vedas, he is constrained to demonstrate the validity of Advaita on the basis of the reasonableness of its propositions.

The decline of the significance of the Vedas as a *pramana* and its characterisation as second-hand religion has contributed to the devaluing of scriptural scholarship. Its study, exegesis and interpretation are not of utmost significance. Vivekananda contemptuously dismisses scriptural scholarship as an activity at the theoretical and intellectual level. With an emphasis in contemporary Hinduism on the gain of knowledge through the transcendence of reason and not on its mediation, reason, argument and intellectual activity, all-important qualities of interreligious dialogue assume more of an obstructive character. There is an impassioned derogation and belittlement of the human intellect in Vivekananda, the leading Neo-Vedanta interpreter, which is not at all found in his classical predecessors: "The intellect is only the street-cleaner, cleansing the path for us, a secondary worker, the policeman; but the policeman is not a positive necessity for the workings of society" *(CW* 2:306). Paradoxically, it would seem that where the Vedas are upheld as a valid means of knowledge, reason has a more positive role to play in clarifying, explaining and defending its propositions. Where the attempt is made, on the other hand, to supersede the necessity for faith in the scripture in the interest of being more rational, reason becomes almost insignificant.

The rejection of the primary authority of scripture, the derision of scholarship, the ridicule of dogma and doctrine and the belittling of reason, which we see in so many modern interpreters of Hinduism, have other important implications for Hindu-Christian dialogue. Perhaps most important is the tendency to overlook the significance of doctrinal differences. Because conclusive insight is understood to be gained through an experience which transcends reason, interpreters like Vivekananda are able to dismiss what they perceive to be a

---

15 For a discussion of the method of Shankara see Rambachan, A. (1991) *Accomplishing the Accomplished: The Vedas as a Source of Valid Knowledge in Shankara* Honolulu: University of Hawaii Press.

preoccupation of the rational mind. It is only by overlooking and dismissing the importance of different doctrinal claims that one can so easily assert, as many Hindus do, that all paths lead to the same goal. Such scant regard for differences of doctrine is often frustrating for many Christians who engage with Hindus in dialogue.

I do not wish to deny the vital role of the experiential dimension in the human search for truth or to claim that it is without significance in the Hindu tradition. Shankara himself, at various points in his commentary on the *Brahma-sutra*, acknowledges this role.[16] While Shankara, as I believe, acknowledges the ultimacy of scriptural revelation for our knowledge of the absolute, his understanding of the relationship between scripture and personal experience *(anubhava)* is dynamic and creative. It offers scope for a vigorous life of the intellect by preserving for it a necessary role in the spiritual quest. By being more faithful to the Upanishadic ideal of the unity of learning *(srotriya)* and commitment to spiritual truth *(brahmanistham)* it offers a more promising and rewarding model for Hindu dialogue with Christianity and other religions. The complete subordination, on the other hand, of scriptural revelation to the authority of personal experience and the associated vilification of reason, the role of the intellect, discussion and language, have sadly engendered scepticism about the worth of dialogue in which these have a prominent role. The devaluation of learning and intellectual skills in a prominent heroic interpreter of Hinduism, like Vivekananda, must not go unchallenged.

Since the latter half of the 1960's the Hindu population of the United States has been growing steadily. Until that time, the doors of welcome were virtually shut to immigrants from Asia. The Chinese exclusion act of 1882 was applied broadly to include all people of Asian origin. In 1965, a new immigration law, initiated by John F. Kennedy, abolished quotas based on national origins and opened the country to immigrants from India. Today, there are lively and flourishing communities of Hindus in most of the major cities of North America, and temple construction has been rapidly following the establishment of such communities. Hindus are prominently among those whom W.C. Smith described as "our neighbors, our colleagues, our competitors, our fellows".[17]

The context of interrelated living offers fruitful opportunities for the 'dialogue of life' between Hindus and Christians and this is clearly taking place. I think that most Hindus in North America will easily identify occasions and moments in their lives when they had to articulate some aspect of their faith and practice to people of other religions. Hindus, on the whole, usually embrace the opportunity to do this. Our interrelated lives in communities of diversity will also require of us more engagement in the 'dialogue of action' through which we will be called upon to work with others for the advancement of mutual interests. While there are many groups in North America whose beliefs and

---

16  See, for example, his commentary on *Brahma-sutra* I.i.2.
17  Smith, W.C. (1972) *The Faith of Other Men* New York: Harper and Row, 11.

practices are influenced by elements of Hinduism, the 'dialogue of spirituality' which Ariarajah describes as involving participation in each other's worship and meditation is still exceptional for Hindus. There is only one Hindu-based organisation of which I am aware, The International Society of Krishna Consciousness in West Virginia, which prominently promotes dialogue of this kind. Ariarajah points to the concerns that many people have about the possibility of meaningfully entering the worship of another tradition and fears of uncritical syncretism.

The dialogue of discourse between Hinduism and Christianity in North America is lacking both in frequency and depth, and in this essay I have offered another reason for what many have discerned to be the lack of Hindu interest and initiative for such dialogue. The questioning of uncritical attitudes about the supremacy of personal experience, and the recovery of its existing but overshadowed traditions of vibrant learning and spirituality seem to me to be a necessary condition for fruitful dialogue of discourse between both traditions. Modern Hindu commentators have not only upheld the authority of personal experience but they have affirmed this to be the uniqueness of Hinduism. I am convinced that the affirmation of a more creative relationship between revelation, reason and experience will reveal many more exciting areas of common interest for discussion between our two religions.

# Dialogue in Buddhism

*Carola Roloff (Jampa Tsedroen)*

# Interreligious Dialogue in Buddhism from a Gender Perspective

## Introduction

In 1991 during the International Year of Tibet, on behalf of the Tibetan Centre Hamburg together with H. H. the 14ᵗʰ Dalai Lama I organised the "Hamburg Tibet Week", a platform that provided interesting insights on dialogue. During his talks not only Carl-Friedrich von Weizsäcker (1912–2007), the famous German physicist and philosopher, was present but also the late Hamburg Protestant Bishop, Prof. Peter Krusche (1924–2000). The Dalai Lama spoke on the issue of Peace for the World and Peace for Tibet, and later, when this talk was published, in a foreword, Bishop Krusche added some thoughts about their meeting[1]. He particularly remembered that the Dalai Lama had said: "We should not conceal the differences: We Buddhists do not believe in a Creator God like you as a Christian." Krusche's comment was that he considered himself very fortunate that, to his understanding, precisely this difference served as a connecting piece: "The Christian belief in a Creator God enables us to see each person as an image of God. God the Creator of heaven and earth I can also meet in people of different religions. It makes me curious, and makes me open for surprises."

I will explain at the end of this paper, why I think that from a Buddhist perspective, such an inclusive approach towards dialogue – inclusive in the sense that all are included in the dialogue regardless of one's religious position – seems to me to be a realistic and feasible one.[2]

But before I go deeper into this, let me first introduce my topic: Dialogue in Buddhism includes not only dialogue with religions, but also dialogue with scientists, dialogue with other Buddhist traditions and even dialogue within their own tradition on controversial issues such as gender equity. However, here I will concentrate on interreligious dialogue in Buddhism and how gender issues could become a driving force for the dialogue between religions.

The Dalai Lama is of course not the only leading Buddhist involved in interreligious dialogue and taking a pluralist approach toward other religions, but he is the one with whom I am most familiar. In his New Millennium Message on January 1ˢᵗ, 2000 he said: "Human problems will, of course, always remain,

---

1    Krusche, D. P. (1993) Gedanken über die Begegnung mit S.H. Dalai Lama am 6. Oktober 1991. In: Dalai Lama *Frieden für die Welt Frieden für Tibet* Hamburg: dharma edition, 7–9.

2    The present paper is based on a lecture I delivered during my visiting professorship at the Academy of World Religions in Hamburg in 2012. I would like to thank Prof. Perry Schmidt-Leukel for a number of most valuable comments, corrections, indications and references on two earlier versions of this article, which lead to further research and insights and which will hopefully be of some benefit for the readers.

but the way to resolve them should be through dialogue and discussion. The next century should be a century of dialogue and discussion rather than one of war and bloodshed."[3] In a conversation with the diplomat Stéphane Hessel (1917–2013), an observer of the editing process of the Universal Declaration of Human Rights, the Dalai Lama stressed that the two main goals he will follow to the end of his life, are the promotion of a harmonious coexistence of religions and of the reflection on inner values.[4] And in forewords to two recent publications he stated:

> Today more and more people realize that the way of resolving difference is through dialogue, compromise and negotiations, through human understanding and humility.[5] Whatever we are trying to achieve, under whatever circumstances, we must develop confidence that dialogue and friendly co-operation are a valid alternative to violence and destruction. (…) The authors of this timely book, my old friend and veteran Gandhian, the late Ravindra Varma, and Anna Alomes, recognise that there is not only a need, but also a growing desire for change in the world. A change that ushers in a renewed commitment to ethical and spiritual values, that resolves conflicts peaceably, employing dialogue and non-violence, that upholds human rights and human dignity as well as human responsibility.[6]

We see this view echoed throughout the Buddhist belief system. Before exploring this background I consider the following four key points:

1  The term 'dialogue' from a Buddhist viewpoint and Buddhist approaches toward inter- and intra-religious dialogues
2  Texts used for interreligious dialogue and how Buddhist approaches to dialogue are anchored in them
3  Examples of various forms of interreligious dialogue in Buddhism
4  Future prospects on how gender issues could become a driving force for interreligious dialogue taking the Buddhist Nuns Ordination Restoration Movement (Buddhist NORM) as an example

## The Term 'Dialogue' from a Buddhist Viewpoint and Buddhist Approaches toward Inter- and Intra-religious Dialogues

There are various ways in which you could translate the term dialogue. As a Tibetologist, let me take recourse to the Tibetan language. 'Dialogue' is a mod-

---

3   http://dalailama.com/messages/world-peace/millennium-message (accessed May 30, 2012).
4   Crossman, S. & Barou, J.-P. (Eds.) (2010) *Stéphane Hessel, Dalai Lama: Wir erklären den Frieden!* Berlin: Ullstein, 58.
5   Alomes, A. (2012a) Power in Philosophy: two arguments for nonviolence today Dharamsala: Library of Tibetan Works and Archives, v.
6   Varma, R. & Alomes, A. (2012b) Towards a nonviolent mind Dharamsala: Library of Tibetan Works and Archives, v.

ern term and synonym to conversation[7]which simply means to talk (to each other), to debate, to discuss – neither of which might be sufficient to define interreligious dialogue.[8] Classical Indian Buddhist literature as well as Tibetan autochthonous literature contains discussions with regard to other Buddhist or non-Buddhist religious traditions. Such discussions are formulated in the very typical style of philosophical debate of Indian logicians. The term 'debate', or philosophical (honest) debate (Tib. *rtsod pa*, Skt. *vāda*) is quite common to Buddhist scholars and it may be what they would first associate when it comes to having a dialogue with other religious traditions.[9] What is meant is an honest debate on religious and philosophical subjects; cross-culturally we can call to mind the dialogues of Plato. In Buddhism, debate is mainly based on the works by Dignāga (480–540), the 6th century father of Indian logic, and his main commentator Dharmakīrti (600–660). Buddhist logic is a vast field on which many Indian and Tibetan authors have published. The aim of debates is the ascertainment of truth. Whether and how far these ancient forms of debate, which in the Tibetan tradition are still practiced on a daily basis, are useful for interreligious dialogue has not yet been analysed.[10] It is definitely not useful if applied with an attitude to prove to others that one's own view is the best and the only correct view.

Thus, to develop a definition of interreligious dialogue may be very helpful for gaining mutual understanding and clearing the ground. According to Sallie B. King, interreligious dialogue is an "intentional encounter and interaction between members of different religions *as* members of different religions."[11] Therefore, a meeting with followers of different religions might be helpful not only in order to learn about examples of good exchanges already experienced,

---

7   Tibetan terms for dialogue, conversation: sbst. *skad cha*, resp. *bka'mol, gleng brjod, gleng brjod, gleng mo*; to talk, converse, debate, discuss: verbs *sgro ba, gleng ba, chos kyi sgro(g) gleng byed pa* (resp. *mdzad pa*).

8   However, nowadays in Tibetan it is referred to as *chos kyi sgro(g) gleng,* i.e., conversation or exchange on religion (dharma).

9   McClintock, S. L. (2010) *Omniscience and the Rhetoric of Reason: Śāntarakṣita and Kamalaśīla on Rationality, Argumentation, & Religious Authority* Boston: Wisdom Publications, 69.

10  For a detailed study on philosophical debate as a living practice in contemporary Tibetan monasticism: Dreyfus, G. B. J. (2003) *The Sound of Two Hands Clapping. The Education of a Tibetan Buddhist Monk* Berkley, Los Angeles, London: University of California Press. Dreyfus, 306–307 argues that he would not go that far as to say that debate is not a valuable pedagogical tool. For him debate is rather a way of reaching greater understanding requiring a certain degree of freedom, which in the Tibetan tradition is real, but limited: "The very authority of the tradition requires that participants be able to find meaningful ways to use the resources offered by the past; otherwise, tradition degenerates into mere traditionalism. But inquiry within it cannot go too far; otherwise, participants will feel that the authority of the past is being undermined."

11  King, S. B. (2011) Interreligous Dialogue. In: Chad V. Meister (Ed.) *The Oxford Handbook of Religious Diversity* Oxford, New York: Oxford University Press, 101–114.

but also in order to jointly define the criteria of what dialogue is and what it is not.

My focus here is on the dialogue between religions which became common in the second half of the twentieth century and is supposed to have started in an organised way with the World's Parliament of Religions, held in Chicago in 1893.[12] At that time Buddhism was represented by the famous Sinhalese Buddhist Anagarika Dharmapala[13] (1864–1933), pioneer in the revival of Buddhism in India and of the Buddhist pilgrimage, which today brings together Buddhists from all traditions and provides for intra-Buddhist and intercultural dialogue. The Buddha's 2,500th death anniversary, his Parinirvāṇa (at the age of 80), was celebrated by Buddhists around the world in 1956 in India.[14] The 2,600th anniversary of his enlightenment (when he was 35 years old) was celebrated in December 2011, during the Global Buddhist Congregation in New Delhi. Buddhists from all traditions celebrated the 2,600 years of Buddha's enlightenment together. During this event, funded by the Indian government, the International Buddhist Confederation (IBC) was formed to preserve and promote Buddhist heritage worldwide, particularly in India and Nepal.

And then in January 2013, the Minister of the State of Bihar organised an International Buddhist Saṅgha Conference on "The role of Buddhist Saṅgha [monastic community] in the 21st century" at Buddha Smriti Park in Patna, known as Pataliputra, the ancient capital of the Magadha Empire. From there, between the 3rd century BCE up to the 7th century CE, Buddhism had started to spread all over Asia. The Patna conference was inaugurated by highly placed dignitaries representing various "Buddhist countries"[15] with the chief guest and main speaker among the dignitaries being H.H. the Dalai Lama. A two-day academic conference programme followed and the whole event was coordinated by the Bodhgaya Temple Management Committee.

Bodhgaya is significant as it is the place where the Buddha attained his enlightenment (*bodhi*) and it is the largest of India's eight main Buddhist pil-

---

12  Dehn, U. (2008) Interreligiöser Dialog. Grundüberlegungen. In: M. Klöcker & U. Two-ruschka (Eds.) *Praktische Religionswissenschaft. Ein Handbuch für Studium und Beruf* Köln, Weimar, Wien: Böhlau Verlag, 238–250.

13  Although the Buddhist world owes a lot to Dharmapala's activities, it should not go unmentioned that it seems that in his heart Dharmapala was not a dialogical person. Dharmapala had received an English education at Christian school and Colleges in Sri Lanka, which was the British colony Ceylon then, and was strongly influenced by the Theosophists Blavatsky and Olcott. He rejected certain aspects of Christianity and is described as an agressive Sinhala chauvinist. Toward the end of his life he was ordained as a Theravāda *bhikkhu* (monk). Trevithick even speaks about his "evident disregard for Hindu feeling" (cf. Trevithick, A. *The Revival of Buddhist Pilgrimage at Bodh Gaya (1811–1949). Anagarika Dharmapala and the Mahabodhi Temple* Delhi: Motilal Banarsidass, 50–57, 88.).

14  Thus the Buddha lived 624–544 BC. From a scientific point of view this dating is considered too early.

15  The fact that they are still referred to as "Buddhist countries" clearly shows that even if the constitutions of those countries may provide a separation of religion and state the amendment has not yet reached the base.

grimage places. In 2002 the Mahabodhi Temple Complex at Bodhgaya became a UNESCO World Heritage Site. Since then, whether related or unrelated to the listing, India witnessed an unprecedented expansion of tourism. The north-eastern state of India, Bihar, where most of the famous Buddhist sites are located, became one of the major attractions for international travellers. At the same time, Bihar is one of the poorest states of India, lacking proper infrastructure, and the number of resident Buddhist practitioners there is relatively small. Since not many native Buddhists live at those Buddhist sites, it is difficult to comply with the needs of the many Buddhist pilgrims visiting. Ever since the decline of Buddhism, which is usually dated around the end of the 12th and the beginning of the 13th century CE and attributed to the gradual Muslim conquest[16] in the Indian subcontinent led by Muhammad Ghuri, India no longer has strong native Buddhist communities. Therefore the Indian government is increasingly seeking support from Buddhist leaders of the various traditions outside India to help develop the Buddhist Heritage according to the needs of their adherents, which includes not only spiritual guidance but also practical aspects like ease of visa re-entry norms for pilgrims.

The IBC is planning to serve as a common platform for Buddhists worldwide with the main Buddhist traditions being well-represented, thus speaking with a strong and united Buddhist voice. It wants to give priority to reviving, developing and training Buddhist communities and *saṅghas* in India and ex-

---

16 From the 8th century onward the Turkic Muslim conquest of northwestern India had begun, reaching the east of India by the end of the 12th / beginning of the 13th century CE. At that time the Buddhist major centres of learning Nālandā (1197) and Vikramaśīla (1203) together with their large libraries were destroyed. These monastic universities had an especially strong influence on Tibetan Buddhism. Thapar points out that in 8th century CE Buddhism had nowhere been more prevalent than in north-western and eastern India (cf. Thapar, R. (2003) *The Penguin history of early India: from the origins to AD 1300*, 433–435, 482–489, London: Penguin.). The conversion of these areas to Islam was a gradual process and the decline of Buddhism had actually already occurred before the Turkish conquest. Its decline requires a wider explanation than just a change in religion. The exact circumstances, however, are unknown. It seems to have been a combination of factors that led to the decay of Buddhism in its country of origin. It was not only due to the coming of Islam and the attack on the main monastery Nālandā, but Buddhism was also gradually replaced by "Puranic Hinduism" involving hostility between Buddhists and some sects of Śaivas. Sectarianism encouraged rivalry and hostility between the various sects of Buddhism, Jainism and Hinduism and contributed to the decline. Furthermore the strong focus of Buddhism on monasticism was no longer attractive to ordinary persons. Tantrism, opposing the Brahmanical ordering of the society, became increasingly popular. It influenced not only Buddhism, but also the other older religions, and eventually by the 13th century Buddhism had lost its status of even a minor religion in India. How these interreligious conflicts between Buddhists, Hindus and Muslims are reflected in the religious literature of those centuries and how they have led to apocalyptic eschatological beliefs is shown very convincingly in Schmidt-Leukel, P. (2013) Drei Kalkins und die Frage nach den Wurzeln religiöser Gewalt. In: *Zeitschrift für Missions- und Religionswissenschaft* 97, 89–99. Only since the 20th century a revival of Buddhism in India can be observed, which in turn has a variety of causes.

plicitly wants to emphasise and advance the role of women in both the lay and ordained communities. It seems that after more than a millennium, practical needs on all sides combined with governmental financial support have led to the foundation of this umbrella organisation of the various strands of Buddhism in its country of origin.

In September 2013 for four days, 250 representatives from Buddhist national *saṅghas*, organisations, institutions and monastic bodies gathered in New Delhi for the 1ˢᵗ Founding Members Conclave. The first panel to the plenary was on Interfaith Relations (A Meeting of Hearts & Minds). Another major event dealt with Changing Times (Buddhism in the 21ˢᵗ Century) and gave a choice of workshops such as: Buddhism in the Global Discourse, Working with Governments & International Bodies, Ordination of Buddhist Nuns, Women in Buddhism, Environment & the Natural World, Buddhist Youth Outreach, Buddhism & Media, and Interfaith Relations. Despite the many doctrinal differences there seems to be the willingness for dialogue and cooperation on common issues, which may lead to a new Buddhist sense of community. During the last session the "Joint Statements of Intent and Purpose Plans" were presented by the chairs of the workshops. "The IBC Statement on Interfaith Relations" stresses that the newly founded organisation acknowledges that "conflict, tensions and mis-understandings between people of different faiths is a major area of concern" and asserts "the right of all individuals to follow their chosen faith." Diversity is reflected in the way that "the IBC does not aspire to find agreement between followers of different religious faiths on tenets of belief, creed or practice". However, the delegates who participated in the workshop came to the conclusion that they believe "that religious leaders of all faiths can subscribe and promote a code of fundamental conduct of respect and non-harming without causing offence to their constituencies". They addressed various challenges faced by followers of religions such as violence in the name of religion, religious extremism, prejudice, stereotyping and generalisation toward other religious traditions. Therefore the IBC resolved to foster interfaith engagement and greater understanding through better education on other religious traditions and endorsed the *Dusit Declaration* of Bangkok 2006, which was re-affirmed in June 2013 as well as the International Movement for a Just World (JUST) to protect all places of worship and to speak out against attacks on religious sites and monuments.

## Texts Used for the Interreligious Dialogue and how Buddhist Approaches are Anchored in them

Depending on the themes of each dialogue there is a great variety of texts to turn to. For example, if the dialogue focuses on saints in the world's religions, there are plenty of hagiographies that can be used. If it is on compassion, there are canonical texts as well as ancient and modern commentaries on compassion, which can be employed, only to name a few.

### Attempts towards a Joint Declaration by the Buddhist Mainstream Traditions

However, contrary to the Catholic Church, no Buddhist tradition seems to have formulated an official declaration such as the *Nostra Aetate*. The *Nostra Aetate* was promulgated by the Vatican Second Council in 1965 to describe the relation of the Catholic Church to non-Christian religions.[17]

In general, Buddhism does not have a central overarching hierarchy with a spiritual leader who can speak with one voice for all Buddhist traditions. Similar to the Catholic and Protestant Churches, there are three mainstream traditions of Buddhism: Theravāda, East Asian and Tibetan Buddhism. Within these traditions there are many Nikāyas, i.e., monk orders and/or schools, and each of them seems to enjoy considerable autonomy. Unless it comes to innovations such as the revival of the Buddhist nuns order – an ongoing issue since the 1970s –a common approach seems to be desired (for details see below).

In Tibetan Buddhism, for example, since 1642 the Dalai Lamas have been the political and spiritual leaders.[18] Additionally, each tradition continued to have its own religious leader, also the Gelugpa, the school the Dalai Lamas belong to. The head of the school of the Gelugpas is the Ganden Tripa, not the Dalai Lama.[19] The Ganden Tripa is an appointed office not determined by reincarnation and they are the followers of Tsongkhapa Lobsang Drakpa (1357–1419), who was the founder of the Gelugpa school, and of his direct successor and disciple Gyaltsab Dharma Rinchen (1364–1432). The First Dalai Lama (*posthumous*) was another close disciple of Tsongkhapa: Gendun Drub (Dalai Lama I, 1391–1474). The present Dalai Lama Tenzin Gyatso is considered to be the 14th incarnation of Gendun Drub, and does not refer to himself as Gelugpa, but as *rime* (non-sectarian).

Although a council of Tibetan religious leaders exists, they meet only on an irregular basis. The last meeting was the 11th Conference of Religious Leaders of Tibetan Buddhism and the Bon Tradition, held from September 22 to 24,

---

17  Hoga, J. P. & McLean, G. F. (2005) *Multiple Paths to God: Nostra Aetate, 40 Years Later* Washington: The Council for Research in Values and Philosophy, 266.

18  See the biography of the 5th Dalai Lama summarised on the website of the present 14th Dalai Lama: www.dalailama.com/biography/the-dalai-lamas#5 (last accessed December 11, 2013). The Dalai Lama had been the spiritual and political head of Tibet since 1642. On November 7, 2011 the 14th Dalai Lama handed over the affairs of the Tibetan government in exile to the new prime minister Lobsang Sangay. See: www.nzz.ch/aktuell/international/neuer-chef-der-tibetischen-exilregierung-vereidigt-1.11820113 (last accessed December 11, 2013), but is still considered to be the head of Tibetan Buddhism.

19  See also Powers, J. & Templeman D. (2012) *Historical Dictionary of Tibet.* Lanham, Toronto, Plymouth, UK: The Scarecrow Press, 199.

2011 in Dharamsala.[20] By protocol, obviously, when all heads of the traditions are present, the Dalai Lama is considered the highest, but this does not mean that he can make overarching decisions on his own. Thus, in case a joint dialogue declaration is considered necessary, this could be signed by the Dalai Lama for Tibetan Buddhism only – provided that the heads of the various Tibetan traditions have agreed on it. A joint declaration could also come from new organisations such as the above-mentioned IBC, representing all major Buddhist traditions. Alternatively the initiative could come from leading Buddhists, individual traditions of Buddhism, or international Buddhist networks such as the Sakyadhita International Association of Buddhist Women or the International Network of Engaged Buddhists (INEB). The above-mentioned *Dusit Declaration* of Bangkok (2006) is an International Buddhist-Muslim Joint Statement, which was drawn up during a dialogue between Buddhists and Muslims in Southeast Asia working towards justice and peace, organised by the Santi Pracha Dhamma Institute (SPDI), INEB, JUST and RfP (Religions for Peace).[21]

In the West there have already been some first attempts. For example, in 1987 a conference on 'World Buddhism in North America' was held at the University of Michigan during which a 'Statement of Consensus' was promulgated for four major reasons:[22]

1. to create the conditions necessary for tolerance and understanding among Buddhists and non-Buddhists alike, 2. to initiate a dialogue among Buddhists in North America in order to further mutual understanding, growth in understanding, and co-operation, 3. to increase their sense of community by recognising

---

20  For the work of the council, taking the revival of Buddhist nuns ordination movement as an example, see Roloff, C. (2013) Buddhistische Nonnen brauchen eine Lobby. In: *Tibet und Buddhismus* 26 (2), 35–37. For an English translation see: www.buddhistwomen.eu/EN/uploads/Documentation/Artikel_TiBu_Feb2012_eng.pdf (last accessed December 11, 2013).

21  Available from http://www.parliamentofreligions.org/news/wp-content/uploads/2013/07/International-Buddhist-Muslim-Joint-Statement.pdf (last accessed December 11, 2013). It has been signed by 26 people, mainly Muslims and Buddhists from countries such as Burma/Myanmar, Sri Lanka, Malaysia, Indonesia and Thailand. One of them is Parichart Suwanbubbha who has also contributed to this volume with the article "Dialogue in Buddhism. A Case Study in Addressing in Southern Thailand", p. 309. I am indebted to Perry Schmidt-Leukel for the information that during the last years there have been important dialogue declarations in Judaism (*Dabru Emet*) and in Islam (*A Common Word*), which did not come from a certain institution. Furthermore see the more recent publication by: Shah Kazemi, R. (2010) *Common Ground Between Islam and Buddhism* Louisville: Fons Vitae. For an online publication see: http://www.islambuddhism.com/docs/CommonGround.pdf (last accessed December 11, 2013).

22  It was held at the Ann Arbor Zen Center in July 1987. The statement of consensus was drafted by a panel comprising, Ven. Havanpola Ratanasara, Ven. U Silananda, Ven. Samu Sunim, Bishop D. Nakamura and Prof. Dr. Luis O. Gómez, with Ven. Mahaghosananda, Ven. Vivekananda and Bishop S. Yamaoka as consultants. Source: http://www.urbandharma.org/udharma/consensus.html (last accessed December 11, 2013).

and understanding their differences as well as their common beliefs and practices, and 4. to cultivate thoughts and actions of friendliness towards others, whether they accept their beliefs or not, and in so doing approach the world as the proper field of Dharma, not as a sphere of conduct irreconcilable with the practice of Dharma.[23]

Luis Gómez notes:[24] "not much came out of the enthusiasm of those days. Perhaps it is part of the Nation's long flirtation with right-wing Christian intolerance, perhaps it is the result of a certain retrenchment among Buddhist groups in the States, but the truth is that there is not as much ferment in the interreligious dialogue as we had, say, in the eighties." According to Prebish and Keown[25] "perhaps the greatest challenge for socially engaged Buddhism in the West is organisational. It is far less developed in its organisational patterns and strategies than its Christian or Jewish counterparts. As such, it is still learning from the many experiments in interfaith dialogue, such as the Society for Buddhist-Christian Studies."

## Some Buddhist Texts and Concepts Applicable for Interreligious Dialogue

Nevertheless, an ongoing and well-accepted interreligious dialogue with various religions is under way. In general, many Buddhists believe that your *karma* decides what religion you meet in this life. The Dalai Lama often states that due to different inner predispositions it is good to have a great variety of religions, so that everybody can find the one that bests suits him or her. This approach seems to be based on or linked to the Buddhist concept of the Buddha's 'skill in means' (*upāyakauśalya*).[26] A Buddha teaches skilfully, since different people need different means, in accordance with the level of his audience.[27] It seems that the Dalai Lama is using a special Mahāyāna methodology for justifying a contemporary and non-sectarian, open approach to other religious traditions, whether Buddhist or non-Buddhist.

For the Theravāda such an approach is for example well expressed in the *Kālāma Sutta,* a canonical text against sectarianism towards other Buddhist

23  Also: Prebish, C. & Keown, D. (2010) *Buddhism – the ebook. An online introduction* (4th edition) Pennsylvania: State College, 214.

24  Personal communication March 25, 2013.

25  Prebish, C. & Keown, D. (2010), 219.

26  Cf. Lopez, D. S. Jr. (1988) Introduction. In: D. S. Jr. Lopez (Ed.) *Buddhist Hermeneutics* Honolulu: University of Hawaii Press, 3–5.

27  Lopez, D. S. Jr. (1988), 5–6, indicates that while seeking to determine the final view of the Buddha, the doctrine of *upāya* caused problems in the interpretation of scripture becoming itself a hermeneutical principle by which interpretation was undertaken. For a detailed discussion of the term and its occurrence in Pāli and Mahāyāna literature Federman, A. (2009) Literal Means and Hidden Meanings: A New Analysis of Skilful Means. In: *Philosophy East & West,* 59 (2), 125–141.

traditions as well as towards other religions.[28] Although among Buddhists there is a lot of discussion about how to interpret this *sutta* correctly in accordance with its context, most may agree that it shows that freedom of an own opinion, the use of sound reasoning as well as making one's own experience is very important.[29] The importance of making one's own experience is one of the strong potentials of Buddhism with regard to dialogue ability.

Tibetans very often quote another canonical text, where the Buddha says:

> Like gold that is melted, cut, and polished,
> So should monks and scholars
> Analyze my words [before] accepting them;
> They should not do so out of respect [for me].[30]

This advice – at least in theory – seems to give space to question even the words of the Buddha, let alone the later commentators, and to develop one's own ideas based on insight as long as they are in accordance with the spirit of the

28  *Aṅguttara Nikāya* 3.65 (Pali Text Society I 188). It is important to note that this *sutta* similar to most of the Pāli canon has not been translated into Tibetan and thus does not belong to the Tibetan Buddhist canon. Thus it cannot be used for argumentation in regard to Buddhism in general. For an English translation of the *Kālama Sutta*, see: Bodhi, B. (2012) (Ed.) *The Numerical Discourses of the Buddha. A Translation of the Aṅguttara Nikāya* Boston: Wisdom Publications, 279–283.

29  Anālayo, B. (2009) The Scope of Free Inquiry According to the *Vīmaṃsaka-Sutta* and its *Madhyama-āgama* Parallel. In: *Rivista di studi sudasiatici* 4 (4), 7–20, states that although the *Kālāma-sutta* is often referred to "as the example par excellence for the advocacy of a principle of free inquiry, expressing a non-authoritarian and pragmatic attitude. Yet, compared with the *Kālāma-sutta* the *Vīmaṃsaka-Sutta* could lay an even greater claim to presenting a remarkable advocacy of free inquiry."

30  I follow here the translation of Lopez 1988: 5. Although everybody knows this quotation, it still needs to be proven that it comes from a sūtra ascribed to the Buddha. Some say that it comes from the Arya-ghanavyūha-nāma-mahāyāna-sūtra ('Phags pa rgyan stug po bkod pa zhes bya ba theg pa chen po'i mdo), P. No. 0778, mdo sna tshogs, cu 1b1–62b8 (vol.29, p.131), D. No. 0110, mngon sde, cha 1b1–55b7. I have checked an electronic version of this long Mahāyānasūtra, but cannot confirm this information. Thurman, Robert A. F. (Ed.) (1984) notes in his annotated full translation of Tsong Khapa's Speech of gold in the Essence of true eloquence: reason and enlightenment in the central philosophy of Tibet, 190. Princeton, NJ: Princeton University Press, that "this verse is known to the commentators as being the Vimalaprabhā commentary on the Kālacakra, although it appears in the Pali Canon as well", but he does not give the respective evidence. For the Sanskrit he refers to a quotation in D. Shastri's edition of Śāntarakṣita's Tattvasaṃgraha (Varanasi: Bauddhabharati, 1968), k, 3587: tapācchedacca nika śātsuvarṇam iva pānditaib / parikṣyā bhikṣavo grāhyam mad vaco na tu gauravāt. The Tibetan reads in Tsongkhapa's famous treatise on the two truths, Essence of True Elloquence, Distinguishing the Provisional and Definitive (Drang ba dang nges pa'i don rnam par phye ba'i bstan bcos legs bshad snying po), Gsung 'bum, Sku 'bum Byams pa gling Par khang edition, TBRC 22272014, vol. 14, p. 445, 3a3: dge slong dag gam mkhas rnams kyis/ /bsregs bcad brdar ba'i gser bzhin du/ /legs par brtags la nga yi bka'/ /blang bar bya yi gus phyir min. Although the Tattvasaṃgraha does not belong to the Kangyur (Translation of the Words of the Buddha), but to the Tengyur (Translation of the Commentaries) it is considered to be canonical.

Buddha's teachings. This is what happened during the First International Congress on Buddhist Women's Role in the Saṅgha at the University of Hamburg in 2007. Discussing the possibilities of the revival of the Buddhist nuns order, some of the speakers argued that the revival would be "reviving the real spirit of the Buddha"[31] or "appeal to the spirit of the Dharma itself"[32]. As Bhikkhu Bodhi pointed out:[33]

> In working out a solution to our own problem, therefore, we have these two guidelines to follow. One is to be true to the spirit of the Dhamma — true to both the letter and the spirit, but above all to the spirit. The other is to be responsive to the social, intellectual, and cultural horizons of humanity in this particular period of history in which we live, this age in which we forge our own future destinies and the future destiny of Buddhism.

Similarly, the Theravāda nun Bhikkhunī Dhammananda, a former professor for philosophy and women studies at the Thammasat University in Bangkok, suggested that[34]

> "in order to preserve Buddhism we need to take into account that the Buddha reminded us on his death bed that it was the Dhamma and Vinaya that will be the lights upon ourselves. Do not insist blindly on only paying attention to the words of the Vinaya, as there is a great need to also apply Dhamma in order to provide us with an understanding of the Vinaya in its true spirit."

She comes to the final conclusion: "Ordination of both genders is one form of expression of true equality that was given to us by the Buddha; we only need to retain its essence and spirit to be true Buddhists."[35]

In this context also the Dalai Lama demanded that in the twenty-first century,

> We need conflict resolution, and the capacity to respect different perspectives, take others' rights seriously, and find ways to promote the spirit of dialogue (...) Given that women are fully capable of achieving the ultimate goal of the Buddha's teachings, in harmony with the spirit of the modern age, the means and opportunity to achieve this goal should be completely accessible to them.[36]

---

31  Krey, G. (2010) Some Remarks on the Status of Nuns and Laywomen in Early Buddhism. In: T. Mohr & J. Tsedroen (C. Roloff) *Dignity & Discipline: Reviving Full Ordination for Buddhist Nuns* Boston: Wisdom Publications, 55.

32  Bodhi, B. (2010) The Revival of Bhikkhunī Ordination in the Theravāda Tradition. In: T. Mohr & J. Tsedroen (C. Roloff) *Dignity & Discipline: Reviving Full Ordination for Buddhist Nuns* Boston: Wisdom Publications, 99–142, 111.

33  Ibid., 134.

34  Dhammananda, B. (2010) A Need to Take a Fresh Look at Popular Interpretations of the Tripiṭaka. Theravāda Context in Thailand. In: T. Mohr & J. Tsedroen (C. Roloff) *Dignity & Discipline: Reviving Full Ordination for Buddhist Nuns* Boston: Wisdom Publications, 158.

35  Ibid., 160.

36  Dalai Lama, XIV (2010) Human Rights and the Status of Women in Buddhism. In: T. Mohr & J. Tsedroen (C. Roloff) *Dignity & Discipline: Reviving Full Ordination for Buddhist Nuns* Boston: Wisdom Publications, 253–280, 274, 278.

No doubt we can find more Buddhist texts that will be helpful to encourage interreligious dialogue and develop a "Theology of Dialogue", although it will not be an easy undertaking.[37] Bhikkhu Bodhi, being one of the leading translators of the Pāli canon, ascertains: "The fourth chapter of the *Sutta-nipāta* contains several *suttas* that describe how the sage can avoid doctrinal disputes. See particularly *Sutta-nipāta, Atthakavagga suttas* 3, 4, 5, 8, 11, 12, 13. The true sage should not praise his own teachings and disparage the teachings of others. He recognises how disputes over views only cause distress and blow up conceit and clinging. If one triumphs in debate, one feels superior to others; if one loses in debate, one feels miserable. Thus, valuing equanimity, the sage avoids debates and disputes over doctrines."[38]

In these texts, for example, we find sayings by the Buddha such as:

> They say their own teaching is perfect
> while the doctrine of others is lowly.
> Thus quarreling, they dispute,
> each saying his agreed-on opinion is true.
> If something, because of an opponent's say-so,
> were lowly,
> then none among teachings would be superlative,
> for many say that another's teaching's inferior
> when firmly asserting their own.
> If their worship of their teaching were true,
> in line with the way they praise their own path,
> then all doctrines would be true —
> for purity's theirs, according to each.[39]

---

37  See for example – as a parallel to the parable of the elephant in the dark house, mentioned by Katajun Amirpur in her article "Straight Paths" in this volume – the Tittha sutta (Udāna 6.4): http://www.accesstoinsight.org/tipitaka/kn/ud/ud.6.04.than.html (last accessed December 11, 2013). Islam must have picked this parable up from India, perhaps through the Sufis. In the Buddhist canon, according to Bhikkhu Bodhi (personal correspondence March 23–25, 2013) "the famous parable of the elephant (Udāna 6.4) is offered not to show that each blind man has found a part of the truth, but that all the other teachers are like blind men who make foolish claims because they cannot see the truth. The Buddha alone sees the elephant and thus can describe it accurately. The view that each blind man knows a part of the truth is the interpretation that the Jains give to this parable, which they include in their own scriptures." As John D'Arcy May and Perry Schmidt-Leukel point out in their Introduction: Buddhism and its "Others" (2008), 11, "Each religious tradition has its own ways, sometimes subtle, sometimes crude, of asserting not only its own uniqueness but also its superiority over all others." In: P. Schmidt-Leukel (Ed.) (2008) *Buddhist Attitudes to Other Religions.* St. Ottilien: EOS Editions, 9–22.

38  Personal correspondence March 23, 2013. For the full texts see: http://www.sacred-texts.com/bud/sbe10/sbe1036.htm (last accessed December 11, 2013). For the best German translation see Nyanaponika (Ed.) (1955) *Sutta-Nipāta: Früh-buddhistische Lehr-Dichtungen aus dem Pāli-Kanon. Mit Auszügen aus den alten Kommentaren. Übersetzt, eingeleitet und erläutert von Nyanaponika.* Konstanz: Christiani, 173, 174, 175, 179, 185, 188, 191.

39  Sutta-nipāta 4.13. For the German translation see Nyanaponika (1955), 192, Verse 903–905. This is also one of the sources selected by the German Buddhist teacher Paul H. Köppler

However, although Bhikkhu Bodhi agrees that in the contemporary world "it is important for different religions to look upon one another with respect and appreciation, and to discover the truth and value behind the outward forms of other systems of faith, so different from one's own", he comes to the self-critical conclusion:

> I can't think offhand of any suttas in the Pali Canon in which the Buddha encourages the monks to be receptive of the teachings of 'the wanderers who belong to other sects' (aññatitthiya paribbajaka). I have not found any suttas that propose dialogue with other spiritual followers in order to learn from them and to broaden one's point of view.[40]

Thus, in order to find texts, which are suitable to develop a dialogue oriented theology[41] we also need to consider the Mahāyāna literature[42] as well as the writings of more recent Buddhist scholars. For example, the Dalai Lama as

---

for his book So spricht der Buddha (Thus speaks the Buddha). For his chapter 8 on "Andere Lehren" (Other Teachings) he selected extracts of discourses, which in his view demonstrate the Buddha's maximum tolerance with regard to other teachings or religions. He is retelling the stories in his own contemporary (euphemistic) words.

40  Although this self-perception of a Theravādin monk may conflict with the widespread perception of Buddhism by others as particularly tolerant, it also shows that Buddhism in context of changed framework conditions may adapt over time and will reconsider its traditional position towards other religions. Contemporary Buddhist scholars or theologians cannot change the body of source material, but they can take a more suitable approach based on Buddhist principles by dissociating themselves in accordance to the different contexts. For a discussion on the very critical perception of followers of other religions in many Pāli discourses see chapter 4 of Grünschloß, A. (1999) Der eigene und der fremde Glaube. Studien zur interreligiösen Fremdwahrnehmung in Islam, Hinduismus, Buddhismus und Christentum Tübingen: Mohr Siebeck, 189–230. For an English summary of that work see: http://wwwuser.gwdg.de/~agruens/summ_efg.html (accessed August 20, 2013).

41  Regarding the term 'theology' D'Arcy May and Schmidt-Leukel (2008), 10–11 state: "Though Buddhists are usually reluctant to adopt the term 'theology', they nevertheless affirm the existence and need for the kind of reflective effort to which this term in its broader sense refers. (…) 'theology of religions' too has its counterpart within each of the major religious traditions, and so in Buddhism as well."

42  See for example the teachings on "Exchanging Self and Other" based on the *Bodhisattvacaryāvatāra* and the *Śikṣasamuccaya* by the 8th-century Indian Buddhist scholar: Śāntideva. J. W.C. Cutler & G. Newland (Eds.) (2004) *Tsong-kha-pa: Lam rim chen mo. The Great Treatise on the Stages of the Path to Enlightenment* Translated by the Lamrim Chenmo Translation Committee, Vol. 2, Ithaca et al.: Snow Lion Publications, 53–60. Another important topic is "hospitality in Buddhism". In his teaching material, Geshe Thubten Ngawang mentions in the context of Vasubandhu's *Abhidharmakośa* IV.9: Systematisches Studium des Buddhismus. Part 1: Die Vaibhāṣika-Lehrmeinung (vols. I-II, transcript 1–360, sources 1–167), sources 47, Hamburg: Tibetisches Zentrum e.V. 1988–2001: "sieben aus Materie entstandene Verdienstarten": "Die Gabe von (1) Hainen, (2) Tempeln, (3) Liegen und Sitzen, (4) ständigem Lebensunterhalt, [Gaben] an (5) Reisende, (6) Kranke und Krankendiener sowie (7) zu Notzeiten im Land. Diese sind die sieben aus Materie entstandenen Verdienste." For the source see the *Vinayavibhaṅga* of the Mūlasarvāstivādins: Lhasa Kangyur, 'Dul ba, *ca* 204b (*rdzas las byung ba'i bsod nams bya ba'i gzhi bdun po*).

well as other Tibetan masters frequently refer to what is known as the "four reliances":

1. Rely on the teaching, not the person. 2. Rely on the meaning not the letter. 3. Rely on the definitive meaning, not the interpretable meaning. 4. Rely on wisdom, not on [ordinary] consciousness.[43]

As Lopez[44] points out, for Lamotte, this wisdom "constitutes the single and indispensable instrument of true exegesis,"[45] which means "that enlightenment provides the final criterion for interpretation".[46] This leads to the question as to "whether enlightenment obviates hermeneutics."[47] For Lopez "it seems certain that without enlightenment, there must be hermeneutics – (...). Those who are not yet enlightened must interpret. (...) The exegete is constantly in search of his place in the absent circle, and his hermeneutics[48] provide the compass."[49]

Accordingly, for dialogue one possible approach may be to simply admit that only those who have reached the final spiritual goal will experience what is ultimately true, while for common practitioners the question of truth remains open.[50] My Tibetan teacher, the late Geshe Thubten Ngawang (1932–2003) used to say: "If their views agree they are no [true] scholars. If their thoughts

---

43  Tib. *rton pa bzhi*, Skt. *catvāri pratisaraṇāni*. Tib. *gang zag la mi rton chos la rton, tshig la mi rton don la rton, rnam shes la mi rton ye shes la rton, drang don la mi rton nges don la rton pa'o*. Also: Dalai Lama, XIV & Hopkins, J. W. (1988) *The Dalai Lama at Harvard* Ithaca, NY: Snow Lion Publications, 22; Stearns, C. (1999) *The Buddha from Dolpo* Albany, NY: State University of New York Press, 86. For further discussion see Lopez, D. S. Jr. (1988) Introduction. In: D. S. Jr. Lopez (Ed.) *Buddhist Hermeneutics* Honolulu: University of Hawaii Press, 3–8 and Lamotte, E. (1988) Assessment of Textual Interpretation in Buddhism. In: D. S. Jr. Lopez (Ed.) *Buddhist Hermeneutics* Honolulu: University of Hawaii Press, 11–27. The *Mahāvyutpatti* (Ed. R. Sakakai, nos. 1545–1549) gives a different order.
44  Lopez, D. S. Jr. (1988), 7.
45  Lamotte, E. (1988), 24.
46  Lopez, D. S. Jr. (1988), 8.
47  Lopez, D. S. Jr. (1988), 9.
48  For a discussion of the propriety of using the term "hermeneutics" in Buddhist philosophy: Powers, J. (1993) *Hermeneutics and Tradition in the Saṃdhinirmocana-Sūtra* Leiden et al.: E. J. Brill.
49  Lopez, D. S. Jr. (1988), 9.
50  Schmidt-Leukel, P. (2011) Interkulturelle Theologie als interreligiöse Theologie. In: *Evangelische Theologie* 71 (1), 4–16, 12, states: "Niemand kann als einzelner alle Perspektiven in sich vereinigen und daher kann auch niemand im Alleingang so etwas wie eine interreligiöse Theologie abschließend erarbeiten. Interreligiöse Theologie ist daher notwendigerweise nicht nur ein dialogischer oder kolloquialer, sondern auch ein unabgeschlossener Prozess." Here I see a possible approach for dialogue as well as the capacity for dialogue in Buddhism. For an English version of this statement see Perry Schmidt-Leukel's article "Intercultural Theology as Interreligious Theology" in this volume, p. 101: "Interreligious theology, then, takes place in the context of a broadly understood interreligious colloquy.– No one individually can synthesise all its perspectives, which means it is impossible for any single person to produce something like a finished interreligious theology. Interreligious theology is necessarily not only a dialogical and or colloquial, but also an unfinished process."

disagree they are no [true] yogis."[51] This is an old Tibetan saying, which I understand as follows: differing views on what the Buddha is supposed to have said can be seen as expressions of various interpretative approaches of past and present Buddhist scholars in order to understand what the Buddha meant.[52] Yogis or Yoginīs (Buddhist mystics) have internalised the Buddha's teachings and, based on their deep insights, would easily agree when it comes to the 'taste' of ultimate truth,[53] although they rarely speak about their attainments, and if so, they may face difficulties in finding the right words to explain it to others.

In Buddhism, Nirvāṇa is the ultimate truth. Nirvāṇa is described as peaceful (friedvoll) or tranquil[54], unimaginable (unvorstellbar) and inexpressible (unausdrückbar)[55]. Not only in Mahāyāna texts but also in the Pāli canon of the

---

51  Tib. *lta ba (Skt. dṛṣṭi) mthun na mkhas pa min. dgongs pa (āśaya) ma mthun na grub thob min.*

52  I believe that this is close to what Alomes (2012a), 113, describes as follows: "Gandhi holds that Truth is not something at which we can arrive in isolation, waiting for a moment of revelation. Truth is discovered by persons in relation with others. The individual agent can only use objective truth as an unattainable guiding principle -- what is achievable is truth in relative terms; and in this respect, the individual searches for truth in terms of the community of which s/he is part. Through power relations with others, guided by the operation of reason, the agent comes to an understanding or 'a measure of reality' which may be true at that time, but is open to modification and refinement. This allows the individual to participate in a creative or dynamic process in which they can move increasingly closer to the truth over a lifetime. It is this progressive sense of truth that best describes Gandhi's life as an ongoing 'experiment'."

53  D'Arcy May and Schmidt-Leukel (2008), 15 state: "The pluralistic option in the interpretation of religious diversity is often compared to different paths leading to the same summit. this neither entails that all religions are the same (the image is still one of *different paths*!), nor that they are converging in the same kind of experience (the image suggests that they approach the summit from *different directions*)", while Alomes (2012b), 80 describes 'unity through diversity' by the following ancient Japanese saying: "There are many paths to the top of the mountain, but the view from the top is always the same."

54  Vasubandhu (4./5. Jh.), La Vallée Poussin, L. d. (1869–1938) (French trans.), Pruden, L. M. (Engl. trans.) (1988–1990), *Abhidharmakośabhāṣyam.* Berkeley: Asian Humanities Press, II, 72b, 322: all *saṃskāras* are impermanent, all dharmas are impersonal, Nirvāṇa is tranquil.

55  Frauwallner, E. (1898–1974) (2010) *Die Philosophie des Buddhismus. Mit einem Vorwort von Eli Franco und Karin Preisendanz* (5ᵗʰ edition) Berlin: Akademie Verlag, 110: "Dieses [*nirvāṇa*] ist ohne Entstehen und Vergehen, ohne Aufhören und auch nicht ewig. Und vor allem ist es weder seiend noch nicht seiend, da Sein und Nichtsein als gegensätzliche Begriffe der Welt der Abhängigkeit angehören. Ferner ist das Nirvāna frei von jeder Vielfalt, bietet also unseren Vorstellungen keine Grundlage und ist daher unvorstellbar und unausdrückbar. In ihm ist somit die Mannigfaltigkeit der Erscheinungen und das Gesetz des abhängigen Entstehens aufgehoben. Es ist von Natur aus friedvoll *(śāntam).*" For an English translation see: Frauwallner, E. (2010) *The philosophy of Buddhism* translated by Gelong Lodrö Sangpo with the assistance of Jigme Sheldrön under the supervision of Ernst Steinkellner. New Delhi: Motilal Banarsidass, 187: "The latter is without arising and passing away, without ending, and also is not permanent. Most importantly, it is neither existent nor non-existent, since existence and non-existence, as opposing concepts, belong to the world of dependence. Furthermore, *nirvāṇa* is free from all diversity and so offers no

Theravādins, Nirvāṇa (Pā. Nibbāna) is considered to be peace.[56] Among theologians of other religions there seems to be a widespread misunderstanding that Nirvāṇa means nil or nothingness (Nichts) and that this is what Buddhists are trying to attain: nothing, which understandably would make a dialogue with the monotheistic religions very difficult, since for them God is the ultimate truth. But as Rupert Gethin points out:

> Nirvāṇa, as the post-mortem condition of the Buddha and arhats, cannot be characterized as non-existence, but nor can it be characterized as existence. In fact to characterize it in either of these ways is to fall foul of one of the two basic wrong views (dṛṣṭi/ diṭṭhi) between which Buddhist thought tries to steer a middle course: the annhilationist view (uccheda-vāda) and the eternalist view (śāṣvata-/sassata-vāda). (…) Although some of the things one might say about nirvāṇa will certainly be more misleading than others, ultimately whatever one says will be misleading; the last resort must be the 'silence of the Āryas', the silence of the ones who have directly known the ultimate truth, for ultimately 'in such matters syllables, words and concepts are of no use'.[57]

Furthermore, it is important to keep in mind that various Buddhists traditions follow different canonical text collections as well as different philosophers who again lived at different times in different places within the context of different texts. And even then, for example in Tibetan Buddhism, following the same Indian Buddhist school of thought and the same Indian Buddhist philosophers, there are different Tibetan interpretations. Therefore some Tibetan scholars relate the above-mentioned Tibetan saying to the *Rime* 'movement', which started in the 19th century in eastern Tibet as a reaction to "institutional paralysis and dogmatic adherence" and "represents a paradigm with much earlier antecedents".[58]

## Buddhist Approaches towards Pluralism

The Tibetan term Rime (*ris med*), usually translated as non-sectarian or Nonsectarianism, consists of two syllables *ri* and *me*, *ri* (Tib. *ris*, Skt. *nikāya*) means 'school' and *me (pa)* (Tib. *med pa;* Skt. *asat*) means 'not existent'. Thus *Rime* refers to the approach of practitioners who have 'no [single] school affiliation' and could also be considered the Tibetan equivalent for a multiple religious belonging. It is the short form of Tibetan *ris su bcad pa med pa* or *phyogs ris med pa.* In fact, it has not only the meaning 'non-sectarian', but various additional

---

basis for our concepts and is thus unimaginable and inexpressible. In it the manifoldness of appearances and the law of dependent origination are thus set aside. It is by nature peaceful (*śānta*)." See also Nāgārjuna, *MMK* 18.7–9, 25.3.

56 AN III.32.
57 Gethin, R. (1998) The Foundations of Buddhism Oxford, New York: Oxford University Press, 78–79.
58 Powers, J. & Templeman D. (2012), 586.

connotations such as 'impartial', 'non-partisan', 'unbiased', 'encylopaedic' and 'eclectic'.

For example, Je Tsongkhapa (1357–1419), the founder of the Gelugpa school, could be considered Rime, since he studied with leading scholars of all schools of his time, which towards the end of his life resulted in the foundation of three new monastic universities starting with Ganden monastery in 1409/1410. But Tsongkhapa himself and his direct disciples did not think of themselves as Gelugpa yet.[59] Eventually the tradition was shaped by their successors. The present Dalai Lama, who was mainly trained and ordained in the Gelugpa school, was also trained by leading scholars of the main other schools. During his public talks in Hamburg in 2007 he clearly stated that he considers himself to be Rime. Not all of the Gelugpa scholars present may have been happy to hear this, because some are afraid that the Dalai Lama's pluralist Rime approach could lead to the extinction of the Gelugpa school itself while others are convinced that this re-opening is important for its long-lasting survival and unity among the Tibetan people.

For further exploration on the capacity of Buddhism for pluralism, it could be very rewarding to especially consider works of Buddhist *Rime* scholars as well as comparable approaches in other religious traditions. Thus we can learn from contemporary representatives of the world religions about how they justify their engagement with inter- and intra-religious dialogues. With regard to Buddhism, in addition to the canonical texts, the ancient Indian commentaries and the authoritative autochthonous commentaries of the various Buddhist traditions, there are some contemporary texts such as the Dalai Lama's *Towards the True Kinship of Faiths. How the world's religions can come together*. Here the Dalai Lama deals with Hinduism, Christianity, Islam and Judaism from his Buddhist perspective and he reaches the conclusion that all faiths turn to compassion as a guiding principle for living a good life and that "indeed, finding a balance between single-pointed commitment to one's own faith and genuine openness to the value of other faiths has come to be a deep personal quest. (…) None of us can any longer remain secure behind the walls and narrow confines of our specific culture and faith."[60]

For the last fifteen years, Buddhism in interreligious dialogue has also been subject of academic studies.[61] At least two recent comprehensive works on Bud-

---

59 Roloff, C. (2009) *Red mda'ba. Buddhist Yogi Scholar of the Fourteenth Century. The Forgotten Reviver of Madhamaka Philosophy in Tibet* (Contributions to Tibetan Studies, vol. 7) Wiesbaden: Dr. Ludwig Reichert Verlag, 2, 323n45.

60 London: Abacus (2010), 179–180.

61 As we can see from the detailed bibliographies given in: Brück, M. v. & Lai, W. (1997) *Buddhismus und Christentum. Geschichte, Konfrontation, Dialog* München: Verlag C. H. Beck, 765–774; Schmidt-Leukel, P. (2009) *Transformation by Integration. How Inter-faith Encounter Changes Christianity* London: SCM Press, 195–211, first approaches towards dialogue between Buddhism and Christianity date back to the 1950ies and 1960ies. Early works by German Christian theologians are for example Waldenfels, H. (1976) *Absolutes*

dhist approaches to interreligious dialogue are available: Kristin Kiblinger's *Buddhist Inclusivism. Attitudes Towards Religious Others*[62] and *Buddhist Attitudes to Other Religions*, edited by Perry Schmidt-Leukel[63]. The latter can also be considered a very good summary regarding the dialogue of Buddhists with other religions and may function as a springboard for further research in this area. It includes not only articles on Buddhist 'Theologies of Religions', inclusivism, Buddhist pluralism and Buddhist and Christian attitudes to other religions, but also a chapter on Buddhist relations to the religious other, i.e., on intra-Buddhist relationships, Buddhist-Hindu relations, Buddhist-Chinese religions' relations, Buddhist-Muslim relations, Buddhist-Christian relations and Buddhist-Jewish relations. The volume is meant to contribute "to a *contemporary Buddhist theology of religions* and provides some of the historical information which such a theology needs to take into account."[64] In their introduction the editors also discuss whether there can be something like a 'Buddhist pluralism', "that is, the recognition of another religious path as being different but nevertheless equally liberative, equally salvic".[65]

The best-known book on Jewish-Buddhist dialogue is *The Jew in the Lotus* by Rodger Kamenetz.[66] This is an account of an historic dialogue between a group of eight Rabbis accompanied by Kamenetz and the Dalai Lama in 1990, the first recorded major dialogue between experts in Judaism and Buddhism. In his introduction, Kamenetz states that "the main organizers of the encounter in Dharamsala were two American Buddhists from Jewish background". Actually a number of famous Buddhist teachers today, mainly living in the US, have left Judaism or consider themselves to be both, Buddhist and Jew. In the academic literature those who have a bi-religious identity, are also referred to as 'JuBu'.[67] In 1996 Kamenetz visited Dharamsala a second time and provided the Dalai Lama with a copy of his book: "I was a little afraid he might be offended by the title which plays on 'the jewel in the lotus' – om mani padme hum – the Tibetan's favorite mantra. I had found that Jews often did not understand the pun and some Western Buddhists were too pious to laugh. But the Dalai Lama

---

   *Nichts. Zur Grundlegung des Dialogs zwischen Buddhismus und Christentum* Freiburg: Herder; Küng, H. (1984) *Christentum und Weltreligionen* München: Piper.

62 Kiblinger, K. (2005) *Buddhist Inclusivism. Attitudes Towards Religious Others* Aldershot: Ashgate.

63 Schmidt-Leukel, P. (Ed.) (2008) *Buddhist Attitudes to Other Religions* St. Ottilien: EOS-Verlag.

64 D'Arcy May and Schmidt-Leukel (2008), 11.

65 Ibid., 14–16.

66 Kamenetz, R. (2010) *The Jew in the Lotus* London: Abacus.

67 For a detailed discussion of the origin of the term and its later variants see Drescher, F. (2012) *Von der Tora zum Dharma -- und wieder zurück? Jüdische Konvertiten zum Buddhismus und das "JuBu"-Phänomen.* In R. Laudage-Kleeberg, H. Sulzenbacher (Eds.) (2012) *Treten Sie ein! Treten Sie aus! Warum Menschen ihre Religionen wechseln.*Edited for the Jüdische Museen Hohenems, Frankfurt am Main and München. Berlin: Parthas Verlag, 276–285.

seemed to think it was hilarious. He touched the book to his forehead in the Tibetan gesture of acceptance."[68]

The famous Buddhist teacher Bhikṣuṇī Thubten Chodron, spending as much time as she could with the group during their brief stay in Dharamsala 1990, refers to herself as 'JuBu' (Jewish-Buddhist), but then makes a remark, which indicates the potential of dialogue to help clarifying one's own identity and location: "My personal reaction to the Jewish-Tibetan dialogue was interesting. I came to see that I'm neither a Jew nor a Tibetan culturally, although I am a Buddhist. I understand the Jewish culture because I grew up in it and understand the Tibetan culture because I've lived many years in it. I've lived with Chinese also and feel at home with them. However, none of these are my cultural group. This has its advantages and disadvantages: everywhere I've lived in the world I've met kind people and have felt comfortable. On the other hand, no place is really home, with 'my' people. I see good points and bad points in both Western and Asian cultures and values, and am somehow trying to incorporate the best of both into my personal life."[69]

Ayya Khema (Ilse Kussel; 1923–1997), who was born in Berlin as a daughter of Jewish parents and converted to Buddhism in 1974, also refers to the influence the *Jew in the Lotus* had on her identity formation.[70] While in her autobiography she explains that she failed to find access to the *Kabbala* and the *Zohar* and thus gave up that path[71], in the final years of her life she confirmed being a Jew[72]. She is recorded to have adhered to her Jewish identity not feeling it a contradiction to her life as a Buddhist nun.[73]

There are also a few other important works by young scholars such as Ellen Posman's dissertation *"There is no place like home": an analysis of exile in Judaism and Tibetan Buddhism*[74], a comparative study of the Tibetan Buddhist exile and the Jewish exile, which refines theories of religious exile.

---

68  Available from: http://www.thubtenchodron.org/InterreligiousDialogue/what_i_learned_about_judaism.html (last accessed December 11, 2013).

69  See: http://www.thubtenchodron.org/InterreligiousDialogue/the_origin_of_the_jew_in_the_lotus.html (last accessed December 11, 2013).

70  "Was mich besonders berührt hat, ist die Beschreibung des Zusammentreffens dieser Konferenzteilnehmer mit Dutzenden von westlichen Nonnen und Mönchen jüdischer Herkunft, ordiniert in der tibetischen Tradition. Sie lebten und lernten jetzt in Dharamsala. Jede diese Nonnen und jeder dieser Mönche berichtete das Gleiche, was mir passiert war. Sie hatten nach dem tiefen, mystischen Aspekt ihrer eigenen Religion gesucht und sich dann, als sie keinen Zugang fanden, vertrauensvoll dem Buddhismus zugewandt." Khema, A. (1997) *Ich schenke euch mein Leben* Uttenbühl: Jhana Verlag, 155.

71  Khema, A. (1997), 154–155.

72  "Of course I'm still Jewish. What else could I be? (…) Jewish is something you *are*, and I am proud of our heritage." Katz, Nathan (2008) Buddhist–Jewish Relations. In: P. Schmidt-Leukel (Ed.) *Buddhist Attitudes to Other Religions* St. Ottilien: EOS Editions, 269–293, 279. Also in: Cornille, C. (2013) *The Wiley-Blackwell Companion to Inter-Religious Dialogue* Hobroken, NJ: Wiley-Blackwell, 394–409.

73  Drescher, F. (2012), 279.

74  Santa Barbara: University of California (2004).

A gateway and major new research tool in Buddhism's relationship with other religions is decidedly the recent four-volume collection *Buddhism and Religious diversity* from Routledge's acclaimed 'Critical Concepts in Religious Studies' series, edited by Perry Schmidt-Leukel.[75] It contains 216 articles on 1,512 pages not only with a general introduction by the editor, but also an introduction by him to each volume: "Buddhism's Encounter and Interaction with Eastern Religions" (Vol. I), "Buddhism's Encounter and Interaction with Christianity" (Vol. II), "Buddhism's Encounter and Interaction with Islam and Judaism" (Vol. III), and "Buddhism and the Challenge of Religious Pluralism" (Volume IV). The well-selected classic and contemporary contributions reflect the editor's in-depth study of the various Buddhist traditions in the context of interreligious dialogue. Some of the articles reach back to the 1950/60s. The authors are not only Indologists and scholars from the field of science of religion like Ernst Steinkellner and Hans-Joachim Klimkeit, but there are also contributions by both traditional and academic Buddhist 'theologians' like the Dalai Lama, Thich Nhat Hanh, Bhikkhu Buddhadāsa, Masao Abe, José Ignacio Cabezón, John Makransky and Rita Gross. In his introduction to the final volume focusing on Buddhist approaches to religious diversity as such, Schmidt-Leukel points out:

> While the challenge of religious diversity concerns the need to find ways of cohabiting a common territory (today increasingly conceived of as our planet), the cognitive challenge consists in the twofold question of how to understand and interpret other religious traditions in the light of one's own tradition, and one's own tradition in the light of the others. More specifically, the challenge of 'religious pluralism' – if we take this phrase as more than just an equivalent to actual 'religious' diversity' or 'plurality' – consists in whether one can make positive sense (in terms of one's own religious values) of religious diversity, or even whether one can welcome that diversity as, to some extent, a diversity of equals. Ultimately, the challenge of religious diversity amounts to the question of whether to abandon traditional claims to the exclusive or inclusive superiority of one's own tradition, thus rejecting the idea that, ideally, all should become members of one's own faith, so that religious diversity would disappear.[76]

Another important resource when dealing with similarities and differences between modern Buddhist traditions and other world religions as well as with cross-cultural hermeneutics is the *Journal of Global Buddhism*. Here we can find some interesting articles on the Western reception of Buddhism, investments in religious capital, and 'Buddhist theology' vs. distanced and non-aligned Buddhist studies considering different cultural locations.[77]

75  London/New York: Routledge (2013).

76  Schmidt-Leukel, P. (2013) Introduction. In: Ibid., Vol. IV, 1.

77  See for example the first three articles in: *Journal of Global Buddhism*, 2, (2001): http://www.globalbuddhism.org/toc.html (last accessed December 11, 2013): Baumann, M. Global Buddhism: Developmental Periods, Regional Histories, and a New Analytical Perspective. 1–43; Fenn, M. Teaching Buddhism in the West: (Mostly) North American Universities and Colleges. 44–58; Freiberger, O. The Meeting of Traditions: Inter-Buddhist

## Examples of Various Forms of Interreligious Dialogue in Buddhism

Theorising about dialogue from a Buddhist perspective does not seem to be very common among Buddhists themselves to date. At first glance I have the impression that the Dalai Lama believes in the Human ('Buberian') dialogue, in the sense "that it is possible for human beings to meet purely and simply as human beings, irrespective of the beliefs that separate them".[78] The Dalai Lama's system of secular ethics, outlined in his recent publication *Beyond Religion* may be considered a draft for 'secular dialogue'.[79] According to Eric Sharpe, 'secular dialogue' stresses "that where there are tasks to be performed in the world, believers in different creeds may share in a program of joint action, without regard to their respective convictions".[80] Although while the Dalai Lama, drawing up his system of secular ethics, does not leave Buddhist ground, he filters out values, which may find general acceptance, not only among followers of other religions but even among non-believers.[81] It is important to note that the Dalai Lama has a very special understanding of the term 'secular'. In the above-mentioned conversation with Stéphane Hessel[82] he explains that under secular ethics he understands universal values such as compassion, tolerance and incorruptibility. He points out that he uses the term 'secular' in the sense

---

and Inter-Religious Relations in the West. 59–71. Other examples are: Barker, M. (2007) Investments in Religious Capital: An explorative case study of Australian Buddhists. In: *JGB*, 8, 68–80. The *JGB* 9 (2008) contains three articles that discuss questions such as "What is the place of advocacy or 'theology' in Buddhist Studies? Where is it implicit in contemporary scholarship? Should the study of Buddhism remain 'distanced' and 'non-aligned'? Is there a definite line demarcating the two modes of scholarship? How does this distinction apply in different cultural locations?" From an empirical perspective Negru, J. H. (2013) Highlights from the Survey of Canadian Buddhist Organisations. In: *JGB*, 14, 1–18, should be of interest too.

78  Sharpe, E. J. (1987) Dialogue of Religions. In: *The Encyclopedia of Religion, vol. 4*, New York: Macmillan, 347.

79  For details see Alomes, A. (2014) Multifaith Dialogue. Considering a Buddhist Perspective on Reaching the 22nd Century Through Universal Responsibility. In: this volume.

80  Sharpe (1987), 347.

81  Dalai Lama, XIV & Norman, A. (2011) *Beyond Religion. Ethics for a Whole World* Boston/New York: Houghton Mifflin Harcourt, 57–58. Note that the Dalai Lama's approach seems to match the "Hamburger Handlungskonzept zur Integration von Zuwanderern" (Hamburg's action plan for the integration of immigrants), edited by the Behörde für Soziales, Familie, Gesundheit und Verbraucherschutz, Februar 2007, 39, which reads: "Es gehört daher zu den Grundlagen der Integration, gemeinsame Grundwerte herauszuarbeiten und Verständnis für religiöse Vielfalt sowie deren Gewährleistung durch die grundgesetzliche Ordnung zu entwickeln." (It is therefore one of the fundamentals of integration to draw up shared core values and to develop a positive attitude toward religious diversity and its guarantee by the constitutional order.)

82  Crossman, S. & Barou, J.-P. (Eds.) (2012) *Stéphane Hessel, Dalai Lama: Wir erklären den Frieden!* Berlin: Ullstein, 46.

of the constitution of India, where it does not mean disrespect or contempt of religion, but on the contrary, respect for all believers and non-believers:

> Secular does not mean disrespect of religion. Rather secular ethics respects all religions as well as non-believers. Individually there is a perception of 'one religion, one truth', but if we take the whole community into consideration, we must always argue for 'multiple religions, multiple truths'.[83]

Similar to many other leading Asian and Western Buddhist teachers, the Dalai Lama is engaged in 'spiritual dialogue', "advocated chiefly by those who have been trained in the contemplative and monastic traditions".[84] One of his earliest dialogues must have been in 1968 when he first met with the Christian monk Thomas Merton, who wrote that "the whole conversation was about religion and philosophy and especially ways of meditation".[85]

Brevity does not allow a deeper exploration of the many different kinds of dialogues Buddhists have been or are still involved in, but we can summarise them in various categories.[86] For example:

1. Interreligious summit meetings such as the first World Day of Prayer for Peace in Assisi in 1986.
2. Non-public meetings of high ranking religious leaders such as the Dalai Lama's meetings with the Archbishops of Canterbury in the U.K. in 1973, 1984 and 1993 as well as his eight meetings with Pope John Paul II in the Vatican between 1980 and 2003, and his meeting with Bishop Desmond Tutu in South Africa (1996), in Canada (2004), and in Dharamsala (2012).
3. Regular local meetings of religious leaders such as the Interreligious Forum Hamburg (IFH), which since 2000 meets twice a year. In 2012 the Forum

---

83  Ibid., 15. It is important to consider that secularism has different meanings in different contexts. The United Nations Research Institute for Social Developments (2011) Religion, Politics and Gender Equality. In: UNRISD Research and Policy Brief 11, GE.11–00619–May 2011–2, 100, divides the plural secularisms across the world into two categories: "Assertive" secularisms like in France, Mexico and Turkey, where "the state played an assertive role to confine religion to the private sphere (also referred to as laïcité) (…) The banning of religion from political party platforms, and from the public arena more broadly, have been contested issues in all three countries", and "Passive" secularisms: "The Indian Constitution does not mandate a strict separation of religion and state, nor is there an established 'state religion'. Rather, given the country's multi-religious population, the state chose to interpret secularism as the responsibility to ensure the protection and equality of all religions. In the United States, while the First Amendment to the Constitution officially separates religion from the state, and guarantees the free exercise of religion (as in India), Protestant ideas and presumptions operate within the legal and political system." The full text is available from http://www.unrisd.org/publications/rpb11e (last accessed December 11, 2013).
84  Sharpe (1987), 347.
85  http://www.thomasmertonsociety.org/altany2.htm (last accessed December 11, 2013).
86  As I found out after the completion of my list for this paper, King (2011) has chosen a similar approach giving a different, more general list of seven types of interreligious dialogue.

prepared a joint action during the International Garden Festival IGS 2013 in Hamburg, which included five religions, five gardens and one common well.

4. Monastic dialogues such as the Monastic Interreligious Dialogue sponsored by North American Benedictine and Cistercian Monasteries of Men and Women.[87]

5. Dialogues between two religions such as the European Network of Buddhist Christian Studies,[88] the Buddhist-Muslim Dialogue (as organised by the Museum of World Religions in Taiwan[89] or by INEB[90]), the Bahá'í Faith and Buddhism Dialogue, or the Dialogue between Hinduism and Buddhism[91].

6. Meetings of experts such as the Study Group Interreligious Dialogue (Arbeitskreis Interreligiöser Dialog) at the University of Hamburg, initiated by Olaf Schumann and Brigitte Werner from the Department of Protestant Theology at the University of Hamburg and now based at the Academy of World Religions. This dialogue started in 1984 and since then discusses a different theme of dialogue related to theology or society each term. In the beginning the dialogue included Protestantism, Islam, Judaism and Buddhism, and later also Hinduism.[92]

7. Meetings during both the Protestant and Catholic Church Days in Germany. For example, in 1987 the participants were able to retreat in a common

---

87  http://www.monasticdialog.com/ (last accessed December 11, 2013). See also the Ven. Thubten Chodron's Home Page as an example of just one Buddhist nun's engagement in interfaith dialogue with Buddhism, but also with Judaism, Islam and Hinduism: http://www.thubtenchodron.org/InterreligiousDialogue/index.html (last accessed December 11, 2013).

88  Although the European Network of Buddhist-Christian Studies is a typical case of dialogue between experts, I list it here separately from no. 6, because it focuses on Buddhism and Christianity only. The Seventh Conference 2007 seems to have been different since it dealt more in general with "Buddhist Attitudes to Other Religions" and contributions were published by Schmidt-Leukel as mentioned above.

89  See for example the Buddhist-Muslim Dialogue in Ladakh, 2010 (http://irdialogue.org/journal/buddhist-muslim-dialogue-in-ladakh-2010-by-maria-reis-habito/ accessed June 11, 2012).

90  "Inter-Faith Dialogue for Peace and Sustainablity" in Kuala Lumpur, Malaysia 2013. For more information see: http://www.inebnetwork.org/background-and-rationale (last accessed December 11, 2013).

91  Brück, M. v. (1986) *Einheit der Wirklichkeit. Gott, Gotteserfahrung und Meditation im hinduistisch-christlichen Dialog* (2nd edition 1987) München: Chr. Kaiser. Brück, M. v. (1992) Sharing Religious Experience in Hindu-Christian Encounter. In: J.D.Gort, H.Vroom et al. (eds.) *On Sharing Religious Experience. Possibilities of Interfaith Mutuality* Grand Rapids (Michigan): Eerdmans Publishing Company, 136–150. Schmidt-Leukel, P. (2008) Buddhist-Hindu Relations. In: P. Schmidt-Leukel (Ed.), *Buddhist Attitudes to Other Religions* St. Ottilien: EOS-Verlag, 143–71.

92  For a detailed report: Petersen, O. (2011) Erfahrungen eines Buddhisten im interreligiösen Dialog in Hamburg. In: C. Roloff , W. Weiße & M. Zimmermann (Eds.) *Buddhismus im Westen. Ein Dialog zwischen Religion und Wissenschaft*, vol 6, series "Religionen im Dialog", Schriftenreihe der Akademie der Weltreligionen, in Kooperation mit dem Zentrum für Buddhismuskunde der Universität Hamburg und dem Tibetischen Zentrum e.V., Münster: Waxmann Münster: Waxmann, 141–154.

house of meditation including Christians, Hindus, and Buddhists. Rooms for silent prayer and meditation have also become a matter of course in almost all airports around the world as well as in most universities.

8. Grass-root dialogue, meaning interreligious dialogue in one's own family, with friends, colleagues, neighbours, at school, when visiting other countries and so on. In 2010 the University of Hamburg, in cooperation with the Tibetan Centre Hamburg, organised the symposium "Buddhism in the West: A dialogue between religion and science" where it was discussed whether Buddhism is a religion or a philosophy and whether one can have a dual religious affiliation. One of the speakers, a Buddhist, married to a Christian theologian, spoke about her daily interreligious dialogue at home.[93]

9. Active participation in online interfaith dialogue such as Interfaithing.com, an online interfaith community with daily interfaith news, positive news, videos, an extensive interfaith resource and the largest interfaith group directory on the Internet.[94]

10. Interreligious dialogue related to a common cultural and spiritual interest such as music. For example, the Herbert-Batliner-Europainstitut in cooperation with the opening event *Ouverture spirituelle* of the Salzburg Festival (Salzburger Festspiele) 2013 organised disputations and concerts under the sign of dialogue between Christianity and Buddhism.

This list certainly is not intended to be exhaustive, but it gives some idea of what kind of initiatives need to be studied in order to find out the possibilities and limitations of dialogue between Buddhism and other religions. An evaluation of the present situation of interreligious dialogue in Buddhism, its results, potential and possible strength requires establishing respective research projects.

## Future Prospects on How Gender Issues Could Become a Driving Force for Interreligious Dialogue, Taking the Buddhist Nuns Ordination Restoration Movement (Buddhist NORM) as an Example

As I have shown in detail in my article "Women's Rights in the Vajrayana Tradition"[95], at least since the Fourth World Conference on Women in Beijing (1995), it is controversial whether – in light of the freedom of religion – women's rights should be put into perspective according to culture and religion.[96]

---

93  Koch, E.-M. (2011) Kann man gleichzeitig Buddhist und Christ sein? In: C. Roloff, W. Weiße & M. Zimmermann (Eds.), 93–98.

94  http://www.interfaithing.com/ (last accessed December 11, 2013).

95  Published in: Meinert, C. & Zöllner, H.-B. (2010) *Buddhist Approaches to Human Rights. Dissonances and Resonances* Bielefeld: transcript Verlag, 195–210.

96  See also: Joy, M. (2008) Women's Human Rights in the Context of Religious Studies. In: M.-L. Keinänen (Ed.) *Svensk religionshistorisk årsskrift 2006–2007* Göteborg: Svenska

Is it appropriate and reasonable to demand that all religions respect the human rights charter as a universally valid minimum consensus on human values, or would this rather be a sign of increasing secularisation of religion? For the last five years this debate has also been taking place within Buddhist circles.[97] Some say that discussing human rights would mix religion with politics. Others take it for granted that in a society that sees human rights as a given, religions would lose their credibility if they did not fully respect them. How can we judge whether gender equity in religion does exist? From a Buddhist perspective I would say: gender equity is reached when women do not only have the same chance to attain the final spiritual goal, but can also – here and now, in everyday life – participate in preserving and spreading their religion by equally holding religious leadership positions including independent performance of all obligations, rules and rituals.[98] Assuming that the number of male and female followers is fifty-fifty, I believe that modern society can only adequately benefit from religion if the gender perspective is fully incorporated. Therefore, during a meeting of the Interreligious Forum Hamburg in 2012, I was quite pleasantly surprised when Wolfram Weisse made the cursory note that by selecting female guest professors for the Academy of World Religions he wanted to give religions a female face. I truly believe that this is exactly what societies and religions need today.

## The Main Gender Issue Debated in Buddhism:
## Full Ordination of Nuns

Just in brief, to help you understand the main gender issue debated in Buddhism at present: over the centuries, full ordination of nuns, comparable to women's priesthood, was either lost or never transmitted to the countries where Theravāda and Tibetan Buddhist traditions are practiced. But it continued to exist in China, Korea and Vietnam. However, even in those places, gender equity is no longer fully reflected in the leadership of Buddhist institutions. This fact stands in stark contrast to the assumptions made by large parts of the West: that Buddhism fits best with democratic principles and modern life styles since all

---

samfundet för religionshistorisk forskning, 15, 181–199.

97 For example: Kawanami, H. (2007) The *bhikkhuni* ordination debate: global aspirations, local concerns, with special emphasis on the views of the monastic community in Burma. In: *Buddhist Studies Review*, 24 (2), 226–244.

98 For a discussion whether or not equal access to salvation is close to modern gendered equality see Casanova, J. (2009) Religion, Politics and Gender Equality: Public Religions Revisited, DRAFT WORKING DOCUMENT April 2009, 18–19 (cannot be cited without the author's approval). Available from http://www.unrisd.org/80256B3C005BCCF9/searc h/010F9FB4F1E75408C12575D70031F321 (last accessed December 11, 2013). Cf. Birnbaum, M. (2010) Religion Revisited: Women's Rights and the Political Instrumentalisation of Religion. Tagung vom 5.-6. Juni 2009 in Berlin. In: *GENDER. Zeitschrift für Geschlecht, Kultur und Gesellschaft* (2) 1, 161–166.

beings have equal potential and equal chances to attain enlightenment. Instead, Western Buddhist circles are beginning to realise that, together with the transfer of Buddhism to the West, almost imperceptibly, an ancient hierarchical model of social structure is seeping through, constantly creating irritations and leading Western Buddhist nuns as well as lay people to feel set back and valued less by monks. In the Buddhist hierarchy, women are subordinate to men. Devout Buddhists believe that only if this principle of seniority and gender subordination is followed, the parish will be in harmony and the teaching of the Buddha will survive. This implies that when questioning this Buddhist hierarchy, for example, by requiring gender equality, the harmony of Buddhist society and even peace and happiness in the country may seem at risk.[99]

Not only Westerners but also Buddhists in the East have recognised this and are beginning to reject these kinds of roles or are calling for a change.[100] A hierarchical model according to seniority and gender, which puts monks and high ranking lay men on top of society and disparages women, nuns as well as laywomen to second-class citizens, is not in line with the structure of modern societies. It will never be accepted as it is, neither in accordance with the ideals of European enlightenment nor with the Universal Declaration of Human Rights, which already in its first sentence stresses the equal rights of *every* human being: "Whereas recognition of the inherent dignity and of the equal and inalienable rights of all members of the human family is the foundation of freedom, justice and peace in the world …".[101]

Thus it does not come as a surprise that an International Buddhist Women's movement, which started in the late 1970s, attracted wide interest and finally led to the restoration of the Buddhist nuns order in Sri Lanka where it had died out in the 11th/12th century.[102] It may be interesting to note that this shift did not start from within the country, but from Sri Lankan circles outside the country. The first ordinations took place in Los Angeles 1988, followed by the

---

99  For details: Roloff, C. (Tsedroen, Jampa) (forthcoming) The Buddhist Nuns Order Resto-
      ration Movement and its Implications for Modern Society. In: S. Warner (Ed.) *A Buddhist
      Response to Global Concerns* Delhi: Motilal Banarsidass.

100  Prebish and Keown (2010), 75–76 critically remark that "there is some tension surroun-
      ding the high visibility of Western and upper-class Asian women in the movement. Some
      Asian women see Western participation as evidence of a lack of humility and an aggressive
      individualism combined with a colonial attitude that assumes they need help in order to
      improve their situation. Some Western women feel that Asian religious women have been
      trained to be too shy, humble, and deferential, and need to acknowledge their own talents.
      Regardless of this tension, there has been a great deal of East–West dialogue between nuns
      and other religious women in the past fifteen or so years and progress has been made in
      improving both the living and educational opportunities of religious women throughout
      Asia."

101  See the Preamble of *The Universal Declaration of Human Rights*: http://www.un.org/en/
      documents/udhr/ (last accessed December 11, 2013).

102  For details see Petra Kieffer-Pülz's unpublished article *The Restoration of the
      bhikkhunīsaṅgha in the Theravāda tradition* (PDF) for free download available at: http://
      www.congress-on-buddhist-women.org/29.0.html (last accessed December 11, 2013).

first ordination involving native Sri Lankan monks from the Mahābodhi Society in India (Sarnath 1996 and Bodh Gaya 1998), and now there are several large training centres in Sri Lanka organising full ordination for women on Sri Lankan soil by Theravādin monks and nuns according to their own Vinaya (legal text collection of the monastic community). The lineage re-established there has grown over one decade and *bhikkhunīs* (Pā. fully ordained nuns) in this lineage have already participated in ordinations for Theravādin women in other countries, including Thailand and the United States. Thus the *bhikkhunī* order in the Theravāda tradition is now at over one thousand in Sri Lanka, and more than fifty[103] in Thailand, Nepal, Indonesia, Singapore, Europe and North America, and India, and therefore, a few steps ahead of the Tibetan tradition, where – although the number of *bhikṣuṇīs* (Skt. fully ordained nuns) ordained in the Chinese Dharmaguptaka tradition is higher – Tibetan Mūlasarvāstivāda ordination has not been established yet.

However, a similar movement has started among Tibetan-Buddhist communities in India, requesting the Dalai Lama, the heads of the various Tibetan Buddhist traditions and individual teachers as well as committees of Buddhist monk scholars to verify the possibilities of having such ordinations established. As Lobsang Dechen, co-director of the Tibetan Nuns Project, Dharamsala (India), pointed out during the Congress on Buddhist Women's Role in the Saṅgha in Hamburg (2007), in her experience the "commonly held view that Tibetan nuns are not interested in receiving *bhikṣuṇī* ordination" is a misconception. Rather, having not studied the relevant texts, "they have often lacked confidence when discussing the possibilities for *bhikṣuṇī* ordination (…) There are now a great number of Tibetan nuns who are educated and understand the importance of *bhikṣuṇī* ordination. (…) It is now apparent that the nuns are ready and able to receive *bhikṣuṇī* ordination and hold the vows, if a means of conferring them can be found in accordance with the Vinaya [the Buddhist monastic law]."[104]

Although the number of fully ordained nuns is small compared to the number of monks, it is constantly growing and many people believe that the momentum can no longer be stopped. Owing to globalisation, this recent transnational movement has been discussed from many perspectives and raises many questions. Not only in the West, but also in Asia, on a social and political level democratic structures increasingly prevail, while Buddhist communities still seem to be structured according to gender and seniority. There is a mismatch between these two different models and thus adaptation is needed.

The process involves legal, political, social, and psychological aspects. To put it simply, whether manifesting consciously or unconsciously it seems that a majority of men are afraid that gender equity would result in sharing power

---

103  The number is highest in Thailand. Susie (2013) The first meeting of Theravada Thai bhikkhunis. In: *Yashodhara,* 30 (4), 12–13, reports about "40 local bhikkhunis and sramaneris from at least 11 provinces in Thailand" who attended the meeting.

104  L. Dechen (2010) Buddhist Women's Role in the Saṅgha. In: Mohr & Tsedroen (Eds.) *Dignity & Discipline,* 207–210.

and resources or even splitting the society. Others seem to be afraid of women in general and believe that their full ordination would lead to a fast decline of Buddhism, perhaps because from an early age on monks, keeping celibacy, are told to beware of women. However, such thoughts publicly remain undisclosed. An outdated view toward women utilised as a creative approach to maintain monastic celibacy originating thousands of years ago cannot hope to transfer to accepted values of respect, dignity, and justice in the 21st century. Instead, although the Buddha himself almost 2,600 years ago granted women full ordination, today, in the 21st century, it is hotly debated whether according to the Vinaya full ordination of women is possible at all.

## Discourse on Reviving Full Ordination for Nuns with Tibetan Monk Scholars

In 2005 during the First Conference on Tibetan Buddhism in Europe His Holiness the Dalai Lama called on the Western nuns to support him by conducting Vinaya research and by discussing the issue of *bhikṣuṇī* ordination in the international community. To that end, he made a donation and together with a few other Western nuns, I established the Committee for *Bhikṣuṇī* Ordination.[105] In 2006, His Holiness asked me to intensify my research in the *bhikṣuṇī vinaya* and the related *vinaya* ordination lineages.[106] Meanwhile there is a large network of resources across all traditions, as demonstrated during the First International Congress on Buddhist Women's Role in the Saṅgha, held at the University of Hamburg in 2007, which brought together monastic and academic scholars from around the world to share research findings from many backgrounds and disciplines that each influence women's ordination, touching a broad spectrum of areas in Buddhist Studies, Gender Studies and beyond.[107] In 2010, after I had concluded my PhD studies and published my thesis, I became a principal investigator at the University of Hamburg to conduct research on *bhikṣuṇī* ordination

---

105  http://www.bhiksuniordination.net/ (last accessed December 11, 2013).

106  Letter signed by the Dalai Lama dated May 23, 2006.

107  The anthology (2010) *Dignity & Discipline: Reviving Full Ordination for Buddhist Nuns* Boston: Wisdom Publications, is a good reflection of that network. It contains a selection of the papers delivered at this gathering, compiled and edited by Thea Mohr and Jampa Tsedroen. In her review in Mari Jyväsjärvi states: "What made the Hamburg conference so unique is that it constituted a public dialogue on a global scale: it brought together Buddhist scholars and practitioners, Asian and Western, across sectarian boundaries, to discuss a shared and pressing concern that has larger implications for how Buddhism will adapt to changing socio-historical contexts." *JGB*, 13 (2012): 3–7. The anthology has also been translated into German: Tsedroen, J. (Carola Roloff) & Mohr, T. (2011) *Mit Würde und Beharrlichkeit. Die Erneuerung buddhistischer Nonnenorden* Berlin: edition steinrich. For papers presented during the congress, but not included in *Dignity and Discipline* or its German version, as well as other essays related to the congress' topic, please see the congress website: http://www.congress-on-buddhist-women.org/ (last accessed December 11, 2013).

in the Tibetan *vinaya* on behalf of the DFG (Deutsche Forschungsgemein-schaft). Since then I have been mainly concerned with researching the ordination of nuns in the Tibetan Buddhist canon and its presentation in the Tibetan commentaries, analysing the *Bhikṣuṇīskandhaka* in the *Vinayakṣudrakavastu*, based on different editions of the Tibetan Kangyur and an ancient manuscript from the 11ᵗʰ century, the Sanskrit *Mūlasarvāstivāda Bhikṣuṇīkarmavācanā.*

In November 2011 the religious heads of the four major schools of Tibetan Buddhism decided to form a subcommittee of experts, representing all the traditions "in order to reach a final conclusion as to whether or not there is a method to revive the *bhikṣuṇī* lineage and to make a clear statement". This 'high-level scholarly committee' consisted of ten Geshes (monk scholars) – including two representatives from each of the four major schools of Tibetan Buddhism and two additional (male) scholars representing the nuns. The committee convened on August 6, 2012 in Dharamsala. The opening speech was delivered by Prof. Samdhong Rinpoche, the former Prime Minister of the Tibetan Government in Exile, himself a monk and the founder of the Central University of Tibetan Studies in Sarnath/Varanasi. In his speech he summarised the current state of research and suggested questions for the committee to concentrate on.

For more than three months, the monk scholars met at the Sarah Institute in Dharamsala and worked through all thirteen volumes of the Tibetan Mūla-sarvāstivāda Vinaya, taking note of every place in the texts that referred to nuns and their ordinations. Unlike previous meetings, which only lasted a few days and did not go beyond presenting contradictory interpretations in the *commentaries* to the Tibetan texts, priority was now given to the canonical texts themselves and the Indian commentaries.

In October 2012, just prior to the finalisation of the committee's 219-page report, I was invited to present my research to this committee. Different from previous meetings, like the important seminar on the issue in 2006, the atmosphere of this meeting was quite friendly and constructive. The monks were seriously interested in finding a solution and pledged that no material would be withheld. This was the first time that I gave an academic talk in Tibetan, which was quite a challenge. My presentation was followed by intensive discussions and a very lively exchange on different evidences.

Let me briefly summarise the two possible solutions I suggested there of how to revive the *bhikṣuṇī* ordination lineage in Tibetan Buddhism. The critical link for change or transformation, i.e. textual evidence, must come from the direct and original source: the authoritative religious texts themselves.[108]

---

108 During the Hamburg Congress 2007 Samdhong Rinpoche (Mohr & Tsedroen (2010), 156) stated: "Our efforts toward re-establishing the Mūlasarvāstivāda *bhikṣuṇī* ordination are not driven by Western influence or feminist concerns about the equality of the sexes — this issue cannot be determined by social or political considerations. The solution must be found within the context of the Vinaya codes." Interestingly, according to Birnbaum, M. (2010), 164, a similar approach has been suggested by José Casanova (2009). See on this also Phillips, A. (2009), Religion: Ally, Threat, Or Just Religion? DRAFT WORKING

The Mūlasarvāstivāda Vinaya presents gradual steps towards women's full ordination. First, as a lay follower one receives *prarvrajyā*, pre-novice initiation. Then one becomes a *śrāmaṇerikā* or novice nun. *Pravrajyā* and *śrāmaṇerikā* ordination can be given either on the same day or separately. Today most Tibetan nuns are well-educated *śrāmaṇerikās*. The other two steps of female ordination, *śikṣamāṇā* and *bhikṣuṇī*, are not currently extant in the Mūlasarvāstivāda tradition. In ancient India, for two years nuns became *śikṣamāṇā*, trainees, followed by full *bhikṣuṇī* ordination.

According to the Mūlasarvāstivāda Vinaya, both the *prarvrajyā*, pre-novice initiation, and the novice ordination as a *śrāmaṇerikā* should be given by *bhikṣuṇīs* only. For the ordination of a *śikṣamāṇā*, a *bhikṣuṇī saṅgha* of twelve nuns is required. On the day of full ordination – and this is a peculiarity of the Mūlasarvāstivāda Vinaya – initially, a *saṅgha* of twelve nuns needs to give *brahmacāryopasthānasaṃvṛti* to the trainee, literally a "vow of celibate lifestyle". There has been much discussion about this term and its meaning.[109] To my understanding it means that the *bhikṣuṇī saṅgha* has to approve that the trainee is ready for full ordination and for keeping a lifetime vow of chastity before the ordainee is remitted to the monks order (*bhikṣu saṅgha*), which then, accompanied by the *bhikṣuṇī saṅgha*, confers full ordination on the same day. Thus, different from the Theravāda tradition, full ordination is not conferred by monks and nuns in two separate acts; instead, they conduct it in one joint act. The rite is headed by a *bhikṣu karmakāraka*, a monk who acts as the conductor of the ritual. There is no male master (*upādhyāya*) and since the new *bhikṣuṇī* will continue to stay with the female community, she is required to state the name of her female master (*upādhyāyikā*). This seems to have led to some confusion among Tibetan monk scholars, because it is unclear who is superior in the ritual, the female master or the male conductor of ritual.[110] Furthermore, due to this, it is unclear whether the lineage depends mainly on the *bhikṣus* or on the *bhikṣuṇīs*. Therefore, it is unclear whether a Mūlasarvāstivāda *bhikṣuṇī* lineage

DOCUMENT May 2009 (cannot be cited without the author's approval). Available from http://www.unrisd.org/80256B3C005BCCF9/(httpAuxPages)/B585808EFB5EF3D2C125 75D70032A30F/$file/WEBPhilipdftII.pdf (last accessed December 11, 2013).

109 See especially Kieffer-Pülz, P. (2010) Presuppositions for a Valid Ordination with Respect to the Restoration of the Bhiksuni Ordination in the Mulasarvastivada Tradition. In: Mohr & Tsedroen (2010), 217–225.

110 Tsedroen, J. (2010) Generation to Generation: Transmitting the Bhikṣuṇī Lineage in the Tibetan Tradition. In: K. L. Tsomo (Ed.) *Buddhist Women in a Global Multicultural Community* 9th Sakyadhita International Conference, Kuala Lumpur: Sukhi Hotu Publications, 205–215. Also published in R. Pabitrakumar (2009) Buddhism, World Culture and Human Values, 20–33. See also the following unpublished manuscripts of talks presented at the University of Hamburg: Roloff, C. (2002) Bhikṣuṇī-Ordination. Available at: http://www.buddhismuskunde.uni-hamburg.de/fileadmin/pdf/digitale_texte/Bd8-K02Roloff.pdf (last accessed December 11, 2013); Roloff, C. (2006) Wiederbelebung der Bhiksuni-Gelübde im Tibetischen Buddhismus – Aktuelle Entwicklungen. Available at: http://www.buddhismuskunde.uni-hamburg.de/fileadmin/pdf/digitale_texte/Bd11-K09Roloff.pdf (last accessed December 11, 2013).

can be revived by Mūlasarvāstivāda *bhikṣus* alone or together with Dharmaguptaka *bhikṣunīs,* who still exist in the Chinese, Korean and Vietnamese Buddhist
traditions. However, from the Mūlasarvāstivāda ritual itself, it seems pretty
clear:

> After the whole bhikṣu saṅgha consisting of at least ten bhikṣus has gathered and is
> seated in a small boundary ('khor, maṇḍalaka) and the entire bhikṣuṇī saṅgha consist-
> ing of at least twelve bhikṣuṇīs has gathered and is seated in a small boundary, [the
> ordainee] should go in front of the karmakāraka-bhikṣu, [kneel] on a bunch of grass
> (rtsa chun po, viṇḍaka) or on a cushion (khong tshangs can, masūrikā), put her palms
> together and request upasaṃpad from both saṅghas.
> She says: "Venerable members of both saṅghas, please listen! I, named so-and-so, for
> a [special] purpose say the name of upādhyāyikā so-and-so, under whom I am seeking
> full ordination. I named so-and-so request full ordination from both saṅghas."[111]

I think it is clear that the master who promotes the ordainee for full ordination
and takes responsibility for her training must be female, because training is
given while attending to her teacher around the clock for at least twelve years
and nuns are not supposed to stay under the same roof with a male overnight.
But when the two *saṅghas* meet, the monk community takes the lead, as is
shown by the ordainee kneeling before the *karmakāraka-bhikṣu* in the *bhikṣu
saṅgha.* Thus the conductor of ritual is a monk and the lineage mainly depends
on the monks involved.

The research conducted in the Tibetan tradition during the last 30 years has
been narrowed down to two possibilities regarding how to conduct the full ordination of nuns, either similar to male ordination by a *bhikṣu saṅgha* only, or in
accordance with the current rite (*da ltar byung ba'i cho ga, vartamānakalpa*),
by a joint act conducted by two *saṅgha*s, a male Mūlasarvāstivāda *saṅgha* and
a female Dharmaguptaka *saṅgha.* The first is considered to involve a procedural
error, but has the advantage that there is no doubt with regard to lineage. If the
latter method is chosen, questions arise as to whether the new *bhiksuni*s will be
Mūlasarvāstivāda or Dharmaguptaka and whether the ordination will be valid,
since traditionally it is believed that *saṅgha*s of different *vinaya* schools hold
different views on how to keep their precepts. Due to this, the question arises as
to whether the two *saṅgha*s can be considered to be in harmony, which is one
of the requirements for a valid ordination.

Although there are minor differences between the Vinayapitakas of the
Mūlasarvāstivādins, Dharmaguptakas, and Theravādins, there is no difference
in their nature, because they go back to the same source, the Buddha himself
and his earliest monastic community. In addition, in all Vinayas it is expressed
that the *bhikṣu* and *bhikṣuṇī* precepts are of the same nature. School affiliation
mainly depends on place, time, language, and the ordination masters (*ācāryas*).
Having different schools does not necessarily entail disharmony; they may still

---

111 Derge, 'Dul ba, da, 111a 2–6.

be in harmony, harmony being one of the basic conditions for the validity of a legal act. Weighing advantages and disadvantages, in certain circumstances it would be appropriate to perform *saṅgha* acts together.

The proceedings of the meeting with the Research Committee in Dharamsala in 2012 were quite technical. They focused on finding ways and means to assure that the ordination will be 'flawless and perfect' and to assure that the nuns, like the monks, will become Mūlasarvāstivāda. I was very impressed by the enthusiasm and the honesty of the monks sent by the heads of the various Tibetan Buddhist traditions to discuss this issue for three months. They were sincerely interested in my presentation and expressed that my contribution has been very helpful. A few weeks after our meeting, the committee finalised a research report, which is in print and "going to come soon" in Tibetan language.[112]

In conclusion, in my view there are two ways to generate the flawless and perfect Mūlasarvāstivāda *bhikṣuṇī* vow:

1) Suppose there are no *bhikṣuṇīs* and either a fully qualified *śrāmaṇerikā* or *śikṣamāṇā* as an exception receives full ordination (*upasaṃpadā*) by a Mūlasarvāstivāda *bhikṣu saṅgha* alone, the flawless and perfect vow of a *bhikṣuṇī* will arise, because in the Vinayapiṭaka there is permission to receive *bhikṣuṇī* ordination from the *bhikṣu saṅgha* if there are no *bhikṣuṇīs*.[113]

2) Suppose Dharmaguptaka *bhikṣuṇīs* function as the *bhikṣuṇī saṅgha* and a fully qualified *śikṣamāṇā* receives full ordination from both *saṅghas*, a *bhikṣu* and a *bhikṣuṇī saṅgha*, the *bhikṣuṇī* vow will arise. Furthermore, provided the Mūlasarvāstivāda *bhikṣu saṅgha* is suitable, for a threefold reason the vow that is generated will be a flawless and perfect Mūlasarvāstivāda vow. The threefold or better put three-part reason why a flawless and perfect Mūlasarvāstivāda *bhikṣuṇī* vow can arise when given by a Mūlasarvāstivāda *bhikṣu saṅgha* together with a Dharmaguptaka *bhikṣuṇī saṅgha* is:

   a) *Even if two saṅghas apply the current rite (da ltar byung ba'i cho ga, vartamānakalpa) only one vow arises and the male saṅgha is foremost;*

   b) *Although the generation of a perfect vow depends on many conditions, a prātimokṣa vow arises from its specific substantial cause (nye bar len pa'i rgyu, upādānakāraṇa) within the continuum of the ordainee. It is not transferred from outside, from another person's continuum;*

   c) *The school affiliation depends on the monastic rite (las kyi cho ga, karmavidhi). If both the monastic rite and the bhikṣu saṅgha are Mūlasarvāstivāda and the accompanying bhikṣuṇī saṅgha agrees, a perfect Mūlasarvāstivāda vow arises. For the vow to arise, most important are the ordainee's thought of renunciation (nges par 'byung ba, niḥsaraṇa) and the thought "I have received it" at the time when the Mūlasarvāstivāda*

---

112 Personal correspondence with Thupten Tsering, Department of Religion & Culture, Dharamsala (dated March 16, 2013) and Tibetan Nuns Project, Dharamsala (dated July 31, 2013).

113 The detailed sources will be published in 2014 in a different place, because it is beyond the scope of this paper.

vow (sdom pa, saṃvara) of a fully ordained person (bsnyen par rdzogs
pa, upasaṃpanna) arises.

This is in summary the reasoning established, tabled together with the evidence
from the authoritative texts themselves. In any case, whether ordination would
be applied in one or the other way, i.e. by monks only or with the help of nuns of
another Vinaya tradition, after the required time period of twelve years[114] those
Mūlasarvāstivāda *bhikṣuṇīs*, together with the Mūlasarvāstivāda *bhikṣus*, would
be qualified to perform the Mūlasarvāstivāda *bhikṣuṇī* ordination rite according
to the current rite. Thus the two ways suggested represent only a transitional
arrangement. Although one does not find this answer so explicitly spelled out
in the ancient Vinaya or Vinaya commentaries, the reason is simply because
it was not an issue of controversy during those times. There were no different
Buddhist traditions during the life time of the Buddha. Only from the 1960s
onwards, after their flight from Tibet and while getting in contact with modern
Buddhist societies, Tibetan Buddhists became aware that East Asian Buddhist
traditions still have fully ordained nuns of the slightly different Dharmaguptaka
Vinaya school and thus it became a pressing issue as to whether with their help
the ancient Mūlasarvāstivāda *bhikṣuṇī* lineage could be revived. A 're-reading'
of the texts is therefore required. The texts need to be read with a critical but at
the same time constructive attitude involving the willingness to find a solution,
which will help Buddhist women to practice today in accordance with what the
Buddha taught a long time back.[115]

## How Buddhists Can Learn from Other Religious Traditions

I am sure theologians having read this will find parallels between my own
approach and hermeneutics and exegeses applied in Feminist Theology or
Theological Women's Studies, which is well established within the Christian
Theologies and also in Islam and Judaism.

Christian feminist theological studies are far ahead of "Buddhist feminist
theological" studies.[116] There is still a great need for comparable research in the

---

114 In the Theravāda and Dharmaguptaka traditions not only for the ordination of monks, but
   also for the ordination of nuns, only ten years are required.
115 It seems that the UNRISD conference in Berlin 2009 came to a similar conclusion. Birnbaum (2010), 165 summarises: "Stattdessen sollten Informationen und Argumente zu-
   gänglich gemacht werden, neue Lesarten von Texten, Kritik an Normen etc., um Religion
   in den sozialen, politischen und historischen Bedingungen zu kontextualisieren. (…) Die
   Forderung, Religion ernst zu nehmen, sollte allerdings nicht vor politischen Forderungen
   zurückschrecken, die an die religiösen Institutionen gestellt werden."
116 The notion 'theology' is with regard to Buddhism not without controversy. It seems like a
   contradiction in terms. For a detailed discussion of this question see the collection of essays by: R. Jackson & J. Makranksy (Eds.) (2000) *Buddhist Theology. Critical Reflections
   by Contemporary Buddhist Scholars* Richmond: Curzon. In June 2013 an Interdisciplinary

field of re-reading the Buddhist canonical texts from a gender perspective. Pub-lications which include contributions from three non-Christian world religions (Islam, Judaism, Buddhism) are still the exception.[117]

It is not only necessary to seek dialogue with other religions but also with other traditions within the same religion. For example, in Hamburg there are more than 40 different Buddhist centres and temples linked to eight different countries and thus at least eight different currents of the three Buddhist main-stream traditions Theravāda, East Asian and Tibetan Buddhism. Furthermore, Germany's largest Vietnamese Buddhist nunnery as well as the first order of Tibetan Buddhist *bhikṣuṇīs* in Europe are based in Hamburg.

But what is the extent to which intra-Buddhist dialogue itself has been the object of research? This question was posed earlier and will now be considered to explain why one of the major focuses of "Buddhist Theology" in Hamburg should be on gender. Buddhist women are engaged in an ongoing global in-tra-Buddhist dialogue (as distinct say from Buddhist men), having begun active goal-oriented networking more than 25 years ago, in 1987.[118] This is mainly

---

Colloquium "Research, Dialogue and Understanding across Religions: Women and Gen-der Issues as an Organizing Point for Scholarship, Followed by a Co-Creative Workshop for a Programme on Women in Buddhism" took place at the University of Hamburg. Du-ring one of the workshops on Buddhism the scholars present, whether practitioners of Buddhism or not, mostly agreed that the term 'theology' – similar to the term 'feminist' – is an unfortunate choice of word for academic studies of Buddhism but agreed to accept it so not to be excluded from dialogue with other religions. A year before, at the same univer-sity, in a different colloquium it was mentioned but not discussed that a leading Indologist and Tibetologist present had suggested to reserve the term 'Buddhologist' as equivalent to 'Theologian'. But there is no consensus since some linguists working on Indian Buddhism, mainly not practitioners of Buddhism, wish to continue to use the term for themselves but do not want to become confused with scholar practitioners.

117 Gerber, C. Petersen, S., Weiße, W. (Eds.) (2011) *Unbeschreiblich weiblich? Neue Frage-stellungen zur Geschlechterdifferenz in den Religionen* Münster: LIT Verlag. Fundamental works on Gender and Buddhism are: Paul, D. Y. (1979) *Women in Buddhism. Images of the Feminine in Mahāyāna Tradition* Berkley: Asian Humanities Press; J. I. Cabezón (Ed.) (1992) *Buddhism, Sexuality and Gender* Delhi: Satguru Publications; Sponberg, A. (1992) Attitudes toward Women and the Feminine in Early Buddhism. In: Cabezón (Ed.) (1992); Gross, R. M. (1993) *Buddhism after Patriarchy. A Feminist History, Analysis and Reconstruction of Buddhism* Albany: SUNY Press; Joy, M. & Neumaier-Dargyay, Eva. K. (Eds.) (1995) *Gender, Genre and Religion. Feminist Reflections.* Waterloo, Ontario, Canada: The Calgary Institute for the Humanities; Mrozik, S. (2007) *Virtuous Bodies: The Physical Dimensions of Morality in Buddhist Ethics* Oxford: University Press; Powers, J. (2009) *A Bull of a Man: Images of Masculinity, Sex, and the Body in Indian Buddhism Cambridge*, MA: Harvard University Press. From these publications it is evident that gen-der in Buddhist literature is not only treated ambivalently but was also treated differently over the centuries within the various Buddhist traditions.

118 Roloff, C. (1987) Erste internationale Konferenz buddhistischer Nonnen 1987. In: *Tibet-Forum*, 6.2, 15–22; Id. (1988) Das Wiedererwachen buddhistischer Frauenorden. In: *Uni-versale Religion: die spirituelle Zeitschrift; ein Forum für die Weltreligionen*, 4.4 (1988), 55–62; Id. (1992) The First International Conference on Buddhist Women. In: *Internatio-nales Asienforum*, 23, 1–2.

due to the fact that Buddhist women around the globe share a common interest: to achieve gender equity and equal opportunities in the field of education and training for the estimated 300 million Buddhist women worldwide, including more than 130,000 nuns of whom many live in poverty.

A first major analysis of this Buddhist women's movement in the context of Christianity and Feminism has been conducted by Thea Mohr.[119] Her study is based on papers given during the first seven of so far thirteen International Sakyadhita conferences held between 1987 and 2013 in various Buddhist countries throughout Asia. Selections of the conference papers have been published until 2008. An analysis of all volumes, especially the last five volumes, is desirable in order to understand which topics have been the focus of dialogue among Buddhist women.[120]

Their dialogue has reached a point where they are now well-educated and ready to take their points of view into dialogue with women of other religions. From a Western Buddhist perspective, although it is important to respect various cultures and religions, women's rights should not be relativised when weighing religious freedom against women's human rights. But Asian women may feel differently about it or may change their mind when becoming aware that subordination of women within religious communities is not only something to be found in Buddhist communities but also in communities of other religions. It will be interesting to learn where there are parallels or differences and how religious women in modern societies relate to them. As the Canadian scholar Morny Joy has shown, "in a backlash against women's rights, fundamentalist elements of a number of religions are using this evasive ploy in the guise of 'tradition' or 'culture' to challenge the rights that have been gained by women so as to prevent any further progress (...)".[121]

---

119 Mohr, T. (2002) *Weibliche Identität und Leerheit. Eine ideengeschichtliche Rekonstruktion der buddhistischen Frauenbewegung Sakyadhītā International* Frankfurt a. M.: Peter Lang. See also Fenn, M. L. & Koppedrayer, K. (2008) Sakyadhita: A Transnational Gathering Place for Buddhist Women. In: *Journal of Global Buddhism* 9, 45–79. Available from: http://www.globalbuddhism.org/toc.html (last accessed December 11, 2013).

120 See especially: Tsomo, K. L. (Ed.) (2008) *Buddhist Women in a Global Multicultural Community* Malaysia: Sukhi Hotu. The editor is a Buddhist nun and Associate Professor at the Department of Theology & Religious Studies of the University of San Diego. The earlier four volumes are Tsomo, K. L. (Ed.) (2006) *Out of the Shadows: Socially Engaged Buddhist Women in the Global Community* Delhi: Sri Satguru Publication; (2004) *Buddhist Women and Social Justice: Ideals, Challenges, and Achievements* Albany, NY: State University of New York Press; (2004) *Discipline and Practice: Buddhist Women Past and Present* Honolulu: Sakyadita; (2004) *Bridging Worlds: Buddhist Women's Voices Across Generations* Taipei: Yuan Chuan Press; (1999) *Buddhist Women Across Cultures: Realisations* Albany, NY: State University of New York Press; (1989) *Sakyadhita: Daughters of the Buddha* Ithaca, NY: Snow Lion Publications.

121 Joy, M. (2008), 194 further states: "The Vatican has been particularly active. It has attempted to influence members of the Catholic communities from a number of countries (especially in Central and South America). In addition, it has made strategic coalitions between Catholic and Islamist countries to support its own position."

There are already a number of comparative studies of intra-Buddhist and interreligious dialogue as well as on transnational women initiatives in modern society with a special focus on women's ordination and women in religious leadership roles before the background of Human Rights and Women's Rights to build on.[122]

Furthermore, as findings from the UNRISD project *Religion, Politics and Gender Equality* (2007–2010) show, "politicized religion impinges on women's rights in problematic ways. The challenge to gender equality comes not just from fundamentalist agendas, but also from those who instrumentalize women's rights for political ends".[123] But although for this study "countries were selected for maximum variation with respect to religious tradition", the focus has been on "Christianity, Hinduism, Islam and Judaism" only, while Buddhism, despite being one of the world's four largest religions, has not been included. This fact in itself makes clear that more dialogue between Buddhism and other religions is needed to understand the apparent reservation to include it.

## Conclusion

Gender issues could become a driving force for the dialogue between religions. Today, the Buddhist traditions have no choice but to acknowledge that the social roles of women have changed over millennia. Not only in Western countries have societies changed, but rapid change in Asia is evident in the debates in response to the 2012 Delhi gang-rape case and sex-selective abortion, especially in China and India. Religious leaders and communities have the moral authority and responsibility to set good examples to protect the dignity of women and

---

122 For academic literature on interreligious feminism from a Buddhist perspective see: King, U. (ed.) (2005) *Gender, Religion and Diversity: Cross-Cultural Perspectives*; Gross, R. & Radford Ruether, R. (2001) Religious Feminism and the Future of the Planet. A Buddhist-Christian Conversation; Pieris, A. (1994) *Feuer und Wasser. Frau, Gesellschaft, Spiritualität in Buddhismus und Christentum*; Pieris, A. (Ed.) (1992–93) Special Issue on Woman and Man in Buddhism and Christianity dedicated to Lakshmi and Lynn, co-founders of this journal. In: *Dialogue (New Series)*, vol. 19/20; It is interesting to note that the editors mention in their introduction that they hope this issue of *Dialogue* will reach the hands of their readers "before the opening of the Third Sakyadhita Buddhist Women's Conference scheduled to be held in Sri Lanka in October this year (1993) as announced in the news column of this issue". Similar to the preceding Second Sakyadhita Conference in Bangkok I was the main speaker on *vinaya* and the *bhikṣuṇī* issue then. I remember a very large group of Sinhalese Dasasilamatas attending the workshop on the issue, where together with Prof. Chatsumarn Kabilsingh, still a Buddhist lay woman, but also a Vinaya scholar, we answered the many questions of those *de facto* nuns lacking the formal ordination and thus not considered to be part of the *saṅgha*. The conference and the foundation of Sakyadhita Sri Lanka finally lead to the revival of the *bhikkhunī* ordination in Sri Lanka as well as in Thailand.

123 UNRISD (2011) Research and Policy Brief 11: *Religion, Politics and Gender Equality.*

to respond to the changing needs and roles of women in modern societies. It is not acceptable in the 21st century for Buddhism to fail to live up to what the Buddha himself allowed a long time ago. For modern, well-educated women who want to fully devote their lives to study, meditation and daily practice of Buddhism need access to the same opportunities as their male counterparts to create the causes to attain liberation. The importance of religious women in the democratisation process and in the educational field – especially their roles in counselling, conflict resolution, peace-making and religious education – should not be underestimated either. Today it is extremely important to integrate the gender perspective in order to preserve and spread religious teachings.

After having spent many years thoroughly investigating the matter at hand, I have reached the conclusion that for change or transformation, textual evidence must come from the direct and original source: the authoritative religious texts themselves. It is the cultural attitudes that need to be transformed. Many with deeply engrained conservative patterns of behaviour will resist change, with an attempt to justify their beliefs and actions by an appeal to the authoritative or canonical texts. Thus it is necessary to appeal to the repository of the very texts themselves to dismantle the wrong views and to advance this matter.

This is the reason, why in the introduction to this paper I quoted Bishop Krusche. I think, to avoid any possible criticism of his public meeting with the Dalai Lama on equal footing, quite skilfully, *a priori*, he gave evidence from the direct and original source by stating "the Christian belief in a Creator God enables to see each person as an image of God. God the Creator of heaven and earth I can also meet in people of different religions". To me this means in my own words: since God is the creator of everything he must have also created the Buddhists in His image.

Similarly, in the intra-Buddhist dialogue, the Dalai Lama says:[124] "There is no point in discussing whether to revive the *bhikṣuṇī* ordination; the Buddha clearly intended for there to be *bhikṣuṇīs*. The question is merely how to do so properly within the context of the Vinaya."

Against this background I sincerely hope that the Academy of World Religions will also become a place where scientists can analyse such equivalent or comparable processes in the world religions and a place where exchanges on the various concepts and aspects of female leadership in the respective religions can take place. Taking Buddhism as an example, the re-introduction of the highest ordination of Buddhist women would not only lead to the appreciation of women's status in Asia but also of Buddhist women's status in today's increasing multi-religious society worldwide. In this way it could also become a momentum for other religions to further consider gender mainstreaming in religion insofar as it has not been realised. Thus we may develop a true theology in dialogue.

---

124 Tsedroen & Mohr (2010), 254.

*André van der Braak*

# Buddhism and Dialogue: On Zen and the West

From the beginning of the twentieth century, the academic discipline of inter-cultural philosophy and theology has taken root. In his history of this discipline, J.J. Clarke distinguishes three historical phases, which can be loosely connected to three methodological approaches.[1] The first approach was the universalist one. The universalists attempted a grand synthesis between East and West. They grossly schematised and simplified the various traditions: the West was rationalistic and materialist, the East was intuitive and spiritual. This universalising approach was characterised by a 'will to truth': a will to find the one overarching perspective under which all philosophical and religious traditions can be subsumed. The second approach, comparativism in a more restricted sense, has been more modest. It has aimed to compare the views of individual Western and non-Western thinkers, mapping out similarities and differences. The comparativists abandoned the ambition of a great synthesis.

Over the past decennia, the cross-cultural hermeneutical framework has gained influence as a third approach. The thinker most often associated with philosophical hermeneutics, Hans-Georg Gadamer (1900–2002), was a well-known proponent of intercultural dialogue, and a major source of inspiration for the study of cross-cultural philosophy in the West. Philosophical hermeneutics stresses the importance of interpreting religious traditions within their temporal and cultural context, and of keeping in mind that every interpretation constitutes another re-contextualisation. The aim is not to arrive at some static 'objective truth' about reality, but to expand the range of possible interpretations, and in this way to contribute to the ongoing conversation of global philosophy. Philosophical hermeneutics recognises a plurality of different traditions, and stresses that one's own tradition needs to be continuously both reinterpreted and strengthened in light of its exposure to what is foreign to it. Cross-cultural hermeneutics aims not so much at comparison per se, but at deconstructing fixed perspectives and opening up a plurality of interpretations, in order to enhance the fullness of our understanding.

In the global context of interculturality today, hermeneutics must undergo a fundamental change, according to some. Since every hermeneutics has its own culturally sedimented roots and cannot claim a universal acceptance uncondi-tionally, the fundamental principle of intercultural hermeneutics is the view that an interpretation is always determined in terms of culture. Therefore, in-tercultural hermeneutics attempts to always recognise and respect the 'foreign'

---

1  Clarke, J. J. (1997) *Oriental Enlightenment. The Encounter Between Asian and Western Thought* London/New York: Routledge, 119–129.

element.[2] Fostering a cross-cultural dialogue between Western and Buddhist religious traditions can help to provide the kind of regeneration that our own traditions are in dire need of. The French sinologist François Jullien stresses that, through the detour of non-Western thought, we can regain access to lost or underemphasised dimensions of our own Western tradition:

> However taken it may be with surpassing itself, Western philosophy never questions itself except from within. However radical it may wish to be, this criticism is always relatively integrated, remaining within the limits of an implicit understanding from which certain positions may emerge. There is always that on the basis of which we question ourselves, which, for that very reason, we cannot question.[3]

To step back from the Western tradition and criticise it from without can allow us to assume a more truly global position. Interreligious dialogue is, therefore, especially valuable and helpful in undercutting assumptions about one's own tradition. In this essay, the various attempts to initiate a dialogue between Western thought and the Buddhist Zen tradition over the past century will be used as a case study in order to study the pitfalls and possibilities for a dialogue with Buddhism.

## Zen and the West

Zen has exercised a fascination over Western philosophers, theologians, psychologists and spiritual seekers. Since it made its entry in Western culture around 1920, in the writings of the Japanese religious scholar D.T. Suzuki (1870–1966), it has captured the imagination of many.

Suzuki's presentation of Zen was heavily influenced by Western Romanticism. It hailed Zen as a universal religion, founded on individual experience rather than conformity to church structures, meditation rather than ritual, critical investigation leading up to 'the Great Doubt' rather than belief in religious dogmas. For many intellectuals, Zen served as a perfect replacement for a Western Christianity that was perceived as outmoded. It was viewed as an exponent of the mystical East, as epitomised in Eugen Herrigel's *Zen in the Art of Archery* (1953).[4] This Romantic form of Zen was embraced in the fifties by artists and intellectuals like Jack Kerouac, Allen Ginsberg and Alan Watts, who formed

---

2    Mall, R. A. (1995) *Philosophie im Vergleich der Kulturen: Interkulturelle Philosophie, eine neue Orientierung* Darmstadt: Wissenschaftliche Buchgesellschaft.

3    Jullien, F. (2000) Detour and Access: Strategies of Meaning in China and Greece New York: Zone Books, 371.

4    Herrigel, a German philosophy professor and student of archery in Japan, was famously instructed by his Japanese teacher to practice until it was no longer he himself, but 'it', that would shoot the arrow. For a more detailed discussion of this work, see: Yamada, S. (2001) The myth of Zen in the art of archery. In: *Journal of Japanese Religious Studies*, 28 (1–2), 1–30.

the Beat Zen Generation. The counter revolution of the sixties established Zen as part of the Western spiritual landscape. Japanese Zen masters (*roshis*) came to teach in the West (Yasutani, Maezumi, Shunryu Suzuki, Sasaki), and their Western students became *roshis* as well (Richard Baker, Robert Aitken, Philip Kapleau, Dennis Merzel, Bernie Glassman, Daido Loori). In the seventies and eighties, with the rise of humanistic and transpersonal psychology, Zen became ever more popular.

But Zen was also approached very critically. Arthur Koestler criticised the deliberate obscurity of the Zen texts in his book *The Lotus and the Robot*.[5] The Japanese novelist Yukio Mishima portrayed the Zen monastery in his novel *The Temple of the Golden Pavilion* as a power-infested, authoritarian community.[6] In line with this critical approach, the Chinese historian Hu Shi approached Zen as merely one religious sect among others, and attempted to describe the Zen tradition within the context of larger political and social developments in the Chinese historical tradition.

In the seventies and eighties, the Japanese Zen scholar Yanagida Seizan introduced a philological approach. Together with Western students, he carefully researched many Zen texts that had been discovered in the early twentieth century in a cave in Dunhuang. Their results led to a questioning of many established Zen myths, and to critical considerations about the nature of the spirituality of Zen. A 1995 publication, *Rude Awakenings*, stressed the need for a self-understanding of the Zen tradition itself.[7] Western Zen priest Brian Victoria published in 1997 *Zen at War*, documenting nationalism and war crimes by Japanese Zen masters, throwing doubt on the universality of Zen spirituality.[8]

In a recent publication, Steven Heine has attempted to clarify the conflict between these two competing perspectives on Zen. As Heine points out, these days nearly everyone agrees that Zen is generally sorely misunderstood and in need of clarification.[9] Discussion has arisen as to what constitutes the 'real' Zen. Heine's book *Zen Skin, Zen Marrow* therefore carries the ironical subtitle 'Will the real Zen Buddhism please stand up?'.

As Heine points out, the Western study of Zen Buddhism has all too often been a reflection of the preoccupations of Western modernity. The critical approach to Zen is part of a reaction to the wider phenomenon of Orientalism, the stereotypical approach of Western scholars to Oriental culture based on thinly disguised, hegemonic agendas.[10] Whereas the colonial West has tended

---

5   Koestler, A. (1961) *The lotus and the robot* New York: Macmillan.

6   Mishima, Y. (1959) *The temple of the Golden Pavilion* New York: Knopf.

7   Heisig, J. W. & Maraldo, J. C. (Eds.) (1995) *Rude awakenings: Zen, the Kyoto School, and the question of nationalism* Honolulu: University of Hawaii Press.

8   Victoria, B. D. (1997) *Zen at war* New York: Weatherhill.

9   Heine, S. (2008) *Zen skin, Zen marrow: Will the real Zen Buddhism please stand up?* Oxford: University Press, 3.

10  Said, E. (1979) *Orientalism* New York: Vintage.

to portray the East as generally inferior and degenerate compared to Western civilisation, the field of religious studies (more dominated by the temperament and outlook of Romanticism) has often shown a seemingly opposite pattern of thought. The spirituality of the East is considered superior to Western varieties (reverse Orientalism). Those two opposed perspectives are both a gross distortion. According to Heine, "Buddhism is seen either as a sublime and quaint form of meditative mysticism, based on mind-purification and self-transformation, or as the hollow shell of a sequestered ancient cult that broods on death and decay yet thrives on monastic political intrigue".[11]

Heine contributes to a cross-cultural hermeneutical approach by providing more information about the actual social and political context within which Zen functioned as a religion in Japan. By investigating the actual practice of Zen, 'Zen on the ground' rather than relying only on published accounts of doctrine and soteriology, he attempts to elucidate the common self-understanding of the Japanese culture that surrounded Zen. This is surely an important step to a less biased current understanding of Zen.

The other half of such a hermeneutical investigation would be to bring to light our own common self-understanding out of which we attempt to make sense of 'Zen'. Let us investigate, therefore, how our various current understandings of Zen have been shaped by our contemporary self-understanding, not taken as a theory of what we are and what spirituality is, but as our lived and sensed understanding that precedes our conscious interpretations.

The original Romantic interpretation of Zen by Suzuki, Herrigel and others, labeled by Heine as 'the Traditional Zen Narrative' (TZN), regards Zen as a universal kind of spirituality that could be practiced regardless of the religious tradition one belonged to, a counterforce to the Western one-sided focus on Cartesian rationality. No small amount of Romanticism and Reverse Orientalism was present in this early dialogue with Zen.

The criticisms of Hu Shi, Koestler and Mishima, labeled by Heine as 'Historical and Cultural Criticism' (HCC), consider Zen to be a remnant of the past, an authoritarian Buddhist sect that shows all the trappings of organised religion. Initially, much academic Zen scholarship fell into this category. As Zen scholar Carl Bielefeldt puts it:

> The postwar Japanese scholarship copied by American Zen academics was based on a 'modernist' ideal of historical objectivity that sought to rule out of bounds normative judgments about the validity of Zen claims or the authenticity of Zen experience. The question of the inner states of the Zen masters was banished beyond the purview of the responsible historian of the Zen documentary record.[12]

---

11  Heine (2008), 4.
12  Bielefeldt, C. (1998) Zen wars III: Revenge of the West Lecture delivered at Lund University, Sweden. Quoted in: A. van der Braak (2008) Zen Spirituality in a Secular Age. In: Studies in Spirituality, 18 (50).

Zen scholars from recent years operate, like Nietzsche, as 'masters of suspicion', deconstructing and unmasking not only the traditional self-understanding of the Zen tradition through genealogical analysis, but also the modernist attempt to reconstruct the objective textual history of Zen ideas. Zen scholars have gone from modernity to postmodernity. But this does not imply a return to Suzuki's transcendentalist Zen. On the contrary, as Bielefeldt notes, in postmodern Zen research,

> the very suggestion that such [Zen] ideas might express a spiritual experience (let alone a spiritual truth) has come itself to be seen as a reactionary political gesture. If our reintroduction of subjectivity into historical narrative has permitted us to imagine once again the inner states of the Zen masters, we can no longer imagine their enlightened insights but only their mundane motives.[13]

As a result, the religious position of the Zen tradition has become unstable and fragmented in much the same manner as that of its Western religious counterparts. Zen is coming of age.

## Toward a Cross-Cultural Hermeneutical Dialogue with Zen

The American philosopher Dale Wright has recently attempted to engage Zen philosophically from a perspective that is informed by the tradition of philosophical hermeneutics.[14] He tries to overcome the opposition of historicist and Romantic perspectives on Zen by showing that both approaches share a set of unquestioned presuppositions, a common worldview: they both think it possible to gain access to 'the way things really are'. The historicists with their analyses aim at a true and accurate picture of Zen as a historical and sociological phenomenon, and the true interpretation of Zen texts. The Romantics try to go 'beyond the mind', and aim at directly beholding 'spirit', possibly through a faculty of mystical intuition or other extra-rational means. Both parties are convinced they can get through to the thing itself, as it exists objectively, independent of the mind of the one who understands. Some kind of pure understanding is considered possible, either through eliminating bias in true scientific fashion, or through transcending rational understanding (seen as inherently limited) altogether.

Wright's aim is not to arrive at a 'clear and simple' picture of what Zen is, or what Zen texts mean. Instead of reaching for the transcultural, transhistorical 'truth' of Zen (a truth often considered to be beyond language as well), his meditations are primarily 'readings'. What happens when we read and interpret a text, a Zen text? Apart from our own work, our attempt at interpretation, the

---

13  Ibid.
14  Wright, D. S. (1998) *Philosophical Meditations on Zen Buddhism* Cambridge: Cambridge University Press.

text also 'works' on us. We become changed by the texts we read, we can't be impassive observers of texts, especially not of Zen texts, that expressly aim at changing the reader. And beyond our own work, and the work of the text, is the work done by the larger cultural and historical forces that we inevitably operate within. To become more aware of those inner and outer workings is the aim of his philosophical meditations.

Both the historicist and the Romantic avoid being targeted and challenged by the Zen text, Wright notices.[15] The scientist keeps a safe distance from the text: it is about someone else in another time and place. There is no need for himself to be impacted by the text, or to assume that it could be relevant to his own life circumstances. The Romantic avoids the impact of the Zen text in a very different way: he already knows that the text is about enlightenment, and that it contains a very deep understanding of an ahistoric truth. The Romantic projects his own, relatively safe, meaning onto the text, and leaves the vastly differing contexts of time and place out of the picture.[16]

## A Different Understanding of 'Understanding'

Practicing philosophical hermeneutics implies a different conception of truth and understanding. When the myth of the given is dispelled, a correspondence theory of truth (*adequatio intellectus et rei*) is no longer relevant. There are no 'things' out there, no 'facts' to be discovered. As Nietzsche said, "there are no facts, only interpretations".[17] Understanding, in the hermeneutic sense of the word, does not refer to being able to grasp facts or concepts, but to an ongoing, preconscious activity. As Wright expresses it:

> Understanding, in this sense, is our most practical attunement to the world, the way we are embedded in the world, oriented to it, and engaged with it. Although the particular shape of understanding differs from person to person and from culture to culture, it is always there as the essential background out of which we live and work.[18]

We understand each thing through its various relations to others, through countless interconnections and juxtapositions. This process is as much a social practice as it is an individual, subjective activity. We are socialised into a vast store of understanding that is culturally established. In a way we do not produce

---

15  Wright (1998), 39.
16  Incidentally, as Zen texts make clear, the world of interpretation extends way beyond texts. Zen koan texts are full of gestures, movements, signals, sounds, behaviors and situations that require interpretation. Anything in a Zen story can become a sign that needs to be 'read' properly.
17  Nietzsche, F. (1967–1977) *Sämtliche Werke, Kritische Studienausgabe (KSA)* Berlin: De Gruyter, book 12, 315.
18  Wright (1998), 41.

understanding, we are immersed in it. No matter how isolated we are, we belong to traditions of understanding and engage in them socially.

To our modern minds, a Zen text must be the product of an individual mind, arising out of a personal inner subjectivity. The Romantic approach has always portrayed Zen as a movement of radical individualism. But this might tell us more about our own Romantic preoccupations with inner depths of subjectivity than about Zen. In 9th century China, for example, very different notions of subjectivity and individuality were current. Zen was very much a communal phenomenon, a particular 'form of life'. All activity in a Zen monastery was directed to the collective matter of awakening. The meaning of such terms was invisibly structured by a shared common understanding, based on the narratives on the Buddha and the Zen patriarchs.

Therefore, in order to be able to say something meaningful about a Zen text, we need to be initiated into the particular forms of understanding, the social, religious, philosophical and cultural contexts that gave rise to this particular text. As Wright notices:

> We need to work our way into the language and customs of local practice before we can share in the subtleties of understanding. This is hard work, and typically not even attempted unless it appears that something important is to be gained from it. In our time, Romanticism has supplied this justification, and the tradition of historicism has initiated the quest for a background of understanding sufficient for reading Zen.[19]

This opens up an interesting conundrum. Once our Romantic hopes for finding a profound absolute truth in Zen, or even for gaining enlightenment from reading the Zen texts, start to fade, what will motivate us to engage in dialogue with them?

## A Different Interpretation of 'Interpretation'

Given this new understanding of understanding, what does it mean when we speak of interpretation? Philosophical hermeneutics distinguishes the relationship between understanding and interpretation in a reversed way: it's not that our interpretations lead to understanding, as is usually thought; our interpretations are based on the pre-conscious forms of understanding that constitute our world. As Heidegger puts it in section 32 of *Being and Time*:

> Interpretation is grounded existentially in understanding: the latter does not arise from the former. Nor is interpretation the acquiring of information about what is understood; it is rather the working-out of possibilities projected in understanding.[20]

---

19 Ibid., 47.
20 Heidegger, M. (1962) Being and Time New York: Harper and Row, 188.

Unless the object of interpretation is understood in some sense already (pre-understanding), there neither would, nor could, be any interpretation of it. In interpretation we come to consciously know what we have understood pre-consciously. Interpretation makes our implicit understanding explicit. Wright puts it as follows:

> When we understand something, we understand it 'in terms of' something else already familiar and available within our world. [...] Interpretations are exercises in connecting one thing to another, a phenomenon to an image in our minds, and that connection to the totality of our understanding.[21]

This is why the scientific focus on eliminating preconceptions doesn't work. Without preconceptions, we would never be able to understand something foreign. Only by connecting it to something already known, can it become meaningful to us. Therefore, truthful interpretation consists not in the avoidance of projection and prejudice, but rather in their critical appraisal. We have to locate our inappropriate projections so that they can be revised or replaced by more appropriate ones. The criteria for such more appropriate projections can ultimately only be pragmatic in nature.

Both the Romantic and the historicist approach tend to assume that there must be some original meaning that can be used as a measure to decide which interpretation is correct. The Romantic, in his search for true Zen, in his interpretation of its texts tries to capture the authentic voice of their author. The historian tries to find out 'what really happened', what it was really like to be a 9th century Chinese Zen master. But what if there is no original meaning, but only a series of consecutive re-interpretations? Zen texts, like any texts, stand in a long history of interpretation, just like our understanding of them is only possible in the terms given to us by our own long history of interpretation (the Romantic and scientific ideologies that have shaped us into the interpreting subjects that we are now).

Becoming aware of this fact opens up another methodological approach: a genealogical one. First introduced by Nietzsche in his *Genealogy of Morality*, and applied by Foucault in his works, genealogy digs up the string of interpretations that hides underneath a seemingly unified phenomenon.

## The Role of Language

Crucial for engaging in dialogue with the Zen tradition is coming to terms with its obvious paradoxes with respect to language. Time and again we read that the true matter of Zen cannot be grasped by language. Zen claims to be a transmission outside the scriptures. This is the rhetoric that defines the movement as a separate school. And yet all such utterances are being made in language, over

---

21  Wright (1998), 50.

and over again. Zen is the most literate Chinese Buddhist tradition. The Zen masters don't follow Wittgenstein's famous dictum that what one cannot speak of, one must be silent of. And in the Zen koans, language is often claimed to have a transformative, liberating effect.

Many interpreters have attempted to come to terms with this paradox by as-cribing an instrumentalist theory of language to Zen: language is an instrument or tool available for our use in achieving certain specific communicative goals. It is a means to an end. Although language can never describe the state of en-lightenment (which is beyond thought and language), it can still be a useful tool to point towards it. The famous Zen metaphor speaks of 'the finger pointing to the moon'. Language is an exoteric tool that can prepare the uninitiated Zen practitioner to the esoteric reality of enlightenment.

Wright points out that, if one interprets the enlightenment experience from within such an instrumentalist theory of language, it is tempting to conclude that it is not linguistically and culturally mediated.[22] It corresponds to some kind of universal depth structure that underlies the various cultural and reli-gious surface structures. The instrumentalist view of language seems to nat-urally lead to a universalist theory of religious experience. Enlightenment is not only beyond language, but also beyond cultural differences. An interesting consequence would be that Zen enlightenment would not be any different from Christian enlightenment, or Platonic enlightenment. Such a view amounts to a denial of the otherness of Zen. It is a safe and reassuring thought that in Zen, we won't find anything fundamentally new, but merely a confirmation of our own highest experiences. What the Zen masters teach us, Meister Eckhart already wrote about.

But is language best conceived of as an instrument? Although we often use language as a tool, it also often uses us. It determines the range of what we can perceive and experience. According to modern theories of language, language is already embedded in the content of our experience. Perception, experience and language are closely interwoven. We always experience something *as* something. Anything not experienced *as* something in particular is simply not experienced. A famous anthropological story tells us that when European ships first visited the South Pacific, the native islanders never saw them coming. They simply didn't perceive the ships, because they were too unfamiliar to them. The islanders didn't have the concept 'ship'.

Through language games we are socialised into forms of life. Seen from this perspective, we are interested in 'enlightenment' because it is a meaningful concept to us, due to the religious and philosophical language games that we have been brought up in. If not, Buddhist texts would probably be rather irrele-vant to us (as they were to the Western world until the 19th century).

---

22  Wright (1998), 67.

## Discussion

The main points of this paper can be summarised as three recommendations for coming to a fuller and richer dialogue with Buddhist traditions.

(1) We have to investigate Buddhist traditions in comparison to our own religious and philosophical traditions. Only then will we be able to come to any interpretations at all. And the more consciously we undertake this, the more appropriate our projections will be. Only by means of comparison and contrast, Wright notes, only by seeing identity and difference, and thus by relation to one's own culture's customs and practices, will one be able to see what a foreign cultural phenomenon is. The Western researcher, who is sensitive to issues and forms of thought in his own tradition, will be able to ask good questions, and to see what is worthy of reflection or further inquiry. He will notice which questions are asked in Buddhist traditions that are lacking in Western traditions, and which Western philosophical and religious questions are not asked or not answered, and he will be interested in asking why and to what effect.

(2) It is important on one hand to appreciate how truly foreign and 'other' Buddhist traditions are (it takes a lot of time and effort to discern otherness), and not jump to interpretations too quickly: this would be just a case of uncritically projecting our own preconceptions onto them (the dangers of a Romantic approach). On the other hand, the attempt to approach them without preconceptions (the impossible striving of the historicists) will make any meaningful interpretation impossible. Buddhist texts will appear just as strange artefacts from a distant time in a faraway country, perhaps of interest to historians, but not as a vital contribution to philosophy today that can have a meaningful impact on our lives.

(3) We have to be more sensitive to the role that language plays. When we recognise, for example, how the term 'enlightenment' peaks our interest because of the way it fits within our language games, we become more open to contemplate the otherness of the Buddhist traditions, and their use of enlightenment. In that case, it would be exactly the difference and uniqueness of Zen that would make it worthwhile to study it. We would no longer be interested in Buddhists because 'they' have what 'we' have too, but because 'they' experience something that 'we' don't, and because their language has opened up a very interesting set of possibilities for them. In *Beyond Good and Evil*, Nietzsche already called attention to the fact that different language families would be able to disclose very different aspects of reality to us:

> It is precisely where a relationship between languages is present that we cannot avoid, thanks to the common philosophy of grammar – I mean thanks to the unconscious mastery and guidance exercised by the same grammatical functions – everything has been prepared from the beginning for a similar development and order of philosophical systems, just as the road to certain other possibilities of interpreting the world seems sealed off. [...] There will be a greater probability that philosophers from the region of the Ural-Altaic language (in which the idea of the subject is most poorly developed)

will look differently "into the world" and will be found on other pathways than In-do-Germans or Muslims.[23]

Although the Romantic projection of enlightenment as a universal mystical experience beyond thought and language is no longer acceptable to current philosophical sensibilities, this doesn't condemn us to a kind of historicist relativism. Reading Buddhist texts with a comparative application of the insights of philosophical hermeneutics may yield various new and previously unknown aspects and perspectives on reality. Precisely because Buddhism may turn out to be much more 'other' and foreign than we could ever imagine, its study could be very fruitful, yes even enlightening indeed. In this way, Western and Eastern enlightenment could come together in very unexpected and unforeseen ways.[24]

---

23  Nietzsche (1967–1977), book 5, 34 f.

24  Parts of this essay were earlier published as part of: A. van der Braak (2008) Zen Spirituality in a Secular Age. In: *Studies in Spirituality*, 18, 39–60, and as part of: Id. (2008) Enlightenment Revisited: Romantic, historicist, hermeneutic and comparative perspectives on Zen. In: *Acta Comparanda* XIX, 87–97.

*Anna Alomes*

# Multifaith Dialogue

## Considering a Buddhist Perspective on Reaching the 22nd Century Through Universal Responsibility

Since Buddhism holds that the problem of violence, disconnection and religious intolerance is a cognitive one (as harmful negative emotions drive intention and subsequent action), the solution requires the agent to work from within; to reduce the level of violence and increase the level of tolerance, compassion and mindfulness of others. In this article I will refer to empirical findings, which show how this process is now being measured and reported. The Tibetan spiritual leader, the Dalai Lama refers to this as 'internal disarmament' and insists that it is just as useful as the more commonly known term of 'external disarmament' – in fact, even more so as it must precede it. Here we see the requirement for 'inner peace' before we can have 'outer peace'. The benefits to the individual include achieving an immediate sense of calm, reduced levels of stress and frustration, an increased sense of well-being and self-worth, and the capacity and genuine desire to assist others.

In this view, ethics is not simply a matter of knowing. More importantly it is about doing. For this reason, even the most sophisticated ethical understanding, if it is not applied in daily life, is somewhat pointless. Living ethically requires not only the conscious adoption of an ethical outlook but also a commitment to developing and applying inner values in our daily lives. And when we do just this, says the Dalai Lama there will be a more optimistic outcome:

> So far, of the twenty-first century, just over a decade has gone; the major part of it is yet to come. It is my hope that this will be the century of peace, a century of dialogue – a century when a more caring, responsible and compassionate humanity will emerge. This is my prayer as well.[1]

## A Time of Change

According to scholars like the German Philosopher, Karl Jaspers, we are now at the right place and right time to make positive change in the world and I propose that we view interfaith dialogue as an important process to assist that change.

Jaspers coined the term 'axial age' (*Achsenzeit*) to describe the period 800–200 BCE when revolutionary thinking appeared in India, China and the

---

1 Gyatso, T. 14th Dalai Lama (2011) *Beyond Religion: Ethics for a Whole World* New York: Random House, 188.

Occident: "the spiritual foundations of humanity were laid simultaneously and independently in China, India, Persia, Judea, and Greece. And these are the foundations upon which humanity still subsists today."[2] He includes, Plato, Aristotle, the historical Buddha, Ashoka, writers of the Upanishads, Lao Tzu, Homer, Socrates, Archimedes, Elijah, Isaiah, and Jeremiah to name only a few figures that rose during the axial age.

This wellspring of thought, spontaneously arising across one period of time is the most important aspect here. By way of making a contemporary connection, it has been suggested that the modern era is a new axial age, wherein traditional relationships between religion, secularity, and traditional thought are changing. We have arrived at a particular moment in time where the threat of human extinction is real and the place to look for part of the solution lies in enhancing the set of relationships between religion, secularity, and traditional thought – relationships that are rapidly shifting. Amidst that shift, we are trying to articulate the limitations of interfaith dialogue and search for ways of overcoming these limitations in order to bring religion, secularity and traditional thought together on an international platform in a way that results in a significant, beneficial and practical impact at the grass-roots level in communities. It is important to revisit key questions like: what aspects of multifaith dialogue cause obstacles, and what aspects promote harmony and realise successful outcomes?

## The Buddhist Keys to Successful Interfaith Dialogue

Revisiting these key questions with Māhayāna Buddhist thinkers[3] produces a very helpful contribution. The proposition is that interfaith dialogue in order to produce successful outcomes requires the presence of three essential ingredients: (i) empathy, (ii) respect and (iii) trust (outlined below). A useful line of enquiry is: how do we ensure that these three building blocks are present? And how do we build them into transferable skills for the classroom and the wider community?

In the Buddhist view, the first key to successful interfaith dialogue is the generation of empathy. But before we take a look at the results of experiments by American scientists like Richard Davidson and colleagues to demonstrate how Buddhist practitioners master that skill, consider the following snapshot from my own field research on the critical role that empathy plays in dialogue and transformation. Colleagues involved in the Israeli/Palestinian struggle, the Truth and Reconciliation Commission in South Africa and the Christian/Muslim struggle say that you can bring all parties into one room, but unless there is

---

2   Jaspers, K. (1953) *The Origin and Goal of History (Vom Ursprung und Ziel der Geschichte)* Yale: University Press.

3   It is with sincere gratitude that I acknowledge the key role played by mentor and friend, Professor Jay Garfield in establishing the connection to senior Tibetan academics, which has grown and flourished for the past 15 years.

a genuine attempt to empathise with each other during the dialogue, there will be no productive outcome. Therefore, one of the factors which limits interfaith dialogue is lack of empathy. This observation is highlighted by my own experience at the Truth and Reconciliation Commission hearings in South Africa in the late 1990's. Consider the following two examples:

## Snapshot from the TRC

Two people sit opposite each other. One, a survivor and the other a perpetrator of unspeakable horrors. This is an amnesty hearing, and in order to be successful in his application, the perpetrator must give all of the facts of the matter and tell the truth. Nothing is scripted. The atmosphere is electric… the hall is packed with family members of the survivor, staff members to support and assist them, lawyers, members of the international media, and Commissioners listening to the testimony. No one knows what will happen but for the first time, sometimes in 30 years, those without a voice, with no recourse to action, and often no knowledge of what happened to loved ones who disappeared, sit on a level playing field, equal to the one who sits opposite them. The perpetrator no longer has the benefit of a powerful military uniform or membership of a ruling party to hide behind – it is simply one person sitting opposite another person. When the differences are taken away, what remains is the common ground – membership of the human race, where membership entails respect and dignity. In this case (i.e. the 'Gugulethu Seven' hearing in Cape Town), an astonishing act of human transformation took place. The perpetrator gave details of events, why he had acted in such a way, and acknowledged that the action was wrong. He had no expectations of forgiveness from the other party, but spoke of regret and sorrow for the harm committed to loved ones. The surviving family member spoke of the anguish and despair, the years of not knowing, the ruination of life and hope, but the relief of now knowing, of trying desperately to understand how it must have been for the other person and offered unconditional forgiveness so that both of their lives might move forward.

This was an astonishing public moment, both parties genuinely trying to understand the point of view of the other, the empathy present, speaking and listening leading to understanding and forgiveness. One week later, the opposite effect could be seen:

It is the special hearing of Winnie Mandikizela-Mandela (the former wife of Nelson Mandela) and the Mandela United Football Team in relation to the murder of Stompie Sepei and the imprisonment of Katiza Cebakulu (Johannesburg)[4]. Summer temperatures are soaring and the air conditioning in the public hall has failed. Hundreds of members of the international press are

---

4    Bridgland, F. (1997) *Katiza's Journey: Beneath the surface of South Africa's Shame* London: Sidgwick & Jackson.

literally climbing the walls for a view; members of the public are crammed shoulder-to-shoulder in the hall and two people sit opposite one another: Winnie M-M on one side and Bishop Paul Verryn on the other. At issue is the death of a 14 year-old boy Stompie Sepei. Bishop Verryn in whose Methodist manse he had resided asked for her forgiveness, for not having cared for the child in a better way (surprisingly, as it was Winnie who had unjustifiably ruined the Bishop's reputation). Winnie M-M who did not want to be at this hearing but had been subpoenaed would not listen to him, saying this was "a circus" and a "farce". Bishop Tutu who was chairing the hearing begged her, not as a Commissioner, but as a long-time family friend to treat this person and the process with respect. She would not. The dialogue broke down, Bishop Verryn did not receive closure or an end to his suffering, Winnie M-M did not offer any empathy, only hostility and bitterness.

What can be said about the two processes? The first had a successful outcome, both parties entered into the dialogue, empathy was present, a space was created where two people with a seemingly vast range of differences could come together in a shared moment, and transformation occurred. Change took place where both parties benefited from the exchange. The second certainly had dialogue, but without any desire for empathy from one side, the process hit a dead-end and neither party benefited from the exchange.

## Improving Empathy

But what if a method to deliberately increase activity in the brain responsible for generating empathy existed? The implications not only for the process of multifaith dialogue, but for the whole of humanity would be enormous.

The lessons from Buddhism that can be brought to bear here take the form of empirical studies that outline: (i) a process for enabling productive dialogue by generating empathy – literary changing our brain states – described in terms of 'neuroplasticity'; and (ii) a mechanism for dialogue through Universal Responsibility (and the soon to be released 'Charter of Universal Responsibility').

## Broadening Interfaith Dialogue to Include Scientists and Other Specialist Knowledge Groups

In order to really drill down to the heart of 'converting understanding into practice', the Dalai Lama has broadened his forums to expand beyond interfaith groups alone, to incorporate scientists and others with specialist knowledge. The empirical studies previewed here will be taken from research presented at the 'Mind and Life Forum' with Western scientists, conducted annually over the past 20 years by the Nobel Peace Prize Laureate in his home town of Dharamsala, India.

# Case Study: Joining Forces – Western Scientists and Tibetan Buddhist Monks

Richard Davidson and his American team of neuroscientists came together with Buddhist practitioners for the now famous empirical study.[5] The study aimed to measure the changes in the brain of long-term practitioners engaged in the practice of meditation for the purpose of generating empathy and compassion.

For roughly 2,500 years, this lineage of meditation adepts explored the brain's plasticity, systematised specific techniques for transformation – 'this is how you can wash away mental pollution like anger, hatred and fear and turn it into compassion, kindness and empathy' – passed rigorous instructions for spiritual practice down through generations to the present day. This interaction enabled scientists to look into the brains of practitioners and see what was going on – and the results were astonishing. The human brain – regarded as the most complex entity in the universe – can be changed as the result of something as seemingly insignificant as applying daily practice to our thoughts.[6] We are not talking here about the cellular changes that underlie the formation of memory and hence learning. In this sense, the brain undergoes continuous physical change. Rather, the oversimplified bottom line in neuroplasticity is that the brain real estate that has one purpose is reassigned and begins to do another.

The Western scientists selected monk practitioners and particularly adepts recommended by the Dalai Lama who had spent their lives in solitude meditating in caves in the Himalayan hills for between 15 and 40 years. They hoped to uncover clear effects of meditation – or, more generally mental training – on brain functions. From those who volunteered, the Dalai Lama chose ten senior meditators. For comparison, the scientists[7] would also study ordinary Tibetans in the same Himalayan hillside town of Dharamsala. Sharon Begley, author of the book *The Plastic Mind – New science reveals our extraordinary potential to transform ourselves,* states:

(From a Western perspective), meditation is typically viewed as a means of stress reduction. Some forms of it are. But from the point of view of Tibetan

---

5    Lutz, A. et al. (2004) Long-Term Meditators Self-Induce High-Amplitude Gamma Synchrony During Mental Practice. In: *Proceedings of the National Academy of Sciences*, 101, 69–73.

6    Davidson, R. J. et al. (2003) Alterations in brain and immune function produced by mindfulness meditation. In: *Psychosomatic Medicine*, 65, 564–570; also in Siegel, D. (2007) *The Mindful Brain – Reflection & Attunement in the Cultivation of Wellbeing* New York: Norton.

7    The scientists included Cliff Saron, now a neuroscientist at the University of California – Davis, Center for Mind and Brain; Francisco Varela, cofounder of the Mind and Life Institute; Richard J Davidson who would join the Mind and Life dialogues in 1994 and was on the verge of seminal discoveries about patterns of brain activity that correspond to happiness and depression; Alan Wallace would smooth the way into the lamas huts after himself meditating there in 1980. Wallace later served as interpreter for the Dalai Lama in Mind and Life meetings.

Buddhism, meditation is a rigorous regime of mental training, in which the mind observes itself. Through introspection and other techniques, the mind tries to free itself of afflictive tendencies such as hatred and jealousy and develop wholesome tendencies such as the power of attention and the capacity for empathy and compassion.[8]

Within the course of 20 years, by 2001, each of the master meditators, one at a time, had made the trek to the West. The tale is recounted that all accomplished monks[9] participated in Davidson's experiments. "They would lie in the cacophonous fMRI, sit still with electrodes plastered all over their scalp and turn their meditative state on and off like a light bulb,"[10] Begley relates. This work proved that states such as happiness, compassion, empathy, enthusiasm, joy and other positive emotions are trainable.[11] Richard Davidson's hypothesis was that meditation or other forms of mental training, can, by exploiting the brain's neuroplasticity, produce changes – most likely in patterns of neural activation, but perhaps even in the structure of neural circuitry, in the sense of what is connected to what and how strong those connections are – that underlie enduring happiness and other positive emotions. If that is so, then by exploiting the brain's potential to change its wiring, therapists or even individuals might restore the brain and hence the mind to emotional health.[12]

"The question we ask ourselves when challenged by the Buddhist view is, are we all stuck at our happiness set point, or is change possible?"[13] says Davidson. He concludes that in the Buddhist view, radical change is possible but from the Western perspective, we haven't given it a chance. The month after the 2004 Mind and Life Meeting, the prestigious science journal Proceedings of the National Academy of Sciences published the report of Davidson's study[14] of the effects of mental training on the brains of eight accomplished Tibetan Buddhist meditators. This was the first scientific study of the meditative state of pure compassion.

The experiments showed that the gamma waves in the brain of the meditators were off the charts in comparison to anything seen before[15] (scientists argue that brainwaves of this frequency reflect activation and recruitment of

---

8   Begley, S. (2009) *The Plastic Mind – New science reveals our extraordinary potential to transform ourselves* London: Constable, 244.

9   All had practiced meditation for at least ten thousand hours. One had racked up fifty-five thousand hours. All had gone on at least one three-year retreat living apart from society and passing all waking hours in meditation.

10  Begley (2009), 275.

11  Ibid.

12  Ibid.

13  Davidson et al. (2003).

14  Lutz et al. (2004).

15  As shown in the two slide presentations held by J. Brefczynski-Lewis, A. Lutz, & R. J. Davidson at the 34th annual meeting of the Society for Neuroscience, held 23–27 October 2004 in San Diego, entitled "A Neural Correlate of Attentional Expertise in Long-time Buddhist Practitioners" and "Loving-kindness and Compassion Meditation Results in Unique

neural resources, and generally, mental effort). They are also a signature of neuronal activity that knits together far-flung brain circuits – consciousness in a sense – even when they were not meditating, and their brains registered a large increase in the gamma signal. When they were not meditating, brains of the monks were different from the non-meditator control group[16] (almost like a continual aha!-moment). It was a hint of what Davidson and the other scientists had been seeking since their treks to the yogi's huts (permanent change in the brain as a result of mental training).[17]

The Dalai Lama, after listening to the results of the findings, responded: "What seems to be very clear is that a purely mental process – for example deliberately cultivating this aspiration of empathy and compassion – can have an effect that is observable in the brain level."[18] This also holds true for the continual practice of more destructive patterns of thought like anger, hatred, jealousy and fear – it changes the brain, but in different ways. Areas traditionally used to host activity related to insecurity, anxiety, hopelessness and depression light up and recruit more brain space on the dark side of town. The Dalai Lama is well-known for his comment, "doing violence to a perceived enemy is only doing violence to yourself".[19] Tests like this and further scientific research highlight that this undesirable effect on our own brain regions can be an expected consequence of such destructive behaviour.

During the discussion of the test results and in support of the reason why we should pursue training in techniques that are life-affirming rather than harm-causing, the Dalai Lama spoke of a 7th-century Buddhist thinker who argued that no matter how much training an athlete, for example, may engage in, and no matter how great an athlete may be, there will be a finite potential beyond which that person will not be able to jump or sprint. In contrast, he said, qualities like compassion, empathy and loving kindness have in principle the potential for limitless enhancement. "This may indicate that, in certain domains, there's limitless neuroplasticity", Davidson said, and the Dalai Lama emphatically agreed.[20]

The power of neuroplasticity to transform the brain opens up new worlds of possibility. We are not stuck with the brains we are born with but have the capacity to willfully direct which functions will flower and which will wither;

---

Patterns of fMRI Activation and Enhances the Reactivity of the Insula/Cingulate Neural Circuitry to Negative Stimuli in Meditators".

16  The control group comprised 10 non-meditating Wisconsin undergraduates who received an intensive course and a week's worth of practice in compassion meditation.

17  As shown in the two slide presentations held by J. Brefczynski-Lewis, A. Lutz, & R. J. Davidson at the 34th annual meeting of the Society for Neuroscience, held 23–27 October 2004 in San Diego.

18  Begley (2009), 276.

19  Conversation with author, Dharamsala 2008, various other places including Gyatso, T. (1999) *The Heart of Compassion* New Delhi: Full Circle, 67; The Hindu newspaper November 25, 2012.

20  Begley (2009), 292.

which moral capacities emerge and which do not, which emotions flourish and which are stilled.[21]

Davidson's research supports the idea long maintained by Buddhist meditation adepts: the mental training that lies at the core of meditative practice can alter the brain and thus the mind in an enduring way. Simpkins and Simpkins[22] concur, suggesting that this presents great hope and possibility: we can change at any age, and the change can involve a verifiable, structural alteration. In the concluding remarks to this paper, suggestions will be made as to how training to increase empathy can be utilised for several roles involved in the process of multifaith dialogue.

## Providing a Mechanism for Interfaith Dialogue through the Idea of 'Universal Responsibility' and Guidelines from 'A Charter for Universal Responsibility'

The Tibetan Spiritual Leader, the Dalai Lama, has been the driving force behind a great deal of interfaith dialogue across the globe for the past 20 years, and a large part of his daily activities for the past 10 years has been to address the concern about the continuation of human existence through the message of Universal Responsibility. He embodies and epitomises a new kind of global and universal consciousness with ancient spiritual roots, which is fully attuned to the modern mind and the key issues we face today. One of his main points is that we face these together, that our concerns and aspirations are in fact global, and that we all have equal rights by birth as free individuals, and mutual responsibilities as members of humanity. We share, for better or worse, a common destiny.

> I believe that to meet the challenge of our times, human beings will have to develop a greater sense of universal responsibility. Each of us must learn to work not just for his or her own self, family or nation but also for the benefit of all mankind. Universal responsibility is the real key to human survival. It is the best foundation for world peace, the equitable use of natural resources and through concern for future generations, the proper care of the environment.[23][24]

Another limitation to successful outcomes from interfaith dialogue is the perception that we alone or the group we belong to is right, and others are to be treated with suspicion; to be treated as different or even to be treated as 'the

---

21  Ibid., 300.

22  Simpkins, C. A. & Simpkins, A. M. (2010) *The Dao of Neuroscience: Combining Eastern and Western Principles for Optimal Therapeutic Change* New York: Norton.

23  HH the Dalai Lama "Stages of Meditation" June 15, 2008 address in Sydney Australia.

24  Also the arguments in the field of human ecology by Stephen Boyden (ANU) about the urgent change needed to promote our understanding of a 'biosensitive future' if we are to have a hope of preserving the human species.

enemy'. How many times has this view derailed bilateral talks on the international stage or caused a stalling of multilateral peace accords, or has even been the motivator for war?

While it could be argued that this perception has been the predominant one for thousands of years, the current shift in focus is driven in part by an increasingly global support for the notion of 'responsibility' echoing through all levels of society including the political: responsibility for the global economic crisis and the ethical questions arising from it. In every country, the destructive effects on the environment must be reversed. There are dire warnings from colleagues working on existential risk, that if we fail to make the right choices now, the human species as we now know it could be extinct within a hundred years. This brings us to the second major point and the great benefit to be had from Buddhist practitioners – the understanding of and set of guiding principles for 'Universal Responsibility'.

## Enabling Successful Outcomes from Interfaith Dialogue: Fostering Respect and Trust through Universal Responsibility

We have dealt with the major building block of empathy and now turn to consider ways of fostering the additional foundation stones of 'respect' and 'trust'. This involves diminishing the spotlight on 'difference' and instead highlighting 'common ground'. Regardless of our different belief systems, we are united by membership of one species, the human race. Jampa Tsedroen (Carola Roloff) in 'Dialogue in Buddhism' reflects: "At first glance I have the impression that the Dalai Lama believes in the Human (Buberian) dialogue, in the sense 'that it is possible for human beings to meet purely and simply as human beings, irrespective of the beliefs that separate them'."[25]

As part of the Nobel Peace Laureate group, the Dalai Lama proposes that realising our inseparable connection to 'Universal Responsibility' is a key understanding that will allow continuation of the human race, can reduce obstacles to the progress of multifaith dialogue and rests in the cultivation of inner values:

> Inner values…are the source of both an ethically harmonious world and the individual peace of mind, confidence and happiness we all seek… all the world's major religions, with their emphasis on love, compassion, patience, tolerance and forgiveness, can and do promote inner values. But the reality of the world today is that grounding ethics in religion is no longer adequate. This is why I believe the time has come to find a way of thinking about spirituality and ethics that is beyond religion.[26]

---

25  Jampa Tsedroen (Carola Roloff) quoting Sharpe, E. J. (1987) Dialogue of Religions. In: *The Encyclopedia of Religion*, vol. 4, New York: Macmillan Publishing Company, 347. See her contribution in this volume.
26  Gyatso (2011), xv.

He urges a move toward secularism, not to imply an antagonism toward religion, nor a reduction in the importance of religious identity, rather mutual
valuing and respect for all faiths as well as for those of no faith. From this
neutral ground, compassion can be built, and compassion draws power from
the understanding of universal responsibility. For those already formulating the
objection that compassion must surely founder on the challenge of justice, the
Dalai Lama's response speaks to the apparent conflict between the principle of
compassion, which implies forgiveness, and the exercise of justice, which requires punishment for wrongdoing. To give priority to compassion and forgiveness, they argue would allow perpetrators of harm to go unpunished and hand
a victory to the aggressors. The ethic of compassion, they say, amounts to little
more than an ethic of victimhood, under which aggression always triumphs,
wrongdoing is always forgiven, and the weak are defenceless.

The Dalai Lama proposes that this objection rests on a fundamental misunderstanding of what compassion entails in practice. Nothing in the principle of
compassion – the wish to see others relieved of suffering – involves surrendering
to the misdeeds of others. Nor does compassion demand that we meekly accept
injustice. Some of the greatest fighters against injustice in recent times, people
of strong character and determination like Mahatma Gandhi, Mother Theresa,
Nelson Mandela, Martin Luther King Jr, Vaclav Havel and others – have been
motivated by universal compassion. He observes that we could not describe
such people as meek or retiring just because they combine their devotion to the
welfare of others with a commitment to nonviolence. When an unjust situation
demands a strong response, as in the case of Apartheid, compassion does not
demand that we accept injustice but rather that we take a stand against it. "So
in answer to those who insist that justice, rather than compassion, should lie at
the heart of any system of ethics, I suggest that in reality there is no conflict
between the principle of justice and the practice of compassion and forgiveness.
Indeed, in my understanding the very concept of justice is itself based on compassion."[27]

## A Charter of Universal Responsibility

In order to provide practical guidelines for dialogue, the Dalai Lama and Professor Samdhong Rinpoche have led a group to construct a 'Charter of Universal Responsibility'. The document (which has not been publicly released,
and therefore it is not appropriate to comment on the detailed content) is a
magnificent piece of work, uplifting, practical, engaging and inclusive of all
faith groups and those with secular values. It provides not only a reminder of
the core elements of respect and trust, but clear guidelines to maintain them.
When this is publicly released in the near future, it will be an extraordinary

---

27  Gyatso (2011), 70.

tool to guide discussion and debate for interfaith groups and community-based organisations, for political entities and school children alike.

## Implications of the Research, the Way Forward and Concluding Remarks

It is conceivable that a dialogue on Universal Responsibility could ideally take place within all schools, respectful of all belief systems represented, which would be one 'educational impulse' in response to the project's call. Another would be to create a secular 15-minute meditation program to fit within the existing school curriculum. The training could easily fit into the peace studies program, human values curriculum, communication program, anti-bullying program, health education, conflict management & problem-solving program, and the social science and community welfare curriculum just to name a few from an extensive list. This program would increase empathy and compassion – similar projects have already been conducted successfully in the United States, Canada, India, France, and beyond. Likewise, the 'Charter of Universal Responsibility' could be used as a framework to guide interfaith forums through their own discussion points and frame commonalities for interfaith dialogue where participants find themselves at a dead-end on points of difference. It can also be utilised to construct a set of interview questions for use in school and community groups.

We salute the hard work to promote dialogue currently underway, and through the application of these understandings and methods we look forward to a time when a more caring, responsible and compassionate humanity will emerge.

*Parichart Suwanbubbha*

# Dialogue in Buddhism

## A Case Study in Addressing Violence in Southern Thailand

## Introduction

This paper comprises two parts: an effort to understand a concept of dialogue founded in Buddhist teachings and practices, and an example of deploying re-al-world dialogue as a tool for conflict transformation. The first element relates to our understanding of dialogue as a form of 'deep listening' which includes
1. Welcoming all shades of difference,
2. Emphasising human-to-human relationships,
3. Listening with loving kindness,
4. Listening without prejudgement,
5. Listening with empathy and
6. Dialogue as a continuing process needing to be practised in our everyday life.

The Buddhist tenets of *kamma* – interconnectedness, the law of change, im-permanence – and teachings supporting the concept of human dignity can all be read to encourage the practice of both interreligious and intrareligious dia-logue. Above all, they affirm that putting Buddhist teachings into practice can help make such dialogues effective. The second part recounts experiences in a dialogue initiative between relatives of insurgents (inmates) and the victims of violence in Southern Thailand through which we will explore the effectiveness of dialogue in transforming conflicts.

## What is Dialogue[1]?

Most people associate dialogue with a conversation between two individuals or groups of people. This is generally correct, but the understanding foreshortens the dimensions of dialogue by focusing on its binary polarity. As David Bohm points out, the word 'dialogue' derives from the Greek root of *dia,* which means 'through', and *logos* which means 'the word', or more particularly 'the mean-ing of the word'.[2] Therefore dialogue refers to meaning flowing around and through us.

1   Suwanbubbha, P. (2006) Moving together through Action and Dialogue. In: Hans Ucko et al. (Eds.) *Changing the Present, Dreaming the Future: A Critical Movement in the Interre-ligious Dialogue* Geneva: World Council of Churches, 46–53.
2   Bohm, D. (1996) *On Dialogue* (ed. by Lee Nichol) London: Routledge.

In order to have meaning flowing through us, we need to practice 'deep listening', i.e. listening with loving kindness, listening without any prejudgement and bias, and listening with empathy. Listening in this manner – and not only 'hearing' – can be encouraged by the practice of any religion, whether it is Buddhism, Christianity or Islam. That is to say, listening is a basic element of learning and understanding the teachings of one's religion. Listening with respect, readiness to learn and with an effort to understand is fundamental to the practice of all religions.

How can religious teachings make dialogue effective? Usually, people who are interested in listening find it easier to understand each other's stories. This leads them towards what is referred to as the state of 'I in me'. By listening to other people's convictions with loving kindness and without any prejudgement, we can start to eliminate bias and misunderstanding. This can lead to what I refer to as the state of 'I in it'. When we further listen with our hearts, we can enter into a condition of empathy with others that brings us close to 'I in you'. Such listening from heart to heart will take us beyond the constraints of the 'you and me', towards a state of awareness I call 'I in now' that transcends any difference. Dialogue parties at this point will be mindful of the present moment and realise the common value of humanity they all access. In other words, listening in a process of dialogue will enable us to learn about the differentness of others, to increase our understanding of their different identities, and to subvert any bias.[3] These forms of listening require us to embrace the values of respect, patience, inclusiveness, self-criticism, empathy, honesty and mindfulness. All religions, including Buddhism, teach these values. If we can regard dialogue, and especially interreligious dialogue, as an effort to learn, then Buddhism helps support dialogue. Indeed, we can regard engaging in the process of dialogue as putting Buddhist teachings into practice.

## Listening in Buddhism

In Buddhism, one of the conditions for the right view arising is called *parato ghoṣa* which means 'hearing or learning from others'[4]. To be able to understand other views, we need to have a *parato ghoṣa.* From the Buddhist perspective, the condition of hearing or learning from others can be understood as underly-

---

3    Swidler, L. (Ed.) (1987) *Toward a Universal Theology of Religion,* New York: Orbis Books, 6.

4    *Majjhima Nikāya* I.43; Pali Text Society I 294; For the English translation see: Ñāṇamoli, B. & Bodhi, B. (Eds.) (1995/2005) *The Middle Length Discourses of the Buddha. A Translation of the Majjhima Nikāya* Boston: Wisdom, 390. There *parato ghoṣa* is translated as "The voice of another". See also *Aṅguttara Nikāya* I.87. For the English translation, see: Bodhi, B. (2012) (Ed.) *The Numerical Discourses of the Buddha. A Translation of the Aṅguttara Nikāya* Boston: Wisdom Publications, 178: 126 (9) "Bhikkhus, there are these two conditions for the arising of the right view. What two? The utterance of another [person] and careful attention. These are the two conditions for the arising of right view."

ing the openness to hear and learn from people of different faiths. Moreover, knowledge or wisdom resulting from listening to and learning from others will lead to *sutamayā paññā*, one of the three important wisdoms in Buddhism:
1. *cintāmaya paññā*, wisdom based on thought,
2. *sutamayā paññā*, wisdom based on listening [learning], and
3. *bhāvanāmaya paññā*, wisdom based on mental development [meditation].[5]

Buddhist teachings support the progression from listening to deep listening. Therefore, Buddhism can be a party to, and an asset for, effective interreligious dialogue.

## Teachings of Loving Kindness and Compassion in Buddhism

Where Christianity embraces *agape,* an unconditional love or equal concern for everyone, Buddhism has the teaching of *mettā*, loving kindness and *karuṇā*, compassion. Both concepts are meant to extend to all living beings beyond any limited realms of existence. This means that even those who oppose us, differ from us or even wronged us are to be included in this unlimited compassion. To apply this teaching to the process of dialogue requires openness and willingness to welcome what others say. For religions, that means we need to listen to what is different in other religions, even if it is unfamiliar to our own ears and traditions, on terms of loving kindness and compassion. This understanding goes well with the abovementioned concept of 'deep listening'.

Moreover, the Buddhist approach of 'seeing everything as it is' represents a mindful mode of accepting things both similar to and different from our own feelings and perceptions. It implies the acceptance of diversity, including different identities of others. In other words, the ability to welcome all facets of different identities including religion, language and belief is a central precondition of dialogue. Differences should be viewed as matters of beauty instead of problems. By simply approaching differences without any prejudgements, the dialogue partners should be able to exercise empathy with other people's belief and conviction. Putting this Buddhist teaching into practice can enable us to sympathetically listen to what followers of other religions believe.

At the same time, it can be difficult to sympathise with others if we cannot use our sympathic imagination, as it were putting ourselves in other people's shoes. Doing this, and listening with empathy in the process of dialogue, is supported by the following Buddhist teaching:

> What is displeasing and disagreeable to me
> is displeasing and disagreeable to the other too.

---

5    *Dīgha Nikāya* III 33.43, Pali Text Society III 219. For the English translation see: Walshe, M. (1995) (Ed.) *The Long Discourses of the Buddha. A Translation of the Dīgha Nikāya* Boston: Wisdom Publications, 486.

How can I inflict upon another
what is displeasing and disagreeable to me?[6]

## Human-to-Human Relationships

A vital and unique characteristic of dialogue is the realisation of the dignity of a partner who is 'there' in front of us. This is one of the main foci of the Buddha's teachings. Buddhism does not believe in an all-powerful creator God, but rather focuses on the human being, as exemplified by:

> It is, friend, just this fathom-high carcass endowed with perception
> and mind that I make known the world, the origin of the
> world, the cessation of the world and the way leading
> to the cessation of the world.[7]

Thus, Buddhism puts the human being at the centre of any spiritual development. Moreover, human beings are enjoined to respect and open themselves to each other. All of us exist under the same law of nature, of 'arising, maintaining and disappearing'. Each of us is also under the law of *kamma* (all actions have consequences). This law of cause and effect means that, from a Buddhist perspective, we must respect each other regardless of different social, economic and political status or convictions. For Buddhists, only spiritual attainments, i.e. virtue achieved, should count. The morality (evidenced by correct actions) of each person indicates their true quality. Buddhists should not judge a person by his or her caste, social status or other extraneous characteristics.

In sum, Buddhism places prior confidence in the potential and dignity of all human beings and their religious behaviour. Buddhists believe that all people are under the same law of *kamma* and the same law of impermanence. Buddhist teaching emphasises that all are equal in terms of being under the natural law of cause and effect, and therefore everyone deserves equal dignity. In the process of dialogue, we focus on realising the 'equal to equal' encounter of human nature (human dignity) more than just comparing the logic or the scriptures of our respective religions.

As a result, circles of dialogue which welcome all kinds of difference need to encourage all stakeholders to touch and feel the human nature of seeking happiness and avoiding suffering. This human nature is shared by everyone, whether soldiers or insurgents, Buddhists or Muslims, rich or poor. Dialogue, therefore, means sharing with each other and listening to others in awareness

---

6   Saṃyuta Nikāya V 55.7. For the English translation see: Bodhi, B. (2000) (Ed.) The Connected Discourses of the Buddha. A Translation of the Saṃyuta Nikāya Boston: Wisdom Publications, 1799.

7   Saṃyuta Nikāya I 2.26. For the English translation see: Bodhi, B. (2000) (Ed.) The Connected Discourses of the Buddha. A Translation of the Saṃyuta Nikāya Boston: Wisdom Publications, 158.

of the existence of common human values. The concept of dialogue provides a safe space for all to touch authentic common humanity. This is one of the emphases in Buddhism as understood in the tradition I am coming from.

## Dialogue as a Process of Doing both 'Outer' and 'Inner Work'

It is said that participating in a process of dialogue means searching for, understanding and practising spiritual value in one's own religion. That is to say, all partners in dialogue need to display loving kindness, honesty, a broad and open mind, patience, self-criticism and other important values in listening to other people's different convictions and beliefs. It means that dialogue is not only 'hearing' but also listening to the feelings and values that underlie words. The practice of all the above values is then a key challenge for all stakeholders while they learn to accept different points of view. Thereby, greater understanding may grow and in the long run, bias and prejudice be overcome.[8] In other words, dialogue can be understood as a test each follower of Buddhism has to undergo. It shows how far he or she is able to translate the good teachings of the Buddha into action when encountering difficult situations, being confronted with different reasonings and convictions of adherents of other religions. These are the fruitful outcomes of outer work. Such constructive and positive changes are considered to be a reflection of a positive inner progress due to the own practice of inner values. All religions, not only Buddhism, teach the moral behaviour which is necessary for an effective conduct of dialogue.

## Interreligious Dialogue in Buddhism

The Buddha himself often interacted with followers of other religions. For example, he was in contact with and listened to the teachings and ideas of Jainism and Brahmanism. He always welcomed differences and urged his followers to consider all opinions and choose whichever belief would lead to the cessation of suffering. On the other hand, the Buddha never encouraged his followers to embrace strongly-held convictions which could result in extreme beliefs and practices.

> The skilful ones call that a bond, when one is attached to something and regards other things as inferior.
> Therefore, as to what is seen, heard, or thought,
> [or] rules-and-observances, a monk should not be attached.[9]

---

8    Ibid.
9    Sutta-Nipāta IV.5, 798. For the Pāli text see: Andersen, D. & Smith, H. (eds.) (1913) Sutta-Nipāta. New Edition (Published for the Pali Text Society by Geoffrey Cumberlege) London: Oxford University Press, 156.

The Buddhist attitude of openness towards others and of welcoming their different beliefs is implicit in the above teaching.

## Interreligious Dialogue in the Edicts of Aśoka

King Aśoka (3rd century BCE; reigned 273/267–237/232), a great supporter of and convert to Buddhism, reflected on his experiences and understanding of the essence of Buddhism to support 'deep listening' and the proper attitudes towards others in his famous 'Rock Edict':

> One should not honour only one's own religion
> and condemn the religions of others, but one
> should honour others' religions for this or that
> reason to grow and render service to the
> religions of others too. In acting otherwise one
> digs the grave of one's own religion and also
> does harm to other religions. Whoever honors
> his (her) own religion and condemns other
> religions, does so indeed through devotion
> to his own religion, thinking 'I will glorify my
> own religion'. But on the contrary, in so doing
> he (she) injures his (her) own religion more
> gravely. So concord is good: Let all listen, and
> be willing to listen to the doctrines professed
> by others.[10]

By adhering to this teaching, we will be able to understand others through listening to their beliefs while maintaining our own position and conviction. Interreligious dialogue should not be limited to pleasant conversations and photo opportunities. Although followers of each religion may mention the good points of their faith, the crucial question is to what extent they 'walk the walk', i.e. practise what their religion teaches. Dialogue must be practised in everyday life and applied to the conflicts arising each day. We must therefore encourage embedding dialogue within the fabric of our existence, not merely using it in the educational sphere or as the subject of occasional, amicable meetings.

## Historical Examples of Interreligious and Intrareligious Dialogue

During the time of the Buddha, he himself conducted dialogues with people of different beliefs as is evidenced by many stories in *Suttantapiṭaka,* the collection of sermons of the Pali Canon, containing such discourses. For instance, the Buddha had a dialogue with a group of ascetics and teachers called *Kālāmas* about the criteria applied to judge which teachings were right or wrong. Ac-

---

10  Rahula, W. (2005) What the Buddha Taught Bangkok: Haw Trai, 4 f.

cording to the sources, the Buddha always respectfully interacted with people of different beliefs. He thus conducted interreligious dialogue, specifically dialogues of study which focus on doctrines.

On the other hand, dialogues also took place within the community of Buddhist followers. One prominent example stems from the communication between the Indo-Greek king Milinda (Menander I) of Bactria and Bhikkhu Nāgasena. They conducted intrareligious dialogue on important teachings such as *anatta* (no-self) which was recorded in the '*Milindapañha*' (Milinda's Questions) from approximately 100 BCE to 400 CE.

> Said King Milinda to the sage Nagasena: "Reverend
> Nagasena, are there any things that exist which come
> out of things that did not exist?" "There are not, great
> king, any things that exist which come out of things that
> did not exist. Only out of things that existed, great king,
> come things that exist." "Give me an illustration."[11]

We must consider, though, whether these are the authentic dialogues or not. In the general understanding, dialogues are more than mere exchanges of information of religious teachings. Therefore, the questions and answers between King Milinda and Bhikkhu Nāgasena are less important than the question whether the parties practised authentic deep listening or not.

By considering the content of the dialogues and the possibility of *Dhamma* practices, we may assume a natural state of awareness on the part of both the Bhikkhu and the King. The practice of dialogue would then be composed of outer work (learning about religious contents) and of inner work (the action of no-self attachment). Therefore it is possible to say that *Milinda's Questions* is an example of intrareligious dialogue in the history of Buddhism. It thus may illustrate a historical instance of practising good teachings, experiencing religious values and translating Buddhist teachings into action while engaging in authentic dialogue.

Today, a famous Vietnamese Zen Buddhist leader, Thich Nhat Hanh, who encourages people to attend to the development of their mind in the present instant, constantly advocates the concept of 'compassionate listening'. His concept of compassionate listening is similar to 'deep listening' in a process of dialogue. In fact, as Thich Nhat Hanh teaches that 'interconnectedness' means "as long as you continue to breathe, I continue to be in",[12] he confirms people in their 'power of understanding other people's suffering' and their 'power of loving kindness'. In order to understand other people's needs and their suffering, we need to compassionately listen to their stories with empathy and mindfulness. According to Thich Nhat Hanh, his act can be thought of as an

---

11  Stryk, L. (Ed.) (1982) *World of the Buddha: An Introduction to Buddhist Literature* New York: Grove Press, 101.

12  Ellsberg, R. (Ed.) (2001) *Thich Nhat Hanh: Essential Writings* New York: Orbis Books, 55.

authentic source of power. Authentic leadership requires 'compassionate listening' or 'deep listening' in order to understand others and win their hearts
and cooperation. The exercise of such power can assure that Buddhist practices
enable a true process of dialogue.

## An Example of Implementing Dialogue in Southern Thailand

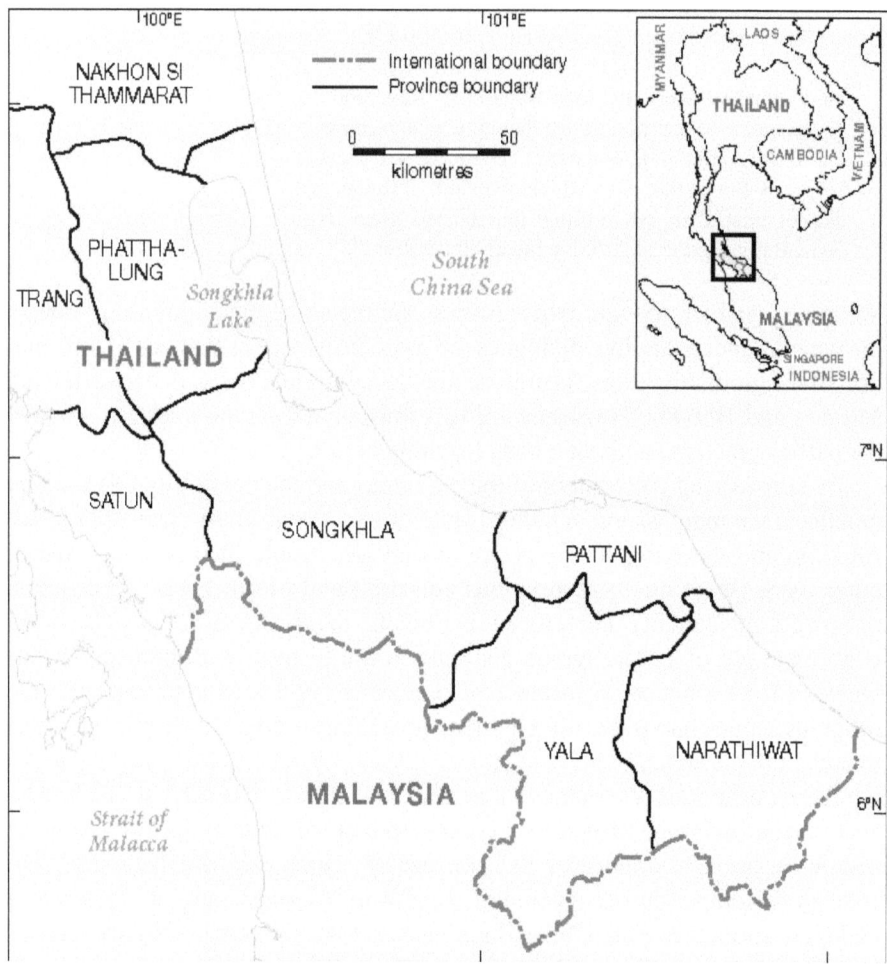

Map of the region (source: http://asiapacific.anu.edu.au)

Since 2004, violence related to the insurgency in Southern Thailand, predominantly in the Malay Pattani region encompassing the provinces of Yala, Pattani,
Narathiwat and some districts of Songkhla Province, has been escalating. Historically, this region was part of the independent Pattani Kingdom. The current
spate of violence began with the robbery of military weapons from an army
camp in Narathiwat. Since then, daily attacks have been part of our lives.

According to figures by the NGO Deep South Watch[13] from January 2004 to September 2012 there were a total of 12,377 violent events resulting in 14,890 casualties (5,377 dead and 9,513 injured). Both Muslims and Buddhists, government security officers as well as innocent victims, have lost their lives in this conflict. Civil society, including peace scholars and activists, have been trying to counter it by developing a peace process through dialogue circles.

It is widely assumed that the root cause of the current violence is found in a sense of being colonised by hostile Thais on the part of some Malayu Muslims. Some Malayu Muslims have even called for independence. At present, the majority of people in the deep south of Thailand are Muslims, while 20 per cent are Buddhists. It has also been claimed that Muslims are being victimised and unjustly singled out by Thai security forces. Some officers may even be involved in smuggling and drug-running, which motivates them to exacerbate the violence in order to provide greater opportunities to profit from these illegal activities.

We must understand, however, that political competition for power at both local and national level is a key driver of violence. In this context it is important to realise the role of both ignorance of other religions and cultures and of the instrumentalisation of religious belief to destroy inter-community trust. Many religious leaders and prominent figures, both Buddhist and Muslim, have been injured or killed in the clashes.

In order to develop peace and reconciliation, dialogue can be deployed to transform conflict[14] if all participants are given the opportunity to express and understand the content and context of the violence by freely expressing their feelings and needs and relating their stories. This holds the promise for a possible improvement of relationships through interpersonal relationships. The following case study presents an example of dialogue between relatives of victims of the violence and those of insurgent inmates detained on grounds of national security.

This dialogue process is part of an action research project on 'Reconciliation and the Culture of Peace: The Case of Central Songkhla Prison' conducted by the Institute of Human Rights and Peace Studies at Mahidol University, Thailand. We are a group of facilitators who have designed a three-day dialogue process consisting of a preparation stage to build trust, a stage devoted to learning about the necessary concepts for dialogue such as interconnectedness and a concept of 'power', and one of practicing heart-to-heart listening in pairs, in threes and in groups. This dialogue process has been going on continually since the first meeting on 9–11 June 2012 which included relatives of inmates considered national security risks.

---

13  www.deepsouthwatch.org, last accessed December 11, 2013.
14  Lederach, J.-P. (2003) *The Little Book of Conflict Transformation* PA: Rotary Center for Peace and Conflict Studies.

The facilitators designed a process of dialogue for relatives of inmates in order that they may develop more self-esteem and know about the nature of this dialogue, i.e. that every voice is important and is welcome by the group. Then they were prepared to accept the different reasons and feelings of others (in this context those of the relatives of victims). Whenever they meet each other, they are encouraged to express freely and comfortably their human emotions such as fear, loneliness, worries, sympathy and so on. Deep listening is practised through different kinds of activities. Moreover, they learnt how to conduct and participate in 'fishbowl dialogue', which combines the concept of deep listening and knowledge management to jointly consider the question "how to help a scapegoat after being seized by the authority". When the first group was ready to meet the relatives of victims, the facilitators planned for the next dialogue.

This second dialogue took place on 12–14 June 2012 and consisted of two parts: 1) one and a half days of introductory training for relatives of victims of the violence in the South and 2) one and a half days to conduct dialogue between relatives of inmates (national security cases) and relatives of victims. The objectives were to create 'a safe space' for both relatives of victims and of inmates to share their stories and listen deeply to their suffering, their feelings and needs in order to find solutions for peace. At the same time, this dialogue aims to strengthen an improved relationship between both sides and to encourage them to apply the process of dialogue as a tool for 'conflict transformation' in their future lives.

The process of dialogue focuses on transcending 'the edge' of any differences – be they based on political preference or religion, ethnicity or language. Participants should encounter each other at the level of 'human nature' that strives for happiness and avoids suffering and dissatisfaction. In this case, both the relatives of victims and of inmates learned how to conduct 'fishbowl dialogues'. It was amazing that both sides would not accept or condone injustice towards innocents. Human nature was vindicated in their refusal to accept any form of unjust solution. Both sides went beyond the boundaries of different political identity in their shared common character of humanity. They also proposed various practical ways to help a 'scapegoat', in the end developing an informal network and exchanging telephone numbers to spread such news and create a display of unity to help innocents victimised by security forces.

It must be stressed that the success of dialogue processes is measured by the improvement in relationships among participants who came in holding different convictions and attitudes towards the violence in Thailand. The participants reported understanding each other better and emphasised that they were all 'in the same boat', or rather, 'all in this together'. "We belong to the same family", they said. They transcended the boundaries of opposing sides as relatives of victims and inmates. A possible explanation for this is that all participants from both sides had the opportunity to share their feelings, needs, fears and suffering as human beings. They shared common concerns of being human and were thus able to develop mutual sympathy and empathy.

On the final day, we observed not only improved relationships, but even a form of loose and unofficial networking among them, resulting from deep listening in the 'fishbowl dialogue'.

Moreover, many of them said that they had had the opportunity to listen to and learn about different attitudes, other people's suffering, and concepts of non-violence. Some of them said that as soon as they heard the incredibly sad and painful stories of others, they realised that the stories of their own suffering became smaller or looked like nothing in comparison to others. As to us, we are pleased to find that a process of dialogue made the participants understand themselves and others better through listening to others and through the results of reflecting on themselves and others.

Participating in such a dialogue offers individuals the opportunity to engage in compassionate listening. Each person is enabled to open their heart and 'be there', to be receptive and respectful towards others with different convictions. As a result, people came to value themselves and others more. Our three-day dialogues between relatives of inmates and of victims of violence confirmed the importance of dialogical encounter as an effective tool for conflict transformation, not only through transforming feelings of hatred, fear, anger and vengefulness into better relationships based on shared fates and greater mutual understanding, but also through violence prevention. The teachings and practice of Buddhism, Islam and other religions play an important role in guiding the thoughts and actions of their followers. They support and sustain dialogue. This is the beginning of a process which we hope will eventually lead us towards a sustainable peace.

# List of Authors

*Alomes, Anna*, Dr., is Contemplative Education Officer at "Mind and Life Europe" in Zurich, Switzerland: mapping exemplary contemplative practices and growing the Mind and Life Institute presence throughout 12 countries across Europe. Key research interests: human transformation, applied ethics, mindfulness, neuroscience, interfaith dialogue, nonviolence and reconciliation.

*Amirpur, Katajun*, Prof. Dr., is Professor of Islamic Studies and Islamic Theology, Associate Coordinator of the international research project "Religion and Dialogue in Modern Societies" and Associate Director of the Academy of World Religions, University of Hamburg, Germany. Main research areas: Islam in contemporary society, Iran, gender, interreligious dialogue.

*Aydın, Mahmut*, Prof. Dr., is Professor of History of Religions and currently Vice Rector of the University of Ondokuz Mayis, Samsun, Turkey. Main research areas: interfaith and intercultural dialogue, religious pluralism, coexistence and contemporary Christian theology and the historical Jesus.

*Ayoub, Mahmoud Mustafa*, Prof. Dr., is Professor Emeritus of Islamic Studies and Christian-Muslim Relations, Hartford Seminary, Temple University, Philadelphia, USA.

*Bernhardt, Reinhold*, Prof. Dr., is Professor of Systematic Theology / Dogmatics at the University of Basel, Switzerland, and a specialist in theology of religions and interreligious studies.

*Beyer, Peter*, Prof. Dr., is Professor of Religious Studies at the University of Ottawa, Canada. Since 2001 he has been conducting research on the religious expression of second generation immigrant young adults in Canada.

*van der Braak, André*, Prof. Dr., is Professor of Buddhist Philosophy in Dialogue with other World Views, project leader of the research project "Multiple religious belonging: hermeneutical and empirical explorations of hybrid religiosity", and coordinator of the Buddhist Studies program, Vrije University, Amsterdam, Netherlands.

*Casanova, José*, Prof. Dr., is Professor of Sociology of Religions at the Berkley Center for Religion, Peace and World Affairs at Georgetown University, Washington DC, USA, and heads the Berkley Center's Program on Globalization, Religion and the Secular.

*Friedrichs, Nils*, M.A., is a doctoral candidate and research assistant at the graduate school of the Cluster of Excellence "Religion and Politics in Modern and Pre-Modern Cultures" at the University of Münster, Germany.

*Ghasempour, Morteza*, Dr., is Lecturer in Philosophy at the University of Cologne, Germany. Main research areas: aesthetics, ethics, hermeneutics, intercultural philosophy. He is a founding member of the international Society of Intercultural Philosophy.

*Ipgrave, Julia*, Dr., is Senior Research Fellow, Warwick Religions and Education Research Unit, University of Warwick, U.K. Her research interests include religion in education and inter religious relations. She is member of the national Christian and Muslim Forum in England.

*Joas, Hans*, Prof. Dr. Dr. h.c., is Permanent Fellow at the Freiburg Institute for Advanced Studies, University of Freiburg, Germany, and Professor of Sociology and Social Thought, University of Chicago, USA. Main interests: social theory, sociology and history of religion, sociology of war and violence.

*Kalender, Mehmet*, M.A., Master in Study of Religion and Islamic Studies. He works as researcher and Ph.D. student in the BMBF project "Religion and Dialogue in Modern Societies (ReDi)", Academy of World Religions, University of Hamburg, Germany. His main research interests are interactions, materiality and spatial aspects in interfaith dialogue and qualitative research of religion.

*Kalsky, Manuela*, Prof. Dr., is Professor of Theology and Society at Vrije University and director of the Dominican Study Centre for Theology and Society in Amsterdam, Netherlands. She is also director of the multimedia website Nieuwwij.nl. Research areas: religion in a pluralist society, dialogical theology, multiple religious belonging, feminist and postcolonial studies.

*Klinkhammer, Gritt*, Prof. Dr., is Professor of Religious Studies at Bremen University, Germany. Her main research interests are: religion and migration, Islam in the West and religious pluralism.

*Körs, Anna*, Dr., is Senior Researcher in the field of sociology with focus on religious pluralism and interreligious dialogue, Associate Coordinator of the international research project "Religion and Dialogue in Modern Societies" and scientific manager of the Academy of World Religions, University of Hamburg, Germany.

*Meir, Ephraim*, Prof. Dr., is Professor of modern Jewish philosophy at Bar-Ilan University, Israel, and Chair of the Department of Jewish Philosophy. He has been a guest professor in Strasbourg, Heidelberg, and Phoenix, and is the

Lévinas guest professor for dialogical philosophy and interreligious theology at Hamburg University.

*Nagel, Alexander-Kenneth*, Jun.-Prof. Dr., is Assistant Professor of Religious Studies at the Ruhr University Bochum, Germany. He is currently supervising a junior research group on the civic potentials of religious migrant communities. Main research areas: religion and migration, interfaith activities and diversity governance, interfaith spaces.

*Rambachan, Anantanand*, Prof. Dr., is Professor of Religion at Saint Olaf College, Minnesota, USA. Main research areas: Advaita Vedanta, interreligious dialogue, theology of religions, Hinduism in the contemporary world and liberation theology.

*Roloff, Carola*, Dr., is Post-doc Research Fellow in the project 'Religion and Dialogue' of the Academy of World Religions at the University of Hamburg, and principal investigator on Buddhist nuns ordination (DFG project). Main research interests: Buddhism in modernity; intra-Buddhist and interfaith dialogue; gender, human and women's rights in Buddhism.

*Schmidt-Leukel, Perry,* Prof. Dr., is Professor of Religious Studies and Intercultural Theology at the University of Münster, Germany. His main focus of research is in theology of religions, inter-faith relations and Buddhist-Christian dialogue.

*Suwanbubbha, Parichart*, Dr., is Assistant Professor and Director of the Institute of Human Rights and Peace Studies, Mahidol University, Thailand, and serves as a secretary of Religions for Peace Interreligious Council of Thailand and is member of the board of Globethics.net, Geneva, Switzerland.

*Vieregge, Dörthe*, Dr., is Senior Researcher in the field of religion and education and Associate Coordinator of the international research project "Religion and Dialogue in Modern Societies" at the Academy of World Religions, University of Hamburg, Germany. Main research fields: empirical studies on youth and religions.

*Weisse, Wolfram*, Prof. Dr., is Professor of religion, education and dialogue, Coordinator of the international research project "Religion and Dialogue in Modern Societies" and Director of the Academy of World Religions, University of Hamburg, Germany.

*Yendell, Alexander,* M.A., is Research Associate at the Institute of Practical Theology, Leipzig University, Germany. Main research areas: quantitative social research, sociology of immigration, sociology of religion and sociology of education.